HENRY ANSGAR KELLY received his A.B., A.M., and Ph.L. degrees from St. Louis University and his Ph.D. from Harvard University. A former Jesuit seminarian, he is now Professor of English and Medieval–Renaissance Studies at the University of California, Los Angeles.

The Devil at Baptism

The Devil, Demonology, and Witchcraft. British edition, *Towards the Death of Satan*. Italian edition, *La morte di Satana*. French edition, *Le diable et ses démons*.

Divine Providence in the England of Shakespeare's Histories

Love and Marriage in the Age of Chaucer

The Matrimonial Trials of Henry VIII

Canon Law and the Archpriest of Hita

Chaucer and the Cult of Saint Valentine

THE DEVIL
AT BAPTISM

Ritual, Theology, and Drama

HENRY ANSGAR KELLY

Cornell University Press

ITHACA AND LONDON

BT
981
.K44
1985

Cornell University Press gratefully acknowledges a grant from the Andrew W. Mellon Foundation that aided in bringing this book to publication.

The Society of Fellows of Harvard University supported the early research for this book.

First published 1985 by Cornell University Press.

International Standard Book Number 0-8014-1806-2
Library of Congress Catalog Card Number 85-404
Printed in the United States of America
*Librarians: Library of Congress cataloging information
appears on the last page of the book.*

*The paper in this book is acid-free and meets the guidelines for
permanence and durability of the Committee on Production Guidelines
for Book Longevity of the Council on Library Resources.*

*For my friends and
mentors in the
Society of Jesus*

Contents

Preface

We have all eaten of the tree of the knowledge of good and evil. No matter how we have come to our awareness of the difference between right and wrong, we have all experienced the sense of guilt that comes from wrongdoing and the fear of being called to account for it. We have felt the need to be pardoned and to be strengthened and protected from further lapses. Furthermore, we are fascinated by these feelings and experiences in others. This fascination is a primary basis of the appeal of much serious drama.

In religious rituals of repentance, pardon, and initiation, the reality and the dramatic presentation of experiences of guilt and their resolution are combined. To people of European heritage, the Christian ceremonies of redemption are the most important instances of such rituals. They reveal some of the more important preoccupations of our forebears, and they also give evidence of dramaturgical impulses corresponding to those that later inspired the religious, and much of the secular, drama of the Middle Ages and Renaissance. (For the purposes of this study, I define drama as "the formal acting out of events." The drama to be found in initiation rituals includes both the reenactment of historical events and the symbolic representation of supernatural realities, whether past or present.)[1]

[1]For a criticism of the usual criteria of drama (action, dialogue, impersonation), see O. B. Hardison, Jr., *Christian Rite and Christian Drama in the Middle Ages* (Baltimore 1965) 30–33. Hardison rightly insists that "no simple line can be drawn between art and life" and that most actors identify with, rather than impersonate, the characters they play. But Hardison may go too far in considering the liturgy of the Mass and

9

Much of the fear from which the Church of Christ promised deliverance centered on the evil spirits who victimized mankind. (Christianity had its origins at a time when Jewish demonology had reached a point of extensive elaboration. This demonology had little effect on the more solemn ceremonies of the Hebrew religion. But the followers of Jesus incorporated much of it into the Gospels and other documents that were gathered together to form the New Testament. As a result, the activity of malignant spirits became an important matter of concern for succeeding generations and has remained so even to this day; and the theories that evolved from this concern have exercised a great deal of influence upon both doctrine and liturgy. The liturgical practices most affected were those by which neophytes were received into the Church.)

In the New Testament the rite of baptism affords passage from the world of sin to the kingdom of God. Even though this rescue was often preached in terms of escape from Satan and the spiritual rulers of this world, the baptismal service was originally very simple and had no reference to the spirits of evil. At the beginning of the third century, however, it suddenly appeared transformed into an elaborate ritual, the most striking new element of which was the diabolic dimension. The initiation ceremonies were now a drama of resolute and sometimes fierce struggle against the devil, man's spiritual oppressor and the instigator of his sins. Eventually the complex of rites came to be regarded as designed primarily to remove the inherited guilt of the original sin of mankind and to take away, or at least reduce, the satanic influence that accompanied it.

Divine Office to be a drama in the full sense of the word. On this point, see Jerome Taylor, "Critics, Mutations, and Historians of Medieval English Drama," in *Medieval English Drama,* ed. Jerome Taylor and Alan H. Nelson (Chicago 1974) 1–27, esp. 3–13. My own use of "drama" may not completely fulfill all of Taylor's criteria, but it does, I feel, come closer to them than Hardison's does. See also Raymond Firth, "Society and Its Symbols," a review of Victor Turner, *Dramas, Fields, and Metaphors: Symbolic Action in Human Society,* in the *Times Literary Supplement* 3784 (13 September 1974) 965–966. An extended analysis of baptismal ritual as drama is made by Hugh M. Riley, *Christian Initiation: A Comparative Study of the Interpretation of the Baptismal Liturgy in the Mystagogical Writings of Cyril of Jerusalem, John Chrysostom, Theodore of Mopsuestia, and Ambrose of Milan,* Catholic University of America Studies in Christian Antiquity 17 (Washington, D.C., 1974). But Riley neglects a good deal of the dramatic aspects of the liturgies he treats by not taking into consideration the exorcisms and other practices of the catechumenate. Thus, in his account, the rite described by Theodore of Mopsuestia is the least dramatic of all, whereas it is in fact the most dramatic when viewed as a whole.

Much of the dramatic action of the service had to be supplied by faith, of course, for the most important participants, namely Satan and his minions and God in his trinitarian *personae* of creator, redeemer, and sanctifier, were invisible, and their actions were usually—though not always—imperceptible to the observers and the other participants. The latter always included several ministers, and one of their functions was to denounce the evil spirits and utter terrible threats against them, commanding and forcing them to remove their power and even their personal presence from within the candidates and sometimes from the water, salt, and oil that were used in the ceremony. In one form of the service, the devil was elaborately summoned to court and was legally convicted of entertaining false claims over the candidates. The candidates themselves were then confiscated and were taken under the protection of Christ, who by dying *incognito* had deceived Satan into forfeiting his rights to tyrannize over the human race.

The candidates themselves took part in the drama not only by their passive submission to hours of exorcism but also by their active pronunciation of a formal renouncement of Satan, as if they had hitherto been his followers and loyal subjects. To make this change of allegiance even more dramatic, the candidates in some rites turned toward the west, the realm of the setting sun and death, the ritual seat of the prince of the world, "who has the power of death," and rejected him and his pomps directly with gestures of mockery, even spitting at him in scorn; and then they turned towards the east and professed their belief in God the Father and his Son, their Redeemer, and in the Holy Spirit. They were anointed with exorcized oil, in some cases were given exorcized salt, and were then baptized with exorcized water and finally anointed with another variety of exorcized oil to strengthen them for their future struggles against the powerful spirits of evil.

In such ways, then, the real-life drama of the struggle with Satan became ritualized and liturgized. Centuries later, in the West, the ritual and liturgy of the Church became dramatized in mimetic representations of the history of salvation. From early Christian times, of course, man's fall and his subsequent delivery by Christ had been repeated in daily and yearly cycles of the mass and office, and in the Lenten and Easter seasons it had been merged with the actual ceremonies of the liberation of the baptismal candidates from Satan. The day of baptism was Holy Saturday, when the Savior's harrowing of hell was commemorated. On the day that Jesus released the souls of the just from the power of Satan in hell, the souls of the living were justified by the Savior's merits. Beginning about the turn of the tenth century, the salvific events of history began to be acted out, in varying degrees of representation. In addition to the well-known unacted *Quem quaeritis* dialogue, which was expanded to take in other scenes and was eventually acted out,[2] a formal deposition of the crucified Christ was often staged, as well as an "elevation" of the resurrected Christ, in the course of which there was sometimes a hell-harrowing episode. Finally, the vernacular drama, centered on the feast of Corpus Christi, sixty days after Easter, gave the complete story, beginning with the fall of Lucifer and Adam and continuing through the Old Testament into the New and on past the time of Christ to the Day of Judgment at the end of the world.

During all of these developments, the baptismal ritual continued virtually unchanged, in the forms that had developed centuries before. Much of its dramatic impact had been blunted, of course, and there was rarely any explicit reference to it in the new drama. But it remained as a relic of earlier dramaturgical impulses, and along with the rest of the liturgy it served as a backdrop for later productions.

In the pages that follow, then, I examine the initiation rites of Christendom in their conceptual and dramatic aspects. My primary concern is the ritual reaction against evil spirits and the interaction of the liturgical forms with developing concepts of demonology in the Church. I point out the ways in which the faithful expressed their concern by acting out their resistance, in a ceremonial and (they piously believed and hoped) efficacious fashion, against the pervasive forces of evil in the world. The ultimate purpose of the initiation rites was not negative but positive, of course; they were intended to effect and demonstrate the adherence of the new Christian to Christ and his Church and to permit him to receive the pardon, assistance, and protection of God in becoming a temple of the Holy Spirit. But the antidemonic elements, the moments of combat with and victory over the great antagonist, provide the dramatic focus of the rites.

HENRY ANSGAR KELLY

Los Angeles, California

---

[2]Hardison postulates the reverse sequence for the *Quem quaeritis:* it was first a play, then a trope. See below, Chapter 12 n. 64.

Abbreviations

ALW	*Archiv für Liturgiewissenschaft.*
Andrieu	Michel Andrieu, ed. *Les ordines romani du haut moyen âge.* 5 vols. SSL 11, 23–24, 28–29 (vol. 5 was posthumously edited by A. van Roey and A. H. Thomas). Louvain 1931–1961.
ANF	*The Ante-Nicene Fathers.* New York 1890.
APOT	R. H. Charles, ed. *The Apocrypha and Pseudepigrapha of the Old Testament.* 2 vols. Oxford 1913.
Bartsch	Elmar Bartsch. *Die Sachbeschwörungen der römischen Liturgie.* LQF 46. Münster 1967.
BNT	Augustin Grail et al. *Baptism in the New Testament,* translation by David Askew of two numbers of *Lumière et vie* for 1956. Baltimore 1964.
CCL	Corpus christianorum. Series latina.
CSCO	Corpus scriptorum christianorum orientalium.
CSEL	Corpus scriptorum ecclesiasticorum latinorum.
DACL	*Dictionnaire d'archéologie chrétienne et de liturgie.*
Dölger, *Exorzismus*	Franz Josef Dölger. *Der exorzismus im altchristlichen Taufritual.* Studien zur Geschichte und Kultur des Altertums 3.1–2. Paderborn 1909.
GCS	Die griechischen christlichen Schriftsteller der ersten drei Jahrhunderte.
Gel	The Gelasian liturgy as found in Vatican Library MS reg. lat. 316, ed. L. C. Mohlberg et al., *Liber sacramentorum romanae aeclesiae ordinis anni circuli.* REDsmf 4. Rome 1960. The numbers cited refer to the paragraphs of this edition.
Greg, Greg sup	The Gregorian liturgy of the *Hadrianum* and the Supplement of Benedict of Aniane in *Le sacramentaire grégorien,* ed. Jean Deshusses. Vol. 1, *Le sacramentaire; le supplement d'Aniane.*

13

	Spicilegium friburgense 16. Fribourg 1971. The numbers cited refer to the paragraphs of this edition.
HBS	Henry Bradshaw Society.
Kelly, *Devil*	Henry Ansgar Kelly. *The Devil, Demonology, and Witchcraft.* Rev. ed. New York 1974.
LQF	Liturgiewissenschaftliche Quellen und Forschungen.
Lukken	G. M. Lukken. *Original Sin in the Roman Liturgy: Research into the Theology of Original Sin in the Roman Sacramentaria and the Early Baptismal Liturgy.* Leiden 1973.
MGH	Monumenta Germaniae historica.
OR	*Ordo romanus.* (See Andrieu.)
OTP	James H. Charlesworth, ed. *The Old Testament Pseudepigrapha.* 2 vols. New York 1983–1985.
PG	Patrologia graeca.
PL	Patrologia latina.
PLS	Patrologiae latinae supplementum.
PO	Patrologia orientalis.
1QS	*The Rule of Qumran.*
Quasten	Johannes Quasten. *Patrology.* Vols. 1–3. Utrecht 1950–1960.
REDsmf	Rerum ecclesiasticarum documenta. Series maior, Fontes.
SC	Sources chrétiennes.
SSL	Spicilegium sacrum lovaniense. Etudes et documents.
Strack-Billerbeck	Herman L. Strack, Paul Billerbeck, et al. *Kommentar zum neuen Testament aus Talmud und Midrasch.* 6 vols. Munich 1922–1961.
TU	Texte und Untersuchungen zur Geschichte der altchristlichen Literatur.

PART I /

THE BACKGROUND

I /

Evil Spirits and Conversion to Christ in the New Testament

Before considering the formal rituals of Christian initiation, I must examine the context in which they developed. I shall start with the New Testament, saving for Chapter 2 a fuller discussion of the Jewish background of the emergence of Christian demonology and baptismal practices. Chapter 3 will address developments during the first two centuries after Christ; Chapter 4 will take special notice of the Egyptian gnostics, among whom first appeared many of the anti-demonic rituals that later came into use in Christian communities in various parts of the world.

The New Testament reflects various speculations concerning the spirit world, speculations that are in most of their details very different from the systematized formulations of later angelology and demonology: that is, the patristic doctrines that were inherited and elaborated by the Church of the Middle Ages. For instance, the Fathers eventually developed the theory that the evil spirits who continually plagued mankind were originally angels who had sinned and were cast out of heaven. Specifically, the pre-cosmic fall of Lucifer and other angels was first conceived by Origen at the turn of the third century. At the time when the New Testament was written, fallen angels of this sort were unknown. Fallen angels of another kind were known, but they figured only in an episode of the remote past. Pseudepigraphous works such as the *Book of Enoch* told the story of certain angels called Watchers who, in the days before the Deluge, had been captivated by women and had mated with them, against the will of God. As punishment, they were imprisoned in the chasms of the earth, to be kept there until the great Day of Judgment, when they were to be cast into the fiery abyss forever. They had no further dealings with men and were therefore of no contemporary social or religious concern except as an example of the visitation of divine wrath upon sinners. It is for this purpose that their tragedy is alluded to in the New Testament, in the Epistle of Jude and in the Second Epistle of Peter, where they are described along with other transgressors of Old Testament times.[1]

One aspect of the story of the fallen Watchers, however, did have some bearing upon everyday life. According to this tradition the offspring of the union between the angels and their human wives were the giants or "mighty men" of Genesis 6.4 who, after killing each other off, lived on in the form of evil spirits or demons. In this guise they afflicted mankind and would continue to do so until the end of the world. There may be some traces of this conception of demons in the unclean spirits that appear prominently in the synoptic Gospels (Matthew, Mark, and Luke), but, if so, their function as tempters is nowhere in evidence. Their origin is not discussed, but like the disease germs of modern medicine they are definitely parasitic in nature; Jesus speaks of the unclean spirit who when he has gone out of a man "passes through waterless places seeking rest, but he finds none" and eventually returns to his human host.[2] Though they are called evil, the evil they cause is limited to the physical and mental disturbances that their inhabitation of the human body produces.

In the *Book of Jubilees,* another pre-Christian pseudepigraphous

[1]Many scholars have asserted that the idea of Satan as Lucifer (who fell before the creation of man and for some reason not connected with man) was contemporary with the New Testament era, because it appears in the longer recension of the *Book of the Secrets of Enoch* (2 *Enoch*) 29.4–5 (*OTP* 1.148). This recension was dated by R. A. Charles to A.D. 1–50 (*APOT* 2.429), but in more recent times it has generally been redated to the Middle Ages. The matter is still not settled (see F. I. Andersen, *OTP* 1.93–96); but all dates and theories based on the early dating must be reassessed. On the Satan-Lucifer question, see H. A. Kelly, "The Devil in the Desert," *Catholic Biblical Quarterly* 26 (1964) 190–220, esp. 203–204; Jeffrey Burton Russell, *Satan: The Early Christian Tradition* (Ithaca 1981) 130 n. 59, and my review of Russell in the *Journal of Religious History* 12 (1983) 331–333. For these and other aspects of the development of demonology, see H. A. Kelly, *The Devil, Demonology, and Witchcraft,* rev. ed. (New York 1974) or, as translated and further revised, *Le diable et ses démons* (Paris 1977).

[2]Matthew 12.43.

work (purportedly dictated by an angel to Moses), the evil spirits are under the supervision of Mastema, or Satan, one of God's angelic assistants, who is in charge of disciplining mankind.[3] Similarly, in the Gospels Satan seems to be in charge of inflicting all diseases upon men, and, accordingly, he has control over the unclean spirits.

The Satan of the New Testament is no longer the angel or "son of God" on familiar terms with God who appears in the book of Job. Though he still has access to God's throne to bring charges against men, his character has become more malignant and his functions enlarged. He is now the ruler of this world, to whom all the authority and glory of the kingdoms of the world have been delivered and who has the power of death.[4] The latter office was that of the angel of death, who was often identified as a satan figure and who, at least in one account in the *Midrash Rabbah* attributed to Eliezer the Galilean (ca. A.D. 150), was called "world ruler" because of the universality and inexorability of his operations.[5] Satan's complete dominion over the world had to give way to the rule of the Messiah, which he opposed with every means in his power. But he was not to be totally ousted from his roles, and there are indications in the New Testament that he is considered, at times at least, to be motivated by an excessive zeal to enforce the law and punish wrongdoers in terms of the Mosaic and civil law.[6]

Such developments in the portrayal of Satan caused a partial merging of his nature and functions with those of the guardian angels of the nations, another Jewish tradition that finds an especially prominent place in the writings of Saint Paul. According to this conception, which is already present in the Old Testament,[7] all of the pagan nations had their own angelic rulers, who shared in the faults as well as in the virtues of the human governments, and who, in the tradition as Paul received it, also controlled the material universe and were the

[3] *Jubilees* 10.18 (*APOT* 2.28).
[4] Revelation 12.10; John 12.31; Luke 4.5–6; Hebrews 2.14.
[5] *Midrash Rabbah*, ed. and trans. H. Freedman and M. Simon (London 1939–1961) 4.230–231 (*Leviticus* 18.3); cf. Strack-Billerbeck 1.149; Kelly, "Devil in the Desert" 210; James S. Ackerman, "The Rabbinic Interpretation of Psalm 82 and the Gospel of John: John 10.34," *Harvard Theological Review* 59 (1966) 186–91; Hamish Swanston, "The Lukan Temptation Narrative," *Journal of Theological Studies* 2.17 (1966) 71.
[6] See G. B. Caird, *Principalities and Powers: A Study in Pauline Theology* (Oxford 1956) chap. 2: "The Great Accuser" (31ff.).
[7] Deuteronomy 32.8–9, emended according to the Septuagint and one of the Qumran texts; see Caird, *Principalities* 5 n. 1; D. S. Russell, *The Method and Message of Jewish Apocalyptic, 200 B.C.–A.D. 100* (London 1964) 248.

mediators or administrators of the Jewish law. They are by no means to be identified with the angels who sinned with women nor, for that matter, with the stars who were punished, according to the *Book of Enoch,* for failing to rise on time.[8] In their role as civil authorities these angels were still owed honor and obedience by Christians. But even though Paul seems to have arrived at a hope for the redemption of these powers, he still recognized that many of the things they required in the name of the law had been abrogated by Christ and must be actively resisted by his followers.

These, then, are the main ingredients of Jewish demonology as it appears in the New Testament. They will supply much of the raw material for later speculation on the world of invisible spirits, even though, as I emphasized at the beginning, this speculation radically altered the original significance of the biblical data. It should be pointed out that, of the malign spirits discussed above, only the "unclean spirits" are called demons in the Scriptures; but I have nevertheless applied the term "demonology" (or "demonic" and "antidemonic") not only to them but to the devil (Satan) and the other wicked angels as well, rather than invent a term such as "cacopneumatology" (the study of evil spirits), which would be technically more accurate for this early stage of development.

The followers of Christ developed three basic processes or forms of conduct for dealing with harmful spirits, those of expulsion, renunciation, and repulsion. The spirits that caused injury by their physical presence, especially by dwelling within the human body, had to be driven out and away; the evil principles and way of life espoused by the spirits had to be repudiated; and once the spirits were removed, physically and morally, their attempts to regain control had to be resisted. Eventually these processes would be combined into a dramatic unity in the baptismal services, in which the candidates would gain freedom from and ascendancy over their spiritual antagonists. In the time of Jesus and in the apostolic age, however, these strategies had not yet been formally united to the initiation ceremonies or

---

[8] *Enoch* 18.12–16 (*APOT* 2.200; *OTP* 1.23). A new edition and translation of *1 Enoch* has been produced by Michael A. Knibb with Edward Ullendorff, *The Ethiopic Book of Enoch,* 2 vols. (Oxford 1978), and the new translation in *OTP* is by E. Isaac; see also J. T. Milik with Matthew Black, *The Books of Enoch: Aramaic Fragments of Qumran Cave 4* (Oxford 1976). Many recent works on Jewish-Christian angelology are defective because they combine different traditions prematurely. See Kelly, *Devil* 25 n. 1.

grouped together into a systematic antidemonic therapy, but they can be observed individually in the New Testament as follows.

Expulsion. The usual method of expulsion was that of exorcism, that is, a command or series of commands addressed to the harmful spirits, which was designed to induce or force them to depart, either because of an appeal to some authority with the explicit or implicit threat of punishment for disobedience or because of some intrinsic power in the formula of command itself. In the synoptic Gospels Jesus forced the unclean spirits to leave their victims by a simple word of rebuke, and on one occasion he characterized his method by saying that he cast out demons by the spirit of God or by the finger of God, rather than, as the Pharisees charged, by Beelzebul, the prince of demons.[9] His followers, on the other hand, and even those who were not his followers, cast out demons by invoking the name of Jesus.

Renunciation. When a man was thought to be possessed by an evil spirit, he was considered incapable of helping himself, and had to be assisted by someone with the power of exorcism. The situation was different in the moral sphere, where there was a question of voluntary allegiance to or repudiation of what the spirits offered in opposition to the will of God. In the imaginary drama of his temptation in the desert, Jesus provided, in a three-act tableau, an example of how to reject the offers of the devil even when they included all the kingdoms of the world.[10] The First Epistle of John says that "he who commits sin is of the devil," but the meaning is obviously that a person can alter this unfortunate genealogy simply by refraining from committing sin.[11] In the Pauline view, before the coming of Christ there was indeed a subjection of men to spiritual powers hostile to God's plan of salvation, a subjection so complete as to be almost involuntary and regarded as a state of slavery. But Jesus took on flesh "that through death he might destroy him who has the power of death, that is, the devil, and deliver all those who through fear of death were subject to lifelong bondage."[12] Saint Paul says, "When we were children, we were slaves to the principals of the universe.

[9]Matthew 12.28; Luke 11.20; Mark 3.22. See S. Vernon McCasland, *By the Finger of God: Demon Possession and Exorcism in Early Christianity in the Light of Modern Views of Mental Illness* (New York 1951). Cf. Adolf Deissmann, *Light from the Ancient East,* trans. L. R. M. Strachan (London 1927) 306.

[10]For the Jewish precedents for this kind of dramatization, see my "Devil in the Desert."

[11]1 John 3.8.

[12]Hebrews 2.14–15.

But when the time had fully come, God sent forth his Son, born of woman, born under the law, to redeem those who were under the law, so that we might receive adoption as sons." He goes on to point out to his readers that once they have participated in the liberation effected by Jesus, they have it in their power to accept or reject the demands of their former masters, the angels who were the intermediaries of the Mosaic law.) "Formerly," he says, "when you did not know God, you were in bondage to beings that by nature are no gods; but now that you have come to know God, how can you turn back again to the weak and beggarly principals, whose slaves you want to be once more? You observe days, and months, and seasons, and years!"[13]

Repulsion (Apotropaism). To a certain extent the process of renunciation coincides with that of repulsion. Saint Paul warns against a return to the regime of the powers and exposes the fallaciousness of the arguments whereby the regulations of the law were justified: "These have indeed an appearance of wisdom in promoting rigor of devotion and self-abasement and severity to the body, but they are of no value in checking the indulgence of the flesh." (The first Epistle of Peter urges alertness in overcoming future trials: "Be sober, be watchful. Your adversary the devil prowls around like a roaring lion, seeking someone to devour. Resist him, firm in your faith." Divine aid is also to be sought, as when Jesus tells the apostles to "watch and pray that you may not enter into temptation."[14] But it is in the Epistle to the Ephesians that there is the most detailed set of instructions for making use of spiritual aids against the advances of the devil and the other spiritual rulers of the world.) It is worth quoting in detail.

> Be strong in the Lord and in the strength of his might. Put on the whole armor of God, that you may be able to stand against the wiles of the devil. For we are not contending against flesh and blood, but against the principalities, against the powers, against the world rulers of this present darkness, against the spiritual armies of wickedness in the heavens. Therefore take the whole armor of God, that you may be able to withstand in the evil day, and having done all, to remain standing. Stand therefore, having girded your loins with truth, and having put on the breastplate of righteousness, and having shod your feet with the eagerness to spread the gospel of peace; above all holding up the shield

[13]Galatians 4.3–10; cf. 3.19.
[14]Colossians 2.23; 1 Peter 5.8–9; Mark 14.38.

of faith, with which you can quench all the flaming darts of the Evil
One. And take the helmet of salvation, and the sword of the Spirit,
which is the word of God. Pray at all times in the Spirit, with all prayer
and supplication. To that end keep alert with all perseverance, making
supplication for all the saints.[15]

These instructions are apotropaic only on the moral or religious level;
they are not designed to prevent the physical occupation or injury of a
person's body by evil spirits. Possession or demonic disease is a
concern only in the synoptic Gospels and in the Acts of the Apostles.
It is sometimes suggested that such afflictions of the body and mind
are the result of sin and can be prevented from recurring by leading an
upright life. But the only mention of the return of an evil spirit occurs
in the parable of Jesus mentioned above: "When the unclean spirit has
gone out of a man, he passes through waterless places seeking rest,
but he finds none. Then he says, 'I will return to my house from
which I came.' And when he comes he finds it empty, swept, and put
in order. Then he goes and brings with him seven other spirits more
evil than himself, and they enter and dwell there; and the last state of
that man becomes worse than the first."[16] In Matthew, Jesus adds:
"So it shall be also with this evil generation." In this application it is
clear that the worse state is caused by continued evildoing. But it is
more difficult to know what concept of demonic possession and
repossession is involved on the literal level. Furthermore, there is no
indication that the unclean spirit was authoritatively driven out in the
first place; he seems to have left his host of his own accord.

In short, (the sort of demoniacal possession that we find in the
Scriptures is not likely to have been the primary inspiration for the
rites of prebaptismal exorcism and postbaptismal apotropaism that
emerged in later times. We shall see that the doctrine of sin demons,
which had developed among some Jewish sectarians about the time of
Christ, is a far more likely source. We should not conclude, however,
that the data of the Gospels and the Acts of the Apostles would not
have been interpreted as evidence for the necessity of such rites. The
same is true of some of the other passages that I have just cited. For
instance, the exhortation of Ephesians could easily be taken as a
libretto for a ritual of "moral rearmament" against the forces of evil
at the time of baptism. Similarly, Jesus's decisive repudiation of the

---

[15]Ephesians 6.10–18.
[16]Matthew 12.43–45; Luke 11.24–26.

devil's temptations comes immediately after his baptism and forty-day fast; this example may have inspired or at least reinforced the later Christian practice of associating a forty-day fast and a formal renunciation of Satan with baptism, with due allowances for the fact that the order of the events was altered. It is certainly true that the parallel between the baptismal candidates and Jesus was sometimes recognized. Paul, for instance, speaks of the candidates as dying and rising with Christ. It is, then, a clear possibility that the events of his life influenced the form that the rites took, as was obviously the case with the liturgical drama of the Middle Ages.

Apart from the passages in the New Testament that could have inspired the exorcistic, renunciatory, and apotropaic initiation ceremonies of the future, in a number of incidents and themes baptism is associated with the struggle against evil powers in such a way as to suggest that some ceremonial connection had already evolved. It seems at least very natural that such a connection might have been made.

Let us look first at the Acts of the Apostles. At one point we observe that the casting out of demons is followed immediately by the conferral of baptism. When Philip came to Samaria to preach the gospel, he amazed the people with the signs he worked, "for unclean spirits came out of many who were possessed, crying with a loud voice; and many who were paralyzed or lame were healed." They were even more impressed with Philip than they were with Simon Magus, and all were converted, Simon among them, and were baptized.[17] There is, of course, no question here of exorcizing all candidates for baptism, as came to be the practice later; but it can readily be assumed that from the very beginning attempts would have been made to effect the cure of all suspected demoniacs before they proceeded to baptism. What happened later, as we shall see, is that all unbaptized persons came to be regarded as demoniacs of a special kind.

There is another suggestive episode later on in Acts. When Paul describes his ride from Jerusalem to Damascus, he repeats the words of Jesus spoken to him as he lay fallen on the ground: "I have appeared to you for this purpose, to appoint you to serve and bear witness to the things in which you have seen me and to those in which I will appear to you, delivering you from the people and from the Gentiles—to whom I send you to open their eyes, that they may

[17]Acts 8.5–13.

turn from darkness to light and from the power of Satan to God, that they may receive forgiveness of sins and a place among those who are sanctified by faith in me."[18] Paul says specifically that the voice was in the Hebrew language; and the Hebrew parallelism evident in the phrase "from darkness to light and from the power of Satan to God" could well reflect a hymn or liturgical formula describing or acting out the process of redemption. The turning from darkness (Satan) to light (God or Christ) corresponds exactly to the ceremony of the renunciation of Satan (facing the west) and the confession of Christ (toward the east) as it came to be practiced in later times. While it is admittedly more probable that Paul's account (or the hymn that he quoted) inspired the form of the rite than that a rite served as inspiration for the formula, it is evident that such a rite would readily suggest itself.

Other possible fragments of baptismal hymns or liturgies can be isolated elsewhere in the Scriptures. We note, for instance, the parallelism in a passage interpolated into the Second Epistle to the Corinthians, which uses the terminology characteristic of the Essene-like sect of Qumran.

Do not be mismated with unbelievers. For what partnership have righteousness and iniquity? Or what fellowship has light with darkness? What accord has Christ with Belial? Or what has a believer in common with an unbeliever? What agreement has the temple of God with idols? For we are the temple of the living God; as God said,

I will live in them and move among them,
and I will be their God,
and they shall be my people.
Therefore come out from them,
and be separate from them, says the Lord,
and touch nothing unclean;
then I will welcome you,
and I will be a father to you,
and you shall be my sons and daughters,
says the Lord Almighty.

Since we have these promises, beloved, let us cleanse ourselves from every defilement of body and spirit, and make holiness perfect in the fear of God.[19]

---

[18]Acts 26.16–18.
[19] 2 Corinthians 6.14–7.1. Cf. Joseph A. Fitzmyer, "Qumran and the Interpolated

If this exhortation had been dramatized ritually at an initiation ceremony (whether of Essenes or Christians), the result would no doubt have resembled in many ways the baptismal services of the centuries to come.

I shall take up later the question of the ceremonies practiced at Qumran, but here I shall cite one more passage from the New Testament, this time from the Epistle to the Ephesians, which may also reflect the light-darkness motif of the Dead Sea sect:[20]

> Let no one deceive you with empty words, for it is because of these things that the wrath of God comes upon the sons of disobedience. Therefore do not associate with them, for once you were darkness, but now you are light in the Lord; walk as children of light (for the fruit of light is found in all that is good and right and true), and try to learn what is pleasing to the Lord. Take no part in the unfruitful works of darkness, but instead expose them. For it is a shame even to speak of things that they do in secret; but when anything is exposed by the light it becomes visible, for anything that becomes visible is light. Therefore it is said,
>
> Awake, O sleeper, and arise from the dead,
> and Christ shall give you light.

The quotation at the end of this passage is generally thought to be from an early Christian hymn, and it is suggested that it was connected with the rite of baptism, which was often characterized as an illumination.[21]

Paragraph in 2 Cor. 6.14–7.1," *Catholic Biblical Quarterly* 23 (1961) 271–280. For possible references by Paul himself to Qumran, see Constantin Daniel, "Une mention paulinienne des esséniens de Qumran," *Revue de Qumran* 5 (1966) 553–567. According to Robert North, "Qumranica," *Biblica* 61 (1980) 116–120, esp. 118, it is fairly universally held that the Dead Sea Scrolls were in use around 70 B.C. But in his review of B. E. Thiering, *Redating the Teacher of Righteousness* (Sydney 1979), in *Biblica* 63 (1982) 117–118, he admits that attempts at later dating must be taken seriously.

[20]Paul's authorship of Ephesians has often been doubted; for instance, it is categorically assigned to a Qumran-influenced Paulinist, who wrote at Ephesus at the close of the first century after Christ, by Helmut Koester, "*Gnomai diaphoroi:* The Origin and Nature of Diversification in the History of Early Christianity," *Harvard Theological Review* 58 (1965) 279–318, esp. 316. For the similiarities of the epistle to the Qumran writings, see F. M. Cross, *The Ancient Library of Qumran and Modern Biblical Studies,* ed. 2 (New York 1961) 216–217; K. G. Kuhn, "Der Epheserbrief im Licht der Qumrantexte," *New Testament Studies* 7 (1960–1961) 334–346.

[21]Ephesians 5.6–14. See D. Mollat, "Baptismal Symbolism in St. Paul," *BNT* 63–83, esp. 81–83.

In the next chapter of Ephesians, as we have seen, the principalities and powers are called "the world rulers of this present darkness" and "the spiritual hosts of wickedness in the heavenly places." Earlier in the same epistle it is said that God seated Christ in the heavenly places above every principality and power and diverted the Christians from the path of the prince of the power of the air and seated them too in the heavenly places.[22] Baptism is not specified here as the precise moment of the Christian's exaltation above the powers, but his transformation is described in terms of being raised from the dead with Christ, which is very suggestive of Paul's baptismal imagery. Of course, even if the primary meaning of this passage were to specify baptism as the means of deliverance from the angelic rulers, we could not be sure that this concept had a noticeable part in the baptismal ritual itself. In this section of Ephesians redemption is spoken of only in terms of revival from the dead, and not as an illumination. Light imagery is introduced as a symbol of continued spiritual progress after baptism (the author prays that his listeners may have the eyes of their hearts enlightened). In Colossians, however, the figure of light and darkness appears in terms suggesting a juxtaposition of baptism and the theme of Christ's relationship with the powers:

> [The Father] has qualified us to share in the inheritance of the saints in light. He has delivered us from the authority of darkness and transferred us to the kingdom of his beloved Son, in whom we have redemption, the forgiveness of sins. He is the image of the invisible God, the firstborn of all creation; for in him all things were created, in heaven and on earth, visible and invisible, whether thrones or dominions or principalities or authorities—all things were created through him and for him. He is before all things, and in him all things hold together. He is the head of the body, the church; he is the beginning, the first-born from the dead, that in everything he might be preeminent. For in him all the fullness of God was pleased to dwell, and through him to reconcile to himself all things, whether on earth or in heaven, making peace by the blood of his cross.[23]

This passage, it has been alleged, contains the substance of a pre-Christian gnostic hymn that the early Church adapted for its own use in the liturgy of initiation, the baptismal message of which can be paraphrased as follows: "You are reconciled and the cosmos is paci-

[22]Ephesians 1.16–2.7.
[23]Colossians 1.12–20.

fied, because the powers which swayed it have been despoiled and now follow in the train of the triumphal progress of Christ."[24]

The hypothesis that gnosticism had its origins before Christianity is much disputed; but we need not agree with it in order to see a reflection of baptismal ceremonies in Colossians. It is evident that at Colossae Christ's supremacy was being challenged by the role given to the heavenly powers. Paul makes it clear that their dominion over men was taken away from them by Christ's victory, and it is precisely in baptism that the benefits of this victory are made available for the Christian.[25] Once again, if the words of the epistle are not actually based upon a liturgical celebration of liberation from the powers, they could readily have inspired such a usage. The same can be said for 1 John 5.18: "We know that anyone born of God does not sin, but He who was born of God keeps him, and the Evil One does not touch him."

The exhortation of Romans 13.12: "Let us then cast off the works of darkness and put on the armor of light" is a formula that M. E. Boismard believes may have originated in the baptismal catechesis. He finds it very close to the formal renunciation of Satan and his works that later became universal in the Church. Similarly, he says, when the First Epistle of John says that the Son of God came "to destroy the works of the devil," it is possibly echoing an early baptismal formula.[26]

In another study, also highly conjectural, Boismard attempts to extricate a baptismal hymn from the New Testament in which the devil figures by comparing the following passages.

Clothe yourselves, all of you, with humility toward one another, for "God opposes the proud, but gives grace to the humble." Humble yourselves, therefore, under the mighty hand of God, that in due time he may exalt you. Be sober, be watchful. Your adversary the devil prowls around like a roaring lion, seeking someone to devour. Resist him, firm in your faith, knowing that the same experience of suffering is required of your brotherhood throughout the world. [1 Peter 5.5–9]

[24]Ernst Käsemann, "A Primitive Christian Baptismal Liturgy," *Essays on New Testament Themes,* trans. W. J. Montague, Studies in Biblical Theology 41 (Naperville 1964) 149–168, esp. 159, 168.

[25]See Y. B. Tremel, "Baptism—The Incorporation of the Christian into Christ," *BNT* 189–208, esp. 204–205; Wilhelm Heitmüller, *Im Namen Jesu,* Forschungen zur Religion und Literatur des Alten und Neuen Testaments 1.2 (Göttingen 1903) 322.

[26]1 John 3.8; see M. E. Boismard, "I Renounce Satan, His Pomps, and His Works," *BNT* 107–112.

He gives more grace; therefore it says, "God opposes the proud, but gives grace to the humble." Submit yourselves to God. Resist the devil and he will flee from you. Draw near to God and he will draw near to you. Cleanse your hands, you sinners, and purify your hearts, you men of double mind. Be wretched and mourn and weep. Let your laughter be turned to mourning and your joy to dejection. Humble yourselves before the Lord and he will exalt you. [James 4.6–10]

Boismard suggests the following reconstruction of the underlying hymn:

God opposes the proud
but gives grace to the humble.
Humble yourselves before God
and he will exalt you.
Resist the devil
and he will flee from you.
Draw near to God
and he will draw near to you.

Once more he is reminded of the renunciation of Satan, which he believes must go back to a very early period. The hymn, accordingly, may have been addressed to the neophytes before the ceremony of renunciation; or alternatively, it may have been a general exhortation chanted upon the occasion of baptism by the presiding officer.[27]

In sum, if the words of the hypothetical hymn refer to the initial conversion to Christianity, they would be sung before baptism; if, however, they are simply an encouragement to people who are already Christians and if they were used at baptism, they would, as I have already suggested, find their most likely place after baptism, as specifying the way for overcoming the devil in the future; that is, the hymn could be classified under the category of repulsion or apotropaism rather than as an invitation to renunciation.

Elsewhere in the First Epistle of Peter, baptism is closely connected with Christ's subjection of the powers: "Baptism, which corresponds to this [Noah's being saved through water], now saves you, not as a removal of dirt from the body but as an appeal to God for a clear conscience, through the resurrection of Jesus Christ, who has gone into heaven and is at the right hand of God, with angels, authorities,

[27]Boismard, *Quatre hymnes baptismales dans la première épître de Pierre,* Lectio divina 30 (Paris 1961) 134–135.

and powers subject to him."[28] Again, this passage may strike us as reminiscent of the baptismal renunciation,[29] but in this context it would be a renunciation of the requirements of law insisted upon by the powers but made obsolete by the Christian dispensation.

As we shall see, when the formula of renunciation first appears in unambiguous form at the beginning of the third century, it is chiefly the religion of paganism that is being renounced, at a time when the pagan gods had been identified as the demons or fallen angels elaborated by Christian tradition. When Paul recalls how the Thessalonians "turned to God from idols, to serve a living and true God,"[30] it is evident that he does not consider the gods worshiped by idolaters to be either living or true. But once again, such a text might have influenced later practice after the conception of idolatry had changed, and it might have assisted in the formulation of the baptismal renunciation. Something of the sort happens when Cyprian quotes Ezekiel 36.25: "I will sprinkle clean water upon you, and you shall be clean from all your uncleannesses, and from all your idols I will cleanse you." Although Cyprian's immediate point is that the unclean do not possess the power of making clean (that is, the baptism performed by heretics is invalid), presumably he believes that the idols of the text refer to the religion fostered by demons.[31]

The concern for the realms of invisible spirits that is manifested in various forms in the New Testament could thus easily have given rise to initiation ceremonies expressive of opposition to harmful extra-human influences. But whether such rites actually existed by the time the books of the New Testament were compiled is not at all evident, and perhaps we must admit that they probably did not, in view of the lack of corroborative evidence from other documents of the first and second centuries. Or at least if practices of this kind are actually reflected in one or other of the suggestive passages that we have examined, they were probably not in wide use at this early date.

A better case can be made for the use of demonological themes in

---

[28]1 Peter 3.21–22.

[29]Cf. William J. Dalton, *Christ's Proclamation to the Spirits: A Study of 1 Peter 3.18–4.6*, Analecta biblica 23 (Rome 1965) 203.

[30]1 Thessalonians 1.9. See Gerhard Friedrich, "Ein Tauflied hellenistischer Judenchristen: 1 Thess. 1.9f." (1965), in *Auf das Wort kommt es an: Gesammelte Aufsätze* (Göttingen 1978) 236–250; see also his "Das Lied vom Hohenpriester in Zusammenhang von Hebr. 4.14–15.10" (1962), ibid. 277–299, esp. 284–288.

[31]Cyprian, *Epistulae* 69.12, 70.1 (CSEL 3.2.761, 767); cf. his *Quod idola dii non sunt* 6–7 (CSEL 3.1.23–25).

prebaptismal instruction, since the Gospels themselves with all their demonology eventually formed part of this instruction.[32] There have been attempts, moreover, especially by Philip Carrington and Edward Gordon Selwyn, to find traces of definite patterns of baptismal catechesis in use in the Church from very primitive times. We have seen the exhortation of Romans, to cast off the works of darkness and put on the armor of light, interpreted in this context. In fact, this short verse includes a number of the themes that Archbishop Carrington postulates for the early catechism, those namely of "putting off" and "putting on," darkness and light, and armor.[33] Selwyn agrees basically with this analysis except that he sees a "Children of Light" exhortation at an even earlier stage than that projected by Carrington; and though he admits that the armor motif may have entered into the baptismal form, he finds its principal use, along with the commands to "watch" and "stand" (or "resist the devil") in a "persecution-form," an instruction aimed at all the faithful in times of crisis.[34]

It is in the latter context that many of the passages cited above find their place, those passages especially in which the Christian is warned against the wiles and weapons of the devil. If these warnings were delivered at a time preceding baptism, they would not, of course, necessarily characterize the initiation services as demonological in themselves, though the preparatory instructions could easily influence the concept that a person had of baptism. "The putting off of evil would be fitly symbolized by the stripping off of the garments before immersion; the command to stand morally would correspond to standing up in the baptismal service after prostration in prayer";[35] and the reclothing after baptism would suggest the donning of the breastplate of justice and all the other items in the Christian's spiritual armory.

In the texts that Carrington and others cite as reflecting the renunciatory part of the catechesis, that is, the putting off of evil, little

[32]B. Standaert, *L'Evangile selon Marc: Composition et genre littéraire* (Diss. Kath. Univ. Nijmegen 1978), as reported by Burkhard Neunheuser, *ALW* 22 (1980) 262, proposes that the Gospel of Mark was originally intended as the prebaptismal instruction to be read at the Easter Vigil. But see Chap. 3 n.28.

[33]Philip Carrington, *The Primitive Christian Catechism* (Cambridge 1940).

[34]E. G. Selwyn, *The First Epistle of St. Peter* (London 1947) 369–382, 398–400, 439–458.

[35]W. D. Davies, *Paul and Rabbinic Judaism: Some Rabbinic Elements in Pauline Theology* (London 1948) 129.

could be construed as demonological in the sense of an explicit renunciation of Satan or the principalities and powers. More pertinent is one of the forms thought to have been employed for instructing the new followers of Christ in their duties, that is, the schema of the "two ways," which is traceable to various passages in the Old Testament[36] and which definitely took on demonological dimensions. The main witnesses to this tradition, however, are extrabiblical and will be examined in the next chapter.

[36]Selwyn 421.

2 /

Jewish Precedents and
Early Christian Practices

The rite of Christian baptism developed from the ritual washings performed by the Jews on various set occasions. The question naturally arises whether these washings or the other purificatory ceremonies that they practiced had an element of the antidemonic about them. Examination discloses no specific connection with demonology in the cleansings prescribed in orthodox circles in their earliest forms, even in proselyte baptism, that is, the initiatory washing of Gentile converts to Judaism as a supplement to circumcision. The observance of such a rite had become widespread by the first Christian century.[1] As for circumcision itself, in the Targum to the Song of Solomon, part of which may date to pre-Christian times, the seal of circumcision is said to have made the Israelites as strong as a man wearing a sword and therefore unafraid of the evil spirits and demons that moved about in the night.[2] But this apotropaic interpretation of

[1]For the washings in general, see *The Mishnah*, trans. Herbert Danby (Oxford 1933 repr. 1958) 732–745 (*Mikwaoth*); on proselyte baptism, Strack-Billerbeck, *Kommentar* 1.102–112; *Mishnah* 148, 431. A good deal of information can be found in the two books of Otto Böcher, *Dämonenfurcht und Dämonenabwehr: Ein Beitrag zur Vorgeschichte der christlichen Taufe* and *Christus exorcista: Dämonismus und Taufe im Neuen Testament,* Beiträge zur Wissenschaft vom Alten und Neuen Testament 90, 96 (Stuttgart 1970, 1972). But Böcher starts from the assumption that all cleansing and healing procedures are fundamentally antidemonic and can therefore conclude that the stress on ethical purity in the New Testament is a polemic against antidemonic practices.
[2]*The Targum to Canticles* 3.8, ed. Raphael Hai Melamed (Philadelphia 1921) 80; Strack-Billerbeck 4.33; cf. R. Le Déaut, *Introduction à la littérature targumique* (Rome 1966) 140–141.

circumcision is rare. Fulfillment of the law was the chief rabbinic prophylactic against demons.[3]

In one tradition, however, the cleansing ceremonies, though not considered exorcistic, were explained as such. In the *Midrash Rabbah* on Numbers 19.8 we read:

> An idolater asked Rabban Johanan ben Zakkai: "These rites that you perform look like a kind of witchcraft. You bring a heifer, burn it, pound it, and take its ashes. If one of you is defiled by a dead body you sprinkle upon him two or three drops and you say to him: 'Thou art clean!'" Rabban Johanan asked him: "Has the demon of madness ever possessed you?" "No," he replied. "Have you ever seen a man possessed by this demon of madness?" "Yes," said he. "And what do you do in such a case?" "We bring roots," he replied, "and make them smoke under him, then we sprinkle water upon the demon and it flees." Said Rabban Johanan to him: "Let your ears hear what you utter with your mouth! Precisely so is this spirit a spirit of uncleanness; as it is written, *And also I will cause the prophets and the unclean spirit to pass out of the land* [Zechariah 13.2]. Water of purification is sprinkled upon the unclean and the spirit flees." When the idolater had gone Rabban Johanan's disciples said to their master: "Master! This man you have put off with a mere makeshift but what explanation will you give to us?" Said he to them: "By your life! It is not the dead that defiles nor the water that purifies! The Holy One, blessed be he, merely says, 'I have laid down a statute, I have issued a decree. You are not allowed to transgress my decree'; as it is written, *This is the statute of the law*" [Numbers 19.2].[4]

Johanan ben Zakkai lived in the first century of the Christian era, and if the attribution to him of these views has any basis in historical fact (a notion that is very problematical),[5] his public characterization of the washings may have abetted an exorcistic concept of baptism.

When we turn to the heterodox Jewish groups (of which Christianity is one, of course) we expect to find more evidence of interest in evil spirits. But of the sects studied by Joseph Thomas in his work on the baptist movements of Palestine and Syria, only that of Elkasai

[3]See John Bowman, *The Gospel of Mark: The New Christian Jewish Passover Haggadah,* Studia post-biblica 8 (Leiden 1965) 49.

[4]*Midrash Rabbah,* ed. Freedman and Simon (London 1961) 6.757–758 (Numbers 19.8); cf. Jacob Neusner, *A Life of Rabban Yohanan ben Zakkai, Ca. 1–80 C.E.,* Studia post-biblica 6 (Leiden 1962) 61–62, who renders the "demon of madness" as "wandering spirit."

[5]Jacob Neusner, "In Quest of the Historical Rabban Yohanan ben Zakkai," *Harvard Theological Review* 59 (1966) 391–413.

(fl. A.D. 100) and his followers is explicitly associated with baths specifically designed to expel demons. Moreover, even among the Elkasaites the baths or baptisms that were prescribed for the cure of the possessed were on a level with the washings recommended for the cure of diseases not designated as demonic and were distinct from the daily baptisms that forgave sins. For example, one treatment reserved especially for demoniacs and those afflicted with phthisis consisted of a bath taken forty times in cold water within a period of seven days.[6] Thomas suggests that the other sects might also have had similar therapeutic washings,[7] but even if this were so, they would not necessarily have had any influence upon exorcistic initiation rituals, since the presence of demons was treated more from a medical than from a religious or moral point of view—unless, of course, all ailments were to be considered a sign of sin. The concept was current in these times, as we know from the Gospels.

Since the time that Thomas published his study, further information on early baptist practices has come to light in the scrolls of the sectaries of Qumran. Here the baths were concerned with the elimination of the sinful influence of evil spirits. The first bath taken by those seeking full admission to the Qumran community may have been decisive in the training program of the novice, even though it was supplemented by other baths later on.[8] This bath, therefore, or the ensemble of baths taken before a person's final acceptance, could be considered as an initiation rite in the same sense as the exercises undergone by Christian catechumens before baptism. The series of purifications must be seen in terms of the Qumran doctrine of the two spirits, the struggle of the spirit of wickedness with the spirit of truth in the heart of the candidate.

The struggle, however, was not considered to be finished when the

[6]Reported in Hippolytus, *Refutatio omnium haeresium* 9.15.4–16.1, ed. Paul Wendland, GCS 26 (Leipzig 1916) 254. The routine daily washings of the Elkasaites can also be seen from the text reported on by A. Henrichs and L. Koenen, "Ein griechischen Mani-Codex (P. Colon. inv. nr. 4780)," *Zeitschrift für Papyrologie und Epigraphik* 5 (1970) 97–216, esp. 135–144; but there is no demonic dimension indicated in these purificatory ablutions, *pace* Georg Kretschmar, "Recent Research on Christian Initiation," *Studia liturgica* 12 (1977) 87–106, esp. 100.

[7]Joseph Thomas, *Le mouvement baptiste en Palestine et Syrie (150 av. J.-C.–300 ap. J.-C.)* (Gembloux 1935) 141–148, 276–277.

[8]J. A. T. Robinson, "The Baptism of John and the Qumran Community; Testing a Hypothesis," *Harvard Theological Review* 50 (1957) 175–191, esp. 182; cf. John Pryke, "The Sacraments of Holy Baptism and Holy Communion in the Light of the Ritual Washings and Sacred Meals at Qumran," *Revue de Qumran* 5 (1966) 543–552, esp. 543.

candidate was fully admitted into the community—it would go on until the end of time (which was felt to be near at hand). Furthermore, the strategy of the combat did not change from expulsion to repulsion, for the spirit of evil remained within. The washings continued, therefore, and retained their exorcistic character, until the "definitive baptism" of the final purification.[9] This ultimate purgation was characterized in terms of washing, and the text of the *Rule* describing it reads like the rubrics of a great dramatic ritual in which the antagonist is finally met and conquered.

> Then God in his truth will make manifest all the deeds of man and will purify for himself some from mankind, destroying all spirit of perversity, removing all blemishes of his flesh, and purifying him with a spirit of holiness from all deeds of evil. He will sprinkle upon him a spirit of truth like waters for purification from all abominations of falsehood and his contamination with the spirit of uncleanness. Thus will upright ones understand knowledge of the highest and impart the wisdom of the sons of heaven to the perfect of way; for God has chosen them for an eternal covenant, and for them all is all the glory of Adam, all perversity being gone. All deeds of treachery will be put to shame.[10]

Rabbinical Judaism too looked forward to an ultimate moral cleansing in messianic times, supported by the words of Ezekiel that Cyprian was to apply to Christian baptism: "I will sprinkle clear water upon you, and you shall be clean from all your uncleannesses, and from all your idols I will cleanse you."[11] This cleansing was contrasted with the ordinary rites of washing practiced by the Jews, which purified from ritual uncleanness and not from moral guilt.

The idols that Ezekiel referred to would hardly be interpreted in the demonic sense that Christians would give to the word. Ezekiel himself, of course, antedated the invention of the fallen angels and their demon offspring, but even after these creatures appeared in the pseudepigrapha, idolatry was only rarely associated with evil spirits.[12] Such an association was even more rare in mainstream Judaism: "It is not likely that early Rabbinic Jews would do such honor to the

---

[9]J. Delorme, "The Practice of Baptism in Judaism at the Beginning of the Christian Era," *BNT* 25–60, esp. 47–48.

[10]*1QS* 4.20–23, trans. A. R. C. Leaney, *The Rule of Qumran and Its Meaning* (Philadelphia 1966) 154.

[11]Ezekiel 36.25. See Strack-Billerbeck 1.112–113. For Cyprian, see Chap. 1 at n. 31.

[12]As in *Jubilees* 11.4–5 and *1 Enoch* 19.1–2; 99.7. See my review of Birger Gerhardsson's *The Testing of God's Son* in *Theological Studies* 29 (1968) 528–531.

gods of other nations as to make them demons. The official gods of these nations were no gods."[13]

At the beginning of the Christian era, idolatry in the proper sense had long since ceased to be a temptation for Jews, and the prophetic denunciations of idols were applied to the effects of sin or to whatever disrupted an individual's relationship with God. In the *Rule of Qumran*, for instance, there is a strong condemnation of the insincere neophyte, who is cursed in "the idols of his heart" or as Theodor Gaster renders it, "the taint of idolatry in his heart" (Gaster notes that the author no doubt followed the tradition of interpreting *gillulim* [idols] as "filthiness").[14]

I have already touched upon the all-pervasive struggle between the two spirits, the champions of truth and wickedness, in the Qumran ideology. The struggle was carried on not only in the heart of every member but also in the world at large. The spheres of influence of the two spirits were sometimes described as two roads or ways,[15] a theme that appears in the Gospels independently of any discussion of evil spirits ("Strait is the gateway to salvation, and wide the path to destruction"). It is found in the same way in the *Didache*, which contains the earliest surviving liturgical description of baptism; its latest editor places it well within the first century.[16] He, along with many other readers, assumes that this discourse on the two ways was originally an instruction intended for Jewish proselytes, which was taken over by Christians to be used in the baptismal catechesis.[17] The question then arises as to whether the spirit of evil was ever formally associated with the way of evil in a baptismal context.

It must be admitted first of all that we are not even certain that the discourse on the two ways ever constituted a part of the Jewish proselyte instruction. From orthodox sources we know only of an instruction warning of the persecution that is to be expected and detailing some of the laws that must be observed after the candidate's

[13]Bowman 128.

[14]*1QS* 2.11: Leaney 124; T. H. Gaster, *The Scriptures of the Dead Sea Sect* (London 1957) 51, 104 n. 18.

[15]See *1QS* 3.13–4.26.

[16]Jean Paul Audet, *La Didaché: Instructions des apôtres* (Paris 1958) 192–200. Kretschmar (n. 6 above) 94 says it is undisputed that the baptismal instructions go back to the beginning of the second century. On these instructions, see W. Rordorf, "Le baptême selon la *Didaché*," *Mélanges liturgiques offerts au R. P. Dom Bernard Botte, O.S.B.* (Louvain 1972) 499–509.

[17]Audet 188–189; see André Benoit, *Le baptême chrétien au second siècle: La théologie des pères* (Paris 1953) 22–23.

incorporation into Judaism; it also outlines the punishments to be undergone for disobedience and the rewards that obedience will bring.[18] However, even granted that the *Didache* originally reflected a worldview like that of the Qumran rule, it may have been disencumbered of its eschatology and doctrine of the two spirits precisely because it was destined for some locale other than Palestine.[19] But it may also reflect a Jewish tradition, such as that of the good and evil inclination, which was not invariably associated with a cosmological dualism like that of Qumran nor with convert classes, whether in Judaism or Christianity.[20]

If the theme of the two spirits were associated with baptism and incorporated into the ritual, it would more likely have been introduced under the rubric of renunciation than exorcism, since a voluntary abstention from the way of evil was called for. Jean Daniélou even suggests that the actual formula of renunciation that came to be used in the Christian ceremony may have come from the Essene ritual. He points to the double oath required of one who entered the Qumran community, which bound him first to submit to the law of Moses and second "to separate himself from all men of evil ways," or, as Leaney translates, "from all the men of perversity who walk in the way of wickedness."[21] The portion of the *Rule* that Cardinal Daniélou cites resembles a renunciation of the prince of evil only by inference; since the candidate forswears evil men, he is assumed to repudiate the spiritual force behind them. Another description of the ceremonies of initiation in the *Rule*, however, contains a somewhat closer approximation to the Christian renunciation. There is not only a confession of sins committed under the regime of Belial but also a resolution never to follow his way again:

---

[18]*Yebamoth* 47ab, *The Babylonian Talmud: Seder Mashim*, ed. I. Epstein (London 1936) 1.310–311; see also the extracanonical treatise *Gerim* in *The Minor Tractates of the Talmud*, ed. A. Cohen (London 1965) 2.603–613; cf. Strack-Billerbeck, 1.110–111; Benoit 13–15; David Daube, *The New Testament and Rabbinic Judaism*, Jordan Lectures in Comparative Religion 2 (London 1956) 113–138; L. W. Barnard, "The *Epistle of Barnabas* and the Tannaitic Catechism," *Anglican Theological Review* 41 (1959) 177–190.

[19]The suggestion is Audet's, *Didaché* 207.

[20]Cf. Matthew Black, *The Scrolls and Christian Origins: Studies in the Background of the New Testament* (London 1961) 100.

[21]1QS 5.8, 10 (Leaney 169); Jean Daniélou, *The Theology of Jewish Christianity*, ed. and trans. J. A. Baker (London 1964) 322; cf. 142; cf. Klaus Thraede, "Exorzismus," *Reallexikon für Antike und Christentum* 7 (1966) 44–117, esp. 78.

All who enter the order of the community shall enter into a covenant in the presence of God to act according to all that he has commanded and not to withdraw from following him through any fear or terror or trial which take place during the dominion of Belial. . . .

The priests recount the righteous acts of God in the deeds of his power and recite all the gracious acts of mercy towards Israel; and the Levites recount the iniquities of the children of Israel and all their guilty transgressions and their sins under the dominion of Belial. And all who are entering into the convenant confess after them, saying:

"We have committed iniquity,
[We have transgressed],
We [have sinned],
We have done evil,

we and our fathers in conducting our lives [against the covenant of] truth and righteousness [and God has passed] his judgment upon us and upon our fathers, but he has bestowed upon us mercies in his gracious acts from everlasting to everlasting."

The candidates then add their voices to the blessing of the men of God's lot and the cursing of those of Belial's lot. Finally, they assent to the following malediction:

Cursed in the idols of his heart be he who comes to enter into his covenant but sets before his face his iniquitous stumbling-block to draw back by means of it, and when he hears the words of this covenant blesses himself in his own heart with the words "It will be well with me even though I go on in the stubbornness of my heart." Utterly destroyed shall be his spirit, thirsty with all his surfeit, without pardon; and may God's wrath and his zeal for his precepts flare up against him for everlasting destruction! May there cling to him all the curses of this convenant and may God set him apart for evil! Let him be cut off from among the sons of light in his drawing back from God through his idols! And let his iniquitous stumbling-block apportion his lot among those accursed for ever![22]

[22]1QS 1.16–2.1, 11–17 (Leaney 123, 124); Werner Bieder, *Die Verheissung der Taufe im Neuen Testament* (Zurich 1966) 29–30, suggests that the *Sibylline Oracles* at one point (4.162–170) describes the Qumran initiation: "O ill-starred mortals, let not these things be, and drive not the great God to divers deeds of wrath; but have done with swords and moanings and killing of men, and deeds of violence, and wash your whole bodies in ever-running rivers, and, stretching your hands to heaven, seek forgiveness for your former deeds, and with praises ask pardon for your bitter ungodliness. God will grant repentance and will not slay; he will stay his wrath once

The similarity of these passages to the Christian renunciation of Satan is hardly so striking that it could not easily be due to coincidence. We have already seen, however, an instance of the influence that the doctrine of Qumran could have upon the character of Christian formulas, in 2 Corinthians 6: "What accord has Christ with Belial? . . . What agreement has the temple of God with idols?" and so on. Another example can be seen in the *Shepherd* by Hermas: "It is good to follow [*akolouthein*] the angel of righteousness and to renounce [*apotaxasthai*] the angel of wickedness." Neither of these passages occurs in a specifically baptismal context, but it is suggestive that Hermas uses the technical term of renunciation that appears in the later baptismal services.[23]

Idolatry did not normally suggest the worship of evil spirits in Jewish literature; in the passage from the *Rule* of Qumran, "idols" does not even refer to idolatry in the literal sense. The same is no doubt true of the interpolated passage in Second Corinthians. But when, in the second century, Justin spoke of the pagan converts who, "full of joy and faith, renounced [*apetaxanto*] their idols and dedicated themselves to the unbegotten God through Christ,"[24] he did mean that they had forsaken the worship of the demons begotten by the fallen angels; but there is no way of telling whether he was referring to an actual ritual of renunciation connected with their initiation as Christians.

In point of fact, when Justin describes the process of initiation, in terms reminiscent of the *Didache,*[25] he mentions nothing demonic.

We shall explain the way in which we dedicate ourselves to God, once we are fashioned anew through Christ, lest in omitting it we should appear to be acting reprehensibly in our explanation. Whoever are persuaded and believe true what we teach and speak of, and who promise that they can live accordingly, are taught to pray and, while fasting, to beg for forgiveness from God for the sins they have previously commit-

---

more if with one accord ye practice precious godliness in your hearts" (*APOT* 2.396; cf. *OTP* 1.388). We see, however, that the baptismal ritual called for here does not specifically include the demonic dimension.

[23]*Shepherd* 36 (Mandate 6.2), ed. Molly Whitaker, *Der Hirt des Hermas,* GCS: Die apostolischen Väter 1 (Berlin 1956) 33; see Daniélou, *Theology.*

[24]Justin, *1 Apol.* 49, ed. J. C. T. de Otto, *Opera,* ed. 3 (Jena 1876) 1.1.134.

[25]M. A. Smith, "Did Justin Know the *Didache?*" *Studia patristica* 7, ed. F. L. Cross, TU 92 (Berlin 1966) 287–290, suggests that Justin is speaking of the liturgy as practiced in Samaria and that he is acquainted with the *Didache.*

ted, while we pray and fast along with them. Then we lead them to where there is water, and they are regenerated by the same means of regeneration by which we were regenerated; for in the name of the Father of all and of the Lord God Jesus Christ, our Savior, and of the Holy Spirit they then are washed in water.

Demons are never far from Justin's thought, however, and he specifies their connection with baptism in the next chapter: "Now, when the demons had heard this washing proclaimed by the prophet [Isaiah], they brought it about that those who enter their temples to make supplication and to offer libations and sacrifices should sprinkle themselves; and they also have them wash themselves thoroughly before coming into the temples where they are located."[26] That is, the demons anticipated and continue to imitate the Christian baptism in the pagan temples. But Justin does not suggest that they are "participants" in Christian baptism itself.

In the opinion of some modern authorities, the fasts that Justin speaks of, as well as those required by the *Didache,* were exorcistic.[27] But there is little or no evidence to support this interpretation. André Benoit maintains that Judaism attributed to fasting the power to drive away demons, but the only text he can quote is a passage from the Talmud tractate on "Fasts" interpreting the directions of the Mishnah on the times for sounding the alarm to announce the beginning of a fast. The Mishnah states: "The alarm is sounded on the sabbath on account of the following mishaps: if a city is besieged by hostile troops or inundated by the river, or if a ship is foundering on the sea. Rabbi Jose says: the alarm is sounded for help but not for a call to prayers." The Talmud clarifies as follows: "Our rabbis have taught: When a city is surrounded by hostile Gentiles, or threatened with inundation by the river, or when a ship is foundering in the sea, or when an individual is being pursued by Gentiles or robbers or by an evil spirit, the alarm is sounded even on the sabbath; and on account of all these an individual may afflict himself by fasting." A variant reading has "an evil beast" for "an evil spirit."[28] The eleventh-century commentator Rashi read the text as referring to a case of possession, when an evil spirit has entered into a man.[29] Even in the un-

---

[26] *1 Apol.* 61, 62 (Otto 162–164, 168–170).
[27] See especially Benoit 11, 146, and Daniélou, *Theology* 321.
[28] *Ta'anith* 22b (cf. 19a), *Babylonian Talmud* (n. 18 above): *Seder Mo'ed* 113 (cf. 92).
[29] Strack-Billerbeck 1.760.

likely event that someone could demonstrate the antiquity of this rabbinic recommendation of fasting in instances of demonic distur-bances, it would have little bearing on the present discussion. For the fasting has no specifically apotropaic or exorcistic significance, but, like the other fasts prescribed in the tractate, is simply a sign of the admission of guilt and a plea for divine mercy.

In the Gospel of Mark, after the expulsion of the dumb spirit from the epileptic boy, Jesus says, "This kind cannot be driven out by anything but prayer." Some ancient authorities add the words "and fasting," which is usually considered an interpolation into the text, like the whole of the similar verse in Matthew. Even granted the truth of this judgment, however, it is possible that the reference to the fasting was based on an authentic tradition, since Jesus, following the precedent of Moses, had presumably fasted on the mountain of Transfiguration before the cure took place.[30] At all events it is clear that at the time when the Markan saying was formulated in its longer version, fasting was thought to be an aid in the process of exorcism; but it should be noted that it is the exorcist who is to fast and not the demoniac. A similar conception is to be found in a Jewish-influenced ritual of exorcism in the *Paris Magical Papyrus,* which was produced in Egypt about A.D. 300. The passage ends with a dietary direction to the exorcist: "But I adjure [*horkizō*] you who use this adjuration [*horkismos*] not to eat the flesh of swine, and every spirit and demon whatsoever will be subject to you."[31]

In a more general context, prayer and fasting together were used as a means to gain strength against the devil and his supporters. In the *Acts of Peter,* compiled perhaps in Syria or Palestine[32] or in Asia Minor[33] near the end of the second century, Peter appeals for spiritual support in his combat against Simon Magus: "Let us fast together while praying to the Lord. He who drove him from that place is able to root him out of here. And may he give us strength to resist him

---

[30]Mark 9.29; Matthew 17.21; see Bowman 16, 200,203; cf. Herbert Musurillo, "The Problem of Ascetical Fasting in the Greek Patristic Writers," *Traditio* 12 (1956) 21 n. 16 and 46 n. 20.

[31]*Paris Magical Papyrus* lines 3078–3081, ed. A. Deissmann, *Light from the Ancient East* (London 1927) 255–263; cf. F. J. Dölger, *Ichthys* 2 (Münster 1922) 369; C. K. Barrett, *The New Testament Background: Selected Documents* (New York 1961) 31–35.

[32]Quasten, *Patrology* 1.133.

[33]Wilhelm Schneemelcher, trans., *Petrusakten,* Hennecke-Schneemelcher, *Neutesta-mentliche Apokryphen,* ed. 3, 2 (Tübingen 1964) 187–188; Mario Erbetta, trans., *Gli apocrifi del Nuovo Testamento* 2 (Turin 1966) 139.

and his magical incantations and to prove that he is the angel of Satan."[34] According to Matthew and Luke, Jesus himself fasted for forty days before his successful encounter with the devil.

There is some indication that abstinence from certain foods was recommended for epileptics in the ancient world. The author of *The Sacred Disease,* a Greek physician who lived in the third century before Christ, complains that men attributed a divine origin to epilepsy merely to conceal their own ignorance: "They added a plausible story, and established a method of treatment that secured their own position. They used purifications and incantations; they forbade the use of baths, and of many foods that are unsuitable for sick folk—of sea fishes: red mullet, blacktail, hammer, and the eel (these are the most harmful sorts); the flesh of goats, deer, pigs, and dogs (meats that disturb most the digestive organs)," and so on.[35] Diet, including abstinence from certain foods, figures prominently also in the treatments for epilepsy described in the first century after Christ by Celsus and Pliny the Elder.[36] Almost all the other instances of fasting in connection with malignant spirits recorded in classical times manifest an apotropaic rather than an exorcistic purpose; that is, it was feared that the eating of particular foods would bring on demonic possession or molestation, and such foods were accordingly avoided.[37]

In patristic literature the connections between fasting and demons are late, sparse, and vague. Of the writings discussed by Herbert Musurillo,[38] the only clear example of a fast that has an intrinsic link with the expulsion of demons appears in the Pseudo-Clementine *Homilies,* a body of apocryphal material reflecting Ebionite and Elkasaite doctrines and other Jewish-Christian patterns of thought. According to the bizarre demonology elaborated here, the evil spirits are like demonic tapeworms and inhabit men's bodies in order to enjoy the food, drink, and sexuality for which they themselves lack

[34]*Acta Petri cum Simone* 18, ed. R. A. Lipsius, *Acta apostolorum apocrypha* I (Leipzig 1891 repr. Hildesheim 1959) 65; L. Vouaux, ed. and trans., *Les actes de Pierre* (Paris 1922) 334.

[35]*Peri hierēs nousou* 2, ed. and trans. W. H. S. Jones, Loeb *Hippocrates* 2 (London 1923) 140–143.

[36]Celsus, *De medicina* 3.23, ed. W. G. Spencer, Loeb *Celsus* I (London 1935) 332–338; Pliny, *Naturalis historia* 28.63, ed. W. H. S. Jones, Loeb *Pliny* 8 (London 1963) 150–152.

[37]Cf. Rudolf Arbesmann, *Das Fasten bei den Griechen und Römern,* Religionsgeschichtliche Versuche und Vorarbeiten 21.1 (Giessen 1929) 21–62: "Das apotropäische Fasten."

[38]Musurillo 19–23.

the organs; a prolonged abstinence, accordingly, will deprive these parasites of their desires and perhaps induce them to depart.[39] Baptism itself in the Pseudo-Clementine writings has a definite exorcistic aspect, but I shall discuss this subject later on, since the basic narrative upon which these discourses are founded seems to be no earlier than the first part of the third century.[40] It is possible, of course, that echoes of earlier practices are preserved in this literature, but once again we can only conjecture.

Also deserving of mention is the *Apocalypse of Elijah;* it comes from Egypt, and the original Jewish layer is thought to predate the destruction of the Jewish quarter in Alexandria in A.D. 117. In it, God is portrayed as saying that he created a pure fast that forgives sins, heals sicknesses, and drives out demons and that can reach to the very throne of God.[41] There is no suggestion of an initiation ceremony here; but as we shall see, an antidemonic fast can be found in second-century Egypt in the baptismal ceremonies of the Valentinian gnostics.

If it is unlikely that Justin's prebaptismal fasting was meant to combat demons, what, then, is to be said of the speculation that baptism itself was exorcistic for Justin? A reason given for holding this view is that the formula for driving out the demons of the possessed also figures in his accounts of baptism, namely, "in the name of Jesus Christ, crucified under Pontius Pilate."[42] The argument is scarcely convincing; it is far more likely that people who were thought to be possessed by demons would be exorcized and cured before being baptized. There is no indication that Justin accepted the Jewish-Christian theory that all sinners were possessed by demons and so would stand in need of exorcism. But it is time to examine the documents that do reflect such a theory.

[39]Homily 9.10, ed. Bernhard Rehm and Johannes Irmscher, GCS 42 (1953) 135.
[40]See Quasten, *Patrology* 1.62.
[41]*Apocalypse of Elijah* 1.20–22 (*OTP* 1.738). On the date, see O. S. Wintermute, *OTP* 1.730. Cf. also the *Testaments of the Twelve Patriarchs,* Testament of Simeon 3.4, discussed in Chap. 3 at n. 9, in which a sin demon is expelled by the "host's" fear of the Lord accompanied by fasting.
[42]Benoit 182–183, citing *1 Apol.* 61; *2 Apol.* 6; *Dial.* 30, 76, 85.

3 /

Sin Demons and Their Removal

The doctrine of sin demons, or vice demons, according to which commission of various kinds of sins entailed the indwelling of corresponding varieties of evil spirits, is very familiar to students of the early patristic era but less so to those concerned with the literature and drama of later times. It is of particular interest for the tradition of the ("psychomachia," the allegorical battle of the virtues and vices within the soul, and we have been introduced to many aspects of the doctrine in Morton Bloomfield's wide-ranging study of the seven deadly sins.[1] But it will be useful to review some of the relevant texts from the point of view of our present discussion, especially since the topic has been of central importance in accounting for the demon-expelling ceremonies of Christian initiation, notably in Franz Josef Dölger's monumental work on baptismal exorcism.[2] We have seen something of a psychomachia motif already in the Qumran writings, though by no means in a purely allegorical sense; there was thought to be an actual struggle between the spirit of evil and the spirit of truth within a person's heart. Sometimes the sectaries spoke of combating multiple spirits of wickedness within them. This concern is especially evident in the *Testaments of the Twelve Patriarchs*, fragments of which have been discovered in the Qumran library.

The *Testaments* as we possess it today is generally assumed to have been extensively revised by a Christian editor,[3] a factor that is of

[1]Morton W. Bloomfield, *The Seven Deadly Sins* (East Lansing 1952).
[2]F. J. Dölger. *Exorzismus im altchristlichen Taufritual* (Paderborn 1909).
[3]See D. S. Russell, *The Method and Message of Jewish Apocalyptic* (London 1964) 55–

interest for us in attempting to explore the origins of Christian ritual. The demonology of the work is not always consistent. Sometimes the emphasis is upon the common Jewish tradition of the good and evil inclinations, which involved a psychomachia that was neither demonic (insofar as man's inner being was concerned) nor allegorical but simply "psychological." An example can be seen in the Testament of Asher:

> There are two ways of good and evil, and with these are the two inclinations in our breasts discriminating them. Therefore if the soul take pleasure in the good inclination, all its acts are in righteousness; and if it sin, it straightway repenteth. For, having its thoughts set upon righteousness, and casting away wickedness, it straightway over-throweth the evil, and uprooteth the sin. But if it incline to the evil inclination, all its actions are in wickedness, and it driveth away the good, and receiveth the evil, and is ruled by Beliar; even though it work what is good he perverteth it to evil. For whenever it beginneth as though to do good, he forceth the issue of the action into evildoing, seeing that the treasure of the inclination is filled with the poison of the evil spirit.[4]

Elsewhere evil spirits are involved, but they seem to be permanent fixtures within each person, like the evil inclination itself:

> Seven spirits therefore are appointed against man by Beliar, and they are the leader in the works of youth. . . . First, the spirit of fornication is seated in the nature and in the senses; the second, the spirit of in-satiableness, in the belly; the third, the spirit of fighting, in the liver and gall. The fourth is the spirit of obsequiousness and chicanery, that through officious attention one may be fair in seeming. The fifth is the spirit of pride, that one may be boastful and arrogant. The sixth is the spirit of lying in perdition and jealousy to practice deceits and conceal-

---

57. See also Marinus de Jonge, "The Interpretation of the *Testaments of the Twelve Patriarchs* in Recent Years," in *Studies on the Testaments of the Twelve Patriarchs,* ed. de Jonge, Studia in Veteris Testamenti pseudepigrapha 3 (Leiden 1975) 184–192.

[4]Testament of Asher 1.5–9 (*APOT* 2.343). I follow the variants of the Cambridge MS as suggested by M. de Jonge, *Testamenta XII patriarcharum Edited According to Cambridge University Library MS Ff 1.24 fol. 203a–262b,* Pseudepigrapha Veteris Testamenti graece 1 (Leiden 1964) xiii, 63. De Jonge produced a revision of this *editio minima* in 1970 and a critical edition in 1978. See also the introduction and translation by H. C. Kee, *OTP* 1.775–828. In the last sentence of the text cited, Test. Asher 1.9, Kee too freely puts "the devil's storehouse" instead of "the treasure of the inclination" (p. 817).

ments from kindred and friends. The seventh is the spirit of injustice, with which are thefts and acts of rapacity, that a man may do the desire of his heart; for injustice worketh together with the other spirits by the taking of gifts.[5]

Ordinarily, however, it is not specified that the evil spirits actually dwell within a man, but rather it is simply said that they urge the commission of sin: "The spirit of fornication hath wine as a minister to give pleasure to the mind. . . . For discretion needeth the man who drinketh wine, my children; and herein is discretion in drinking wine: that a man should drink so long as he preserveth modesty. But if he go beyond this limit the spirit of deceit attacketh his mind, and it maketh the drunkard to talk filthily, and to transgress and not to be ashamed." It is even said of wine that "there are in it four evil spirits—of lust, of hot desire, of profligacy, of filthy lucre."[6] Complete abstinence from wine is not demanded, but it is recommended in order to avoid the sins it gives rise to.

Normally, it is within a person's own power to escape the influence of the spirits: "If ye do well, even the unclean spirits will flee from you."[7] At one point ritual washing seems to figure as a means to keep off the spirit of fornication. Isaac instructs Levi: "Beware of the spirit of fornication; for this shall continue and shall by thy seed pollute the holy place. Take, therefore, to thyself a wife without blemish or pollution, while yet thou art young, and not of the race of strange nations. And before entering into the holy place, bathe; and when thou offerest the sacrifice, wash; and again, when thou finishest the sacrifice, wash."[8] At another point fasting is brought into play: "And now, my children, hearken unto me and beware of the spirits of deceit and envy. For envy ruleth over the whole mind of a man, and suffereth him neither to eat nor to drink nor to do any good thing. But it ever suggesteth to him to destroy him that he envieth, and so long as he that is envied flourisheth, he that envieth fadeth away. Two years therefore I afflicted my soul with fasting in the fear of the Lord, and I learned that deliverance from envy cometh by the fear of God. For if a man flee to the Lord, the evil spirit runneth away

[5]Testament of Reuben 2.2–3.6 (*APOT* 297–298). Omitted is an interpolated series of seven or eight spirits given to man at his creation, through which all his works are performed and with which are mingled the spirits of error (2.3–3.2).

[6]Testament of Judah 14.2, 7–8; 16.1 (*APOT* 320).

[7]Testament of Benjamin 5.2 (356).

[8]Testament of Levi 9.9–11 (310).

47

from him, and his mind is lightened."⁹ Whereas Judah recommended abstinence or temperance in order to prevent an attack by an evil spirit, Simeon declares that he fasted in his effort to eliminate an evil spirit that had dominated him (it is not clear whether the spirit dwelled within him or merely harassed him externally). Although it is chiefly the fear of God that is said to cause the flight of the spirit, the juxtaposition of fasting with the expulsion of demons in this text is perhaps the most pertinent of all the examples that we have studied in our search for the motivation behind the exorcistic regimen that came to be practiced before baptism.

There is a possible reference to Christian initiation (which would, of course, have been inserted by the Christian editor) in Levi's account of his vision, in which his role as a priest is foretold in terms of an enthroning ceremony: "The first anointed me with holy oil, and gave to me the staff of judgment. The second washed me with pure water, fed me with bread and wine, even the most holy things, and clad me with a holy and glorious robe."¹⁰ The sequence of anointing, baptism, and the eucharist is that of the Syrian Church,¹¹ and the application of oil would come to have apotropaic significance; but such meaning is not in evidence in the present text. Levi's paraphernalia, however, include "the breastplate of understanding" and "the plate of faith,"¹² which recall the anti-satanic armor of the New Testament epistles.

Hermas's *Shepherd,* as has been mentioned, takes over the Qumran demonology in part. When the author demonizes sin, he does so not only in terms of the one spirit of evil, that is, the devil, but also in terms of the manifold spirits of the *Testaments.* The internal combat between the spirits is described only in the second part, the Book of Mandates, and is not even hinted at elsewhere in the work.¹³ The author addresses himself not to baptismal candidates but rather to

⁹Testament of Simeon 3.1–5 (301).

¹⁰Testament of Levi 8.4–5 (309). Cf. H. Ludin Jansen, "The Consecration in the Eighth Chapter of Testamentum Levi," *The Sacral Kingship,* Studies in the History of Religions 4 (Leiden 1959) 356–365.

¹¹See Joseph Ysebaert, *Greek Baptismal Terminology: Its Origins and Early Development,* Graecitas christianorum primaeva 1 (Nijmegen 1962) 313; Georg Kretschmar, "Die Bedeutung der Liturgiegeschichte für die Frage nach der Kontinuität des Judenchristentums in nachapostolischer Zeit," *Aspects du judéo-christianisme,* Colloque de Strasbourg (Paris 1965) 113–136, esp. 124–126.

¹²Testament of Levi 8.2.

¹³Stanislas Giet, *Hermas et les Pasteurs: Les trois auteurs du Pasteur d'Hermas* (Paris 1963), sees a multiplicity of authorship elsewhere in the *Shepherd,* but though he

people who are already Christians, and he elaborates upon the effects of virtue and vice in their lives. For instance, he says:

> If you are patient, the holy spirit dwelling in you will be pure, undarkened by another evil spirit; dwelling in spacious quarters, it will be glad and rejoice in the vessel in which it lives and serve God with great cheerfulness and interior well-being. But if any anger should come, the holy spirit, being tender, is suddenly cramped, and, not having its place pure, seeks to depart from it; for it is stifled by the evil spirit and does not have a place to serve the Lord as it wishes but is soiled by the anger. For the Lord lives in patience, but the devil in anger. Therefore when the two spirits live in the same place it is troublesome and evil for the man in whom they live. . . .
> Therefore the tender spirit, being unaccustomed to live with an evil spirit and with hardness, leaves such a man and seeks to live with gentleness and stillness. Then, when it leaves the man in whom it lived, the man is emptied of the upright spirit and, having its place taken by the evil spirits, he is unstable in everything he does, being dragged here and there by the evil spirits and made completely blind to good thoughts. This then is what happens to all angry men. Depart therefore from anger, that most evil spirit; clothe yourself in patience and resist anger and bitterness, and you will be found with the dignity loved by the Lord.[14]

He goes on to say that each man has two angels with him, one of uprightness and one of evil. Hermas asks how he is to recognize their workings, since both of them dwell with him. His supernatural informer tells him that when the heart is filled with virtuous thoughts it is a sign that the angel of uprightness is with him, and when, on the contrary, he finds himself attracted by forbidden pleasures, it is a sign that the angel of evil is in him. He is to trust in the angel of uprightness and to depart from the angel of evil; "you see, therefore," he is told, "that it is good to follow the angel of uprightness and to renounce the angel of evil."[15]

Daniélou, we saw, finds it significant that the word for renunciation or bidding farewell that is used here is the same term that is used in later texts for the renunciation of Satan before baptism. He is right in attempting to connect Hermas to prebaptismal renunciation rather

---

notices the differences in demonology between the Mandates and the Visions, he does not feel justified in attributing them to different authors (248).

[14]*Shepherd* 33 (Mand. 5.1) 2–4; 34 (5.2) 6–8 (Whittaker 29, 31).
[15]Ibid. 36 (6.2) 1–9 (32–33).

than to prebaptismal exorcism, since the evil spirits of which Hermas treats can be overcome or driven out at will by the person they inhabit, and there is no need to have them exorcized. Hermas, however, is dealing not with a once-for-all renunciation of the devil or the angel of evil but with one that must be repeated whenever necessary, that is, whenever the evil spirit enters a person's heart. He does mention baptism once but only in terms of the simple ceremony, "when we went down into water and received the remission of our previous sins."[16]

The *Shepherd* was accepted as divinely inspired by Irenaeus, Clement of Alexandria, Origen, and Tertullian, though Tertullian repudiated it later in his career.[17] Tertullian does bear witness to the baptismal renunciation of Satan, but, as we shall see, neither this ceremony nor Tertullian's demonology has any connection with the sin demon concept of Hermas. Origen, in contrast to Tertullian, gives special prominence to the theory of sin demons, drawing on the *Testaments* as well as on the *Shepherd*.[18] Did the theory affect his notion of the ceremonies of baptism? His references to the baptismal renunciation suggest nothing of the sort,[19] and he gives no indication that there was a practice of prebaptismal exorcism in the communities of Egypt and Palestine where he lived and worked. It has recently been alleged that he did refer to such a practice in one of his homilies on the Book of Numbers and professed himself to be mystified by the whole procedure.[20] In fact, however, he merely said that it was no easy task to explain the words, actions, and practices, as well as the questions and responses, that occur in the conferral of baptism.[21]

The "questions and responses" suggest not exorcisms (which normally consisted of adjurations to the demons and prayers to God) but rather the ceremonies of renunciation of the devil and the confession

---

[16]Ibid. 31 (4.3) 1 (28).

[17]The passages where these fathers mention Hermas are collected in PG 2.819–826. Cf. R. Joly's edition of Hermas, SC 53 (Paris 1958) 30 n. 1.

[18]See Jean Daniélou, *Gospel Message and Hellenistic Culture,* trans. John Austin Baker (London 1973) 437–441.

[19]See Chap. 6 at nn. 9, 12, 18; cf. Chap. 4 at n. 58.

[20]Thraede, "Exorzismus" 85: "Selbst Origenes hatte die Unverständlichkeit des Tauf-Exorzismus schon beklagt (*Num. hom.* 5.1)."

[21]"Sed et Eucharistiae sive percipiendae sive eo ritu quo geritur explicandae, vel eorum quae geruntur in baptismo verborum gestorumque et ordinum atque interrogationum ac responsionum quis facile explicet rationem?" (Rufinus's translation of the first chapter of the fifth homily on Numbers, PG 12.603; GCS 30.26).

of faith, which were often conducted, at least in the West, in a catechetical or dialogic form. I do not mean to deny any acquaintance on
Origen's part with baptismal exorcism. He was in Rome about the
year 212, where he no doubt met the presbyter Hippolytus, and he
probably witnessed the exorcistic rites recorded in Hippolytus's
Apostolic Tradition. But as we shall see, there is little or no evidence of
such rites in the East until the fourth century and then normally only
under the influence of the *Apostolic Tradition*. If, then, I am correct in
supposing that Origen was referring in his sermon to the practice of
the renunciation of Satan, he was declaring that he was uncertain of
the precise significance of the ritual. But had he been called upon to
offer an explanation, he would presumably have included the demons
of sin as well as the devil in the content of the renunciation, even
though the formulas that he spoke of elsewhere named only the
devil's domain (the world) and his pomps, works, services, and
pleasures.[22]

Irenaeus, like Origen, may have accepted Hermas's demonology
literally; at one point, when commenting upon Matthew 12.29, he
says: "We were his [Satan's] vessels and dwellings when we were in
apostasy, for he used us as he wished, and the unclean spirit dwelled
within us."[23] However, he may be speaking allegorically here and
may accordingly have read Hermas in an allegorical sense; certainly
the concept that all unbaptized persons were the habitations of unclean spirits was not a central one to his thought, and there is no
indication that the doctrine of sin demons was reflected in the initiation ceremonies as he knew them.

A similar conclusion may be in order for the *Epistle of Barnabas* as
well. The author of this work, who poses as the apostle Barnabas,
gives an instruction on the two ways, in which light-bringing angels
of God are said to be stationed over the way of light and angels of
Satan over the way of darkness.[24] But he also makes a number of
references to the entry and dwelling of evil spirits in men. Are these
references anything more than figures of speech? He seems to be
echoing the Gospel account of Satan's entering into Judas when he

[22]See n. 19 above.
[23]Irenaeus, *Adversus haereses* 3.8.2, ed. W. W. Harvey (Cambridge 1857 repr. 1965) 2.28–29.
[24]*Epistle of Barnabas* 18, ed. Funk-Bihlmeyer-Schneemelcher, *Die apostolischen Vät-er,* Sammlung ausgewählter kirchen- und dogmengeschichtlicher Quellenschriften 2.1.1 (Tübingen 1956); cf. John 13.27.

51

warns against the possibility of the Evil One gaining an entrance by deceit and casting us out from our life. He urges a hatred of the works characteristic of the way of wickedness in order to prevent the "Black One" from finding a means of entrance. Later, when speaking of the rebuilding of the temple of God, not physically, but in the hearts of believers, he says: "Before we believed in God, the dwelling of our heart was perishable and weak, just like a temple built by hands, for it was full of idolatry, it was a house of demons because what was done was opposed to God." He goes on to say that the temple of the Lord is rebuilt, since "in receiving the remission of sins and in hoping in the name of the Lord we have become new, remade from the beginning. Therefore in our dwelling God truly lives in us."[25]

Clement of Alexandria opposed the literal interpretation of these words and maintained that Barnabas was simply likening the activity of sinners to that of demons: "He does not say that demons are driven out of us, but that the sins that we, like them, commit before believing are forgiven."[26] Clement may be correct in this interpretation; but even if Pseudo-Barnabas were drawing on a sin-demon theory, we would hardly be justified in stating categorically that baptism had the effect of driving out the demons who made their abode in the man's heart or that exorcism here seems to have become an integral part of the baptismal act itself.[27] Barnabas indicates rather that the heart has ceased to be a house of demons when the individual comes to believe and ceases doing what is opposed to God. Though a case might be made for saying that baptism is the time when God begins to dwell in the soul, there is no real indication that baptism has an exorcistic meaning either here or in the other parts of the epistle where baptism is explicitly discussed.

It has been argued that the whole epistle is a homily that was read during the Easter Vigil service, which would allegedly account for the prominence of baptismal motifs throughout.[28] If so, and if, as is usually thought, it was written in Alexandria in the first third of the

---

[25]*Epistle of Barnabas* 2.10, 4.10, 16.7f.

[26]Clement of Alexandria, *Stromata* 2.20 (116.3–117.3), ed. Stählin-Früchtel, GCS 52 (1960) 176; cf. SC 38 (1954) 122.

[27]So Benoit 38–39.

[28]L. W. Barnard, "The *Epistle of Barnabas*—A Paschal Homily?" *Vigiliae christianae* 15 (1961) 8–22. But the evidences for an early association of baptism with the Easter liturgy have been called into question by S. G. Hall, "Paschal Baptism," *Studia evangelica* 6 (1973) 239–251.

second century,[29] Clement would doubtless have been aware of the exorcistic function of baptism if such had existed in orthodox circles, since he lived and taught in the same city later in the same century.

Clement rejected the doctrine of indwelling sin demons as a gnostic aberration, and since he approved of the canonicity of the *Shepherd,* it follows that he read Hermas as well as Pseudo-Barnabas in a figurative sense. How, then, are we to view the literal acceptance of the doctrine by Origen, Clement's younger contemporary at Alexandria? We should remember that Origen attributed his views on demonic temptation to Jewish-Christian sources, namely the *Testaments of the Twelve Patriarchs* and the *Shepherd.* Furthermore, the fact that the doctrine of sin demons was favored by the gnostics would not be enough to disqualify it in his eyes, since his whole teaching on evil spirits was heavily influenced by gnostic thought.[30]

Let us examine the nature of the aberrations that Clement was opposing. He singled out Basilides, who had taught at Alexandria during the time of Hadrian and Antoninus Pius (A.D. 120–145), and reported:

> The adherents of Basilides are in the habit of calling the passions appendages, saying that these are in essence certain spirits attached to the rational soul, through some original perturbation and confusion, and that, again, other bastard and heterogeneous natures of spirits grow on to them, like that of the wolf, the ape, the lion, the goat, whose properties, showing themselves around the soul (they say), assimilate the lusts of the soul to the likeness of the animals. For they imitate the actions of those whose properties they bear. And not only are they associated with the impulses and perceptions of the irrational animals, but they affect the motions and the beauties of plants, on account of their bearing also the properties of plants attached to them. They have also the properties of a particular state, as the hardness of steel.

Clement mocks this doctrine by alluding to the Trojan horse; Basilides's own son, he notes, perceived that the theory entailed a serious disadvantage.

> Man, according to Basilides, preserves the appearance of a wooden horse, according to the poetic myth, embracing as he does in one body a

[29]Barnard, "The Problem of the *Epistle of Barnabas,*" *Church Quarterly Review* 159 (1958) 211–230; Quasten, *Patrology* 1.89–91.
[30]See Kelly, *Devil* 31–35, 38–39, 104–119.

host of such different spirits. Accordingly, Basilides's son himself, Isidorus, in his book, *About the Soul Attached to Us,* while agreeing in the dogma, as if condemning himself, writes in these words: "For if I persuade anyone that the soul is undivided, and that the passions of the wicked are occasioned by the violence of the appendages, the worthless among men will have no slight pretence for saying, 'I was compelled, I was carried away, I did it against my will, I acted unwillingly,' though he himself led the desire of evil things and did not fight against the assaults of the appendages. But we must, by acquiring superiority in the rational part, show ourselves masters of the inferior creation in us." For he too lays down the hypothesis of two souls in us, like the Pythagoreans.[31]

It is important to note that in the Basilidean psychomachia the spirits of vice and passion within man are always present and are apparently overcome not by being expelled but simply by being held in check.

Such is not the case with Valentinus himself, whose doctrine resembles very much that which we saw in the *Testaments of the Twelve Patriarchs.* Clement, however, seems to consider his words as confirmatory of Basilides's opinions:

Valentinus too, in a letter to certain people, writes in these very words respecting the appendages: "There is one good, by whose presence[32] is the manifestation, which is by the Son, and by him alone can the heart become pure by the expulsion of every evil spirit from the heart; for the multitude of spirits dwelling in it do not suffer it to be pure, but each of them performs his own deeds, insulting it oft with unseemly lusts. And the heart seems to be treated somewhat like a caravanserai. For the latter has holes and ruts made in it, and is often filled with dung, men living filthily in it, and taking no care for the place as belonging to others. So fares it with the heart as long as there is no thought taken for it, being unclean, and the abode of many demons. But when the only good Father visits it, it is sanctified, and gleams with light. And he who possesses such a heart is so blessed, that 'he shall see God.'"[33]

As we shall see in the next chapter, it was Theodotus, a disciple of Valentinus, who left the earliest record of actual rites designed to fend off the influence of evil spirits at baptism, though there is some

[31]Clement, *Stromata* 2.20 (112–114.2); Früchtel 174, *ANF* 2.371.
[32]*Parousia,* Grabe's emendation of MS. *parrēsiae;* Früchtel reads *parrēsia,* "free expression."
[33]*Stromata* 2.20 (114.3–6).

question whether the rites were aimed specifically at the expulsion of indwelling demons.

Clearly, then, in spite of the importance to be attributed to the doctrine of sin demons in laying the groundwork for the practice of prebaptismal exorcism, the concept did not gain a great deal of credit in the Church among the scholars. Clement of Alexandria offered the only orthodox objection to it, but the notion had very few noteworthy proponents. Even in the writings where it appears prominently, its connections with baptism are either very tenuous or simply nonexistent. Moreover, an examination of these works has shown us that when sin demons are eliminated it is almost entirely by means of renunciation rather than by exorcistic procedures. As for the influence of these writings upon later times, there is one definite instance of the *Shepherd*'s doctrine on the two angels being used in a baptismal sense, namely in the third-century *Didascalia,* which I shall discuss in connection with the Church in Syria. It concerns not a prebaptismal exorcism, however, but rather baptism itself, considered as having the effect of replacing the evil spirit with the Holy Spirit. Such is the case even in the Pseudo-Clementine writings, where the theory of sin demons had its most extravagant development.

We cannot say for certain, therefore, that the sin-demon concept was the basis for the evolution of regular rites of exorcism before baptism. It remains, however, a very likely, perhaps the most likely, foundation of the practice. But if so—that is, if the notion did inspire the rites—we would have to postulate that the demons of sin came to be regarded as so securely entrenched in the candidates for baptism that simply renouncing them or the sins they sponsored was insufficient, so that various exercises would have to be performed by the catechumens and also by their spiritual guides in an effort to facilitate the expulsion of the spirits. We may have seen a trace of this attitude already in the Testament of Simeon, where the evil spirit of envy was overcome by its victim after two years of fasting in the fear of the Lord.[34] It is obvious that vicious habits cannot be immediately eliminated by an act of the will, and if they were thought to be caused by the presence of evil spirits, a regimen of prayer and asceticism, as well as exorcism in the strict sense, might understandably have been developed to remove them.

[34]See above at n. 9.

The hero of this story is, of course, Clement of Alexandria, whose common sense delivered the civilized Levant from these outlandish demonic parasites of the soul. He believed in evil spirits, of course; he could not help but be a man of his times to that extent. He rejected the internal pest only to concentrate upon the attack from without, that is, the methods whereby the powers of the devil and the unclean spirits sow their seeds into the sinner's soul. He countered the demonic psychomachia of the gnostics with a Pauline natural psychology: "The vapors of fleshly lusts bring on the soul an evil condition, scattering about the idols of pleasure before the soul."[35] The evil spirits do, naturally, play a definite role in the process.

> The simple word, then, of our philosophy declares the passions to be impressions on the soul that is soft and yielding, and, as it were, signatures of the spiritual powers with whom we have to struggle [cf. Ephesians 6.12]. For it is the business, in my opinion, of the maleficent powers to endeavor to produce somewhat of their own constitution in everything, so as to overcome and make their own those who have renounced [*apeipasthai*] them. And it follows, as might be expected, that some are worsted; but in the case of those who engage in the contest with more athletic energy, the powers mentioned above, after carrying on the conflict in all forms, and advancing even as far as the crown,[36] wading in gore, decline the battle, and admire the victors. . . .
>
> The powers, then, of which we have spoken hold out beautiful sights and honors and adulteries and pleasures and suchlike alluring phantasies before facile souls. . . . And each deceit, by pressing constantly on the soul, impresses its image on it; and the soul unwittingly carries about the image of the passion, which takes its rise from the bait and our consent.[37]

For Clement, then, the struggle continued even after the powers had been renounced; and if the demons did not actually dwell within the soul, they at least left their mark on it.

[35] *Stromata* (116.3; 115.3).

[36] Früchtel follows Lowth's emendation in making the participles *agōnesamenai* and *chōrēsasai* agree with those who defeat the powers and not (as in the *ANF* translation given above) with the powers themselves.

[37] *Stromata* (110.1–3; 111.3–4).

4 /

Gnostic Antidemonic

Initiation Rites

In the second century of the Christian era there appeared on the religious scene the great gnostic heresiarchs, whose teachings were a combination of the Christian Gospel, Hebrew Scriptures, Greek philosophy, and Oriental astrology and mysticism. We have seen Clement of Alexandria single two of them out for attack, namely, Basilides and Valentinus. Valentinus was particularly influential; after a successful career of evangelizing Egypt with his doctrines, he continued his apostolate in Rome, from the time of Hyginus (ca. 136–140) until the reign of Anicetus (ca. 155–160).[1] The writings of Theodotus, a disciple of Valentinus, contain the first substantial description of baptism in terms of liberation from evil spirits, with ceremonies to match. Since Theodotus belonged to the Eastern school of Valentinian gnosticism, as opposed to the Western, or Italian, branch, it might not be unreasonable to assume that he received his instructions before his master departed for Rome and that therefore the dates of Theodotus's own teaching would roughly correspond to the time that Valentinus was in Rome. F. Sagnard, however, conjectures that he flourished slightly later, about 160 to 170.[2]

The writings of Theodotus are preserved only in the excerpts made by Clement of Alexandria in the next generation. The *Extracts from*

[1]Irenaeus, *Adversus haereses* 3.4.3 (Harvey 2.17); Epiphanius, *Panarion* 31.7.1–2, GCS 25.395–396.
[2]F. Sagnard, *Extraits de Théodote,* SC 23 (1948) 6–7; see also Sagnard's *La gnose valentinienne et le témoignage de saint Irénée* (Paris 1947).

the Works of Theodotus and the So-called Oriental Teaching at the Time of Valentinus forms an appendix to Clement's *Stromata* and is sometimes interrupted by Clement's own remarks.[3] In the sections dealing with the sacraments of initiation, Theodotus's chief concern is for the astrological portion of his gnosis. In his view, not the stars and the planets themselves but the invisible powers controlling them influenced the births and lives of men. In spite of the fact that some of the powers were beneficent, the total impact of all the powers (in other words, Fate) upon man was an evil to be escaped from. Theodotus's gnosis showed the way: "From this dissension and battle of the powers the Lord rescues us and supplies peace from the array of powers and angels, in which some are arrayed for us and others against us. For some are like soldiers fighting on our side as servants of God, but others are like brigands. For the evil one girded himself, not taking the sword by the side of the king, but in madly plundering for himself." The beneficent powers, on the other hand, are not endowed with sufficient strength or willpower to prevail against them. "And besides, man, over whom the battle rages, since he is a weak animal, is easily led towards the worse, and aids those who hate him."[4]

The psychomachia envisaged here, then, is one fought not within a man's soul but for a man's soul, and the fight takes place in a cosmic battlefield, the spheres of the planets and the stars. The unfavorable balance against man was rectified by the coming of the Savior, for those who receive the proper knowledge and respond with the requisite faith: "Therefore the Lord came down bringing the peace which is from heaven to those on earth, as the apostle says, 'Peace on the earth and glory in the heights.' Therefore a strange and new star arose doing away with the old astral decree, shining with a new unearthly light, which revolved on a new path of salvation: the Lord himself, men's guide, who came down to earth to transfer from Fate to his providence those who believed in Christ." Man's liberation is effected by the combination of the events of the Savior's life and his own baptism:

[3]For direct citation of the Extracts, I will use the translation of Robert Pierce Casey, *The Excerpta ex Theodoto of Clement of Alexandria,* Studies and Documents 1 (London 1934), as emended according to Sagnard's text, as well as the text edited by Otto Stählin (GCS 17.105–133) and Stählin's review of Casey's edition in *Theologische Literaturzeitung* 60 (1935) 414–416.

[4]Extracts 69–73.

As, therefore, the birth of the Savior released us from "becoming" and from Fate, so also his baptism rescued us from fire, and his Passion rescued us from passion, in order that we might in all things follow him. For he who was baptized unto God advanced toward God and has received "power to walk upon scorpions and snakes" [Luke 10.19], the evil powers. And he commands the apostles, "When ye go about, preach, and baptize those who believe, in the name of the Father, and of the Son, and of the Holy Spirit" [Matt. 28.19] in whom we are born again, becoming higher than all the other powers.

Theodotus explains later what he means by the baptismal release from fire:

The material element of fire lays hold of all material things, and the pure and immaterial element lays hold of immaterial things such as demons, angels of evil, and the devil himself. Thus the heavenly fire is dual in its nature, belonging partly to the mind, partly to the senses. By analogy, therefore, baptism is also dual in its nature; the sensible part works through water, which extinguishes the sensible fire, but the intellectual through Spirit, a defense against the intellectual fire. And the material spirit [i.e., wind], when it is little, becomes a food and kindling for the sensible fire; but when it has increased, it has become an extinguisher. But the Spirit given us from above, since it is immaterial, rules not only over the elements but over the powers and the evil principalities.[5]

The result of this initiation process is the invalidation of astrology for the initiates, since they are no longer under the control of the stars: "Until baptism, Fate is real, but after it the astrologists are no longer right." He describes the change that takes place in technical Valentinian terms: "So long, then, as the seed is yet unformed, it is the offspring of the female, but when it was formed, it was changed to a man and becomes a son of the bridegroom. It is no longer weak and subject to the cosmic [forces], both visible and invisible, but, having been made masculine, it becomes a male fruit."

As for the manner in which this liberation is brought about in the baptismal process, he says: "But it is not only the washing that is liberating, but the knowledge [*gnōsis*] of who we were, and what we have become, where we were or where we were placed, whither we hasten, from what we are redeemed, what birth is and what rebirth." By *gnōsis* here Theodotus means the baptismal catechesis, whereby the candidate is instructed in mankind's original nature (divine) and in

[5]Extracts 74, 76, 81.

what it has become (by the fall); he is told of his true homeland, and the nature of the world where he now is, of his destiny (that is, redemption), the process of generation (birth in the world of evil), and regeneration (incorporation into the true life).[6]

So far, we have baptism pretty much as Saint Paul envisages it; it is the process by which we take advantage of Christ's salvific passion, death, and resurrection and liberate ourselves from the principalities and powers. Paul, however, was speaking of subjection to the powers only in terms of belief and allegiance, which could be simply renounced, whereas Theodotus presumably meant that the water and Spirit in baptism immunized a man from the actual astrological and material pressures that the powers brought to bear on the human race.

Renunciation did play a role in Theodotus's system as well, however, and in fact there may have been an explicit ceremony of renunciation in the baptismal services he describes, to judge from the language of Extract 77. We read: "Therefore baptism is called death and an end of the old life when we take leave of [*apotassesthai*] the evil principalities, but it is also called life according to Christ, of which he is sole Lord. But the power of the transformation of him who is baptized does not concern the body but the soul, for he who comes up [out of the water] is unchanged. From the moment when he comes up from baptism, he is called a servant of God and lord of the unclean spirits, and now they tremble at him whom shortly before they obsessed [*energein*]." We recall that the word used for renunciation here is that which will be employed in the orthodox Christian baptismal formulas found in texts dating from the beginning of the third century. However, saying that the candidates "bid farewell" to the principalities may simply be another way of saying that the faithful are liberated from the powers by baptism. But we have seen Clement of Alexandria use a somewhat similar expression (*apeipasthai*) in speaking of the renunciation of the powers.[7] The latter part of the extract seems to refer to the trembling demons of James 2.19. It is worth noting that the word translated here as referring to obsession is the term later used to designate demonic possession, in the *energoumenoi*.

Theodotus also speaks of a sealing that takes place at baptism,

[6]Extracts 78–79; see Sagnard, *Extraits* 234.

[7]*Stromata* 2.20 (110.1–3). Sagnard (*Extraits* 234) thinks that something of Clement's own ideas may be present in the Theodotus Extract 77.

which gives the candidates ascendance over the evil powers: "For he who has been sealed by Father, Son, and Holy Spirit is beyond the threats of every other power and by the three Names has been released from the whole triad of corruption." In a later passage, which may contain Clement's own doctrine, the seal seems to be identified with the name of God: he speaks of the faithful having this name for purposes of identification, like the seal (brand) on an animal. "Thus also the faithful soul receives the seal of truth and bears about the marks [*stigmata*] of Christ."[8]

It has been assumed that the seal here mentioned is the sign of the cross, and in fact Theodotus does indicate earlier that the sign of the cross divides the faithful from the infidels.[9] When he speaks of those who knew the names of Jesus and Christ even before the Advent but did not know the power of the sign of the cross, he seems to be referring to the Jews and the ordinary (non-Valentinian) Christians.[10] If so, and if there is an allusion to an initiatory marking with the cross, we might have to conclude that this ceremony was observed only among Valentinians, at least in the Egypt of Theodotus's time; but just as likely a conclusion would be that the Valentinians felt that only they performed the sealing in the proper manner.

A cross appears elsewhere in the Theodotan passages, where however it suggests only the Valentinian cosmic principle or personality and seems in fact to be regarded as a barrier that gives way only to those who have the Name and are united to their baptized and redeemed angelic counterparts.[11] But "having the Name" may, as has been mentioned, refer to the seal; and the reference to the seal as the stigmata of Christ, which may be an echo of Galatians 6.17, perhaps supports the view that it was a consignation, that is, a signing with the cross. This signing may also have involved an anointing with oil, to judge from the various unctions practiced by the gnostics, such as those mentioned by Irenaeus in describing the Marcosian redemption services.[12]

When, therefore, the Name is received as the seal in baptism, it has

[8]Extracts 80, 86.

[9]Extract 42; cf. Daniélou, *Theology* 331.

[10]So Sagnard, *Extraits* 148–151, commenting on Extract 43.

[11]Extract 22; cf. Irenaeus, *Adversus haereses* 1.3.5 (Harvey 1.29–30); Casey, "Two Notes on Valentinian Theology," *Harvard Theological Review* 23 (1930) 275–298, esp. 289.

[12]Irenaeus, *Adversus haereses* 1.21 (Harvey 1.180–188); see G. W. H. Lampe, *The Seal of the Spirit: A Study in the Doctrine of Baptism and Confirmation in the New*

the effect of a protective charm and a password; and if this sealing with the Name was a sign of the cross in the Theodotan liturgy, it would be the earliest extant example of the use of the cross as an apotropaic ceremony of Christian initiation. But whether or not the seal and the cross can be identified in this way, the extract in which the cross is said to divide the faithful from the unfaithful (infidel) is the first known instance of the cross being associated with the making of a Christian. F. J. Dölger believes that it refers to the original reception of the catechumen and not to the actual baptismal rite. He estimates that the general apotropaic use of the cross in private devotions, which is reflected in Tertullian's writings, goes back at least to the middle of the second century; and he feels that its use as an initiatory ceremony must be even earlier, perhaps reaching back very close to apostolic times.[13]

Tertullian also refers to the cross used in conjunction with the postbaptismal anointing and not to a preliminary signing.[14] But Origen, preaching at Caesarea in Palestine towards the middle of the third century, indicates that by his time there was a signing with the cross before the ceremony of baptism, since he speaks of it before alluding to the renunciation of Satan and his works.[15] Eventually baptism itself came to be referred to as the cross. It is not clear when this first happened, but the idea may be present in the *Acts of Peter,* which, as we saw before, is placed in the Levant in the last decade of the second century. Here, a person is baptized "in the sign of the Lord."[16] In the *Acts of Paul,* a work written in Asia Minor about A.D. 160, Thecla says, "Only give me the seal in Christ, and temptation

Testament and the Fathers (London 1951 repr. 1967) 126–127. See also the Valentinian fragment *On the Anointing,* trans. John D. Turner, in *The Nag Hammadi Library in English,* ed. James M. Robinson (New York 1977) 440: "It is fitting for [thee at this time] to send thy Son [Jesu]s Christ and anoint us so that we might be able to trample [upon] the [snakes] and [the heads] of the scorpions and [all] the power of the devil" (11.40.11–17).

[13]F. J. Dölger, "Beiträge zur Geschichte des Kreuzzeichens," *Jahrbuch für Antike und Christentum* 1 (1958) 12–13; 4 (1961) 10–11.

[14]Tertullian, *De resurrectione mortuorum* 8.3 (CCL 2.931); Dölger 6 (1963) 7.

[15]Origen, *Selecta in Ps. 38* Homily 2.5 (PG 12.1405); Cf. Dölger, "Beiträge" 4 (1961) 10, who believes the text shows that this usage of consignation was flourishing ca. A.D. 200.

[16]Dölger 5 (1962) 15; in *Acta Petri cum Simone* 5 we read: "Si vis me dignum habere quem intingas in signo domini, habes occasionem." And: "In tuo nomine mox lotus [MS lucutus] et signatus est sancto tuo signo" (Vouaux [above, Chap. 2 n. 34] 258–260).

shall not touch me." The reference is obviously to baptism (Paul answers: "Have patience, Thecla, and thou shalt receive the water"), but whether a cross is involved is not clear.[17]

Possibly, then, Theodotus received the rite of conferring the seal from previous Christian practice. There are other possible influences as well. Though we found only one example of the seal of circumcision as a protection against evil spirits, there were other instances not connected with initiation when Jews regarded seals as prophylactics. Another possible source of influence is the world of Greek religion. In fact, we are assured that "in the gnostic literature we are closer to the notions of Hellenistic religion than to the beliefs of Judaism, and very near the pagan mysteries with their 'sealings' of initiates as a token of their future attainment of a blessed immortality."[18]

It would be a mistake, however, to consider the exorcistic or apotropaic aspects of the seal and other elements in gnostic and orthodox Christianity as primarily indebted to pagan rites. We are rightly warned not to picture the Greco-Roman society as demon-ridden. Exorcism was not a religious practice among the pagans, as it was in Christianity, though sometimes it was a private healing trade pursued for profit. They knew of no spiritual beings with the sheer malevolence of the devil and his demons. True, "paganism had plenty of deities who were to be feared if you did not take the right steps to appease them, but paganism knew the right steps to take."[19]

---

[17]*Acts of Paul* 25, trans. M. R. James, *The Apocryphal New Testament* (Oxford 1924 repr. 1963) 277. Eric Segelberg, "The Coptic-Gnostic Gospel According to Philip and Its Sacramental System," *Numen* 7 (1960) 189–200, esp. 194, suggests a possible gnostic parallel in the *Gospel of Philip* (which may be as early as the second century). However, it relies on H. M. Schenke's heavily restored reading of chapter 49: "If thou sayest 'I am a Jew,' no one will be moved. If thou sayest 'I am a Roman,' no one will be disturbed. If thou sayest 'I am a Greek, a barbarian, a slave, a free man,' no one will be troubled. If thou sayest 'I am a Christian,' [everyone] will tremble. May it be [that I receive] this *sign* [reading *maeine* for MS *meine*, "fashion"] which [the archons] will not be able to endure, [namely,] the Name." This translation was made by R. McL. Wilson, *The Gospel of Philip* (London 1962) 110, who admits that gender considerations would support the reading of *maeine* over *meine* but insists that any restoration must be regarded as purely conjectural. Jacques E. Ménard in his edition, *L'Evangile selon Philippe* (Paris 1967) 165, defends *meine* itself as meaning sign, by taking it as the Akhmimic equivalent of the Sahidic *maeine*. Wesley W. Isenberg, in *Nag Hammadi Library*, ed. Robinson, who dates the work to the second half of the third century, translates the phrase thus: "Would that I [may receive] a name like that!" (p. 138).

[18]Lampe 122–123, cf. 126.

[19]A. D. Nock, *Conversion: The Old and the New in Religion from Alexander the Great to Augustine of Hippo* (Oxford 1933) 104–105.

63

A peculiarity of the seal in Theodotus's conception of it is that the unclean spirits are also able to acquire it: "It is fitting to go to baptism with joy, but, since unclean spirits often go down [into the water] with some and these spirits following and gaining the seal together with the candidate become impossible to cure for the future, fear is joined with joy, in order that only he who is pure may go down [to the water]."[20] The seal spoken of in this and previously quoted texts refers to baptism and not to a rite of confirmation, and accordingly the present passage means that the evil spirits are actually baptized.[21] The seal is certainly a major effect of the gnostic sacramental system; but it is evident that the unclean spirits do not receive the benefits of redemption or freedom from the world that baptism bestows upon men and their guardian angels. They are only strengthened in their ability to oppose man's salvation, and one must take care to eliminate them before one is baptized. Dölger paraphrases the last part of the text in the following way: "With joy is mixed fear, which brings it about that one is moved to penance and humble prayer and emerges at last alone, with a pure heart, to go into the water."

In order to achieve or maintain the purity necessary to keep the unclean spirits from joining in on the act, a number of precautions are taken: "Therefore [let there be] fastings, supplications, prayers, [raising] of hands, kneelings, because a soul is being saved from the world [*kosmos*] and from the 'mouth of lions.'"[22] There is no indication that the fasting mentioned here has a more specific antidemonic purpose than simply to provide the proper accompaniment to the prayers and supplications, and the same can be said of the kneelings or genuflections, as well as of the raising of hands, if this is the meaning of the text. Sagnard reads rather "the imposition of hands." He points out that the laying on of hands can have many different significations but that the notion of the action of a power, efficacious operation, or communication is always implied.[23]

One of the earlier extracts refers to the laying on of hands during the recitation of a prayer that is given in full by Irenaeus: "The Name hidden from every divinity and dominion and truth, which Jesus the

[20]Extract 83.
[21]F. J. Dölger, *Sphragis: Eine altchristliche Taufbezeichnung in ihren Beziehungen zur profanen und religiösen Kultur des Altertums* (Paderborn 1911) 73; Sagnard, *Extraits* 235, 238.
[22]Extract 84.
[23]Sagnard 234.

Nazarene put on in the zones of the light of Christ, Christ living through the Holy Spirit, for the angelic redemption."[24] The imposition of hands here is not a prebaptismal exercise, of course, but is performed in the course of the baptism itself, or perhaps even after baptism, if the "redemption" or *lutrōsis* mentioned in the prayer is to be considered a separate sacrament, as seems to be the case in the *Gospel of Philip:* "The Lord did everything in a mystery, a baptism and a chrism and a eucharist and a redemption and a bride-chamber."[25] On the basis of the data of Irenaeus, who like Theodotus combines the notions of baptism and redemption, it has been suggested that the Valentinian sacrament of redemption would "probably have been either that of the pouring of water and oil over a person's head, perhaps followed by an anointing—the whole rite would then probably be a sacrament for the dying—or a simple anointing."[26]

The imposition of hands as an exorcistic practice first appears, to my knowledge, in the Qumran *Genesis Apocryphon,* where Abraham uses this method to free Pharaoh from an evil spirit,[27] and there is some indication in the New Testament that the curative imposition of hands is also connected with the liberation from demonic oppression. So it is in the case of the woman bound by Satan with a spirit of infirmity (Luke 13.10–13); and one time when Jesus is described as healing the diseased by laying his hands on them, it is said that "demons also came out of many" (Luke 4.40–41). In Palestine in the third century, Origen speaks of the imposition of hands as a procedure used by exorcists against unclean spirits, so that the practice must have been common by his time, along with the "many prayers, many fasts, many invocations of the exorcists" that he speaks of.[28]

Theodotus later speaks of postbaptismal struggles against the powers of evil. After his explanation of the procedure for freeing oneself from the company of unclean spirits, he says that there is "immediate temptation for those who long for the things from which they have been separated, and even if one has foreknowledge to endure them, yet the outward man is shaken." The individual must

[24]Extract 22.5; Irenaeus, *Adversus haereses* 1.21.3 (Harvey 1.184).
[25]*Gospel of Philip* 68 (Wilson 130).
[26]Segelberg (n. 17 above) 191, 197, 199–200; Irenaeus 1.21; cf. Casey, *Excerpta* 7 (n. 2), 21, 118.
[27]*The Genesis Apocryphon of Qumran Cave I* 20.20–29, ed. J. A. Fitzmyer, rev. ed., Biblica et orientalia 18A (Rome 1971) 64–67.
[28]Origen, *Homilies on Joshua* 24.1, trans. Rufinus (GCS 30.1, 448–449).

gather strength from the Savior's example: "Even the Lord after baptism was troubled like as we are and was first with beasts in the desert. Then when he had prevailed over them and their ruler as if already a true king, he was already served by angels. For he who ruled over angels in the flesh was fittingly served already by angels. Therefore we must put on the Lord's armor and keep body and soul invulnerable—armor that is able to quench the darts of the devil, as the apostle says."[29] Theodotus does not seem to be referring to any specific ritual precaution to be taken aginst the evil spirits, either at baptism or after baptism; he is is simply exhorting the faithful to be on their guard.

For a clearer view of the Theodotan drama of salvation, and a more precise understanding of the significance of the rituals of deliverance from the evil powers, I shall review the demonology of the *Extracts*. Of particular interest is the question of whether we are to identify the unclean spirits who attempt to obtain the seal with the principalities and powers.

I have shown that the invisible astral powers, some of whom are beneficent and others maleficent, are designated as angels. The Evil One is associated with the maleficent powers in making external and corporeal attacks on mankind. Baptism rescues man from fire, which is defined in its immaterial aspect as an agent that can act even on demons, angels of evil, and the devil himself. The rite takes its efficacy in this matter from the Spirit, who rules over the elements, the powers, and the evil principalities. The evil principalities are renounced in baptism, and the candidate becomes the master of the unclean spirits, who are now frightened of the man they had previously possessed. Sometimes, however, when a candidate is not single and is himself unclean, the unclean spirits will go down with him and follow beside him (I translate the Greek literally) in order to get the seal with him. To prevent them from doing so, the candidate undergoes a regimen of prayer and fasting, and perhaps he is assisted by ministers who lay their hands upon him; the object is to prepare his soul to be delivered from the world and the mouth of lions. When, however, a man has successfully escaped from the tyranny of the visible and the invisible forces of the world, he may be tempted to return to the things he has been removed from, just as the Lord was tempted after his baptism. But as the Lord prevailed over the beasts

[29]Extracts 84–85.

and imposed his rule upon angels, it behooves his followers to take up his armor and thereby quench the devil's darts. The Savior, by being baptized and advancing towards God, received power to tread upon scorpions and serpents, as the evil powers are called in the Gospel. Everyone who is so baptized, in the Name of Father, Son, and Holy Spirit, becomes higher than all the other powers.

There is obviously an identity of ultimate purpose uniting all of the hostile forces; possibly, however, the invisible powers that guide the course of the stars and govern through them are not considered the same kind of being as the unclean spirits. Perhaps there is a distinction among "demons, angels of evil, and the devil." Practically the same sequence of names occurs in Irenaeus's account of the doctrine of the disciples of Valentinus:

> They further teach that the spirits of wickedness derived their origin from grief. Herein the devil, whom they also call Cosmocrator [ruler of the world], and the demons, and the angels, and every wicked spiritual being that exists found the source of their existence. They represent the Demiurge as being the son of that mother of theirs [Achamoth], and Cosmocrator as the creature of the Demiurge. Cosmocrator has knowledge of what is above himself, because he is a spirit of wickedness; but the Demiurge is ignorant of such things, inasmuch as he is merely *animal*. Their mother dwells in that place which is above the heavens, that is, in the intermediate abode; the Demiurge in the heavenly place, that is, in the hebdomad; but the Cosmocrator in this our world.[30]

It is clear in Theodotus that the devil is the ruler of beasts, who are perhaps identified as angels, just as the scorpions and serpents of the Gospel quotation are identified as evil powers. Theodotus's conception may be comparable in some ways to that of one of the non-Christian gnostic Hermetic writings, where the stars are immortal beings served by demons, who are good or bad according to their activity; each time a man is born, the demons operative at the moment, according to the location of the stars, infest his body and even part of his soul; but if a man receives the divine light in his soul, the demons are reduced to impotence, though it seems they are not necessarily removed from the person.[31]

If the unclean spirits who make men energoumenoi actually "pos-

---

[30]Irenaeus, *Adversus haereses* 1.5.4 (Harvey 1.47–48, ANF 1.323).
[31]*Corpus hermeticum* 16.13–16, ed. A. D. Nock, trans. A. J. Festugière (Paris 1945) 2.236–237.

sess" them in the sense of dwelling in them, the spiritual exercises undertaken before baptism would be exorcistic in the strict sense of attempting to dislodge spirits from the bodies or spirits of men. It is possible, however, that Theodotus had in mind the kind of external harassment visualized at one point in the *Paris Magical Papyrus:* "Let thy angel descend, the implacable one, and let him draw into captivity the demon as he flieth around this creature which God formed in his holy paradise."[32]

We have seen that in the gnostic systems of Basilides and Valentinus himself, various kinds of unwholesome spirits seemingly distinct from the cosmic powers were thought to dwell within men. The same is true of other versions of gnosticism as well—for example, the *Gospel of Philip:* "Among the unclean spirits there are male and female. The male are they which unite with the souls which inhabit a female form; but the female are they which are mingled with those in a male form, through a disobedient [one]. And none shall be able to escape them, since they detain him, if he does not receive a male power or a female, which is the bridegroom or the bride. . . . For if they had the Holy Spirit, the unclean spirits would not cleave unto them."[33] Furthermore, in Clement's characterization of Valentinus's doctrine, there is much the same terminology as that used by Theodotus, though the latter speaks of "demons" and "unclean spirits," whereas Valentinus has "spirits" and "unclean demons." But Clement himself uses the expression "unclean spirits" when trying to show that the doctrine of indwelling spirits is inconsistent with other gnostic beliefs, and he seems to be directing his argument chiefly against Valentinus.[34]

It is tempting to suppose that Theodotus's liturgy deals with the kind of unclean demons that Valentinus describes, though we are properly warned against the danger of filling out Theodotus's teaching from other sources, "since Valentinian systems exhibit characteristic variations at the most unexpected points."[35] We may, however, at least advert to the possibility or even likelihood of there having

[32]Lines 3024–3027 (Deissmann 256, 260). Deissmann believes that the demon has already been freed from the victim by exorcism and is fluttering about him and that now it is to be arrested so as not to enter into him again (256 n. 4).

[33]*Gospel of Philip* 61 (Wilson 41–42, 119–120). Just before the last sentence cited, at the end of a hiatus there occurs the word "demons." See Ménard 74–77 and 177–178 for conjectural emendations.

[34]Clement, *Stromata* 2.20 (115.1).

[35]Casey, *Excerpta* 21.

been in Valentinus's personal practice a series of ceremonies similar to those described by Theodotus. The recently discovered *Gospel of Truth,* which has been ascribed to Valentinus, throws little light upon the subject, though it may be referring to a baptismal exorcism when it warns, "Do not become a place for the devil, for you have already set him at naught,"[36] especially when translated more tendentiously: "because you have already thrown him out."[37] But in fact the text may be no more than a reference to Ephesians 4.27: "Give no place to the devil." Furthermore, even if the dictum did refer to a baptismal expulsion of the devil, the ritual mise-en-scène need not be the same as that presupposed by Theodotus. For example, in the *Prophetic Eclogues,* another gnostic collection similar to the *Excerpta ex Theodoto,* also gathered by Clement of Alexandria, there is the following observation: "Regeneration [comes] immediately from 'water and spirit,' just like the universal creation. 'For the spirit of God was moving over the abyss.' And for this reason our Savior was baptized, even though he stood in no need of it, in order to sanctify all the water for those who are regenerated. In this way, then, we are made clean not only in body but also in soul. A sign that even what is invisible in us is sanctified is the fact that even the unclean spirits entangled with the soul are filtered off by the new and spiritual birth."[38] This passage presupposes a very different situation from that envisaged in the liturgy of the *Excerpta,* for here baptism itself is considered exorcistic, whereas for Theodotus, far from being exorcistic, baptism actually increases the hold of the unclean spirits upon a man, and for this reason it is imperative that the spirits be removed before the baptism takes place.[39]

[36]*Evangelium veritatis* 33.19–21, ed. Michel Malinine et al., trans. R. McL. Wilson, Studien aus dem C. G. Jung-Institut 6 (Zurich 1961) 30. George W. MacRae, in *Nag Hammadi Library,* ed. Robinson, puts: "for you have already destroyed him" (p. 44). J. E. Ménard, ed., *L'évangile de vérité,* Nag Hammadi Studies 2 (Leiden 1972) 60, gives a similar reading.

[37]Eric Segelberg, "The Baptismal Rite According to Some of the Coptic-Gnostic Texts of Nag-Hammadi," *Studia patristica* 5, ed. F. L. Cross, TU 80 (Berlin 1962) 117–128, esp. 120.

[38]Clement of Alexandria, *Eclogae propheticae* 7, ed. O. Stählin, GCS 17.138.

[39]Another passage in the *Eclogae* (no. 46, pp. 149–150) appears to interpret "spirit" in an allegorical sense or at least as not signifying independent personalities. It can be translated: "The passions in the soul are called spirits, not spirits in reality, since an impassioned man is a legion of demons [cf. Luke 8.30], but figuratively. For the same soul as it changes in receiving now some and now other qualities of evil is said to have taken on spirits." If this rendition of the eclogue is correct, it is evident that it

Theodotus alludes to one other ceremony of great interest. After speaking of the sanctification of the bread and oil, that is, the transformation of these substances into spiritual power by the power of the Name, he says that the water too, both in being exorcized and in "becoming baptism," not only keeps off evil but sanctifies as well.[40] That is to say, the water is first exorcized in order to be made usable for baptism. This text provides the first known instance of the word *exorkizein* being applied to a material object. Properly, of course, evil spirits should be the object of exorcism, that is, "adjuration," since it is they who are adjured to leave their unwarranted abodes; however, the word came, naturally enough, to be applied to demoniacs themselves; a minister exorcizes them in the sense of saying exorcisms over them. In later Western baptismal rites, as we shall see, when water is "exorcized" it is simply "exhorted," that is, addressed by way of personification, and the word has no demonic connotation in itself. But the formula that accompanies it often carries the idea that the water is to serve the purpose of expelling or repelling demons; moreover, it is frequently assumed that evil spirits or their influences are actually in the water, and consequently there is a demand or prayer for their removal.

It is not clear which, if any, of these meanings applies to the present text. The first effect of the exorcized water is said to be the elimination of evil, or, literally, "the greater evil," which may refer only to impersonal impurities within the water or in the candidates. The reference could also, however, be to the evil powers; this is the way Sagnard interprets the phrase, though he translates it impersonally as "la séparation de l'élément inférieur."[41]

In the *Prophetic Eclogues,* as previously noted, it is said that Jesus himself sanctified all water so that it would be efficacious for baptism. It must be noted that according to this view no blessing or exorcism of the water would be necessary before its use for individual baptisms. There is a similar concept in the *Gospel of Philip:* "Even as Jesus perfected the water of baptism, so did he pour out death. Because of this we go down indeed into the water, but we do not go down into

---

expresses a point of view very much like that of Clement himself, which I cited at length in the previous chapter; and no doubt the passage should be marked down as his own commentary on the subject and not as a report of gnostic belief.

[40]Extract 82.

[41]Sagnard, *Extraits* 233.

death, in order that we may not be poured out into the spirit of the world. When it blows, it causes the winter to come into being. When the Holy Spirit breathes, then the summer comes."[42]

Earlier in the second century, Ignatius of Antioch said that Christ "was born and baptized in order to cleanse the water by the Passion." One interpretation of this text would rank it as the earliest witness to a tradition that Christ cleared the waters of the demons who lived in them.[43] But it is not evident that this meaning can be found either in Ignatius's statement or in the theological or liturgical writings, whether orthodox or heterodox, of subsequent times. It is true that Psalm 73.13 ("Thou didst break the heads of the dragons on the waters") was sometimes used to describe Christ's defeat of the devil. There may be an example of this usage in a Christian passage in the *Testaments of the Twelve Patriarchs,* where the editor seems to have reworked a purely Jewish tradition: "Ye shall be set at nought in the dispersion, vanishing away as water, until the Most High shall visit the earth, coming himself as man, with men eating and drinking and in peace, breaking the head of the dragon through the water. He shall save Israel and all the Gentiles, God speaking in the person of man."[44] But even when the psalm was used to describe the effect of Christ's baptism, it did not necessarily mean that the devil was thought to inhabit the water. Sometimes, in fact, as we shall see, there is clear evidence to the contrary.

Elaborate attempts have been made[45] to show that baptism in the early Church involved the idea of a descent into the underworld of the demons. In addition to the mistake of demonizing water dragons, that is, serpents,[46] this interpretation relies on another faulty notion:

[42]*Gospel of Philip* 109 (Wilson 167–168).

[43]Ignatius of Antioch, *Epistle to the Ephesians* 18, ed. Funk-Schneemelcher 87. For demonic interpretations, see Benoit 67–69; Daniélou, *Theology* 226–227. For a collection of later texts on Christ's purification of the waters, none of them referring to demon removal, see Sebastian Brock, *The Holy Spirit in the Syrian Baptismal Tradition,* Syrian Church Series 9 (Kottayam 1979) 76–79.

[44]Testament of Asher 7.2–3 (*APOT* 345). See the use made of Psalm 73 by Cyril of Jerusalem, Chap. 9 at n. 28.

[45]Especially by J. H. Bernard, *The Odes of Solomon,* Texts and Studies 8.3 (Cambridge 1912) 32–39, 103–106, and Per Lundberg, *La typologie baptismale dans l'ancienne église* (Leipzig 1942), followed by Benoit and Daniélou, but opposed, at least in part, by Tremel, "Baptism" 202 n. 2, and Dalton, *Christ's Proclamation to the Spirits* 202–203.

[46]It is worth noting that the word "dragon" (that is, the Greek *drakōn*) signified no more than "large serpent." And though these serpents were sometimes endowed with

namely, the idea that in the first two centuries of the Christian era the watery abyss of the Old Testament sea monsters was identified with the fiery abyss where the lustful angels were to be cast at the end of the world[47] or where the dragon devil of the Apocalypse was to be temporarily detained,[48] or with Sheol; and that the devil or demons were thought at this early date to be actually present in Sheol holding the dead captive at the time of Christ's descent. Cardinal Daniélou believes that this last theme first appears in the *Testaments of the Twelve Patriarchs,* but the texts he cites by no means require this meaning, and his reading of the *Odes of Solomon* is equally unconvincing.[49]

The *Odes of Solomon* is a work of such obscure provenance and meaning that any evidence it is thought to provide concerning early baptismal practices must remain very tentative. Robert Grant at first considered these hymns to be Valentinian, but more recently he agrees with Daniélou as to their Jewish-Christian character; F. M. Braun suggests the Syrian gnostic Bardesanes (154–ca. 223) as their author.[50] Much is made of Christ's descent into the lower regions,

---

wings in antiquity, not until the Middle Ages did artists and authors conceive of them and other serpents as having legs. There was one exception, however: according to Jewish and Byzantine tradition, the serpent in Eden originally had legs, but God removed them as part of its punishment for deceiving Adam and Eve. That is, all serpents were legless from that time forward. See H. A. Kelly, "The Metamorphoses of the Eden Serpent during the Middle Ages and Renaissance," *Viator* 2 (1971) 301–327.

[47]As in *1 Enoch* 10.13.

[48]See Revelation 9.1–2; 20.2–3.

[49]Daniélou, *Theology* 239–242, 244–248.

[50]R. M. Grant, *Gnosticism and Early Christianity,* rev. ed. (New York 1966) 134; F. M. Braun, "L'énigme des *Odes de Salomon,*" *Revue thomiste* 57 (1957) 597–625. For more recent defenses of the Christianity of the *Odes,* see Henry Chadwick, "Some Reflections on the Character and Theology of the *Odes of Solomon,*"*Kyriakon: Festschrift Johannes Quasten,* ed. Patrick Granfield and Josef A. Jungmann (Münster 1970) 1.266–270; James H. Charlesworth, "The *Odes of Solomon*—Not Gnostic," *Catholic Biblical Quarterly* 31 (1969) 357–369; and Charlesworth's new edition and translation, *The Odes of Solomon: The Syriac texts* (Oxford 1973; corrected reprint Missoula, Mont., 1977, or Chico, Calif., 1978). For further speculations, see Brian McNeil, "The *Odes of Solomon* and the Sufferings of Christ," *Symposium syriacum 1976,* ed. François Graffin and Antoine Guillaumont, Orientalia christiana analecta 205 (Rome 1978) 31–38; H. J. W. Drijvers, "Die *Oden Salomos* und die Polemik mit den Markioniten im syrischen Christentum," ibid. 39–55; and Brian McNeil, "The *Odes of Solomon* and the Scriptures," *Oriens christianus* 67 (1983) 104–122. In progress is Michael Lattke's *Die Oden Salomos in ihrer Bedeutung für Neues Testament und Gnosis,* vols. 1–2 (Freiburg 1979), vol. 1a (1980); three more volumes are projected. Lattke

where, however, the enemies are Sheol and Death[51] and not Satan. There may be a reference to the devil at one point, where Christ is made to say that God, who raised him up from the depths and slew all his enemies, overthrew by his hands the dragon with seven heads and set him up to destroy the dragon's seed.[52] In another ode, which ends by speaking of the healing benefits of water, it is said that the Spirit of the Lord destroys what is alien so that nothing shall be contrary or rise up against him. There may be some hint here, and in other places adduced by J. H. Bernard,[53] of the apotropaic character of baptism. But these data do not allow us to conclude that Christ descended into a watery hell and defeated its demonic proprietors or to say that Christ purified demon-polluted water and thereby allowed it to be used in baptism.

Another work that deals with the healing power of water is the *Testament of Adam* (or *Apocalypse of Adam*), which may have been known to the gnostics, if it was one of the apocalypses of Adam mentioned by Epiphanius.[54] At the tenth hour of the day, according to "Adam," there is a visitation of the water, when (as the Syriac version reads) "the Holy Spirit comes down and broods upon the waters and the springs. And if the Spririt of the Lord came not down and did not thus brood upon the waters and springs, the race of men would be destroyed and the demons would cause to perish with a look whomsoever they would. And if at this hour a man take water and the priest of God mingle holy oil therewith and anoint the sick therewith, they recover health immediately." The Greek and Arabic versions say that the Spirit sanctifies the waters, and the Arabic adds that it drives away the demons from the waters, and that, if the Holy Spirit did not so brood, "all that drank of them would perish because of the evil operation of the demons." According to the Greek, the mixture of water and holy oil not only cures every disease but purifies

---

sees the work as gnostic in the broad sense and as related to the Gospel of John. See the review by R. Köbert, *Biblica* 61 (1980) 433–434.

[51]*Odes of Solomon* 42.11 (Charlesworth 145).

[52]Ibid. 22.1–5. Bernard (92) believes that the Coptic version makes the allusion to the devil explicit in the following verses (where the dragon's poison is said to be destroyed) by reading "the poison of the slanderer," i.e., *diabolos*.

[53]*Odes* 6.1–5; see Bernard 41. Charlesworth points out that Bernard and others who read "His adversary" in Ode 6.5 are incorrect because there is no pronominal suffix.

[54]Epiphanius (n. 1 above) 26.8.1 (284); cf. F. J. A. Hort, "Adam, Books of" *Dictionary of Christian Biography* 1 (London 1877) 37–38.

demoniacs and drives away demons or, as the Arabic puts it, cures the sick and those who are possessed by unclean spirits.[55] Whether originally gnostic or not, the *Testament of Adam* offers a good example of ancient superstitions about spirits living in water. Beliefs of this sort were to found among Christians, Jews, and pagans alike.[56] It would not be surprising, therefore, if the water exorcism in the service described by Theodotus had the meaning of expelling demons from the water.

In conclusion, the *Extracts of Theodotus* provides the first certain instance of "Christian" antidemonic rituals before baptism, whereby both the candidates and the water were somehow purified of evil spirits. It also contains a possible reference to a ceremony of renunciation, and it speaks of the reception of an apotropaic seal, which was perhaps administered with a sign of the cross. The oil that was used may also have had an antidemonic significance. According to G. W. H. Lampe, it is probable that the gnostic sects of the second century first separated Spirit baptism from water baptism, and "it is to these circles that we probably ought also to look for the introduction of subsidiary ceremonies such as postbaptismal unction; even if these rites did not originate with the gnostic or semi-gnostic sects, they acquired a new and greatly enhanced significance at their hands."[57] Such anointings could easily have acquired an apotropaic character, even in cases where this level of meaning was not originally present.

In more orthodox (that is, nongnostic) Christian communities in Egypt, there is some evidence, from a time slightly later than that of Theodotus, of antidemonic measures taken at baptism or before baptism. We saw that Clement of Alexandria may have known a renunciation of the powers, and when Origen at Caesarea spoke of a sign of the cross made on the forehead, as well as of a renunciation of the devil and his works, or, as he put it elsewhere, a renunciation "of all other gods and lords,"[58] he may have been recalling practices of his earlier days in Alexandria. The baptismal water, we know, was con-

[55]M. R. James, "A Fragment of the Apocalypse of Adam in Greek," *Apocrypha anecdota,* Texts and Studies 2.3 (Cambridge 1893) 141.

[56]Dölger, *Exorzismus* 163. For Jewish beliefs, see Kaufmann Kohler, "Demonology," *Jewish Encyclopedia* 4.514–520, esp. 516–517; Strack-Billerbeck 4.517–518; Bowman, *Gospel of Mark* 46. Tertullian, as we shall see, describes pagan beliefs of this sort that he himself accepted (*De baptismo* 5).

[57]Lampe 127. For other views, see Georg Kretschmar, "Recent Research on Christian Initiation," *Studia liturgica* 12 (1977) 87–106, esp. 87–89.

[58]Origen, *Homilies on Exodus* 8.4 (GCS 29.223); see n. 15 above.

secrated in the Alexandrian liturgy,[59] but there is no sign that the consecration had, in Origen's view, an antidemonic character.

More important, we have seen that there is no indication of a prebaptismal exorcism in Origen's writings, in spite of the fact that he subscribed to the theory of sin demons. He indicated his mind in the matter in an explanation that he gave of Matthew 12.43–45: before we believed, the unclean spirit lived in us, but he was forced to leave when we "came to Christ." He noted that a man was not immediately worthy of having Christ dwell in him unless his life was pure; otherwise the unclean spirit and others worse than it would return.[60] The sinner must repent of his sins before he received baptism, because no one who came to baptism while still a sinner could obtain the remission of his sins.[61] In his view, therefore, exorcism was not necessary for the purification of the ordinary sinner before baptism. It was sufficient simply to stop sinning.

There is, then, no sign of prebaptismal exorcism among orthodox Christians in Egypt or in the adjacent regions of the Levant, in the second or third century. We shall see, however, traces of the idea that baptism itself had an exorcistic (demon-expelling) effect, as in the Syriac *Didascalia,* which contains Hermas's conception of human life as entailing possession either by the evil or by the good spirit.[62] But an orthodox practice of exorcistic rites *before baptism* first appears not in Egypt but in Rome, Valentinus's other stamping ground. From Rome it spread to the rest of the Christian world. Only in Syria and beyond was the novelty successfully resisted.

Before turning to orthodoxy, let us take a last look at Egyptian gnosticism in one of its more advanced forms, that set forth in the *Books of Jeu.* According to this work, which stems from the Barbelo sect in the beginning of the third century, Jesus told his disciples: "I will give to you the three baptisms: the water baptism, the baptism of fire, and the baptism of the Holy Spirit. And I will give to you the mystery of taking away from you the evil of the archons, and after these things I will give to you the mystery of the spiritual inunction

---

[59]Origen, *Catena on John* 3.5 (GCS 512).

[60]Origen, *Homilies on Exodus* 8.4 (GCS 225–226).

[61]Origen, *Homilies on Luke* 21, ed. Max Rauer, ed. 2, GCS 49 (Berlin 1959) 128–129.

[62]Thraede, "Exorzismus" 82: "Hier ist Dasein Besessenheit (von Gott oder Dämonen)." Thraede sees the *Didascalia* as carrying on a Levantine ecclesiastical tradition of initiation exorcism, a theory that I find unlikely.

[*chrisma*]."[63] The disciples' reception of the three baptisms is then described. For the baptism of water, Jesus first set up a sacrificial offering, flanked by vessels of wine; he then added juniper, something called kasdalanthos, and nard. He had the disciples dress in linen clothing, put anemone plant in their mouths, and placed the number of the seven voices, namely 9879, in their hands, along with the sunflower plant, and stationed them before the offering. Next he spread out linen cloths and placed on them a cup of wine and bread, according to the number of the disciples. He laid olive branches on the place of offering and set olive-branch crowns on their heads. Then he sealed them with one of the numerous seals that appear in the book, this one being a kind of cross with extra crossbars; it had the meaning of *thēzōzaz*. Then, keeping close together, all turned to the four corners of the world, while Jesus prayed, "Iōazezēth azazē asazēth, amen, amen, amen," and so on. He addressed his father, the infinite light, and called upon the fifteen helpers (who served the seven light virgins that were placed over the baptism of life) to come and baptize his disciples with the water of life, to forgive their sins, and to purify their iniquities, that they might be counted as heirs of the kingdom of light. He then called for a miracle if his prayer was answered, and immediately the wine in the vessel on the right became water; and Jesus baptized them, had them partake of the offering, and sealed them with another seal, this one looking like a stick man lying on his side, with very short legs and arms and a very long neck.[64]

The same sort of mystification is to be found in the ceremonies for the other two baptisms[65] as well as in the mystery for eliminating the evil of the rulers from the disciples. In the latter rite Jesus set up an incense altar and put incense in the mouths of the disciples. He sealed them with two more seals, and prayed the father to compel Sabaoth, the Adamas, and all his captains to come and take away their evil that was in his disciples. They did so, and the disciples became immortal and followed Jesus wherever they were to go.[66] Jesus then gave in full detail the itinerary of the journey that their souls would take when they had left their bodies and the ways in which the various powers would flee from them or let them pass.[67]

[63]*Books of Jeu* 2.43, ed. Carl Schmidt, trans. Violet Macdermot, Nag Hammadi Studies 13 (Leiden 1978) 102.
[64]Ibid. 45 (107–108).
[65]Ibid. 46–47 (108–114).
[66]Ibid. 48 (114–116).
[67]Ibid. 49–52 (116–138). The end of the book is missing; it no doubt contained much more of the same kind of directions.

The more conventional Christians believed in a far simpler system of hostile spirits than did their gnostic contemporaries. But the elaborate ritual methods by which the gnostics liberated and defended themselves from the forces of evil may have had some influence in inspiring the Church throughout the world to take similar, if less bizarre, measures against Satan and his minions. I shall pose the question of gnostic influence in more detail in the chapters to follow.

PART **II** /

EARLY MAINSTREAM
DEVELOPMENTS

5 /

Hippolytus of Rome and

The *Apostolic Tradition*

In mainstream Christianity of the first two centuries, we have seen, along with some antidemonic interpretations of baptism itself, a number of possible reflections of antidemonic rites surrounding baptism but little or nothing that could be definitely identified as such. It is in the West about the beginning of the third century that we first find clear accounts of initiatory rituals directed against evil spirits. They are described or alluded to in the writings of Tertullian in Carthage and in the *Apostolic Tradition* of Hippolytus in Rome. According to tradition Carthage was evangelized from Rome, and there was always a close relationship between the two cities. Since the baptismal rite as Tertullian knew it followed in its general lines that of the *Apostolic Tradition*,[1] we may begin with an analysis of the rites described by Hippolytus and then compare them with the African practices.

The original text of the *Apostolic Tradition* does not survive, but it is possible to obtain a good idea of its contents from the many translations and adaptations that we do possess. I shall use Dom Bernard Botte's reconstruction of the service as my main text and clarify it where necessary by referring to the editions and translations of the different versions. The text in the Sahidic dialect of the Coptic language is the most important for our study, since it is the chief witness

[1] See the detailed comparison made by Ernest Evans, *Tertullian's Homily on Baptism* (London 1964) xix–xxviii.

81

where the Latin text is lacking, as is the case for most of the initiation ceremonies.[2]

In accepting the *Apostolic Tradition* as the first orthodox scenario of the administration of Christian baptism, we must set liberal boundaries to our notion of orthodoxy. Hippolytus had some ideas that were aberrant from the viewpoint of the doctrines of the Church that eventually won out. From this viewpoint, in fact, he is even considered an antipope. But his differences of opinion with the main community at Rome were mostly in matters of discipline. He was an unforgiving sort, and he accused the Church leaders of excessive leniency towards sinners.

In liturgical matters, Hippolytus no doubt evolved peculiar practices of his own, and the *Tradition* is not to be thought of as providing an exhaustive picture of the liturgy in use in Rome at this period, especially since the rites must still have been in the process of development. Nevertheless, since Hippolytus the theologian was more of a compiler of the ideas of others than a creative thinker, the same may also be true of Hippolytus the liturgist, especially since it was his avowed purpose to hand on the tradition of the apostles.

Did he, then, record a purely Roman rite? It has been urged with great vigor that the liturgy of Alexandria provided the chief inspiration for his services,[3] but this thesis has not met with much favor. One objection is that even though some of the ceremonies can be explained as being at home in the East as well as in the West, the double anointing that takes place after baptism is a practice found only at Rome.[4] In response, it could be alleged that the double

---

[2]Bernard Botte, *La Tradition apostolique de saint Hippolyte: Essai de reconstitution,* LQF 39 (Münster 1963; the 4th printing, 1972, has two pages of corrigenda and addenda). V. Raffa in *Ephemerides liturgicae* 78 (1964) 165–167 questions Botte's assumption that the archetype upon which all the versions are based is very close to the original (cf. Botte xxix); there could be a distance of two centuries, and the content could be very different. Raffa also wishes that Botte had made a more literal translation of the various versions. A new translation and a synoptic presentation of all of the pertinent texts is to be had in Jean Michel Hanssens, "La synopse des ordonnances apparentées à la *Tradition apostolique,*" in *La liturgie d'Hippolyte: Documents et études* (Rome 1970) 1–163. For references to other discussions, see George Kretschmar, "La liturgie ancienne dans les recherches historiques actuelles," *Maison-Dieu* 149 (1982) 57–90, esp. 59.

[3]J. M. Hanssens, *La liturgie d'Hippolyte: Ses documents, son titulaire, ses origines, et son caractère,* Orientalia christiana analecta 155 (Rome 1959) 500.

[4]Botte xiv–xvi. But the later Roman liturgy of John the Deacon may have only one anointing after baptism (see Chap. 7 n. 37). Kretschmar, "La liturgie" 62, objects that

anointing is a sign of the *Tradition's* influence upon Rome and not vice versa. Furthermore, Hippolytus undeniably shows a great familiarity with Eastern thought. He need not have acquired it in the East,[5] of course, for such knowledge was fully available in the Rome of his day. His description of the baptismal rites may show Alexandrian influence even if we hold that they are basically Roman.

The Roman practices before Hippolytus's time may also conceivably have been influenced by some of the peculiar Eastern views of demonology that we have studied. Specifically, Rome was the home of Hermas and his *Shepherd,* with its Essene and Jewish-Christian doctrine of sin demons; and Valentinus would have promulgated his gnostic version of the same doctrine during the two decades that he spent in Rome.

I shall now turn to the text and examine the program that is set up for the candidate who is to be received into the Church. I am, of course, regarding the processes of initiation very selectively, emphasizing the actions that must be performed to free the candidate from the power of the adversary.

In the gnostic rite described by Theodotus, as previously noted, a series of ascetic practices was performed before baptism in order to purify the candidate of unclean spirits. Similar precautions are taken in the *Apostolic Tradition.* We read, in the Coptic (Sahidic) version:

> When they have chosen those who are set apart to be baptized, their life having been examined (whether they have lived seriously as catechumens, whether they have honored the widows, whether they have visited the sick, whether they have completed every good work), and when those who brought them have borne witness to them, that they did thus, then let them hear the gospel; moreover, from the time that they will be separated [from the rest] let hand be laid on them daily, in exorcizing them.[6] And when the day draws near on which they will be baptized, let the bishop exorcize each one of them, that he may know whether they are pure. And if there is one who is not good[7] or pure, let

---

the episcopal structure of the Alexandrian Church would not have been sufficiently formed around the year 200 to have produced the *Tradition.*

[5]Quasten 2.163.

[6]The Ethiopic reads "instructing" rather than "exorcizing."

[7]Omitted by the Arabic and Ethiopic texts. The Coptic (Sahidic) takes over the original Greek word, *kalos,* which means "beautiful" but is here used in its moral sense.

him be put on one side, because he did not hear the word in faith; for it is never possible for the alien to be concealed.[8] Then let those who are set apart to be baptized be instructed to bathe[9] *and make themselves free,*[10] and wash themselves on the fifth day of the week [Thursday]. And if a woman is in the manner of women, let her be put on one side, and let her be baptized on another day. Let them who will be baptized fast on the preparation of the sabbath [Friday]. And on the sabbath [Saturday] when they who will be baptized have assembled in one place by the direction of the bishop, let them all be commanded to pray and bend their knees. And when he has laid his hand upon them, let him exorcize all alien spirits[11] to flee away from them, and not to return to them henceforward. And when he has done exorcizing, let him breathe in their face.[12] And when he has sealed their foreheads and their ears and their noses, let him raise them up. And let them spend all the night in vigil, and let them be read to and instructed.[13]

In the liturgy of Theodotus it is not possible to tell whether the mention of hands refers to the candidate's raising of his own hands in prayer or to the laying on of hands by another person. Here in the *Apostolic Tradition* there is no such ambiguity, for the latter meaning is stated explicitly. Hippolytus does not identify the minister who performs the preliminary exorcisms. But in the previous chapter, when he speaks of the earlier stage of initiation, that is, the time when the catechumens receive instructions, he says that they are dismissed at the end of each session when the instructor, who may be either a cleric (*ekklēsiastikos*) or a layman, places his hand on their heads and prays.[14]

As in the *Excerpta ex Theodoto,* the preliminary rites described by Hippolytus include fasting, prayer, and genuflections, and there is also a direction that to be suitable for baptism one must be pure, or,

---

[8]Arabic: "for it is not possible that an alien should ever be baptized." Ethiopic: "because it is not proper to do to an utter alien."

[9]Ethiopic adds: "and be exorcized."

[10]Arabic and Ethiopic omit the words italicized, which Botte considers an erroneous interpolation in the Sahidic text. Horner (n. 13 below) interprets the text as an instruction to make oneself free "from the alien."

[11]Arabic: "every alien spirit"; Ethiopic: "the unclean spirit."

[12]Ethiopic: "upon them" (rather than "in their face").

[13]*Ap. Trad.* 29 (Botte 42–44), translation adapted from G. Horner, *The Statutes of the Apostles; or, Canones ecclesiastici* (London 1904) 315–316; cf. Walter Till and Johannes Leipoldt, *Der koptische Text der Kirchenordnung Hippolyts,* TU 58 (Berlin 1954) 14–17.

[14]*Ap. Trad.* 19 (Botte 40, Till 15).

literally, "clean" (*katharos*). Earlier we read that "if anyone has a demon, he shall not hear the word of instruction until he is cleansed."[15] There are, however, other ways of being morally unclean than by having a demon. Prostitutes, homosexuals, and self-made eunuchs are designated as such and are to be excluded.[16] But in the case of the person who is discovered not to be good or clean when exorcized by the bishop, it is, we are specifically told, because he has not heard the word in faith.

Some interpreters translate the word "exorcize" in this context as "bind by oath," but it is quite clear that the term is used here in the sense of the exorcism of evil spirits. At one point the alien spirits themselves are the object of exorcism, but elsewhere the candidates are exorcized; that is, words of exorcism are said over them, in order to purify them. Similarly, there are exorcisms of oil and bread.

Hippolytus speaks of another kind of uncleanness, that namely which results from being unwashed or, in the case of women, from menstruation. We must not exclude the possible influence here of Jewish notions of ritual impurity,[17] but perhaps the most likely reason for these rules is that Hippolytus, writing as he was in bath-conscious Rome, did not wish the baptismal water or fountain to be fouled by the candidates' bodies; such in fact was the way in which Augustine explained the tradition.[18]

Let us review Hippolytus's prebaptismal ceremonies in detail. First the candidates are examined to see whether their morals have been above reproach during their catechumenate. Then they are exorcized every day, and near the end by the bishop himself, to see whether they are clean. Anyone who is not good or clean is to be set aside. Botte says that "good" corresponds to the interrogation concerning conduct, and "clean" to the result of the exorcism. But his explanation suggests that a person could be good without being clean, or vice

---

[15]*Ap. Trad.* 15 (Botte 34, Till 11).

[16]*Ap. Trad.* 16 (Botte 36).

[17]See, e.g., Black, *Scrolls* 98–115.

[18]Augustine, *Epist.* 54.7.10 (CSEL 34.2.168): "Si autem quaeris cur etiam lavandi mos ortus sit, nihil mihi de hac re cogitanti probabilius occurrit, nisi quia baptizandorum corpora per observationem quadragesimae sordidata cum offensione sensus ad fontem venirent, nisi aliqua die lavarentur." R. J. Zwi Werblowsky, "On the Baptismal Rite According to St. Hippolytus," *Studia patristica* 2, ed. K. Aland and F. L. Cross, TU 64 (Berlin 1957) 92–105, esp. 97–98, protests against the notion of Jewish ritual influences, but his own notion that a woman was considered to be "still in the grip of the demonic powers" because of her menses is rather unlikely. Even the most liberated of women presumably continued to menstruate.

versa, whereas the same reason is given for both deficiencies, namely, that the individual has not heard the word in faith, seemingly a moral failing that could have been overcome by good will. More likely, then, "good" is simply a synonym for "clean."

The clause that follows reads, in the Sahidic version: "because it is impossible for the foreign one (*sh^emmo*) to remain hidden for ever." Who or what is "the foreign one"? Botte assumes that *sh^emmo,* which he translates as *alienus* in Latin, is a rendering of the Greek word *allotrios,* which the Coptic transcribes twice elsewhere without translating.[19] He also makes the hazardous assumption that it specifies the devil himself. It would be safer, if we understand the word as applying to an evil spirit, to read it as referring simply to one of the alien spirits mentioned in the following lines. The Arabic version, however, which is based on the Sahidic, says that the alien cannot "be baptized," rather than "be hidden," thereby showing that it understands the alien to be the candidate, unless it is saying that evil spirits should not be baptized. The latter reading is unlikely, though it does recall the Egyptian gnostic concept of Theodotus: unless the unclean spirits are removed from the unclean candidates, the spirits can go down and obtain the seal with the candidates. Furthermore, later in the *Tradition* there is a warning against letting anything fall from the chalice during the eucharistic liturgy lest an alien spirit lick it up.[20] More probably, however, the Arabic text has the sense of the Ethiopic, which clearly designates the candidate and not an evil spirit as the alien. It may be that this was Hippolytus's original meaning as well, in which case he would be speaking of a catechumen who was alien because still under the influence or control of an evil spirit.

Whatever the original meaning of the alien in this context was, it seems clear that the bishop's exorcism (performed sometime before the Thursday baths) was thought to be decisive in ferreting out all candidates who were as yet not purified of evil spirits or the influence of evil spirits. It is, then, disconcerting to see that still another exorcism is performed by the bishop on Saturday. And whereas in his first exorcism the presence of the alien among the candidates was the exception, now it is suggested that when the exorcism is undertaken,

[19]*Ap. Trad.* 21 and 38 (Botte 46, 84). The Ethiopic translation of the phrase in chap. 20 (see n. 8 above) is, according to Botte, either based on a MS of the Sahidic-Arabic type and corrected by the more accurate Latin tradition or based on the Latin and adapted to conform to the Sahidic-Arabic line.

[20]Ibid. 38: "ut non spiritus alienus . . . illud delingat." The Coptic text has preserved the original Greek words *pneuma allotrion.*

with the bishop placing his hand, as previously, upon the candidates' heads, there are still many alien spirits present. A possible explanation is that Hippolytus or his scribe mistakenly repeated the instruction for the bishop's first exorcism. As the text stands, however, the assumption seems to be that the candidates are all clean, in spite of the fact that they are still afflicted with evil spirits, since there is no question now of turning back any of the candidates because of what might be brought to light by the exorcism. Perhaps the real explanation for this seeming contradiction is that the final exorcism, like the still later use of exorcized oil, is simply a dramatic recapitulation of what has gone before; it would serve to edify the congregation, strengthen the candidates, and warn the evil spirits not to return.

The bishop then breathes into the faces of the candidates. This ceremony has no specifically indicated exorcistic function, since it occurs after the bishop has stopped exorcizing, when, presumably, all the evil spirits have fled. It may have the purpose of eliminating whatever demonic influence remains. This seems to be the meaning that Augustine attached to the rite of exsufflation in the Africa of his time, as we shall see. To accord with this tradition Botte translates the term as *exsufflare,* "breathe out," rather than as *insufflare,* "breathe upon." We may note, however, that *insufflare* is the word used in a sermon usually ascribed to Quodvultdeus, the fifth-century bishop of Carthage.[21] The ceremony as Hippolytus knew it may have had a meaning more positive than negative; that is, it may have signified a strengthening of the candidate or even an imparting of the Holy Spirit.[22] As will be seen, the prayer that Hippolytus records (as reconstructed by Botte) after baptism renders thanks to God for making the candidates worthy of having their sins forgiven by means of the bath of rebirth and begs him to make them worthy of being filled by the Holy Spirit. But no ceremony or prayer follows to indicate that the Holy Spirit does in fact enter them. Is it possible, then, that the Holy Spirit has already entered them and that God is now asked to keep them worthy of his indwelling in the future?

After the breathing ceremony, the candidate is sealed on the forehead, ears, and nose. Once again we are not told the purpose of this

[21]Pseudo-Augustine (Quodvultdeus), *De symbolo ad catechumenos* 3.1 (PL 40.661). See PLS 3.261.

[22]Thraede, "Exorzismus" 83, speculates that prebaptismal exorcism may have been combined with a prebaptismal imparting of the Spirit. He refers to Acts 10.44–48: as Peter preaches, the Holy Spirit falls on the people, and Peter calls for baptism to be administered.

87

rite. Perhaps it is the ancestor of the later Effeta or opening of the ears. But to judge from one use of the word for sealing (*sphragizein*) later in the *Tradition,* where it means making the sign of the cross on oneself as a protection against the devil,[23] it may have an antidemonic meaning here. If so, it should logically be a prophylactic or apotropaic rather than an exorcistic measure. Logic sometimes gives way to other virtues (or vices), however, and it may have served the dramatic ends of the ceremony to conceive of the antagonist as still present and fighting for control of his victims. Such seems to be the case in the sixth- or seventh-century Gelasian ritual, where the Effeta ritual is accompanied by a typically exorcistic command to the devil to flee.

However, the sealing ceremony of the *Tradition* may not be antidemonic at all. For at another place we are told that signing oneself with one's wet breath and saliva has simply a sanctifying effect upon those who have already been made clean by being washed: "He who has used marriage is not defiled; for those who are washed have no need to wash again, for they are pure. By [as it were] catching thy breath in thine hand and signing thyself with the moisture of thy breath, thy body is purified even unto thy feet. For the gift of the Spirit and the sprinkling of the font, drawn from the heart of the believer as from a fountain, purifies him who has believed."[24] This ritual is a kind of commemorative rebaptism. Is it significant that in referring to baptism here Hippolytus first speaks of the gift of the Spirit and then of the sprinkling of water?

To return to his description of the initiation ceremonies. We have seen the catechumens, most of whom have been under instruction for three years, undergo the exercises of exorcism, bathing, fasting, and the Saturday rituals. Early on Sunday, the baptism itself takes place:

> At the hour, then, when the cock will crow, let them first pray over the water. Let the water be flowing along into the tank or descending upon it. And let it be thus if there is no scarcity; but if there is scarcity continuous and sudden, then use the water which ye shall find. And let them undress themselves. And ye shall first baptize the little ones. Moreover, all who can speak for themselves, let them speak; but for them who cannot speak, let their parents speak for them, or any other belonging to their family. And afterwards ye baptize the adult men, but

[23] *Ap. Trad.* 42 (Botte 98–100).
[24] Ibid. 41 (92–94) trans. of Latin text by Gregory Dix, *The Treatise on the Apostolic Tradition of St. Hippolytus of Rome* (London 1937 repr. 1969 with corrections by Henry Chadwick) 65–66.

last the women, who have all loosed their hair, and laid aside the gold and silver ornaments which they were wearing; let not any take any alien thing [*eidos allotrion*] down to the water with them. And at the hour which is determined for baptizing, let the bishop give thanks over the oil, and put it into a vessel, and call it oil of the thanksgiving, and take also other oil, and exorcize [upon] it and call it the oil of exorcism.[25] And a deacon should carry the oil of exorcism and stand on the left hand of the presbyter, and another deacon shall take the oil of the thanksgiving and stand on the right hand of the presbyter. And when the presbyter has taken hold of each one of those who will be baptized, let him command him to renounce [*apotassesthai*], saying: "I renounce thee, Satanas, and all thy service and all thy works."[26] And when he has renounced all these, let him anoint him with the oil of exorcism,[27] saying, "Let all spirits remove far from thee."[28] And then let him give him to the bishop naked, or [to] the presbyter who stands at the water for baptizing.[29]

It is possible that the direction for the blessing of the water had some connection with the tradition of the apotropaic effect of the crowing of the cock, a tradition found, for instance, in the Mithraic religion of this time.[30] But it is more likely that the cockcrow is simply an indication of time, as it is elsewhere in the *Tradition*.[31] It has been suggested that both the direction for the women to loose their hair and the further command to take off all ornaments have an antidemonic motivation. W. C. van Unnik reviews the evidence and finds it not particularly convincing.[32] Botte, however,

[25]Ethiopic: "exorcize Satan in it, and it is named oil which has been exorcized from every unclean spirit."

[26]Arabic: "I revile thee, O Eblis, and all thy service and all thy impure works." Ethiopic: "I renounce thee, Satan, and all thine angels and all thine unclean works."

[27]Ethiopic: "the oil which he made pure from all evil."

[28]Arabic: "Let every foul spirit remove far from them." Ethiopic: "All unclean spirits shall depart from him."

[29]*Ap. Trad.* 21 (Botte 44–46, trans. Horner 316–317).

[30]See Maarten J. Vermaseren and C. C. van Essen, "The Aventine Mithraeum Adjoining the Church of St. Prisca," *Antiquity and Survival* 1 (1955) 22; *The Excavations in the Mithraeum of the Church of Santa Prisca in Rome* (London 1965) 163.

[31]*Ap. Trad.* 41 (Botte 96). Here cockcrow is specified as the next time of prayer after midnight. Cf. Werblowsky 98–99: "I do not propose to press the cock whose crowing heralds the light of dawn and the end of the nightly rule of demons. Rabbinic law too directs that proselyte baptism should take place in day-time, but again, significantly, for a legalistic reason."

[32]W. C. van Unnik, "Les cheveux défaits des femmes baptisées: Un rite de baptême dans l'ordre ecclésiastique d'Hippolyte," *Vigiliae christianae* 1 (1947) 77–100, esp. 81–85. Cf. Dölger *Exorzismus* 112–114; Lukken 240 n. 319.

assumes, and probably rightly so, that the word *allotrios* here means an object that could be under the power of the evil spirits; at least it may refer to something connected with the service or works of Satan, which are to be renounced.

In the rite of Theodotus, the water was both exorcized and sanctified, and the bread and oil was simply sanctified. In the *Tradition* it is the water that receives no more (it seems) than a simple blessing, whereas bread and at least some oil are exorcized. Exorcized bread is that which is given to the catechumens at the communal meals of the congregation.[33] There is no indication of when it is exorcized, but it is doubtless done immediately before it is distributed, just as the oil of exorcism is exorcized immediately before its use in the baptismal ceremony.

Dölger noticed that the "foods" allowed during times of fast, namely bread, salt, water, and oil, were all exorcized and used in the initiation regimen, and he suggested a connection.[34] There is no known community, however, in which all four items were exorcized. Exorcized bread seems not to have been used outside the circle of influence of the *Apostolic Tradition*. The holy food given to catechumens in Africa is not said to have been exorcized.[35] As for the water and oil, they are exorcized in the *Tradition* not as food but specifically for use in connection with the baptismal ceremony. When Hippolytus mentions oil elsewhere, it is to be blessed, not exorcized, in the same way as the bread and wine at the eucharistic liturgy, with the purpose of having it strengthen those who taste it and give health to those who use it.[36] When salt was first used, in Africa and then in Rome, it was not exorcized, and it is not obvious that it had any kind of antidemonic purpose. That it came to be exorcized later was probably due to the fact that the other ingredients used at baptism were exorcized. It may have been felt that the salt too should have a similar kind of blessing. However, we shall see that in these formulas of the later Roman liturgy the word "exorcize" when addressed to material objects is simply a word of command that does not itself have reference to evil spirits.

There is no evidence in the *Tradition* as to the precise nature of the

[33]*Ap. Trad.* 26, 28 (Botte 68, 72).
[34]Dölger, *Exorzismus* 87–92.
[35]Augustine, *De peccatorum meritis et remissione et de baptismo parvulorum* 2.26.42 (CSEL 60.113).
[36]*Ap. Trad.* 5 (Botte 18).

exorcism of the oil or the bread, whether it was simply an apostrophe to these substances exhorting them to be adequate for holy uses or whether it sought to give them power against evil spirits, or even whether it involved the attempt to free the ingredients themselves from demons or their evil effects. It is obvious that the Ethiopian translator had the last-named purpose in mind for the exorcism of the oil. But since the oil of exorcism has the same function as the exorcism of the candidates, we may consider it likely that the formula for the exorcizing of the oil contained a desire that it might become effective in removing evil spirits from the candidates.

After all of these preliminary ceremonies have been accomplished, the time has finally arrived for the ritual of baptism itself. Each candidate descends into the water, accompanied by a deacon. The minister who performs the baptism places his hand on the candidate and asks: "Dost thou believe in God the Father almighty?" The candidate answers, "I believe," and the baptizer, holding his hand on his head, immerses him for the first time. He then asks: "Dost thou believe in Jesus Christ, the Son of God, who by the Holy Spirit was born of the Virgin Mary, was crucified under Pontius Pilate, died, and rose alive from the dead on the third day, and ascended to heaven and sits on the right hand of the Father, and will come to judge the living and the dead?" When the candidate expresses his belief he is baptized a second time. He is baptized for a third time after assenting to the third question: "Dost thou believe in the Holy Spirit within the holy Church?"

When he has come up from the water, the priest anoints him with the oil of thanksgiving, saying, "I anoint thee with holy oil, in the name of Jesus Christ." Then each candidate dries himself and they all enter the church. The bishop places his hand on them and prays the prayer analyzed above: "O Lord God, as thou hast rendered them worthy of receiving the remission of sins by the bath of regeneration, make them worthy to be filled by the Holy Spirit and send upon them thy grace, so that they may serve thee according to thy will: for to thee is the glory, Father, Son, with the Holy Spirit, in the holy Church, now and through all ages, amen."

Then he pours oil of thanksgiving from his hand onto the head of each candidate and says, "I anoint thee with holy oil in God the Father almighty and in Jesus Christ and in the Holy Spirit." He then seals him on the forehead, presumably with the sign of the cross, kisses him, and says: "The Lord be with thee." The candidate replies,

"And with thy spirit." Next, all the new Christians pray together with the rest of the faithful for the first time and then give the kiss of peace.

Prayers are then offered over the bread and the wine and also over milk mixed with honey, signifying the fulfillment of God's promise to their fathers, and, finally, over water, which represents the bath, so that the interior man, that is, the soul, might receive the same benefits as the body. The bishop then distributes communion, and the service is at an end.[37]

I have described the whole ceremony at length in order to provide a frame of reference for discussions of later rites and also to show the complete absence of allusions to evil spirits once the actual baptism begins. Even though some of the following actions, especially the two anointings and the sealing, could have been considered as defenses against demons, there is no indication at all that this was the case. It is perfectly credible that Hippolytus and his associates believed themselves done with the devil and his servants once the renunciation and the anointing with exorcized oil had occurred and that they took no further thought of this darker side of reality during the rest of the ceremony. If so, the great adversary in this ritual tableau of salvation received the ultimate insult of being ignored once his power over the candidates was severed. The final form of the Roman rite will in fact follow this scenario, but in intervening rites, and especially in Eastern services, due precautions will be taken against a return of the evil spirit after baptism.

Hippolytus mentions the arrangements made for infants only on the morning of the actual baptism. It may not be wrong to infer that very young children were not required to perform the exercises of the catechumenate, such as receiving instruction, undergoing exorcism, and so on. Such would not be the case in later times, for in general the method Hippolytus describes for including infants in the adult ceremony of baptism proper would be extended to the whole process of initiation. That is, attendants or sponsors would hold the children and answer for them and put them through the necessary motions. In the resulting drama, the human protagonists (the infant candidates) would be unconscious of the great reversal of fortune that was being effected, and only the assistants and the "audience" would be aware of what was happening and be moved by it. As before, of course, the

---

[37]Ibid. 21 (Botte 48–58).

triumph would be effected by God himself, not by a mythical god descending in cumbrous stage machinery, but spiritually. The three divine personae would be present and active to the eyes of faith. The adversary too would be present in single or manifold form, a presence that was likewise normally attested only by faith. But sometimes, in the cases of adults, he was evident to the senses as well, in the frenzied contortions of the possessed and in the blasphemous cries of hatred and protest that he uttered from within their bodies.

6 /

The Renunciation of Satan

The renunciation of Satan is the one demonological rite of initiation that the *Apostolic Tradition* of Hippolytus had in common with the practice of the contemporary Church in North Africa, as reflected in the writings of Tertullian. The renunciation, in fact, is the only universal antidemonic Christian initiation ritual; it occurred in liturgies like that of Hippolytus, where there was no postbaptismal prophylaxis, and in the Syrian rites where no prebaptismal exorcism was practiced. Before discussing other African developments, I shall explore the origin, function, and distribution of this dramatic confrontation with, and defiance of, the devil.

The idea of renunciation is, of course, present in all religious conversions and initiations. When a person turns from one form of life to embrace another, the old ways must necessarily be rejected, especially those practices most inimical to the new beliefs and style of life. We have seen an example of renunciation in the ritual of the Qumran sectaries, and similar practices can be found, inferred, or postulated in the ethically centered pagan mysteries and sects. In fact, these pagan religions formed the context of the renunciatory rite of Hippolytus and Tertullian, and without question it was influenced by them, certainly as far as the content of the renouncement was concerned and perhaps in the form of the ritual as well.

Some scholars, as I have already mentioned in a previous chapter, like to think that the basic ritual of the renunciation of Satan developed quite early, in the context of Jewish Christianity. Since the devil and other evil spirits were considered to be prominent opponents of the kingdom of God, it is not unnatural that the New Testament should yield analogies to the formal renunciation of Satan and all his works. Nevertheless, we cannot, in my opinion, safely assert that any ritualized form of renunciation had yet evolved by the time that the canonical books were compiled.

One particularly intriguing Jewish-Christian hypothesis, however, deserves mention. M. E. Boismard has conjectured that, since the terms "works," "pomp," "angels," and "worship" (or "service") seem to be interchangeable in the various formulas of renunciation,[1] they are all translations or mistranslations of a term in a very early baptismal liturgy formulated in Hebrew or Aramaic. He suggests the word *mela'kah,* which is often translated by "works" (*erga*) in the Septuagint,[2] and on one occasion as "service" or "worship" (*leitourgia*).[3] The original formula would have been "the devil and his works" (*ml'ktw*), which could have been read as "his angels" (*ml'kyw*) or "his mission," that is, as the Greek *pompē* (*ml'kwtw*). Boismard depends heavily upon the analogy between Pharaoh and Satan, which is not well attested to at the early date he postulates for his hypothetical liturgy, and the fact that there are no clear references to the standard pattern of the renunciation ("of Satan and his _____") until the turn of the third century also makes his theory less probable.[4]

A more likely, or at least equally likely, source of influence is the practices of the gnostics. We have seen that, in the ritual described by Theodotus, baptism is characterized as consisting of or involving a renunciation of the evil principalities (Extract 77). The followers of Simon Magus, according to Irenaeus, asserted that Simon "pledged himself that the world should be dissolved, and that those who are his should be freed from the rule of them who made the world," that is, the angels.[5] The idea that the elect were to be freed from the world as well as from the world rulers is very important, as can be seen from the ceremonies of the Marcosian gnostics: "He who is initiated replies

---

[1]For a collection of the formulas, see Hans Kirsten, *Die Taufabsage: Eine Untersuchung zu Gestalt und Geschichte der Taufe nach den altkirchlichen Taufliturgie* (Berlin 1960) 39–51.

[2]E.g., Genesis 2.2–3; Exodus 31.3–15; 1 Kings 5.16 (= MT 1 Kings 5.30, LXX 3 Kings 5.30).

[3]1Chronicles 26.30.

[4]See M. E. Boismard, "I Renounce Satan" 107–112.

[5]Irenaeus, *Adversus haereses* 1.23.2 (Harvey 1.194), trans. *ANF.*

as follows: 'I am established and I am redeemed, I redeem my soul from this world [*aiōn*] and from all things connected with it, in the name of Iao, who redeemed his own soul into redemption in Christ who liveth.' "[6]

The devil was associated with the rule of the world both by Theodotus and by Christian and Jewish tradition,[7] so that, if orthodox Christians began to renounce both the world and the world ruler Satan in imitation of the gnostic precedent, they could do so with no suggestion of heterodoxy. Even before the time of Theodotus, in fact, Justin Martyr said that Christians had renounced (*apotassesthai*) the things that were in the world (*kosmos*); and as I noted earlier, he also spoke of their renunciation of idols, which he regarded, so to speak, as *machinae ex diabolo*.[8] The so-called *Second Letter of Clement to the Corinthians* also mentions a renunciation of the world, using the word *aiōn,* meaning "age." Tertullian, Augustine, and Rufinus (the latter as translator of Origen) use the corresponding Latin word *saeculum* (rather than *mundus,* the equivalent of *kosmos*) when speaking of renunciation of the world, which they linked to baptism.[9]

The actual formula of renunciation spoken by the candidate probably did not ordinarily include the world. It appears rather to have been a tripartite naming of the devil together with two groups of associated evils. In Africa, from the time of Tertullian onwards, it was the devil, his pomps, and his angels.[10] But it is likely that the minister of baptism in his address to the candidate specified this

[6]Ibid. 1.21.2 (1.185), cited by Thraede, "Exorzismus" 99.
[7]See Kelly, "Devil in the Desert" 210–211, and *Devil* 16.
[8]Justin, *Dialogue with Trypho* 119 (Otto 2.428); see Chap. 2 at n. 24.
[9]Pseudo-Clement, *2 Cor.* 6.3–4 (Funk-Bihlmeyer-Schneemelcher 73); Tertullian, *Ad martyres* 2.5 (CCL 1.4); Augustine, *De baptismo* 5.20.28 (CSEL 51.285); Origen, *Hom. Josh.* 26.2 (GCS 30.459). The last passage reads: "Quid nos iuvat in baptismo saeculo renuntiasse, et morum nostrorum pristinas sordes ac vitiorum carnalium immunditias retinere?"
[10]Tertullian, *De spectaculis* 4.1–3 (CCL 1.231); *De anima* 35.3 (2.837); *De corona* 3.2 (2.1042); Augustine, *Serm.* 215.1 (PL 38.1072); Quodvultdeus, *De symbolo ad catechumenos* 1.1.2; 2.1.1 (PL 40.637, 652); idem, *Contra Iudaeos, paganos, et Arianos* 1 (PL 42.1117). The *De centesima, sexagesima, tricesima,* ed. R. Reitzenstein, "Eine frühchristliche Schrift von den dreierlei Früchten des christlichen Lebens," *Zeitschrift für die neutestamentliche Wissenschaft* 15 (1914) 60–90 (and PLS 1.53–67), may reflect a bipartite formula. See par. 82 (Reitzenstein 84): "Si renuntiasti diabolo et operibus eius, quid eum lascive vivendo repetis?" Jean Daniélou, *The Origins of Latin Christianity,* trans. David Smith and John Austin Baker (London 1977 repr. 1980) 63, says that the *De centesima* comes "from the sphere of Latin Judaeo-Christian apocalyptic writing of the second century."

renunciation as equivalent to a renunciation of the world, to judge from the frequent apposition of this concept with the renunciation of the devil. Examples can be found in the writings of Cyprian, the third-century bishop of Carthage, and the fourth-century Optatus of Mileve. In the former, we can see traces of a formula, "the world, its pomps, and its delights," which is present also in the second-century treatise *De aleatoribus,* in a modification of Romans 12.2: "Videte, fratres, ne configuremini huic saeculo et pompis et deliciis et voluptatibus eius."[11]

Both Origen and Augustine characterized the devil as prince of this world when they recalled the baptismal renunciation, and thus they made explicit the connection between the two types of formulas. Augustine said, "The devil is cast out when this world is renounced with one's whole heart; for thus is the devil, who is the prince of this world, renounced, when his corrupting influences, pomps, and angels are renounced."[12]

What is the meaning of the curious word "pomp," or "pomps," that appears in almost every formula of renunciation, both in the East and in the West? (A note on the number: the Western practice was to use the plural, whereas in the East the singular was favored. Origen, however, the earliest Eastern witness, uses the plural; and Tertullian, who provides the first testimony from the West, uses the singular— though on one occasion he uses both singular and plural.)[13] Even in the *Apostolic Tradition* series, which the Sahidic gives as "Satan, service, and works," "service" is probably a translation of the singular *pompē* in Hippolytus's original Greek text.[14]

The writings of Tertullian provide a rich context for an attempt to explicate the precise significance of *pompa,* which has, of course, the basic meaning of procession. It is quite clear that this Carthaginian convert to Christianity considered the principal object of the renunciation to be the practices associated with idolatry. Since he accepted the story that the evil angels had fallen through lust for women and

---

[11]*De aleatoribus* 9 (CSEL 3.3.102), and see Daniélou, *Origins* 97; Cyprian, *De habitu virginum* 7 (CSEL 3.1.192); *De dominica oratione* 19 (281); *De lapsis* 8 (242); *Ad Fortunatum de exhortatione martyrii* 7 (328); *De bono patientiae* 12 (406); *Epist.* 13.5 (508); *De mortalitate* 26 (313); Optatus, *Sermo in natali sanctorum innocentium* 12 (PLS 1.294).
[12]Origen, *Hom. Num.* 12.4 (GCS 30.104–106); Augustine, *De agone christiano* 1 (PL 40.291).
[13]Tertullian, *De spectaculis* 4.1–3. The only other exception to the use of the singular form in the East occurs, as we shall see, in the *Apostolic Constitutions.*
[14]Botte, *Tradition apostolique* 47 n.5.

had begotten demons,[15] some scholars have held that the *pompa* in his formula of renunciation referred to the demons among his following, as distinguished from the angels who fathered them. J. H. Waszink, however, shows that the activities of evil angels and demons are practically identified in Tertullian's writings, and *pompa* never has a personal meaning. The word signifies rather, he believes, the procession that took place in the circus, in which statues of gods were carried around the racetrack, and all the activities of idolatry, divination, and vice that came to be associated with it.[16]

A good example of the sort of thing that Tertullian must have had in mind can be seen in one of the love poems of Ovid, written two centuries earlier, in which he describes his systematic seduction of a girl whom he encountered at the races and in which he puts to work all the principles enunciated in his *Art of Love*. He gives a stylized account of his line of patter:

But now the procession [*pompa*] is coming—keep silence all, and attend! The time for applause is here—the golden procession is coming. First in the train is Victory, borne with wings outspread—come hither goddess, and help my love to win! Applaud Neptune, ye who trust o'er-much the wave! Naught will I with the sea; I choose that the land keep me. Applaud thy Mars, O soldier! Arms I detest; peace is my delight, and love that is found in the midst of peace. And Phoebus—let him be gracious to augurs, and Phoebe gracious to huntsmen! Minerva, turn in applause to thee the craftsman's hands. Ye country dwellers, rise to Ceres and tender Bacchus! Let the boxer court Pollux, the horseman Castor. We, winsome Venus, we applaud thee, and thy children potent with the bow; smile, O goddess, upon my undertakings, and put the right mind in my heart's new mistress! Let her endure to be loved. She [Venus] nodded, and by the movement gave favoring sign. What the goddess has promised, yourself promise, I ask: with Venus's permission let me say it, you will be the greater goddess. I swear to you by all these witnesses and by the train [*pompa*] of the gods, I am asking you to be, for all time to come, my queen![17]

[15]Tertullian, *Apologeticum* 22.3 (CCL 1.128).
[16]J. H. Waszink, "Pompa diaboli," *Vigiliae christianae* 1 (1947) 13–41. See also Daniélou, *Origins* 412–418. For patristic comment on public entertainments, see Werner Weismann, *Kirche und Schauspiele im Urteil der lateinische Kirchenväter unter besonderer Berücksichtigung von Augustin,* Cassiacum 27 (Würzburg 1972), and Heiko Jürgens, *Pompa diaboli: Die lateinischen Kirchenväter und das antike Theater,* Tübinger Beiträge zur Altertumswissenschaft 46 (Stuttgart 1972).
[17]Ovid, *Amores* 3.2, trans. Grant Showerman, Loeb (London 1914) 453.

The behavior that Ovid describes and encourages here was offensive even to the pagan guardians of morals in his day; how much more would the puritanical Tertullian find fault with such goings-on, especially since he regarded the whole spectacle as a show produced by Satan to entrap men's souls.

In order to bring home forcefully and dramatically the obligation of converts to the Church of Christ to abjure the devil's religion, which was a mere imitation and mockery of true religion, and to abstain from the corrupting pleasures and sins of his world, the striking ritual of renunciation was evolved. But the Church of Africa, especially in Tertullian's time, did not take full advantage of the dramatic possibilities of the rite, for, to judge by the references to it cited earlier, the devil was renounced in absentia, or, at least, he was not addressed in direct discourse. And since there is no sign of pre-baptismal exorcism in Africa until the middle of the third century, there would be no head-on encounter at all with the powers of evil at the initiation ceremonies. The indirect form of the renunciation continued to be the rule in Africa and eventually came to prevail elsewhere in the West.

In contrast, in the ceremony described by Hippolytus at Rome, the devil was actually confronted and repudiated in person. The same seems to have been true of the service that Origen described when characterizing the devil as prince of sin and the prince of those who had not yet left the world and been converted to the Father: When a man came to the baptismal font he announced to the devil (Rufinus: "denuntiaverit diabolo") that he would make no more use of his pomps and works and would never again submit to his services and pleasures.[18] The direct denunciation of the devil remained the usual practice in the East, but it seems also to have been continued or introduced at times in Italy and elsewhere in Europe. For example, in the treatise on *The Mysteries* by Augustine's mentor, St. Ambrose of Milan, the candidate is described as facing the west, which is symbolic of the realm of darkness, and as speaking as if he stood face to face with the devil. He renounces "the devil and his works, the world and its luxury and pleasures."[19] The world, we notice, has been incorporated into the candidate's formula of renunciation in this case,

[18]Origen, *Hom. Num.* 12.4 (GCS 30.104–106).
[19]Ambrose, *De mysteriis* 2.5, ed. Otto Faller, 1955 (CSEL 73.90–91). Cf. his *De fuga saeculi* 8.45, 9.57 (CSEL 32.199, 206): "Renuntiavimus saeculo et usui eius"; "ut iam mundo nihil debeas, cui semel renuntiasti."

and we shall see occasional examples of the same thing elsewhere. It was once thought that the candidate actually spat at the devil in this ceremony, as in the Byzantine service, but the reading *in os sputaris* that appears in the manuscripts of *The Mysteries* is usually rejected in favor of *in os putaris*. Since the *sputaris* reading does occur, however, it could reflect a local practice of antidemonic expectoration; or, alternatively, the reading could have inspired such a practice.

In Ambrose's *Hexameron,* which according to Jerome was a revision of Origen's work, the devil as prince of the world was addressed directly, but with a different formula: "I renounce you, devil, and your works and your empires."[20] Jerome himself also indicated that the renunciation was to be made toward the west and cited a direct renunciation of the devil and his world, pomp, and works.[21] It has been alleged that Jerome was using the Eastern form, since when he wrote the letter in which the formula occurs he had been established in Bethlehem for twenty-eight years.[22] His use of the singular of *pompa* would support this view. He may, however, have been hearkening back instead to a tradition of his native Illyria (Yugoslavia), since Nicetas of Remesiana, his fellow countryman and contemporary, recorded a similar form: when the candidate was freed of the works or pomps of the devil, he took the chains with which he had been bound and threw them behind his back as if into the enemy's face and then said the creed.[23] Presumably he faced the west and spoke directly to the devil during the renunciation, although, when discussing the formula used during the service, Nicetas merely describes it, instead of quoting it verbatim, so that one cannot tell whether direct address was to be used or not. He does, however, give a direct form of the renunciation when suggesting its use as a help against temptation.[24]

Nicetas's formula names the devil, his angels, and his works. He

---

[20]Ambrose, *Hexameron* 1.4.14 (CSEL 32.12); see Jerome, *Epist.* 84.7 (CSEL 55.130); Hanssens, *Liturgie d'Hippolyte* 456. *Imperia* could be translated "regimen" or "commands" as well as "empires."

[21]Jerome, *In Amos* 3.6 (PL 25.1068); *Epist.* 130.7 (CSEL 56.186); cf. his *Commentary on Matthew* 1.5.27 (PL 26.39): "Renuntio tibi, diabole, et pompae tuae, et vitiis tuis, et mundo tuo qui in maligno positus est." The latter phrase is a reference to 1 John 5.19, which speaks of the world as lying in the power of the Evil One.

[22]Hanssens, *Liturgie* 456.

[23]Nicetas of Remesiana, *Instructio ad competentes* 5.2.8, ed. Klaus Gamber, Textus patristici et liturgici 1 (Regensberg 1964) 112; cf. 5.3.2 (115).

[24]Nicetas, *Instructio* 5.3.35 (122).

explains what is included under the latter two terms: "Confident in Christ his leader, he renounces the enemy and his angels, that is, all the inquisitiveness of magic ("universa magica curiositas") that is maintained by Satan's angels. Then he renounces also his evil works, that is, forms of worship and idols, the casting of lots and auguries, pomps and theaters, thefts and frauds, fornication and drunkenness, dances and lies."[25] Here, then, described in a nutshell, is the dissolute demonic life of the pagans in the provinces at the turn of the fifth century as seen through stern Christian eyes. The pomps of the devil are mentioned only as an instance of his evil works and are not singled out in the formula itself.

A treatise on *The Sacraments,* which obviously draws on Ambrose's *Mysteries* and which has usually been attributed to him, has been claimed by the latest editor of Nicetas as a part of the latter's *Instruction to the Competents* (the competents being those catechumens who were ready for baptism). I am inclined to agree that Ambrose was not the author, from the fact that the formula of renunciation, while similar in content and form to that of *The Mysteries,* is deprived of much of the drama of Ambrose's ceremony (though it does correspond to the later Ambrosian rite). It is no longer an address to the devil but a dialogue between the minister and candidate:

When he asked you, "Do you renounce the devil and his works," what did you reply?

"I do renounce them."

"Do you renounce the world and its pleasures?" What was your reply?

"I do renounce them."[26]

---

[25]Ibid. 5.3.1 (115). Cf. *Tractatus de baptismo* 2 (PL 57.775): "Abrenuntiare omnibus pompis et operibus eius et omni fornicationi diabolicae spopondistis?" The work comes from the Milan area, ca. 550. See Kirsten 65 n. 66. For a specific mention of the devil's idols, see the *Passio sanctae Caeciliae* in Bonino Mombrizio, *Sanctuarium seu Vitae sanctorum* (Milan ca. 1480) fol. 190ᵛ: "ut renuntiet diabolo et pompis eius et idolis eius." The *Passio* was written ca. 500; see Henri Quentin, *DACL* 2.2712–2720. A new edition of Mombrizio's *Sanctuarium* was published in Paris in 1910, 2 vols., introd. A. Burnet.

[26]*De sacramentis* 1.2.5, ed. Faller (CSEL 73.17); ed. Gamber, *Instructio ad competentes* 6.1.5 (126). The word used for "world" is *saeculum,* but later the author equates it with *mundus:* "Ergo abrenuntiasti mundo, abrenuntiasti saeculo" (*De sacr.* 1.2.8, *Instructio* 6.1.8). Gamber's arguments against Ambrose and attribution to Nicetas, as set forth in his book, *Die Autorschaft von De sacramentis* (Regensburg 1966) and earlier writings, are contested in a review by Josef Schmitz, "Zum Autor der Schrift *De sacramentis,*" *Zeitschrift für katholische Theologie* 91 (1969) 59–69, with a response by

It seems that the indirect form of renunciation prevailed elsewhere in Europe, for example in the region of present-day France. There was, however, a great deal of variety in the formulas used. Hilary of Poitiers, writing in the fourth century, says that the devil, the world, and sins are renounced at baptism; and according to an *Exposition of the Catholic Faith,* perhaps authored by Hilary of Arles (401–449), a renunciation is made of the devil and his angels and the pomps of the world (*pompae saeculi*). Hilary of Arles's contemporary, Salvian of Marseilles, who may have come from Cologne, has another formula, one that specifies the devil and his pomps, spectacles, and works.[27] In the next century Caesarius of Arles in his sermons cites a similar formula but omits the *spectacula,* which perhaps had been introduced as an explanation of *pompae.* On one occasion, Caesarius has the same formula that became standard in North Africa, namely, "the devil, his pomps, and his angels."[28]

Eligius of Noyon (d. 660) reflects Caesarius's more common formula and also the explanation of Nicetas: "You have renounced the devil and all his pomps and works, that is, idols, the casting of lots, auguries, thefts, frauds, fornication, drunkenness, and lies."[29] Martin of Braga, who came to Spain in the sixth century from Pannonia (north of Illyria) via Palestine, also seems to be drawing upon Nicetas: "Do you renounce the devil and his angels, his forms of worship and idols, his thefts and frauds, his fornication and drunkenness, and all his evil works?"[30] The only earlier witness to Spanish usage is Pacian of Barcelona in the fourth century, who speaks simply of renouncing the devil and all his angels. In later times, Isidore of

---

Gamber (587–589) and rejoinder by Schmitz (589). Schmitz does not take up the matter of the contradiction between direct and indirect renunciations either here or in his extended analysis of the renunciation in his book *Gottesdienst im altchristlichen Mailand: Eine liturgiewissenschaftliche Untersuchung über Initiation und Messfeier während des Jahres zur Zeit des Bischofs Ambrosius* (†397) (Cologne 1975) 113–126.

[27]Hilary of Poitiers, *Tractatus super psalmos* 14.14.4 (PL 9.306–307); Hilary of Arles (?), *Expositio de fide catholica* (PLS 3.58); Salvian, *De gubernatione Dei* 6.32 (CSEL 8.133). Salvian's formula is definitely indirect: " ' Abrenuntio enim,' inquis, 'diabolo, pompis, spectaculis, et operibus eius.' "

[28]Caesarius of Arles, *Serm.* 12.4 (CCL 103–104.60; cf. 12.3 [59–60]); 119.3 (499); 200.6 (811). The African formula occurs in 178.1 (721–722).

[29]Eligius, *De rectitudine catholicae conversionis* 2 (MGH, Script. rer. merov. 4.749).

[30]Martin of Braga, *De correctione rusticorum* 15, *Opera omnia,* ed. C. W. Barlow, Papers and Monographs of the American Academy in Rome 12 (New Haven 1950) 196.

Seville (d. 636) says that the devil, his pomps, and all his association are renounced; and Taio of Saragossa (d. 683) says, "We promise to renounce the works and all the pomps of the ancient enemy." Ildephonsus of Toledo (d. 667) bears witness to an exception to the tradition of an indirect renunciation of the devil, for the evil spirit is addressed in person: "I renounce you, devil, and your angels, your works, and your empires."[31]

The method of administering the renunciation first found in the treatise on *The Sacraments* became the pattern for the rituals of the West. We recall that this work transformed Ambrose's direct address to the devil into a two-part catechetical dialogue between the minister and the candidate. The later Ambrosian liturgy of Milan follows suit: The infant's sponsor is asked, "Does he renounce the devil and his works?" and "Does he renounce the world and its pomps?" Each question, of course, is answered in the affirmative.[32]

The Spanish and Roman liturgies devised a threefold question for the renunciation, in imitation of the three-part confession of faith and the triple immersion of baptism. The content of the Spanish service was that of Ildephonsus's formula, without its direct address.

The priest addresses each infant by name: "Do you, servant of God, renounce the devil and his angels?"

The ministers reply for the child: "I do."

Priest: "His works?"

Ministers: "I do."

Priest: "His empires?"

Ministers: "I do."[33]

We recall that Hippolytus had a direct renunciation of the devil in the service he described. We have no further witness of Roman practices for the next three centuries. Then a deacon named John (probably the future Pope John I), about the year 500, gave an explanation of the rites of baptism as performed in his day. With regard to the renunciation he simply said that "diabolical snares and pomps are renounced."[34] Our next report comes from the full-blown Gelasian

---

[31]Pacian, *Sermo de baptismo* 7 (PL 13.1094); Isidore, *De ecclesiasticis officiis* 2.25.5 (PL 83.821); Taio, *Sententiae* 2.13 (PL 80.794); Ildephonsus, *De cognitione baptismi* 111 (PL 96.158).

[32]*Manuale ambrosianum,* ed. Marco Magistretti, Monumenta veteris liturgiae ambrosianae 2–3 (Milan 1904–1905) 2.467; cf. 123 n.; 169.

[33]*Liber ordinum,* ed. M. Férotin, Monumenta ecclesiae liturgica 5 (Paris 1904 repr. 1967–1968) 34.

[34]Ioannes Diaconus, *Epistola ad Senarium* 3, ed. André Wilmart, *Analecta reginensia,*

liturgy of the sixth or seventh century. Here the renunciation has developed into a triple question: "Do you renounce Satan?" "And all his works?" "And all his pomps?"[35]

Other formulas appear in the Gallican liturgies of the seventh and eighth centuries. The *Bobbio Missal* has "Do you renounce Satan, his pomps, his luxuries, this world?" and the *Old Gallican Missal* "Do you renounce Satan, the pomps of the world, and its pleasures?"[36] Sometimes the Gelasian phraseology is met with in its unitary form ("Do you renounce the devil and all his works and all his pomps?"),[37] but eventually the Roman form in its totality became universal and remained so to modern times.

The development in the East is more complicated, and I will consider it in detail later. It can be said, however, that most of the services are simply elaborations of the basic formula of Hippolytus's *Apostolic Tradition.*

The many references in the writings of the Fathers to the renunciation of Satan demonstrate the great impact that the ceremony made upon the Christian community; and the varied forms in which it appeared show that the formulas and services were constantly adapted in order to make the repudiation of the things of this world, and of the evil genius who ruled over them, more meaningful to the faithful. Nevertheless, the force of tradition is also evident in the retention of the word *pompa* long after the train of the demon gods to which the word referred had ceased to pass in procession through the moldering circuses of the Roman Empire.

Before considering the other demonological aspects of the rites of Christian initiation in their formative years, let us glance at *The Acts of St. Sebastian,* a fifth-century literary recreation of the life and martyrdom of the soldier-saint who died, it was said, during the last

---

Studi e testi 59 (Vatican City 1933) 172. Cf. Michel Andrieu, *Les Ordines romani du haut moyen âge* 2, SSL 23 (Louvain 1948) 383.

[35]*Liber sacramentorum* (Gel), ed. L. C. Mohlberg et al. REDsmf 4 (Rome 1960) no. 421. See Chap. 12 at n. 63. For a vernacular Germanic version from A.D. 743 in the form of three questions (devil, all devil worship, all devil's works), with the final response naming Thor and other gods, see Jeffrey Burton Russell, *Lucifer: The Devil in the Middle Ages* (Ithaca 1984) 127 n. 74.

[36]*The Bobbio Missal* 2.244, ed. E. A. Lowe (HBS 58.74); *Missale gallicanum vetus* 27.171 (REDsmf 3.17).

[37]E.g., Pirmin (d. 753), *De singulis libris canonicis scarapsus* (PL 89.1035); Boniface of Mainz (d. 754), *Sermo* 15.1 (PL 89.870); cf. Pierre de Puniet, "Baptême," *DACL* 2.251–346, esp. 327–328.

persecution of the Christians before toleration came with Constantine the Great. We can see what the renunciation of Satan meant to the author from his account of the conversion of the prefect Chromatius. The theme of renunciation was worked into the prebaptismal course of instruction that the prefect underwent. He was first asked if he renounced all idols. He affirmed that he did. And all sins? He answered that he promised to renounce all the diabolical sins and pleasures of the world. He was told that Lent was the time for candidates to learn that they were to renounce all the arts of the enemy and the commerces of the world. Finally, after a few days, when he had duly renounced all the affairs of the world, he was baptized.[38]

There is nothing of the "pompous" aspect of the devil's empire in this account; it is not the fashionable and dissolute life of the circus that the author marked out for sacrifice to the cause of Christ and salvation but rather the corruptions and evils of the workaday world.

In this chapter, I have not analyzed the confession of faith and the rituals associated with it, which usually followed immediately upon the renunciation of Satan (as in Hippolytus's *Apostolic Tradition*). But it must be remembered that these ceremonies formed a striking element in this part of the baptismal drama.[39]

---

[38] *Acta sancti Sebastiani* 17.61–63 (PL 17 [1879] 1139–1140).
[39] See Lukken 90–92, 250–253, for dramatic aspects of the *syntaxis,* or confession of faith.

7 /

Africa and Europe

Even though the Carthaginian Church of Tertullian's time seems not to have had the elaborate prebaptismal exorcisms that characterized the rite described by Hippolytus in Rome, baptism as he knew it did have a broader demonological context than that which would be afforded by the renunciation ceremony alone.

If the candidate underwent no course of exorcism at the turn of the third century, there was at least a recommended program of asceticism preceding baptism. Tertullian, however, regarded it not as exorcistic but rather as apotropaic, that is, as directed against lapses into sin in the future. He advised candidates to devote themselves before baptism to much prayer, fasting, kneeling, and watching, and to confess all their previous sins, so that the past might be atoned for and defenses acquired for resisting future temptations ("subsecuturis temptationibus munimenta"). It was even suggested by some that, since Jesus himself was beset by diabolic temptations after fasting for forty days, they too, like him, should fast after as well as before baptism. Tertullian admitted that it would be a good idea, except that it would interfere with the festivity called for on the occasion of their conversion.[1]

In another context, Tertullian contrasted the use of fasting as an exorcistic measure with the fasting that preceded baptism. Alluding to the remark of Jesus that a certain kind of demon could be driven out only by prayer and fasting, he remarked that fasting was an aid to

[1]Tertullian, *De baptismo* 20.1, 3 (CCL 1.294).

fighting against the more recalcitrant possessing demons and was also used before baptism to hurry the coming of the Holy Spirit. For it was no wonder, he said, that the evil spirit was brought out (that is, in cases of possession) by the same method by which the Holy Spirit was brought in (that is, at baptism).[2]

No one was more aware than Tertullian of the demonic influences that surrounded the people of his day. He asked rhetorically at one point, "What man is there to whom an evil spirit does not adhere, even at the very gates of his birth, waiting to ensnare his soul?" He was speaking of the omnipresence of idolatry, which he termed the "universal midwife," and he cited the goddesses invoked at childbirth. "Thus," he said, "a demonic spirit found even Socrates as a child; so too 'geniuses,' which is a name of the demons, are assigned to all men."[3] In spite of all these dangers, however, Tertullian did not indicate the existence of, or feel the need for, any special rite designed to set men free from the demonic influence when they became members of the Christian community—in addition, that is, to the act of renunciation, and, of course, baptism itself, through which the Son of God destroyed the works of the devil.[4] He regarded the liberation of the Israelites from Pharaoh as a type of the rescue of Christians from the world and the devil: "The nations are freed from the world by means of water, and they leave behind [*derelinquunt*] the devil, their former ruler, who is overcome in the water."[5]

He described the baptismal ceremony and interpreted the meaning of each step: "The flesh is washed, so that the soul might be cleansed; the flesh is anointed, in order to consecrate the soul; the flesh is signed, as a fortification for the soul; the flesh is overshadowed by the laying on of hands, so that the soul might be illuminated by the Spirit; the flesh feeds on body and blood, so that the soul too might grow fat on God."[6] It is possible that some of the postbaptismal actions, especially the signing with the cross and the anointing with oil, were antidemonic and that they had the same purpose as the ascetical practices before baptism: namely, that they were demon-repelling, serving as means for coping with future diabolical assaults,

[2]Tertullian, *De ieiunio adversus psychicos* 8.3–4 (CCL 2.1265); cf. Mark 9.29. See Chap. 2 at n. 30.
[3]Tertullian, *De anima* 39.1–3 (CCL 2.842). For Tertullian's demonology in general, see J. B. Russell, *Satan* 88–100.
[4]Tertullian, *De pudicitia* 19.19–20 (CCL 2.1322).
[5]Tertullian, *De bapt.* 9.1 (284).
[6]Tertullian, *De resurrectione mortuorum* 8.3 (CCL 2.931).

and not as exorcisms, for ridding the soul of past or present demonic forces. (Like prayer and fasting, of course, anointing and signing were also used as exorcistic devices in other circumstances, that is, in attempts to liberate demoniacs from the evil spirits that possessed them.)[7]

We are able to derive further knowledge of the early Carthaginian baptismal service, and the significance attached to the rites, from the practices of pagan religions, which Tertullian, like Justin Martyr, believed to be in many instances nothing more than the devil's imitation of Christian rituals: "For the devil too baptizes some of his believers and followers; he promises them the remission of their sins in the font; and, if my memory of Mithra still serves me, it is there that he signs his soldiers on their foreheads."[8] Similarly, he says, unclean spirits often brood upon water, imitating the action of the Holy Spirit in creation: "Without any sacred significance, unclean spirits do settle upon waters, pretending to reproduce that primordial resting of the divine Spirit upon them: as witness shady springs and all sorts of unfrequented streams, pools in bathing places, and channels or storage-tanks in houses, and those wells called snatching-wells—obviously they snatch by the violent action of a malignant spirit; for people also use words like 'esetic' and 'lympathic' and 'hydrophobic' of those whom water has drowned, or has vexed with madness or fear."[9] But in spite of Tertullian's belief in widespread demonic pollution of this sort, there seems to have been no exorcism of the water before it was blessed for baptism. No doubt there was never any question of using the kind of infested water he speaks of.

Tertullian believed that water even by itself had dignity and furthermore that Christ had sanctified water when he was baptized. All water, moreover, when God was invoked, acquired "the sacred significance of conveying sanctity."[10] At baptism an angel of God intervened to make the water suitable for what was to follow. After speaking of the action of the evil spirits upon contaminated water, he

---

[7]Tertullian, *Scorpiace* 1.3: "Nobis fides praesidium, si non et ipsa percutitur diffidentia signandi statim et adiurandi et unguendi bestiae calcem." Ysebaert, *Greek Baptismal Terminology* 306, rejects the correction that would read away "unguendi" (cf. CCL 2.1069).

[8]Tertullian, *De praescriptione haereticorum* 40.1–4 (CCL 1.220).

[9]Tertullian, *De baptismo* 5.4, ed. and trans. Ernest Evans, *Tertullian's Homily on Baptism* (London 1964) 12–13; CCL 1.281.

[10]Tertullian, *De baptismo* 3.1 (CCL 1.278); *Adversus Iudaeos* 8.14 (CCL 2.1362); *De baptismo* 4.4, trans. Evans 11 (CCL 1.280).

says: "Why have I referred to such matters? So that no one should think it overdifficult for God's holy angel to be present to set waters in motion for man's salvation, when an unholy angel of the evil one often does business with that same element with a view to man's perdition." He explains further: "Not that the Holy Spirit is given to us in the water, but that in the water we are made clean by the action of the angel, and made ready for the Holy Spirit."[11]

In the Carthaginian drama of salvation, therefore, the great antagonist was conspicuous by his absence. The candidate simply renounced him, without addressing him, and then was prepared by a celestial minister for the reception of the divine Spirit.

For later developments in North Africa, we are able to extend our view somewhat farther beyond the boundaries of Carthage, though Dido's city remains our chief source of information for some time to come. We know from the records of the council held in Carthage in the year 256 that prebaptismal exorcism, of which there was no trace in the writings of Tertullian, had come to be practiced at least in some regions of Africa. The rite was mentioned by Vincent of Thibari, who found authorization for the practice in the words of Christ himself: "We know that heretics are worse than the pagans. If they are converted and wish to come to the Lord, they have the rule of truth that the Lord delivered to the apostles by divine precept, saying: 'Go, lay on hands in my name, expel demons'; and in another place: 'Go and teach the nations, baptizing them in the name of the Father and the Son and the Holy Spirit.' Therefore they can come to the promise of Christ first by the laying on of hands in exorcism, and secondly by the regeneration of baptism, and only then."[12] Cyprian however says nothing of the practice in his writings, which may mean that the rite had not yet been introduced to Carthage itself. In his description of baptism he seems to leave no place for exorcism except in the case of the violently possessed:

> If anyone is disturbed by the fact that some of these sick persons who are baptized are still tempted by unclean spirits, let him know that the obstinate evil of the devil prevails only up to the salutary water, for in baptism he loses all the poison of his evil. We see a type of this in King Pharaoh, who for a long time offered opposition, and, having held out so long in his perfidy, could resist and prevail until he came to the water, where, once he had arrived, he was defeated and destroyed.

[11]Tertullian, *De baptismo* 5.1, 6.1, Evans 12–15.
[12]In the *Opera omnia* of Cyprian, CSEL 3.1.450.

Now the blessed apostle Paul states that that sea was the sacrament of baptism. . . . The same thing happens even today, when by means of exorcists the devil is scourged and burned and tormented by the voice of man and power of God, and when he says repeatedly that he will go out and leave the men of God, he nevertheless goes back on his word, and with the same lie exercises the kind of obstinacy and deceit that Pharaoh did. But when one comes to the saving water and the sanctification of baptism, we must realize and have confidence that there the devil is overwhelmed and the man dedicated to God is liberated by the divine indulgence. For if scorpions and serpents that thrive on dry land could continue to do so or retain their poison once they are thrown into the water, then too could evil spirits (who are called scorpions and serpents and yet are trodden underfoot by us with the power given by the Lord) continue to remain in the body of a man in which after baptism and sanctification the Holy Spirit has begun to live.

Finally we see this happen in real life; when in emergencies the sick are baptized and receive grace they are relieved of the unclean spirit by which they were previously agitated, and live praiseworthy and upright lives in the Church and day by day achieve a greater addition of celestial grace by increasing their faith; and, on the other hand, many who have been baptized in sound health, if afterwards they begin to commit sin, are troubled by the return of the unclean spirit, so that it is evident that the devil is eliminated in baptism by the faith of the believer, and that he returns subsequently if faith should fail.[13]

In the last part of this passage Cyprian seems to be alluding to the Gospel parable of the unclean spirit that went out of a man and returned with seven worse than itself. We recall that Origen too connected this episode of the Gospel with baptism. The effect of Cyprian's teaching is that baptism itself has an exorcistic result when it is administered to demoniacs in danger of death. Since he does not follow the sin-demon theory of ethical possession, there is no occasion for the exorcistic factor of baptism to come into play in ordinary circumstances. Baptism simply causes the devil to lose his power of tempting the new Christians, unless their faith should grow weak.

When speaking of the baptismal water, Cyprian said that it had to be cleansed as well as sanctified before a man's sins could be washed away. This might refer to some kind of exorcism said over the water. Augustine used the same expression a century and a half later, and we find also in his writings that God's name was invoked over water,

[13]Cyprian, *Epist.* 69.15–16 (CSEL 2.764–765).

and it was consecrated in the name of Christ by being signed with his cross.[14] It seems that there was no set formula for the consecration of the water, since Augustine noted that often errors against the faith were expressed in the prayers over the water because of the inexperience of those who offered them.[15]

In addition to being used for the consecration of the water, the cross was also marked upon the forehead of catechumens at the conclusion of their instructions. Then, too, it figured in the blessing of the oil or chrism (used before or after baptism), as well as in the eucharistic sacrifice. As in the writings of Hippolytus and Tertullian, the cross sometimes had an apotropaic function; and like Hippolytus, Augustine compared the Christian signing of the forehead to the sprinkling of blood on the doorposts to ward off the destroying angel.[16]

When the catechumens were ceremonially certified as properly informed about the Christian faith, they were not only signed with the cross on their foreheads but were also given salt. We do not know the way in which it was administered, whether it was put in their mouths or given to them to keep or use; nor do we know the significance attached to it. It has been reasonably suggested that there may have been some antidemonic intention behind its use, at least in the minds of many of the catechumens,[17] but no indication of this purpose survives in written records. The image that salt most readily brings to mind in connection with Carthage is the absolute destruction inflicted upon the city centuries before by Scipio Africanus Minor, who left no stone upon another and strewed the site of the city with salt to prevent even the herbiage of the natural world from establishing itself there again. In accordance with this line of thought, the salt of the catechumens may have symbolized the destruction of evil and world-

[14]Ibid. 70.1 (767); Augustine, *De baptismo* 5.20.27 (CSEL 51.1.285); ibid. 3.10.15 (205); *Serm.* 352.1.3 (PL 39.1551).

[15]Augustine, *De baptismo* 6.25.47 (323–324). Cf. Frederik van der Meer, *Augustine the Bishop,* trans. Brian Battershaw and G. R. Lamb (New York 1961) 366. For a more recent survey of Augustinian data, see Robert de Latte, "Saint Augustine et le baptême," *Questions liturgiques* 56 (1975) 177–223 (adults) and 57 (1976) 41–55 (infants).

[16]Augustine, *Tractatus in Iohannis evangelium* 118.5 (CCL 36.657); ibid. 50.2 (433–434); cf. Hippolytus, *Apostolic Tradition* 42 (Botte 100). For other instances of Augustine's use of the cross, see Benedictus Busch, "De modo quo S. Augustinus descripserit initiationem christianam," *Ephemerides liturgicae* 52 (1938) 385–483, esp. 413–416.

[17]Van der Meer, *Augustine the Bishop* 356.

ly tendencies. Such a concept leaves room for its use as an exorcistic or apotropaic tool.

But we have another explanation for catechumenal salt, namely that given by John the Deacon in Rome at the end of the fifth century, when Carthage was in the hands of the Vandals. He said that "the catechumen receives blessed salt, over which the sign [of the cross] is made, because, just as all flesh seasoned with salt is preserved, so too the mind, which was damp and drifting in the waves of the world, is preserved by the salt of wisdom and of the preaching of the word of God, to be brought to stable and lasting firmness, once the ooze of corruption is thoroughly cast off by the delightfulness of divine salt."[18] Two centuries later, when Carthage was on the eve of its final destruction at the hands of the Saracens, the "salt of wisdom" maintained its preservative symbolism in the Roman ritual, but it had also taken on a definitely apotropaic meaning: in the prayer that preceded the ceremony of placing it into the mouth of the infant to be baptized, it was said that the salt was consecrated in order to become "a salutary sacrament for putting the enemy to flight."[19]

By Augustine's time, the practice of prebaptismal exorcism had long since become established not only in Africa but everywhere in the West. Closely linked to the exorcism was the exsufflation, which, like the breathing ceremony of the *Apostolic Tradition,* seems to have been performed in Africa after the final exorcism on the night before the baptism was to take place. Augustine names the rites in that order, though on one occasion he speaks of the exsufflation as part of the exorcism.[20] It has been conjectured that there was an earlier exsufflation as well, at the time when the cross and the salt were first conferred, at least in the circle of the stern followers of Bishop Donatus.[21]

Augustine saw these rites of exorcism and exsufflation as a proof of a traditional belief in original sin and concluded that their purpose was to liberate the candidates, even infants, from the "power of darkness" or the "power of the devil."[22] According to Optatus of

[18]John the Deacon, *Epistle to Senarius* 3 (Wilmart 172).

[19]Gel 288–289.

[20]Augustine, *Contra Iulianum opus imperfectum* 3.199 (PL 45.1333).

[21]Van der Meer 454, citing Augustine, *Contra Cresconium* 2.5.7, ed. M. Petschenig (CSEL 52.365–367). It is possible, however, that Augustine is referring here to the ceremony that takes place on the eve of baptism.

[22]For example, Augustine, *Contra Iulianum* 1.4.14 and 3.3.8 (PL 44.649, 705). See the texts given by Dölger, *Exorzismus* 60 n. 2; 70 n. 3.

Mileve, who was writing about the year 375, all men, even those
with Christian parents, were born with an unclean spirit, which had
to be removed before baptism; this was done by exorcism, "by
which the unclean spirit is cast out and made to flee to desert places,"
like the evil spirit of the parable. Optatus used Christ's image of
housecleaning: "An empty home is made in the breast of the believer,
a clean home, where God enters and dwells."[23] Augustine too used
similar language at times; he said that infants were possessed by the
devil, or that the prince of this world was cast out from those who
were regenerated, in order to make God's image a dwelling of the
Holy Spirit.[24] He does not seem to have meant that the devil possessed them corporeally, however, but only that they had been subjected to his law as a result of original sin; their relationship to the
devil was that of captive slaves to their master. Their freedom was
bought through the laver of regeneration and the blood of Christ, and
they passed into the kingdom of their purchaser. "The power of their
captor is frustrated, and they are given power to change from children of this world to children of God."[25] We may conclude that
Augustine considered the prebaptismal exorcism to be not a real
eviction of demons from the bodies of the candidates but a dramatic
metaphor for the redemption of souls from their diabolical oppressor.

We are not told how the exsufflation was performed except that the
breath was blown in the face of the candidates,[26] as in the *Apostolic
Tradition*. As with the exorcism proper, Augustine seems to have
considered this ceremony a symbolic equivalent of the real thing.
That is, it appears to have been an exorcistic technique for use upon
demoniacs, but when applied to baptismal candidates, especially infants, in whom he saw nothing evil or sinful except the results of
original sin, the ceremony would have to take on some kind of
transferred meaning, like the elimination ("blowing away") of the
remnants of the devil's power or the counteracting of his *inspirationes*
or "breathings in" by this breathing out. Or it may be that the
ceremony was meant as an insult to the devil. Augustine said at one
point that blowing at an image of the emperor was considered a
crime,[27] so that perhaps it was meant as an act of contempt and

[23]Optatus, *Libri VII* 4.6 (CSEL 26.110).
[24]Augustine, *De nuptiis et concupiscentia* 2.18.33 (CSEL 42.286–287); cf. *Contra
Iulianum opus imperfectum* 2.181, 4.77 (PL 45.1220, 1383).
[25]Augustine, *De nuptiis* 1.20.22 (235–236).
[26]Augustine, *Contra Iul. op. im.* 3.182 (PL 45. 1323).
[27]Ibid. 3.199 (1333).

defiance that was made efficacious by divine power to bring about the candidate's removal from the rule of Satan. Tertullian spoke of spitting and blowing (*exsufflare*) at the smoking altars in the temples.[28] No doubt this behavior reflected contempt,[29] but perhaps it also had the object of extinguishing the fires. He also said, however, that demons were forced out of bodies by the touch and breath (*afflatus*) of Christians.[30]

Augustine summed up baptism and all the demonological ceremonies that preceded it (exorcism, exsufflation, and renunciation) as "sacred and manifest signs of hidden things by which the candidates are shown to pass from their evil captor to the good redeemer who took on infirmity for us and bound the strong one in order to snatch away his vessels."[31] During the time that the exorcisms were performed, the candidates were to fast and abstain, as an aid to the process of purification. There was also an examination or "scrutiny" of the candidate.[32] To judge from Augustine's phraseology ("they are catechized, exorcized, and scrutinized"), we would expect such an examination to be an inquiry into the results of the instruction that the candidate had received as well as into the effects of the exorcism; and since there was seldom any question of literal demonic possession, the latter aspect of the examination would have focused upon the candidate's behavior and attitudes, to see whether he was really free of the devil's moral influence. However, there are strong indications that the scrutiny, both in Africa and in Europe, was not at all an investigation by the bishop or priest of the candidate's doctrine or morals but rather a part of the exorcism or even the exorcism itself.

---

[28]Tertullian, *De idolatria* 11.7 (CCL 2.1111).

[29]See F. J. Dölger, "Heidnische Begrüssung und christliche Verhöhnung der Heidentempel: *Despuere* und *Exsufflare* in der Dämonbeschwörung: Kultur- und religionsgeschichtliche Bemerkungen zu Tertullian De idolatria 11," *Antike und Christentum* 3 (Münster 1932) 192–203.

[30]Tertullian, *Apologeticum* 23.16 (CCL 1.133).

[31]Augustine, *De gratia Christi et de peccato originali* 2.40.45 (CSEL 42.203). He is referring to the parable of Jesus in the Beelzebul debate, Mark 3.27: "No one can enter a strong man's house and plunder his goods, unless he first bind the strong man; then indeed he may plunder his house."

[32]Augustine, *De fide et operibus* 6.8–9 (CSEL 41.43–44). See van der Meer, *Augustine* 356. On the early development of examination before baptism, see A. Dondeyne, "Les disciplines des scrutins dans l'Eglise latine avant Charlemagne," *Revue d'histoire ecclésiastique* 28 (1932) 5–33, 751–787; E. Molland, "A Lost Scrutiny in the Early Baptismal Rite," *Studia patristica* 5, ed. F. L. Cross, TU 80 (Berlin 1962) 104–108.

In one of his sermons, Augustine recalls the ceremony to the minds of his congregation in these words: "When you were being scrutinized and the persuader of apostasy and desertion was being duly rebuked in the omnipotence of the awesome Trinity, you were not clothed in sackcloth, but you did stand upon it, in symbolic fashion."[33] Earlier in the same sermon, he addressed the candidates in the present tense and spoke of the scrutiny as a silent examination of conscience undertaken by the candidates themselves while the exorcisms were being pronounced: "What we do to you, adjuring you in the name of your redeemer, you are to complete by a scrutiny of your heart and remorse. With prayers to God and rebukes we withstand the wiles of the ancient enemy, while you carry on with your own prayers and heartfelt contrition, so that you may be rescued from the power of darkness and brought to the kingdom of light. This now is your task, this is your labor. We heap upon him the curses that his wickedness deserves; but you on your side declare a most glorious war against him by your aversion and your pious renunciation."[34] During the exorcism, therefore, the candidate was to find in himself the repentence and moral courage necessary to make the formal renunciation of Satan meaningful and lasting.

Not long after Augustine's death, we find Pope Leo the Great in Rome writing to the bishops of Sicily in terms which show that he identified the scrutiny with exorcism: candidates for baptism, "according to the apostolic rule, are to be scrutinized by exorcisms and sanctified by fasting and instructed by frequent sermons."[35]

After the *Apostolic Tradition,* which, as we saw, was compiled in Rome early in the third century, there are only fugitive references to Roman usages for the next few centuries. Pope Siricius, writing to a Spanish bishop in the year 385, said that people who were to be baptized had their names enrolled forty or more days before Easter or Pentecost and were "expiated" by exorcisms and daily prayers and fasts. The *Canons to the Gauls,* which is dated about the year 400, speaks of three scrutinies and says that the candidate who is being scrutinized is anointed with exorcized oil at the third scrutiny. The

---

[33]Augustine, *Serm.* 216.11 (PL 38.1082); cf. Quodvultdeus, *De symbolo* 1.1.1–2 (PL 40.637); 3.1 (660–661); *Contra Iudaeos, paganos, et Arianos* 1 (42.1117). Optatus of Mileve furnishes us with an example of the words used in exorcism, at least by the Donatists, who when rebaptizing would first exorcize the converts and say, "Go out, accursed one" (*Libri* 4.6, CSEL 26.110).

[34]Augustine, *Serm.* 216.6, 10 (PL 38.1080, 1082).

[35]Leo, *Epist.* 16.6 (PL 54.702).

point of the canon is that only one such anointing of the catechumen is sufficient for God's power to operate in him. Pope Celestine I (422–432) stated that none approached the font without first having the unclean spirit driven from them by the exorcisms and exsufflations of clerics.[36]

Apart from the letter of Pope Leo, just cited, we have no further witness until we come to John the Deacon at the turn of the sixth century. He attempted to explain to Senarius the meaning of the terms "catechesis" and "scrutiny" and the reason that infants were scrutinized on the third day before Easter. He described the baptismal ceremonies in the following order.

Catechesis. The minister "instructs" (that is, fortifies) the candidate by a blessing, imparted by the imposition of his hand, showing that he has or will become holy, just, a true son, from being damnable, unjust, and a slave. (John apparently makes no mention of any other kind of instruction because he is speaking chiefly of infants.)

Exsufflation. No description is given of this rite, which is apparently performed before rather than after the exorcism. It is meant as an insult to the devil, "because the ancient apostate deserves such ignominy."

Reception of salt. I have already noted John's views on the significance of this ceremony. He adds that there is a frequent imposition of hands and, with an invocation of the Trinity, a threefold blessing of the Preserver ("Conditor") upon the head of him who is thus preserved ("conditur") by divine salt.

Renunciation of the devil's snares and pomps. Before one is reborn in Christ, "there is no doubt that one is bound by the power of the devil, and unless one renounces his snares with a true profession and is freed from them at the beginning, in the midst of the very rudiments of faith, one does not come to the grace of the laver of salvation."

Reception of the Apostles' Creed. After the exsufflation and the renunciation, the candidate "now merits to receive the words of the symbol handed down by the apostles." At this point the catechumens are called competent or elect.

Scrutiny. "We scrutinize their hearts through faith, to see whether, after the renunciation of the devil, they have fixed the holy words in their minds, whether they acknowledge the future grace of the Re-

[36]Siricius, *Epistola ad Himerium Tarraconensem* 2.3 (PL 13.1135); *Canones ad Gallos* 8, Mansi, *Concilia* 3.1137; Celestine, *Epist.* 21.13 (PL 50.536).

deemer, whether they profess belief in God the Father almighty." (I will discuss this account below.)

First anointing. .The candidate's ears and nostrils are anointed with oil of sanctification. The anointing of the ears symbolizes the fortification of holiness that comes from the word of God, which is to prevent the entry of anything harmful or anything that could summon the candidate to fall away. The anointing of the nostrils serves as an admonition to persevere in God's service as long as the new Christian breathes the breath of this life. It has another meaning, too; since the oil is blessed in the name of the Savior, the candidate is fortified by its spiritual odor to keep out every pleasure of the world and everything that could weaken the mind.

Second anointing. The candidate's breast is anointed with oil of consecration, so that he may understand that he is to follow the commandments of Christ with firm conscience and pure heart, now that the devil has been abandoned.

Unclothing. The candidates "are ordered to proceed with bare feet, and by removing their deathly and carnal clothing to acknowledge that they are setting out on a way of life in which no roughness and nothing injurious can be found." (This is a very optimistic view of the life of a Christian.)

Baptism. They are baptized by a threefold immersion, signifying the Trinity and Christ's resurrection on the third day.

Clothing and final anointing. Each candidate puts on white robes and his head is anointed with sacred chrism to signify that the kingdom and the sacerdotal mystery have come to him. A linen cloth is placed around his head to emphasize further the symbolism of the priestly chrism. The white robes recall Jesus as he was transfigured and foretell the glory of heaven. John defends the practice of reserving the consecration of the chrism to bishops, even though it is said that priests perform this function in Africa.[37]

It has been suggested that John's explanation of the scrutiny as an examination could hardly have had any basis in the practice of his day, since he was speaking of infant baptism, and that therefore his account was probably nothing more than an etymological conjec-

---

[37]John, *Epistle to Senarius* 2–8 (Wilmart 171–175). On the question of whether a further anointing by the bishop after the priest's anointing is assumed by John, see J. D. C. Fisher, *Christian Initiation: Baptism in the Medieval West: A Study in the Disintegration of the Primitive Rite of Initiation,* Alcuin Club Collections 47 (London 1965) 20–22.

ture.[38] We have seen that Leo I, writing a half century before John, spoke of the scrutiny as effected by means of exorcisms. Furthermore, though John speaks of only one action as involving a scrutinization, he spoke of three scrutinies at the beginning of his letter. We recall that the *Canons to the Gauls* specified that an anointing with exorcized oil took place at the third scrutiny. It seems clear that the term "scrutiny" came simply to designate a meeting in which the baptismal candidate participated in a number of ceremonies, notably exorcisms. Later tradition confirms that the primary purpose of the scrutinies in Rome was exorcism and not an examination of the candidate's knowledge or virtue. But John's explanation was repeated in still later times, especially in connection with Charlemagne's questionnaire on the meaning of the baptismal rites; and furthermore, it is possible, if not probable, that such examinations of faith and morals were conducted in the case of adult converts, which would be the rule in missionary contexts.

John specifically speaks of the need to rebaptize converted heretics who had not been previously baptized in the name of the Trinity. Moreover, he indicates that there is no difference between adult and infant baptism: "All of these things are to be done even to infants, who because of their youth can as yet understand nothing. Therefore you should know that while they are being presented by their parents or by anyone else, it is necessary that, as they were damned by another's error, they be saved by another's profession."[39]

It still remains to discuss the ritual or process that John specifically characterized as a scrutinization. He seems to be speaking of the profession of faith that takes place after the renunciation. Traditionally this profession, like the renunciation at times, had the form of a "catechism," an examination consisting of questions and answers, the content of which was the Apostle's Creed, or, as John puts it, "the words of the symbol handed down by the Apostles." We have seen it already in the *Apostolic Tradition:* the candidate was first asked, "Do you believe in God the Father almighty?" and he responded, "I do believe"; the second question dealt with Christ, and the third with the Holy Spirit and the Church. This kind of examination, however, would not fulfill John's requirement of finding out "whether they have fixed the holy words in their mind" if the words were repeated to them and only a simple assent were demanded.

[38]See Andrieu, *Les ordines romani* 2.383–384.
[39]John, *Ep. to Sen.* 7, 9 (175–176).

Perhaps, then, a preliminary memory test would be required of an adult candidate.

It is interesting to see that a hundred years before John the Deacon's time, Nicetas of Remesiana, the Illyrian contemporary of St. Augustine, spoke of the scrutinies in the same terms as John, that is, as examinations of doctrine. But the examinations first occurred during or after the catechumen's course of instruction. Nicetas says: "We think, therefore, that the scrutiny is called an exploration, or examination, because it is necessary after one has heard the doctrine and instruction to explore frequently how well he remembers or understands what he has heard, or with what intention he embraces it." He goes on to say, however, that further scrutinies are to be made after the renunciation of Satan, "to examine frequently how firmly and rootedly he has fixed in his heart the sacred words of faith that he has received."

We are, I think, to take Nicetas to mean not that there was a long period of time between the renunciation and the profession of faith but rather that the creed to be said after the renunciation was committed to memory beforehand and that there were quizzes and dress rehearsals before the actual ceremonies. It will be recalled that the cues were not given in the Remesian service for either the renunciation or the profession. That is, there was no catechetical questioning but rather a recitation. It is an interesting feature of all these dramatic rituals that while the devil is sometimes addressed as if he were present (as at Remesiana), God is always mentioned in the profession as if he were not present: not "I believe in you, O God," but "I believe in God." In other words, the act of faith was treated not as a prayer but as a declaration to the congregation.

Just as the scrutinies were a preparation for the profession of faith, the exorcisms, according to Nicetas, prepared the candidate for the renunciation of Satan: "Once the catechumen is instructed, therefore, and has been fed with the faith of Christ, he is led to be exorcized, so that he may say his repudiation to the devil and prepare himself to be worthy of divine grace. For he cannot become a partaker in spiritual grace before he casts out the filth of the devil from his heart and spits out the falsehoods of idolatry." According to Nicetas's new editor, Klaus Gamber, the sermon *Homo ille* belongs to Nicetas and comes next in his series of instructions. We will see it being used before the exorcisms in the Spanish liturgy. The sermon does not refer directly to exorcisms, but it seems at one point to use the language of exorcism in referring to the objects of renunciation: "You have heard that God is one. Let there depart, therefore, all vain superstition, let there depart the respect given to the devil and his angels, let there depart the worship of idols, let there depart the error of the Gentiles."[40] For this author, therefore (whether Nicetas or someone else), the exorcism had taken on the voluntary aspect of the renunciation. But it also retained its original meaning of a ceremony of expulsion performed by a minister upon the devil's victim. The exorcisms were composed of the words of Jesus taken from the Gospels, and they acted like a cleansing fire upon the candidate.[41] As with Augustine, then, the exorcism was not literally a demon-expelling rite but a symbolic service dramatizing the devil's hold over men and the need to purify oneself of his influence by divine aid.[42]

The service that John the Deacon described differed from that of the *Apostolic Tradition* in having two anointings before baptism and one afterward rather than the reverse. The single anointing before baptism in the *Tradition* made use of oil of exorcism and was performed immediately after the renunciation. It was administered with an exorcistic formula. The corresponding ceremony in John's service is the second anointing, the application of oil of consecration to the candidate's breast. It was performed with no reference to the devil except in the past tense: the devil had been repudiated, and the anointing emphasized the candidate's dedication to Christ. In the later Roman ritual, oil of exorcism was applied to breast and back (with no formula) just before the renunciation.[43] Similarly, the treatise on *The Sacraments,* which, as we saw, drew on *The Mysteries* of Ambrose of Milan, mentioned an anointing administered before the renunciation, the effect of which was to prepare the candidates as athletes of Christ to wrestle in the world. There followed the renunciation of the devil and his works and of the world and its pleasures. Though the renun-

---

[40]Nicetas, *Instructio* 1.1.9; 1.2.12 (Gamber 18, 22). See Chap. 13 at n. 46.

[41]Ibid. 1.1.7 (17).

[42]In an *Explanation of the Creed* that Faller and others attribute to Ambrose but that Gamber gives to Nicetas, the scrutinies are associated and perhaps contrasted with exorcism: in the mysteries of the scrutinies "there was an inquiry as to whether uncleanness cleaved to anyone's body; by exorcism the sanctification not only of the body but also of the soul is sought for and effected" (*Explanatio symboli* 1, ed. Otto Faller, CSEL 73.1; Gamber, *Instructio* 5.1.1). The attribution to Nicetas is unlikely from the fact that the physical inspection that is called for here is not hinted at in the undisputed passages from Nicetas cited above.

[43]Gel 421.

ciation was not a defiance spoken directly to the devil, the devil was obviously the world champion against whom the new Christian would primarily be pitted in the wrestling matches of the future. Augustine, Ambrose's protégé, may have had such a baptismal anointing in mind when he said that Christ had anointed his followers to make them wrestlers against the devil. *The Sacraments* also gives an apotropaic significance to the ceremony of washing the candidate's feet, which comes between the two postbaptismal anointings: they are thereby reinforced so that the devil may not trip them up in the future as he tripped up Adam and poured poison on his feet.[44]

John the Deacon's first anointing corresponded to the sealing of forehead, ears, and nostrils that took place after the final exorcism, properly so called, and the breathing ceremony in the *Apostolic Tradition*. Judging from the context of the *Tradition,* I concluded that the sealing may have involved a protective signing with the cross (and perhaps the protection was thought of only as *ad hoc* or *de praesenti* rather than as *de futuro*); but it may simply have been a confirmation of the candidate's release from the devil and a sign of his coming sanctification. The cognate ceremony in the Gelasian ritual was the Effeta. "Effeta," of course, was the word spoken by Jesus after he put his fingers into the ears of the deaf-mute and touched his tongue with saliva (Mark 7:32–35). The Gelasian service combined this dominical healing procedure with the ritual reported by John. The priest used saliva (not oil) and touched the ears and nose (not the mouth). Instead of referring to the divine words and fragrance that the candidate had experienced, he bade his senses to be opened to the odor of sweetness and at the same time warned the devil to flee before the judgment of God.[45] The anointing with oil of exorcism and the renunciation of Satan followed. The only earlier witness to the Effeta is *The Sacraments,* which gives no details. An obviously similar ceremony known as the "opening of the ears" was practiced in Ravenna. Peter Chrysologus, archbishop of the city in the first half of the fifth century, testified that the rite occurred after the candidate had been cleansed of the demon by the laying on of hands and exorcisms.[46]

The Sacraments is also the only early European witness to the prac-

[44]*De sacramentis* 1.1.4 (Faller 17, Gamber 126); 3.1.7 (Faller 41, Gamber 143); Augustine, *Tractatus in Iohannem* 33.3 (CCL 36.307).

[45]Gel 420.

[46]*De sacramentis* 1.1.2–3 (Faller 15–16, Gamber 125–126); Peter Chrysologus, *Serm.* 52 (PL 52.346–347); cf. 105 (494).

tice of the exorcism of the baptismal water: "After the priest first enters, he makes an exorcism according to the creature of water and then offers an invocation and prayer so that the font might be sanctified and the holy Trinity be present."[47] Probably the reference is to an address to the water beginning with the words, "I exorcize you, O creature of water," such as is found in later rites. But since "exorcism" in this liturgical context is simply a synonym for "exhortation," as we shall see, the formula probably had no antidemonic intent as yet.

I have completed my survey of early baptismal ceremonies in the West, and before I look at later developments I shall make a long detour to the East to study the manifold rituals that evolved in that part of the *oikoumenē*. But at this point let me sum up the Western initiation scenarios by recalling the prototypical plot of exorcism, renunciation, and apotropaism, or to put it in more dramatic terms, rescue, reversal of allegiance, and armament against renewed attack. There was a great development of the first two elements, that is, of preliminary ceremonies intended to drive the devil or demonic influences out or away from the candidate before baptism and, following these rites but also before the baptism proper, a voluntary repudiation of all commerce with the diabolical world. But very little stress was laid upon the apotropaic elements, in terms at least of the great adversary. Rather, thought of the devil seems usually to have been put aside temporarily, so that the ceremonies ended positively with an emphasis upon the solidarity that came from being reborn in Christ.

[47]*De sacramentis* 1.5.18 (Faller 23, Gamber 129).

8 /

First Rites in the East:

I. The Nonexorcistic Tradition

In the West there was a tendency to neglect the final element of the basic scenario of exorcism, renunciation, and apotropaism. In Eastern practices by contrast, the exorcistic aspect is often missing, while there is an emphasis upon the apotropaic measures designed to prevent future attacks from the adversary. This pattern is observable notably in Syria. There was, however, a strong influence from the West upon the East, particularly in the coastal areas of the Levant. The *Apostolic Tradition* of Hippolytus was especially popular, as we have already seen. In these regions, the practice of prebaptismal exorcism was introduced, with the result that all three elements of the antidemonic scenario were given prominence. At times, however, as we shall see in the next chapter, the exorcism was either eliminated or transformed into a quite different ceremony.[1]

[1]I gave a basic outline of these developments in the various versions of my book: *The Devil, Demonology, and Witchcraft*, ed. 1 (New York 1968) 34–40; ed. 2 (1974) 38–44; *Towards the Death of Satan* (London 1968) 34–40; *La morte di Satana* (Milan 1969) 48–56; *Le diable et ses démons* (Paris 1977) 55–63. Some of the differences in the rituals of western and eastern Syria have been noted by Gabriele Winkler, "The Original Meaning of the Prebaptismal Anointing and Its Implications," *Worship* 52 (1978) 24–45, but as far as the antidemonic dimension is concerned, she defines the basic contrast as one of degree rather than of kind. She does not usually distinguish between exorcistic expulsion and present- or future-oriented prophylaxis but rather identifies the exorcisms as both purificatory and apotropaic (see p. 40). Her point is that, in the Syrian hinterland and Armenia, these "cathartic and apotropaic elements" did not receive the same sort of ritualistic development as in the coastal areas. This conclusion

Let us begin our survey of the Orient by studying some early documents demonstrating that Syria was exposed to the same doctrine of sin demons that presumably gave rise to prebaptismal exorcism in Hippolytan Rome. It is most noticeable in two writings that claimed the authority of a much earlier leader of the Roman Church than Hippolytus, namely, Clement I, bishop of Rome at the end of the first century; I mean the Pseudo-Clementine *Homilies* and *Recognitions*, which were produced in the fourth century but were probably based on a work that originated in Syria or East Jordan in the first part of the third century. The source work itself may have stemmed from a writing of the Jewish Ebionite sect of the second century.[2]

One revealing passage in the *Recognitions* demonstrates that baptism itself was thought to effect the expulsion of the unclean spirits that dwelled within idolaters:

> Everyone who has at any time worshiped idols and has adored those whom the pagans call gods, or has eaten of the things sacrificed to them, is not without an unclean spirit; for he has become a guest of demons, and has been partaker with that demon of which he has formed the image in his mind, either through fear or love. And by these means he is not free from an unclean spirit, and therefore needs the purification of baptism, that the unclean spirit may go out of him, which has made its abode in the inmost affections of his soul, and, what is worse, gives no indication that it lurks within, for fear it should be exposed and expelled.[3]

Elsewhere in the *Recognitions* it is said that any kind of immoderateness summons the demons to take up residence in a man. One might conclude from this explanation that even after baptism one could suffer a relapse and again be occupied by demons. But the instruction is addressed to pagans, and the point is that conversion to true religion will liberate them from the evil spirits. The expulsion is

---

is set forth at greater length in her major work, *Das armenische Initiationsrituale: Entwicklungsgeschichtliche und liturgievergleichende Untersuchung der Quellen des 3. bis 10. Jahrhunderts*, Orientalia christiana analecta 217 (Rome 1982). For Sebastian Brock's somewhat more precise distinctions, see n. 15 below.

[2]See Hans Joachim Schoeps, "Die Dämonologie der Pseudoklementinen," *Aus Frühchristlicher Zeit* (Tübingen 1950) 38–81; cf. Dölger, *Exorzismus* 29–32; Berthold Altaner and Alfred Stuiber, *Patrologie*, ed. 8 (Freiburg 1978) 135.

[3]*Recog.* 2.71, translation of Rufinus, ed. Bernhard Rehm and Franz Paschke, GCS 51 (Berlin 1965) 93, trans. *ANF* 8.116.

effected not only by abstaining from impurity but also and primarily by increasing one's belief in God:

> It is necessary for you, who are of the Gentiles, to betake yourselves to God and to keep yourselves from all uncleanness, that the demons may be expelled, and God may dwell in you. And at the same time by prayers commit yourselves to God, and call for his aid against the impudence of the demons; for "whatever things ye ask, believing, ye shall receive." But even the demons themselves, in proportion as they see faith grow in a man, in that proportion they depart from him, residing only in that part in which something of infidelity still remains; but from those who believe with full faith they depart without any delay. For when a soul has come to the faith of God, it obtains the virtue of heavenly water, by which it extinguishes the demon like a spark of fire. There is therefore a measure of faith, which, if it be perfect, drives the demon perfectly from the soul; but if it has any defect, something on the part of the demon still remains in the portion of infidelity; and it is the greatest difficulty for the soul to understand when or how, whether fully or less fully, the demon has been expelled from it.

The reference to the heavenly water seems to indicate that it is in the act of baptism that the deliverance from the demons is completed, though the following words seem to suggest that it is possible for a man who believes himself fully united to the believing community (hence baptized) still to have a demon within him. The author goes on to suggest that moderation in all things, especially in food and drink, helps a person to keep from giving a place to demons.[4]

At another place the initiation process is described.

> If anyone desires it, let him be baptized, that stripped of his former evils, he may for the future, in consequence of his own conduct, become heir of heavenly blessings, as a reward for his good actions. Whosoever will, then, let him come to Zacchaeus and give his name to him, and let him hear from him the mysteries of the kingdom of heaven. Let him attend to frequent fastings, and approve himself in all things, that at the end of these three months he may be baptized on the day of the festival. But every one of you shall be baptized in ever-flowing waters, the name of the Trine Beatitude being invoked over him, he being first anointed with oil sanctified by prayer, that so at length, being consecrated by these things, he may attain a perception of holy things.

[4]Ibid. 4.16–18 (GCS 154, *ANF* 138).

125

The purpose of the fasting is not specified here, and one can only conjecture whether it had as a primary object in the author's mind or in actual practice the driving out of demons. In the corresponding passage from the *Homilies,* the imposition of hands as well as fasting is recommended before baptism: "Whoever of you wish to be baptized, begin from tomorrow to fast, and have hands laid upon you day by day, and inquire about what matters you please."[5]

It would be hard to maintain that such preliminary exercises were purely ascetical and nondemonic in intent, given the peculiar demonology that was in force in these circles. For if demons were brought on by excessive eating, surely it would be discouraging for them, to say the least, if a person abstained from food altogether. We shall see the *Homilies* draw this conclusion explicitly. However, since it was up to the individual to evict the demons by a voluntary change of lifestyle, as was the case in the earlier witnesses to the sin-demon theory (the *Shepherd* of Hermas, for example), the whole process of elimination had more kinship to renunciation than to exorcism. But perhaps, as I conjectured earlier when first meditating upon the origin of prebaptismal exorcism, practices that could be classed as exorcistic may have been added to voluntary renunciation and self-control as an aid in effecting the desired liberation. The exercises named here correspond to those listed by Theodotus in describing the ritual of the Egyptian gnostics. But we recall that for Theodotus it was essential that the demons be removed before baptism, for otherwise the demons themselves would be strengthened by the sacrament. In the Pseudo-Clementines, on the contrary, baptism was considered the coup de grace for any evil spirits that might have escaped expulsion after the candidate's change of heart and habit.

A program for dealing with demons is described and discussed in the *Homilies,* the demonology of which is somewhat different from that of the *Recognitions.* We saw that according to the *Recognitions,* demons enter into a man "when either the mind falls into impiety, or the body is filled with immoderate meat or drink." But according to the *Homilies,* the demons themselves desire to participate in sensual pleasure:

> The reason why the demons delight in entering into men's bodies is this. Being spirits, and having desires after meats and drinks and sexual pleasures, but not being able to partake of these by reasons of their being spirits, and wanting organs fitted for their enjoyment, they enter

[5]*Recog.* 3.67 (GCS 141, ANF 132); *Hom.* 3.73.1 (GCS 42.83, ANF 251).

into the bodies of men in order that, getting organs to minister to them, they may obtain the things that they wish, whether it be meat, by means of men's teeth, or sexual pleasure, by means of men's members. Hence, in order to [effect] the putting of demons to flight, the most useful help is abstinence and fasting and suffering of affliction. For if they enter into men's bodies for the sake of sharing [pleasures], it is manifest that they are put to flight by suffering. But inasmuch as some, being of a more malignant kind, remain by the body that is undergoing punishment, though they are punished with it, therefore it is needful to have recourse to God by prayers and petitions, refraining from every occasion of impurity, that the hand of God may touch him for his cure, as being pure and faithful.[6]

There is nothing exorcistic about this regimen, in the sense of having a minister adjure demons to depart from an afflicted person or having him perform rites toward this effect. But the prayers that are addressed to God in obstinate cases would correspond to "deprecatory" exorcisms, that is, an exorcist's appeals for supernatural aid.

The instruction cited above refers to a person's workaday dealings with the problem of possessing demons, but no doubt a similar program was in order for the baptismal candidates. The question remains: were there formal exorcisms performed in conjunction with the candidate's own prayers and fasting? A passage in the *Homilies* suggests that this kind of treatment was reserved for disease demons. We read that Peter departed from Phoenicia, "having driven away diseases, sufferings, and demons from great multitudes who were persuaded, and having baptized them in the fountains, which are near to the sea, and having celebrated the eucharist."[7]

What, then, are we to say of the imposition of hands and anointing with oil that took place before baptism? With regard to the anointing, we shall see that when it has an antidemonic significance in Eastern rites, it usually looks to the future and not to the past; it is a "confirmation" against being caught again in the snares of the devil, not an aid for escaping from them here and now. As for the imposition of hands, it is true that it was used to cure the sick, which included the violently possessed (*daimonōntes*),[8] but it may also have signified nothing more than a simple blessing.[9]

As in the *Recognitions,* it is specifically stated in the *Homilies* that

---

[6]*Hom.* 9.10 (GCS 135, ANF 277). See Chap. 2 at n. 39.
[7]Ibid. 11.36.2 (GCS 172, ANF 292).
[8]Ibid. 10.26.1 (GCS 152). Cf. Ysebaert, *Greek Baptismal Terminology* 305, 308.
[9]*Hom.* 3.72.1; 16.21.5 (GCS 83, 228).

baptism itself gives the power of driving out demons from the convert; in addition, according to the *Homilies,* it enables the convert to relieve others of demons as well: "Washing in a flowing river or fountain or even in the sea, with the thrice-blessed invocation, you shall not only be able to drive away the spirits which lurk in you, but yourselves no longer sinning and undoubtingly believing God you shall drive out evil spirits and dire demons, with terrible diseases, from others. And sometimes they shall flee when you but look on them. For they know those who have given themselves up to God. Wherefore, honoring them, they flee affrighted."[10]

Let us turn now to more orthodox circles. In the *Teaching of the Apostles (Didascalia apostolorum),* which was written by a bishop for a community in northern Syria in the first part of the third century,[11] we meet briefly with the idea of sin demons in a passage that draws on Hermas. All men are characterized as being filled either with the Good Spirit or with evil spirits; but the picture is colored by the same Gospel parable that we saw being used by Origen, Cyprian, and Optatus, namely, that of the unclean spirit that goes out of a man and wanders in waterless places (Matthew 12.43–45). The Syrian prelate interprets "waterless places" to mean unbaptized men and says that the evil spirit cannot find any place to rest, since every man is filled either with the Holy Spirit or an unclean spirit. "He therefore who has withdrawn and separated himself and departed from the unclean spirit by baptism is filled with the Holy Spirit."[12] It seems then that the unclean spirit is automatically eliminated by baptism, which by its very nature involves a voluntary rejection of what such a spirit stands for.

The author goes on to say, speaking now of baptized Christians, that the Holy Spirit can be driven out by one who fails to do good works or who continues to practice Jewish ritual purifications. Elsewhere too his language seems to indicate a kind of ethical possession of persons who cause the Church trouble; this is particularly true in the case of Simon Magus.[13] Similarly, he speaks of those "who, through envy or jealousy of the enemy and Satan, who works in

[10]Ibid. 9.19.4–5 (GCS 139–140, *ANF* 279).

[11]Quasten 2.147; Altaner-Stuiber, *Patrologie* 84.

[12]*Didascalia apostolorum* 26, trans. R. H. Connolly (Oxford 1929) 246. The Latin of the Verona MS reads: "Qui vero per baptismum reiecit et deposuit et liberatus est ab immundo spiritu, sancto repletur."

[13]Ibid. 23 (200).

them, bring an accusation against any of the brethren falsely" and raise other disturbances. If such a person repents, he is to be received back into the Church in the same way that a heathen is admitted: "As thou baptizest a heathen and then receivest him, so also lay hand upon this man, whilst all pray for him. . . . For the imposition of hand shall be to him in the place of baptism; for whether by the imposition of hand, or by baptism, they receive the communication of the Holy Spirit."[14] It seems clear, then, that there was no prebaptismal exorcism practiced in the circles from which the *Didascalia* came. There is an elaborate ceremony of anointing with oil in the baptismal rite proper, but its significance is not explained, except in its being likened to the Old Testament anointing of priests and kings.[15]

Another orthodox witness to baptismal practices at this time is Origen, who settled permanently in Palestine in the 230s. We recall that even though he too subscribed to the doctrine of sin demons, he made no mention of their ritual elimination at the time of baptism, either by exorcism or by baptism itself, though he had undoubtedly witnessed the exorcistic practices described in the *Apostolic Tradition*

[14]Ibid. 10 (101–104).
[15]Ibid. 16 (146–147). Cf. Ysebaert 360–362. Puniet, "Baptême" 278, thinks that the *Didascalia* in the Latin version is alluding to an exorcistic anointing when it says, "Nulla est alia curatio ut abscedat ab eo spiritus immundus nisi per sacram purgationem et sanctum baptismum" (chap. 26). But it seems more likely that it is a case of hendiadys and that only baptism is meant. The Syriac version reads: "For there is no other power whereby the unclean spirit may depart save by the pure and holy Spirit of God" (Connolly 246). For the motif of priestly and kingly anointing in the *Didascalia*, see Winkler, *Armenische Initiationsrituale* 405–406. Sebastian Brock, in "The Syrian Baptismal *Ordines* (with Special Reference to the Anointings)," *Studia liturgica* 12 (1977) 177–183, esp. 181–182, drawing on Winkler's study in its dissertation form (1977), finds the "charismatic" aspect to be fundamental and the protective function secondary. In "The Transition to a Post-Baptismal Anointing in the Antiochene Rite," in *The Sacrifice of Praise,* ed. Bryan D. Spinks (Rome 1981) 215–225. Brock analyzes the various themes or motifs that can be deduced from Syrian prebaptismal anointings: mark of ownership (like circumcision); a protective mark (on the forehead) or protective body cover; mark conferring royal priesthood; mark conveying sonship. He notes that "only very rarely, as far as the Antiochene area is concerned, is the oil regarded as exorcistic as well as protective. On the other hand it is frequently seen in positive terms as healing and cleansing" (p. 218). That is to say, its cathartic functions are not antidemonic. Brock seems to think it incongruous that the apotropaic aspects of the prebaptismal *rushma* were later associated with the postbaptismal anointing (p. 223). For instance, James of Edessa (d. 708) speaks of myron as armor against demons and evil men; see Brock, "Jacob of Edessa's Discourse on the Myron," *Oriens christianus* 63 (1979) 20–36, nos. 10 and 23 (trans. on pp. 33, 35). But as we have seen, such a placement makes perfect sense, logically and dramatically.

during his visit to Rome twenty years before his coming to the Holy Land. He did, however, speak of a renunciation of the devil; and since, as was suggested earlier, in his view the demons of sin entered the mind because of indulgence in vice, a sincere renunciation of the devil and his pomps, works, services, and delights would presumably result in the expulsion of such demons. Hermas himself, we remember, recommended such a renunciation of the evil angel and the following of the good angel. In extreme instances, of course, as with those whom Origen described as having gone mad for "love," the demonized sinners would not be capable of making the requisite renunciation. It does not follow, however, that prebaptismal exorcism would be employed in such cases. More likely persons such as these would be rejected as unsuitable for incorporation into the Christian community.

Origen cited not Hermas but the *Testaments of the Twelve Patriarchs* as the source of his doctrine on sin demons. He drew on Hermas for another theory, that of the two "guardian angels." He seemed to envisage the operation of these beings in much the way that Christopher Marlowe dramatized it in *Doctor Faustus,* where a good angel and an evil angel alternately suggest good and evil thoughts to Faustus. I have used the term "psychomachia," "war within or over a man's soul," to characterize the maneuverings of the good and evil spirits in Hermas, but perhaps war is too strong a concept; certainly it would apply better to the militant mind of the Qumran sect, with its struggle of the spirits within the heart ("cardomachia," of course, would be a more accurate designation for it in this case). In the *Shepherd* there is not much of a fight in evidence, since the holy spirit, being very delicate and tender, simply gives way when crowded by the tough spirit of evil. The author of the *Didascalia* seems to reduce even this minimal contact. He gives the impression that one spirit leaves its abode in a particular man before its counterpart takes up residence. Origen has even less to say on the mutual relations of the two kinds of angels.[16] There is no sign in any of these authors that exorcism was "brought to the aid" of the good spirit, whether at baptism or in other circumstances. Unlike the two-angel theory, exorcism implied an extremely warlike stance and a marshaling of the forces of good against the spirits of wickedness.

Another, perhaps more heterodox, witness to the baptismal practices of the Syria of Origen's time is the *Acts of Thomas.* This work,

[16]See Chap. 3 at n. 18.

dating from the beginning of the third century, was associated with Edessa in East Syria. In it a rite of initiation is described in which an anointing with oil is followed by a bath in water, which was the usual sequence of baptismal rites in Syria. There has been something of a dispute over the original nature of the work, one view being that it was first written in Syriac and that it contained the oil-water pattern from the beginning.[17] Another view is that it was first written in Greek and described a gnostic sacrament of initiation in which only an anointing with oil was used.[18]

Whether or not the water was added later, it is obvious that the ceremony of the oil constitutes the more important part of the rite. When Thomas applies it, he prays that it may be effective for the remission of sins and for the turning back of the enemy ("eis apotropēn tou enantiou") and for the salvation of their souls.[19] The *apotropē* most likely refers to future combats with the devil, though it is possible that it also involves the elimination of his presence or of the influence that he exerted up to the time of the anointing. Something of this sort is evident in the eucharistic prayer that follows: "For the gall which thou didst drink, let the gall of the devil be removed from us."[20] This is not exorcism in the strict sense, however, since the devil is not thought actually to possess the bodies of the communicants. Though this is the way in which the prebaptismal exorcisms

[17]So A. F. J. Klijn, *The Acts of Thomas* (Leiden 1962) 13–14, 54–57.

[18]Ysebaert, *Greek Bapt. Term.* 4, 308, 342–346, 392. Cf. G. Bornkamm, in Hennecke-Schneemelcher, *Neutestamentliche Apokryphen* 2.299, 305–306, who agrees with Ysebaert on the original nature of the rite but with Klijn on the original language. Dieter Georgi, ibid. 308, disagrees with Klijn's denial of the gnostic nature of the work. Jean Daniélou, "Onction et baptême chez Grégoire de Nysse," *Ephemerides liturgicae* 90 (1976) 440–445, sees it as an orthodox Jewish-Christian work, at least in the anointing ceremony, which he associates with the Spirit's action before baptism, drawing on I. de la Potterie, "L'onction du chrétien par foi," *Biblica* 40 (1959) 12–69, and Georg Kretschmar, "Die Geschichte des Taufgottesdienstes in der alten Kirche," *Leiturgia: Handbuch des evangelischen Gottesdienstes,* ed. Karl Ferdinand Müller and Walter Blankenburg, vol. 5: *Der Taufgottesdienst* (Kassel 1970) 1–348, esp. 24–25. Winkler, *Arm. Init.* 95–96, 136–146, who considers the Syriac version the original, sees the work as orthodox but containing descriptions of baptism at three different stages of development: (1) water baptism (chaps. 49–50); (2) prebaptismal anointing of head and water baptism (chaps. 25–27, 132–133); and (3) prebaptismal anointing of head, anointing of whole body, and water baptism (chaps. 121, 156–158).

[19]*Acta Thomae* 157, ed. of Greek text by Max Bonnet (Leipzig 1883) 82; the Syriac text, ed. W. Wright, *Apocryphal Acts of the Apostles* (London 1871) 1.*skd* [= 324] line 1 (trans. 2.289), reads "destruction" or "abolition" (*butal*) of the enemy.

[20]*Acta Thomae* 158, trans. M. R. James, *Apocryphal New Testament* 433; Wright 2.290.

in the West were rationalized by men like Augustine after the belief in sin demons had evaporated, the same explanation would not apply in a region where there had not been a similar sequence of belief → practice → disbelief → rationalized practice. The anointing in the *Acts of Thomas,* therefore, should no doubt be considered apotropaic rather than exorcistic. This judgment is confirmed in the ceremony of the blessing of the oil. The oil itself is first apostrophized (a practice that was to become popular in the West) and then the Lord is addressed, and one of the petitions of the prayer reads: "Let the gift also come whereby, breathing upon [thine] enemies, thou didst cause them to go backward and fall headlong, and let it rest on this oil."[21]

We have seen that the deacon Philip in the Acts of the Apostles (8.5–13) and Peter in the Pseudo-Clementine *Homilies* used exorcism before baptism only in the case of obvious demoniacs. The same is true in the *Acts of Thomas.* On one occasion a woman who is molested by a lustful demon asks Thomas to set her free, for she is convinced that he has power over evil spirits. Thomas agrees, overruling the demon's objection (derived from the Gospel episode of the Gerasene demoniac, Luke 8.22–39) that his time has not yet come. Then the woman asks for the sign (in the Syriac text) or the seal (Greek text), so that the enemy will not come again.[22] By "sign" or "seal" is meant either the baptismal ceremony as a whole or more specifically the anointing with oil. The episode is another confirmation of the apotropaic concerns of the author.

The same significance can be seen in the writings of the great liturgical poet Ephraem, who though only a deacon dominated Christian thought in East Syria during the fourth century. In one of his hymns for the feast of the Epiphany, Ephraem characterizes Satan as annoyed by the odor of the oil that is used in the baptismal signing and as frightened by the sign itself. He says in another hymn that the Spirit secretly signs his flock with fire in the three names, and these names put the enemy to flight; the oil and the spiritual weapons that a person receives in the baptismal water humble the pride of the Evil One.[23]

---

[21]Ibid. 157, trans. James. Cf. Bartsch 83–86.

[22]*Acta Thomae* 42–49. See Wright I.ryz [= 217] line 20 (*rushma*); Bonnet 165 (*sphragis*). Cf. Winkler, *Arm. Init.* 136–137.

[23]Ephraem Syrus, *Hymni* 3.20, 23; 5.2, 10–11, ed. Edmund Beck, CSCO 187 (Louvain 1959) 138, 145–146. Ephraem call the prebaptismal anointing both sign (*rushma*) and seal (*hatma*). See Winkler 161.

The importance of distinguishing between exorcism and apotropaism in Syrian initiation practices can be seen in discussions of the *Acts of John,* a work written about the turn of the fifth century. The cross that John makes over the candidates before baptizing them is not an exorcistic action, as has been claimed,[24] but rather functions, where evil spirits are concerned, as a sign that they no longer have power to meddle with these new Christians. The apostle himself makes this point clear:

> I will anoint and soften with oil your knees, which you have bent and which the Evil One, our enemy, has lacerated, making them bend before his idols, which have been made by him a dwelling place for his demons; and I will seal you with His cross, which is the mark of life, upon your head, which He has bowed down and which is glad to be bowed down, because it is created in the likeness of Him who created it; and I will place a stamp upon your foreheads, so that when he sees that ye are the asylum of this Lord, he may flee and say: "These were my kids, and were joined unto me that they might become big he-goats, and might butt with their horns all armies; but now the Son of the Father, who bowed himself down and became flesh from the Virgin, has taken them and made white their color, which had been the color of the darkness in which I am shut up; and he has made them new lambs, and lo, they dwell with him."[25]

The cross by itself, that is, apart from baptism, has the same effect. John tells the crowd at one point: "I have made this cross a bulwark for you, that Satan may not come and assemble his demons and make sleep enter into you or heedlessness of mind."[26]

In her survey of early descriptions of baptism in the East, Gabriele Winkler has found no evidence of any antidemonic rituals, apart from the renunciation of Satan, in fourth-century Persia, Armenia, and

---

[24]E.g., by A. F. J. Klijn, "An Ancient Syriac Baptismal Liturgy in the Syriac Acts of John," *Novum testamentum* 6 (1963) 216–228, esp. 224; and by Vincent van Vossel, "Le terme et la notion de 'sceau' dans le rituel baptismal des Syriens orientaux," *L'orient syrien* 10 (1965) 237–260, esp. 247–248. Cf. E. C. Whitaker, "Unction in the Syrian Baptismal Rite," *Church Quarterly Review* 162 (1961) 176–187.

[25]*The History of John, the Son of Zebedee,* trans. adapted from Wright, *Apoc. Acts Apos.* 2.36–37. In this passage, which is not treated by Winkler, the signing is characterized as a sealing (*htam,* verbal form of *hatma*), mark (*nisha*), and stamp (*tab'a*). See Wright, 1.m [= 40] lines 14–17. Eventually there is a renunciation, not of the devil, but of the idols that are staffed by the devil's demons: "We renounce this Artemis" (46) and "Henceforth we renounce all idols" (48).

[26]Ibid. 32.

133

Cappadocia, except that Saint Basil describes the time of preparation as designed to free the candidates from the lordship of Satan.[27] Aphrahat the Persian Sage considers that the waters of baptism provide armor against the devil,[28] but whether this idea was incorporated into a postbaptismal formula or ceremony is not apparent.

As a final instance of an Eastern baptismal ritual in which there is no trace of prebaptismal exorcism or of any other obviously exorcistic rites, let me cite the *Ecclesiastical Hierarchy,* a document that dates from the turn of the sixth century. It was composed by a Syrian monk who posed, in his writings, as Dionysius the Areopagite, the disciple of Saint Paul mentioned in the Acts of the Apostles (17.34). He alleged that he and the apostles Peter and James had been present at the funeral of Mary the mother of Jesus. This fraud gave a solemn authority to his neo-Platonic ideas in the Middle Ages.

Although Pseudo-Dionysius alludes to no rituals of exorcism in the baptismal service he describes, he does give the details of an elaborate rite of renunciation, which can serve to introduce us to the very dramatic and typically Eastern practice of facing the west and delivering a direct and personal defiance to the devil. We recall that direct address in the renunciation is to be found in the *Apostolic Tradition* of Hippolytus, and the practice of facing the west is called for in Ambrose's *Mysteries*. But these exceptions in the West proved to be the rule in the East.

According to the Pseudo-Areopagite, the presiding prelate at the baptismal service asks the candidates whether they are willing to live by the divine norm. When they claim that they are, he places his hand on the head of each and seals him. Then, one by one, the candidates face west with hands outstretched in aversion and breathe on Satan three times and speak the words of renunciation. They then turn to the east to align themselves with Christ. Next the prelate seals them three times with the sacred oil of unction, and the priests anoint their whole body. The water is sanctified by prayer and a triple effusion of the sacred oil *myron* (the Eastern equivalent of chrism) in the form of a

---

[27]Winkler, *Arm. Init.* 345–346, citing Basil's *De baptismo* 1.1.3 (PG 31.1520). One of the Cappadocian Fathers, Gregory Nazianzen, does refer to a lengthy exorcism before baptism, but he was writing from Constantinople (Winkler 347, 352, citing *Oratio* 40.27, PG 36.397). See Dölger, *Exorzismus* 56, 68–69.

[28]Aphrahat, *Demonstrationes* 6.1 (Patrologia syriaca 1.251–254): "Qui armaturam induit ex aquis, arma sua ne proiciat, ne superetur. Qui scutum gestat adversus malignum, a telis quae ille sibi immittit se custodiat." See Brock, *Holy Spirit* 102.

cross, and the prelate proceeds to confer baptism proper.[29] The most interesting development here is the breathing ceremony, which in the Western ceremonies was always (so far as we can tell) an exorcistic or postexorcistic act performed by the minister upon the candidate. Here the candidate is so self-possessed that he can take it upon himself to add this gesture of defiance to his renunciation. There was a precedent for this turn of events: Ephraem, who, as we saw, was active in East Syria a century and a half before the time of Pseudo-Dionysius, said that one renounced the devil while breathing upon him.[30]

Dionysius goes on to give an explanation of the renunciation. He says it amounts to the rejection of dark evil and of what is opposed to becoming godlike.[31] He continues to speak in an impersonal way about the forces of evil, even when talking of the energumens, who, along with catechumens and penitents, are excluded from the mysteries. He seems to think that the state of the energumens is caused basically by their pusillanimity in failing to resist anxieties and passions and that their cure is simply a question of mind over matter (or, rather, mind over "energy"). Whoever is worthy of communion, he says, will not be "energized" by opposing phantasies and fears but will mock them and put them to flight. The only mention of demons in this long discussion comes when he contrasts these energumens who are taking proper steps towards their cure with those who are "energized by a most detestable energy," who desert the God-formed life and come to resemble ruinous demons.[32] That is, demons do enter the picture somehow, but they are not said to be responsible for the condition of the energumens; it is not a question of demonic possession. And once again it must be emphasized that the energumens are distinguished from the baptismal candidates (the catechumens). But even with the energumens, it is a question not of exorcism but of voluntary rejection of evil.

[29]Pseudo-Dionysius, *Ecclesiastical Hierarchy* 2.2.5–7, ed. Johannes Quasten, *Monumenta eucharistica et liturgica vetustissima*, Florilegium patristicum 7 (Bonn 1935–1937) 280–281.
[30]Ephraem, *In secundum adventum Domini*, in *Opera omnia graece et latine* (Rome 1743) 195.
[31]Pseudo-Dionysius, *Ecclesiastical Hierarchy* 2.3.5 (288).
[32]Ibid. 3.3.7 (302–305).

135

9 /

First Rites in the East:

II. Exorcism and Reaction

Let us turn now to the Eastern traditions in which the exorcist played a prominent role before baptism. We need only recall the Oriental versions of the *Apostolic Tradition* to realize that the early Roman exorcistic practices outlined by Hippolytus were adopted *in globo* in the East; and in many areas, not only in Syria but especially in Egypt, the exorcistic and other antidemonic aspects of the *Tradition* were further expanded. Sometimes the changes were small—we have had occasion already to notice some of the variants that appear in the Egyptian (Sahidic, Bohairic, and Arabic) and Ethiopic (made from the Arabic) translations of the work. Another example can be seen in the *Canons of Hippolytus,* a fourth-century Egyptian adaptation of the *Tradition.* One of the rubrics added to Hippolytus's account in this work is that the candidates are to incline their heads toward the east while the bishop is exorcizing them and are to face west during the renunciation of Satan and all his service. Furthermore, the instruction about removing jewelry and loosing hair is definitely given an anti-demonic interpretation: it is to prevent anything belonging to alien spirits from descending with them into the water of the second birth.[1] This direction probably has nothing to do with that earlier Egyptian tradition recorded by the gnostic Theodotus, namely, the

---

[1] *Les canons d'Hippolyte* 19, ed. René Georges Coquin, PO 31 (Paris 1966) 378; cf. Hippolytus, *Ap. Trad.* 20, 21 (Botte 42, 46). George Kretschmar, "La liturgie" 57–90, esp. 58 n. 2, suggests Asia Minor rather than Alexandria as the place of origin for the *Canons.*

fear that the evil spirits would receive the seal of baptism along with the candidates. It seems rather to be a statement of the impropriety of wearing anything that savors of the vanity of this world and the service of Satan.

The *Apostolic Tradition* underwent larger alterations and additions as well. At a very early stage, before any of the extant translations (including the Latin) were made from the original Greek text, the work was combined with another third-century compilation known as the *Canons of the Apostles* or the *Constitutions of the Apostolic Church*.[2] This work is of great interest to us especially because of its highly developed teaching on sin demons. Let us listen, for instance, to what the apostle Philip has to say about the "demoness" of lechery and the demon of wrath:

> My son, be not lustful, because lust leads to fornication, drawing men into it by force. For lust is a female demon, and if the demon of wrath should be united with that of pleasure, they destroy those who will receive them. Now the way of the evil spirit is the sin of the soul. And whenever he sees a little place of rest and goes in, he enlarges the way, and takes with him all the other evil spirits, and goes unto that soul, and he lets not the man look up at all to see the right. Let your wrath have its measure, and check it after a little interval, and draw it back to you, lest it cast you into an evil deed. For wrath and evil pleasure, if they remain always continuing, become demons, and whenever they have dominion over the man, they swell in the soul, and it becomes under derision; and if they should bring him into deeds of wrong, they mock at him, rejoicing over the destruction of that man.[3]

As we can see from this excerpt, the *Canons of the Apostles* simply recommends self-control as a means of preventing the sin demons from taking possession of a man. But what if the advice comes too late or is ignored? The author gives no additional remedy for recovering from demonic domination, but exorcism would surely have been in order. At least, it should have come as no surprise to the user of the *Tradition-Canons* compilation to find in the *Tradition* section the provision that all pagans (who have, of course, been living in sin all their lives) were to be systematically exorcized before they were admitted to baptism.

[2]See Botte, *Tradition apostolique* xvii–xviii, xx. The Greek text of the *Canons* was edited by A. Harnack, TU 2.2 (Leipzig 1884) 225–237.
[3]*Canons* 8, trans. Horner, *Statutes* 298 (Sahidic version); cf. Harnack 228–229.

In the Ethiopic version of the *Apostolic Tradition,* the baptismal ceremonies are considerably expanded. For the rite of renunciation, the candidates are naked, of course, and stand with their arms outstretched towards the west; they face straight ahead without fear and pronounce these words of anathema against the devil: "I curse you, Satan, and all your wicked angels, and all your works, and all your idols, and all your commands."[4] This interpolated section of the Ethiopic text also contains a number of prayers for the consecration of the oil and water, in which it is asked that these elements be given power against spirits. For instance, both apotropaic and exorcistic qualities are sought for the oil: God is first requested to make it "a breastplate of faith against all the work of Satan"; and another prayer asks that it may serve to destroy every diabolical adversary and drive out every evil or unclean spirit. Then the minister breathes into the oil three times and first anoints the candidate's breast, then his shoulders, and finally the rest of his body.[5]

With regard to the water, there is a prayer that purports to exorcize it; but as we read it, we see that the water is not to be de-demonized but rather to be made demon-proof, that is, blessed against all hostile actions and against all magic and enchantment.[6] Another of the rituals has a prayer for the blessing of the water in which God is asked to destroy every evil spirit in the candidates, driving them out according to Christ's promise.[7] It is not clear whether the removal of the evil spirits refers to the actual baptism itself; if so, it would indicate that the anointing and whatever exorcisms preceded it might not have the sought-for effect. But then we recall that in the original *Apostolic Tradition* the demon-expelling ceremonies were continued far beyond the time in which the candidates were pronounced free from the alien spirits.

Formulas comparable to the Ethiopic prayers over the oil and the water can be found in the prayerbook ascribed to Serapion, who was bishop of Thmuis in lower Egypt in the middle of the fourth cen-

---

[4]A. Salles, *Trois antiques rituels du baptême,* SC 59 (Paris 1958) 51; original text in Hugo Duensing, *Der äthiopische Text der Kirchenordnung des Hippolyt* (Göttingen 1946) 108. For an analysis different from Salles's, see Georg Kretschmar, "Beiträge zur Geschichte der Liturgie, insbesondere der Taufliturgie, in Ägypten," *Jahrbuch für Liturgik und Hymnologie* 8 (1963) 1–54.

[5]Salles 47–50.

[6]Ibid. 45.

[7]Ibid. 44.

tury.[8] The prayer over the oil, for instance, asks that by the baptismal anointing Jesus may reveal himself and heal the souls, bodies, and spirits of the candidates of "every mark of sin and lawlessness or satanic fault." In the prayer over the chrism it is said that those who are anointed with it have the sign of the cross impressed upon them, "by which cross Satan and every opposing power was routed and triumphed over."[9] In other words, the chrism has an apotropaic rather than an exorcistic significance; the cross by which Christ defeated the powers of evil is to serve the new Christians as a means of defense. The ordinary oil, on the other hand, does have an exorcistic function, though it is not Satan but rather his influence that is to be eliminated from the candidate. The author, however, employs both oil and water as exorcistic agents in the strict sense but not at baptism: they are rather to be used as part of a general therapeutic regimen, for healing purposes; that is, healing in the normal sense of the word and also in the particular sense of driving out the evil spirits causing illness and disease.[10]

I turn my attention now to Syria, not to the eastern regions this time, but rather to the coastal areas of the west, around the metropolis of Antioch. Just as this city was one of the headquarters of the missionary voyages to Europe in the earliest days of Christianity, so too it was more susceptible to influence from the West in later times than were most inland districts. We may consider first the *Testament of Our Lord,* which was probably composed in the patriarchate of Antioch, though not necessarily in the city itself, in the fifth century.[11] The author took over and elaborated all aspects of the *Apostolic Tradition* of Hippolytus, especially the exorcisms, for which he sometimes supplied words.

First of all he treated of the demoniacs properly so called—that is, those who were noticeably tormented by a demon, which he characterized as a "material spirit" that influenced the mind and prevented it

[8]*Sacramentarium Serapionis,* ed. F. X. Funk, *Didascalia et Constitutiones apostolorum* 2.158–195; trans. John Wordsworth, *Bishop Sarapion's Prayerbook,* ed. 2 (1923 repr. Hamden 1964). Bernard Botte, "L'Eucologe de Sérapion est-il authentique?" *Oriens christianus* 48 (1964) 50–56, ascribes the work to an Arian writing fifty or a hundred years after the time of Serapion; but he concedes that the author may have been revising an authentic work of Serapion.

[9]*Sac. Serap.,* canons 22, 25 (Funk 184, 186; Wordsworth 75, 76).

[10]Ibid. 17, 19 (Funk 180, 192).

[11]See Botte, *Trad. ap.* xxvi.

from receiving the immaterial and sacred word. It is obvious that victims of such spirits had to be cleansed of them before they could receive instruction.[12] Therefore, only candidates who were ostensibly clean or who had been made clean from the torments of material spirits, that is, demons, could be catechized. But once the course of instruction was over, the bishop exorcized each catechumen one by one to see if he were truly clean and not possessed by an unclean spirit. If there was someone who was not clean, his condition would be made evident by the unclean spirit himself (presumably because the spirit would not be able to remain concealed in face of the bishop's spiritual attack). Such a catechumen was not to be cleansed like the demoniacs mentioned above, however, but was rather to depart from their midst in disgrace, "because the evil and alien spirit abided in him." As in the *Tradition,* this kind of occult possession was taken to be purely the catechumen's own fault, "because he has not received the words of command and admonition with faith."[13]

On Saturday, the eve of the baptism proper, there was still another exorcism to be performed. This time it was pronounced over all the candidates together. The bishop first addressed God in a long prayer as the all-powerful ruler before whom all evil forces flee. Then he declared to God that he was exorcizing the candidates in God's name and in the name of Jesus Christ. He did not adjure any demons still present to depart, however, but simply went on to ask God to drive a great many things from the candidates' souls, including various unhealthy or vicious conditions, magic operations (described with all the incoherence of well-worn charms), and "every unclean spirit." It is noteworthy that no pride of place is given to the demons in this list. But let me quote the first part of the formula:

> O Lord God almighty, I exorcize them in your name and in the name of your beloved son Jesus Christ. Drive away from the souls of these your servants every disease and illness; every scandal and every infidelity; all doubt and contempt, every unclean spirit; every magic and death-dealing work that subsists beneath the fiery, dark, malodorous, incantatory, and voluptuous earth; the arrogant greed for gold; the mad greed for silver. Yes, Lord God, bring to an end in these servants of yours, who have received their names in you, the weapons of Satan, all magic,

[12]*Testamentum domini nostri Jesu Christi* 2.1, ed. with Latin trans. I. E. Rahmani (Mayence 1899) 112–113; cf. the rather unreliable English translation by J. Cooper and A. J. McLean, *The Testament of Our Lord* (Edinburgh 1902) 117.
[13]Ibid. 2.6 (Rahmani 120–121; cf. Cooper-McLean 121).

incantations, worship of idols, divination, astrology, necromancy, observance of stars, astronomy, enticements of the passions [and so on].

Even though the previous exorcism was supposed to have uncovered all the unclean spirits, and even though the emphasis of this final exorcism was not upon the spirits themselves, it was still possible for them to be present, to judge from the author's rubrics: "If, while the bishop pronounces this exorcism, anyone should become agitated and suddenly rise up and break into tears or shout, or foam at the mouth or gnash his teeth, or shamelessly stare about, or become excessively uplifted, or be seized by a sudden impulse and rush away, the deacons who detect him are to put him aside to prevent a disturbance from being made while the bishop is speaking. He is to be exorcized by the priests until he is cleansed, and then baptized." Though it is not specifically stated that a disturbed person of this sort is afflicted by an unclean spirit, the remedy to be applied strongly suggests it, and the rubric also indicates that any improvised demonic participation in this dramatic ritual was neither encouraged nor welcomed. The disturbed person was to be treated like those who were vexed by demons before being admitted to the catechumenate rather than being repudiated like the catechumens whose demonic condition was revealed by the bishop's first exorcism.

When the priest has exorcized any candidates thus found to be unclean, and when he has exorcized those too who have been offered (perhaps the author is speaking of infants here), "he insufflates them and signs them on the forehead, nostrils, breast, and ears, and thus arranges them in their proper order." In due course, the candidates face west and speak the words of renunciation: "I renounce you, Satan, and all your service, your displays, your desires, all your works."

Even after the renunciation, as in the *Tradition*, there seems to have been a further possibility that unclean spirits were still remaining, for when the exorcized oil was applied, the priest said: "I anoint you with this oil to deliver you from every wicked and unclean spirit and from every evil."[14]

What of the baptismal liturgy of the city of Antioch itself? We know from the baptismal instructions of St. John Chrysostom that elaborate prebaptismal exorcisms were in use, but there is nothing to

[14]Ibid. 2.7–8 (Rahmani 120–129; Cooper-McLean 121–126).

suggest that the service was modeled on Hippolytus in the manner of the *Testament of Our Lord*.

Two series of Chrysostom's Antiochene catecheses are extant, the first of which was probably delivered during the Lent of 388, and the second in 390. In one of the lectures of the second series, he gave an account of the exorcisms. Exorcists were ordained specifically to perform the exorcisms, and the whole ceremony was amply justified by its effects: the spirits of the candidates were thoroughly purified by the exorcists' formidable cries, which put to flight every contrivance of the Evil One and thereby readied the soul for the coming of the King. And lest his audience should think that the exorcisms were valued only for their psychological effect upon the candidates (that is, in making them determined to resist diabolical allurements), he went on to specify that evil spirits were the object of the attack. He said that no matter how fierce or unmanageable a demon was, he was forced to flee in haste when the exorcists uttered these cries and called upon the universal ruler.[15] From this description it seems that the exorcists used both imprecatory and deprecatory exorcisms: they not only adjured the demons to depart but also addressed supplications to God, asking him to drive off any evil spirit that was in the way, as in the bishop's exorcism in the *Testament of Our Lord*.

In the earlier series of lectures,[16] Chrysostom spoke only of the effect of the exorcisms on the candidates: the frightening and horrible words recalled to their minds the master of them all and his threats of punishment, vengeance, and the fires of hell.[17] Here his tone resembles that of the Western Fathers such as Augustine and Nicetas, who rationalized away the crude idea that the candidates were literally possessed by the devil and regarded the exorcism as dramatic incentives for overcoming the effects of original sin or for preparing the candidates for a fervent renunciation of the devil. Chrysostom does not define the nature of the demonic control of souls before baptism, though in the lecture just cited he says that "the catechumen is a sheep

[15]John Chrysostom, *Huit catéchèses baptismales inédites* 2.12, ed. Antoine Wenger, SC 50 (Paris 1957) 140. All of Chrysostom's catecheses are translated by Paul W. Harkins, *Baptismal Instructions,* Ancient Christian Writers 31 (Westminster 1963); for the passage cited here, see 47–48.

[16]The two catecheses edited by Montfaucon (PG 49.221–240) and the second and third of the four edited by A. Papadopoulos-Kerameus, *Varia graeca sacra* (St. Petersburg 1909) 154–183; the first of the Papadopoulos series coincides with Montfaucon's first. See Wenger 64–65; Harkins 17–18.

[17]Cat. Papadopoulos 2.16 (Harkins 154–155).

without a seal [brand]; he is a deserted inn and a hostel without a
door, which lies open to all, without distinction; he is a lair for
robbers, a refuge for wild beasts, a dwelling place for demons."[18]
Since he is speaking metaphorically in the rest of the sentence, the
image of the house of demons can hardly be taken as evidence of a
belief on his part that all persons before baptism are literally possessed
by demons. At most he would seem to mean that the devil and his
minions are still in the vicinity, attempting to continue exercising
their control over their subjects. Even so, however, the accent seems
to be on a staged or symbolic representation of reality and not upon
the literal facts of the moment.

In continuing his explanation of the exorcisms, in the lecture that I
first cited, Chrysostom says that the attitude of the candidates during
the ceremony has a different purpose from that of the exorcisms
themselves. We saw that the object of the latter was to drive away
demons and purify the candidates. But the candidates, for their part,
by the fact that they stand with bare feet and stretch their hands to
heaven, express their lamentable condition as captives of the devil,
which is emphasized now that they are close to deliverance in order to
foster greater sentiments of gratitude.[19] That is to say, the reality has
been heightened dramatically for the sake of special effects.

After the exorcisms, Satan is renounced by direct address. In the
earlier series of homilies, Chrysostom names Satan's pomp and service, which is the form attested to by Nilus of Ancyra in the fifth
century and Procopius of Gaza in the sixth—though Procopius's
form is much more hostile than a simple renunciation: "I declare war
upon you, O Satan, and upon your pomp and all your service."[20] In
his later series Chrysostom adds the devil's works to the formula; and
after becoming Patriarch of Constantinople in 397, he cites another
formula naming Satan's angels instead of his works.[21] But according

[18]Ibid. (Harkins 155); quoted in Wenger 78–79 n. 1.
[19]Cat. Wenger 2.14 (Harkins 48); cf. Cat. Pap. 2.14 (Harkins 154).
[20]Cat. Montfaucon 2.48 (PG 49.239; Harkins 188); Nilus of Ancyra, *Epist.* 3.287
(PG 79.525); Procopius of Gaza, *Comm. in Gen.* 35.2 (PG 87.463–464). According to
Cat. Papadopoulos 3 (see Wenger 79 for the text), the renunciation took place on
Good Friday, as in the Byzantine liturgy (see Chap. 10 at n. 4). Wenger suggests that
this was a recent development at Antioch and that it was originally set on Holy
Saturday, just before the actual ceremonies of baptism.
[21]Cat. Wenger 2.20 (Harkins 51); *Hom. Colos.* 6.4 (PG 62.342). St. Basil, *De Spiritu
sancto* 11.27 and 27.66 (PG 32.113, 188) speaks simply of renouncing the devil (or
Satan) and his angels.

to Proclus, who was appointed patriarch in 434, all the ingredients of Chrysostom's formulas are included in the Byzantine service: "I renounce you, Satan, and your pomp and your service and your angels and all your works."[22]

To return to the Antiochene liturgy: after the renunciation, apotropaic precautions are taken. The candidate is signed with myron and later anointed with oil as an aid to overcoming the devil in the future.[23] Chrysostom speaks as if the devil were rather taken by surprise to see his former prisoners suddenly freed from his service, and he grinds his teeth and prowls around like a roaring lion when he realizes it.[24] Obviously the saint is using rhetorical exaggeration here—even in dramatic terms it is hardly appropriate, since it would not have taken much intelligence on the devil's part to realize the end to which all the exorcisms and renunciation were tending—especially because the Great Escape was an annual or even more frequent occurrence. But his words do emphasize the playacting quality of the whole ritual.

Our knowledge of baptismal practices in Constantinople is more limited than in the case of Antioch. We do, however, have a clue as to the nature of the preliminary exorcism. According to a directive that seems to come from the fifth century but was later mistakenly designated as the seventh canon of the First Council of Constantinople (A.D. 381), heretics were to be received in the same way as pagans: on the first day they were made Christians (presumably by being enrolled); on the second, they became catechumens; and on the third, they were exorcized. The exorcism consisted, in part at least, of breathing upon the face and ears of the candidates.[25]

[22]Proclus, *Mystagogic Catechesis,* Codex sinaiticus graecus 491.130, cited in Wenger 81, and edited by François Joseph Leroy, *L'homilétique de Proclus de Constantinople,* Studi e testi 247 (Vatican City 1967) 188, hom. 27.2.3.

[23]Cf. H. Benedict Green, "The Significance of the Prebaptismal Seal in St. John Chrysostom," *Studia patristica* 6, ed. F. L. Cross, TU 81 (Berlin 1962) 84–90. Daniélou, "Onction" 445, says that the original Syrian (and Jewish-Christian) association of myron with the action of the Holy Spirit has been lost here and that Chrysostom has confused the purpose of the myron with the purpose of the ordinary oil. But in Syrian tradition, as we saw in the last chapter (see n. 15), the oil was both "charismatic" and apotropaic. Chrysostom makes both oil and myron apotropaic (if indeed myron is not simply used as a synonym for the oil), and he resists the Western idea of the oil as exorcistic.

[24]Cat. Wenger 2.22–24 (Harkins 51–52).

[25]Mansi, *Sacrorum conciliorum nova et amplissima collectio* 3.564; cf. Dölger, *Exorzismus* 119.

We have seen that some kind of exorcistic breathing ceremony was common in the West and in Western-influenced regions of the East from the time of the *Apostolic Tradition* onwards. Such a ceremony was practiced also in Jerusalem, another coastal city of the Levant. In the middle of the fourth century, we find Cyril of Jerusalem telling the audience of his *Catechetical Homilies* to undergo the exorcisms with fervor, for whether they were breathed upon or exorcized it would be for their salvation. The function of the exorcists was to inject fear into the soul, and as a result the hostile demon would flee and the soul would be cleansed of its sins and would win salvation for itself.[26]

Later in his homilies, the question is raised whether sin is something alive, say an angel, or a demon, to do what it does. Cyril answers, seemingly rejecting the Jewish-Christian notion of indwelling vice demons, that it is not an enemy from without that struggles against a man but his own evil offspring growing out of himself. He does, however, admit that we are not entirely alone—there is an evil instigator, the devil, who makes suggestions to all but does not overcome those who do not accede. But at this point Cyril is talking of temptation and sin in general, and he does nothing to explain the mechanism of the exorcisms used in baptism, which seem to employ the same techniques as those used upon persons thought to be possessed by a demon.[27] When he describes baptism itself, he says that it was sanctified by Christ's own baptism. He uses the figurative language of the Bible to show that the devil has no power over the candidates in spite of their sins: since the dragon was in the waters and swallowed the Jordan (Job 40.23) and his heads had to be crushed (Psalm 73.13), Christ descended into the water to bind the Strong One (Matt. 12.29), to give us power to tread on serpents and scorpions (Luke 10.19). Life rushed forward to bind Death, so that we can taunt Death (1 Cor. 15.55) and Hell (cf. Hosea 13.14). When we descend into the water of baptism, the dragon has no power to swallow us, in spite of our sins.[28] Symbolically, then, the devil, though

---

[26]Cyril, *Procatechesis* 9 (PG 33.348–349).

[27]*Cat.* 2.2–3 (384–385). In another context, Cyril speaks of the success enjoyed by a certain man who often subdued, by the words of his prayers, demons who could not be held down by chains. Cyril attributes it to the power of the Holy Spirit within him; his very breath becomes a fire to the invisible foe while he is exorcizing (16.19, 945).

[28]Ibid. 3.11–12(441–444). Cf. Lukken 255–256, who with Dölger believes that Christ was thought to have literally purified the waters of demons. See Chap. 4 at n. 44.

powerless, is still in the water; but Cyril is not speaking of a real presence, or of a real need for the water to be "unbedeviled."

In the *Mystagogical Catecheses,* usually attributed to Cyril but possibly the work of his successor, John of Jerusalem, there is no mention of the exorcisms, but we know from the report of Egeria at the turn of the fifth century that prebaptismal exorcisms were still performed by clerics during Lent even in John's time.[29] The homilies do describe the renunciation, however, and the rites that follow. The candidate faces west and addresses Satan as if he were present, renouncing him and all his works, all his pomp, and his service. In drawing an analogy between the converts and the Israelites fleeing Pharaoh, the author says that the audacious demon has pursued them up to the font, and he disappears in the saving water.[30] The oil used in the ceremony puts to flight, if not precisely Satan or demons, at least every trace of all adverse power. Just as the breath of the saints and the invocation of God's name burns and expels demons like a fierce fire, so too the exorcized oil takes on such power from being prayed over that it not only cleanses away the traces of sins by its burning but also chases away all the invisible powers of the Evil One.[31] The myron that the candidate receives after baptism will enable him to resist the ambushes of the devil and overcome all opposition, just as Christ overcame the adversary after he was baptized and after the Holy Spirit descended upon him.[32]

Neither Cyril of Jerusalem nor John Chrysostom believed that the pagans who presented themselves for baptism were possessed by demons; yet they had inherited a ritual that treated them as if they were so possessed. They therefore gave to the ritual what we might term a "liturgotropic" interpretation, on the analogy of Robert Graves's concept of iconotropy: that is, the reinterpretation of another culture's religious images to suit one's own mythological presuppositions. Prebaptismal exorcisms were a response, it seems, to the theory of sin demons. The Fathers rejected the theory but kept the

---

[29]*Itinerarium Egeriae* 46.1 (CCL 175.87): "Consuetudo est enim his talis ut qui accedunt ad baptismum per ipsos dies quadraginta quibus ieiunatur primum mature a clericis exorcizentur, mox missa facta fuerit de Anastase matutina." On the question of authorship of the catecheses, see Charles Renaux, "Hierosolymitana," pt. 2, *ALW* 23 (1981) 149–175, esp. 149–154.

[30]*Myst. Cat.* 1.2–8, ed. Auguste Piédagnel, *Cyrille de Jérusalem: Catéchèses mystagogiques,* SC 126 (Paris 1966) 84–98.

[31]Ibid. 2.3 (108).

[32]Ibid. 3.4 (126).

practice while giving it another meaning in keeping with their more sophisticated demonology.[33]

Were there no other reactions to the exorcisms? Let us return to the region of Antioch and examine a document known as the *Apostolic Constitutions,* composed about the year 400. It describes a baptismal liturgy that is Antiochene in character but differs from the rites of the city itself, as we know them from Chrysostom's homilies. It does, however, correspond to the service described by Theodoret, who was bishop of the small nearby town of Cyrrhus in the first half of the fifth century.[34] The ritual of the *Constitutions* differs most strikingly from that of Antioch in that it has no prebaptismal exorcism at all— in spite of the fact that the author drew upon Hippolytus's *Apostolic Tradition.* Nor is any use made of exorcized oil in the baptismal ceremony, though there is a general prayer of blessing over water and oil not designed for baptism in which God is asked to bestow the power of healing, expelling diseases, putting demons to flight, and removing every snare.[35]

What is the reason for these omissions? Did the author, like the great doctors of the Church, reject the notion of sin demons and simply eliminate the ceremonies that presupposed it? This hardly seems to be the answer, for he made use of the *Didascalia* and took over the Hermas-like concept that each man was inhabited by either the Holy Spirit or the diabolic spirit.[36] Perhaps the real answer lies in the native Syrian tradition to which the *Didascalia* belongs. We saw that even where the doctrine of sin demons was accepted there was no provision made for ridding sinners of their unwholesome inhabitants by mass exorcisms; rather it was simply a question of the voluntary

---

[33]I draw attention here to Sebastian Brock's edition of "A Baptismal Address Attributed to Athanasius," *Oriens christianus* 61 (1977) 92–102, which Brock thinks was written about the turn of the sixth century in Egypt by a person aware of the Jerusalem catechetical tradition, perhaps the patriarch Athanasius II (488–494). The address contains no demonological references at all; it goes on at length about the purification necessary before baptism, but it is referring only to moral attitudes. The effect of the sweet-smelling myron is to make the candidate a sharer in Christ's own anointing.

[34]See Ysebaert, *Greek Baptismal Terminology* 317–318, who cites the Pseudo-Justinian *Quaestiones et responsiones ad orthodoxos,* now attributed to Theodoret. See also Botte, *Tradition apostolique* xxv.

[35]*Apostolic Constitutions* 8.29.3, ed. F. X. Funk, *Didascalia et Constitutiones apostolorum* (Paderborn 1905) 1.532.

[36]Ibid. 6.27.5 (371–373); cf. 6.7.1 (315).

rejection of sin; and there is, of course, such a rejection in the *Apostolic Constitutions,* in the renunciation of Satan at baptism.

The devil in this service is renounced along with his works, pomps, services, inventions, and everything else that is subject to him.[37] But it is noteworthy that the form of the renunciation is "nondramatic." That is, contrary to the practice of the *Apostolic Tradition* and the city of Antioch, the great adversary is not defied to his face, so to speak, by a direct address but is spoken of in the third person, as if he were not present to hear himself rejected. But this indirect renunciation is characteristic of the later Antiochene liturgies and also of the service of Theodore of Mopsuestia, a one-time resident of Antioch. The baptismal ritual described by Theodore is in many ways, from a dramaturgical point of view, the most interesting that we will encounter. It is pertinent at this point not only because of geographical and chronological congruence but also because it provides a new solution to the problem of the prebaptismal exorcism: the ceremony is completely transformed to meet the needs of current theology.

It has often been assumed that Theodore delivered his *Catechetical Homilies* while he was a priest at Antioch between the years 383 and 392, that is, at the same time that his old classmate John Chrysostom was preaching his own homilies in Antioch. But since the rite that he describes is much different from the one that Chrysostom outlined, it has more plausibly been suggested that Theodore was speaking of the service in force at Mopsuestia in Cilicia, to the north and west of Syria, where he was bishop from 392 to 428.[38]

At first glance it might seem that the two rites are rather similar. Exorcists are used in both, and the words they speak are referred to as exorcisms, and the catechumens dress and behave in such a way as to

---

[37]Ibid. 7.41.1 (444); cf. 3.18.1 (213), where there is an allusion to the renunciation of Satan and his demons and deceits.

[38]Ysebaert 316. Bernard Botte, "L'onction postbaptismale dans l'ancien patriarcat d'Antioche," *Miscellanea liturgica in onore di sua eminenza il cardinale Giacomo Lercaro 2* (Rome 1967) 795–808, suggests that Theodore could have been influenced by the rite of Tarsus, where he lived for a while before becoming bishop of Mopsuestia. Unlike Chrysostom's rite, Theodore's includes a postbaptismal signing (and probably anointing), a feature that is shared with the *Apostolic Constitutions*. A postbaptismal anointing is also called for in canon 48 of the Council of Laodicea (ca. 380). See Sebastian Brock, "Baptismal Themes in the Writings of Jacob of Serugh," *Symposium syriacum 1976,* ed. F. Graffin and A. Guillaumont, Orientalia christiana analecta 205 (Rome 1978) 325–347, esp. 344 n. 117. But it is only in the later rituals that this postbaptismal anointing is given apotropaic meaning; see Brock, "Transition."

emphasize their miserable state of captivity under Satan. But in Theodore's service, the exorcists do not exorcize demons, even ostensibly, but rather play the role of lawyers who plead with God in a suit
on behalf of their clients. The whole ceremony has been transformed
into a courtroom drama. Satan is present as defendant, and God is the
judge. The exorcists are mentioned as the candidates' counsel or
advocates—Theodore uses the technical term *synēgoroi,* which appears in transliterated form in the Syriac version (the original Greek
text is not extant). They make a long appeal to God in a loud voice
and demand that the evil master of the plaintiffs be punished and
removed from his position of authority over them.[39]

Theodore characterizes Satan as answering the charges and plead-
ing his case. (Were his arguments spoken by a devil's advocate?) He
claims that, because of Adam's fall and God's sentence, all men belong to him by right. He is answered that they did not belong to him
from the beginning, but that they came under his control because of
his evil and their negligence; and furthermore, because Satan unjustly
condemned Christ to death, he has been liberated from death, and
with him all humanity.[40]

Each candidate or set of candidates seems to represent the whole of
mankind in Theodore's presentation, and as a result he is somewhat
vague as to the precise causes and implications of Satan's domination
over the unbaptized. Everyone shares in Adam's nature and punish-

---

[39]*Cat. Hom.* 12.22, ed. R. Tonneau and R. Devreesse, *Les homélies catéchétiques de
Théodore de Mopsueste* (Vatican City 1949) 359. A similar conception of the exorcism is
reflected in a commentary edited by Sebastian Brock, "Some Early Syriac Baptismal
Commentaries," *Orientalia christiana periodica* 46 (1980) 20–61, esp. 35: "The adjuration [is] the battle with Satan and a supplication to the judge on behalf of him who
seeks to be freed from evil dominion." But the sentence looks like an afterthought,
for it comes after discussion of the renunciation of Satan and the confession of Christ.
Later adaptations of the commentary (MSS C and D), followed by George, bishop of
the Arabs (d. 724), and others, transfer the sentence so that it follows the renunciation
(where, however, it is still out of place). Narsai has the same order as Theodore (see n.
51 below). Scholars have assumed, without discussion, that Theodore's courtroom
presentation of baptism in his homilies had no basis in reality and that Mopsuestia
used prebaptismal exorcisms like those of Antioch, which Theodore deliberately
"misconstrued" to serve his theological and dramatic interpretation (and that Narsai
was doing the same thing when he gave a similar picture of baptism). But though I
admit that this interpretation is possible, it does not strike me as likely. Another
possible (and less unlikely) explanation is that Theodore eliminated the imprecatory
exorcisms of direct address to the devil and kept only deprecatory forms, as was done
in the new Roman ritual (see Chap. 14 at n. 33).

[40]Theodore, *Cat. hom.* 12.18–30 (351–357).

ment, which involves enslavement by Satan,[41] so that it would seem to be a completely involuntary subjection. However, he tells the candidates that they brought their servitude upon themselves and that men after Adam's time chose to be Satan's slaves of their own accord.[42]

The arguments of the advocates of mankind are found to be decisive, and the divine verdict is handed down condemning the devil, who is adjudged a tyrant. The candidates are thereby freed from his oppression and are allowed to be enrolled without hindrance. Then each of them makes a formal renunciation of his former life: "I renounce Satan, all his angels, all his service, all his illusion, and all his pomp." There follows, still before the baptism itself, an anointing with a sign of the cross, which is meant to frighten off the demons in the future and keep them from coming near these new Christians and inflicting injury upon them.[43]

In discussing the *Apostolic Constitutions* above, I was somewhat hesitant in characterizing the indirect form of the renunciation as undramatic in comparison with a direct address. It is obvious from the Mopsuestian service that in certain circumstances an indirect statement can be just as effective. In this case, it is more proper, given the courtroom setting, for the candidate to announce his severance from the devil's power to the presiding judge or to the assembly as a whole rather than to Satan himself.

We have completed our survey of the early Christian forms of ritual deliverance from the powers of evil. The formal renunciation of Satan became a universal practice, in West and East. Prophylaxis against future attacks was a frequent concern, especially in the East. But it is the preliminary attempt to depose the malign spirits by exorcism that has proved in many ways to be the most interesting facet of the services. The practice spread to all regions of the ecumenical world, except in Syria, and often dominated the initiation procedures, in spite of the fact that it presupposed the awkward notion that all unjustified men were inhabited by demons. Theologians like St. Augustine reinterpreted the exorcisms in the light of the perhaps equally awkward notion of original sin or some other more acceptable demonological concept. Theodore of Mopsuestia

---

[41]Ibid. 1.5 and 12.22 (11, 359).

[42]Ibid. 12.23; 13.6 (361, 377).

[43]Ibid. 12.26; 13.5, 17–18 (361–363, 373, 397–399); on the renunciation see B. Botte, "Le baptême dans l'église syrienne," *L'orient syrien* 1 (1956) 137–155, esp. 143.

seems actually to have changed the ceremony to bring it more into accord with the received teaching. This indeed would have been the wiser course for the other intellectual leaders of the Church to have followed if they wished their concept of man's unjustified state to prevail among the faithful.

As it was, Theodore's lead was not pursued, except in East Syria. Elsewhere, the creative liturgists took their cue not from the liturgotropic rationalizations of the Fathers but from the literal sense of the exorcisms themselves, which had continued to be performed with more attention than the Fathers' homilies had been reread. As a result, this aspect of the confrontation with the adversary, theologically questionable unless symbolically understood, underwent great elaboration, unhindered by the circumstance that these fearsome adjurations came more and more to be pronounced over the heads not of sinful and world-tainted adults but of imperceptive infants. The imaginative formularists devised similar adjurations addressed to the evil spirits residing in the water and other materials used in the ceremonies.

The upshot was that Christian communities were regularly exposed to a large mass of very primitive incantations that would readily lend themselves to dramatic or allegorical interpretations. The unreality of the literal level would suggest an alternative meaning in more acceptable terms, at least for doctrinally sophisticated believers, that is, Augustine's idea of regarding the exorcized infants not as actual but as symbolic demoniacs. By a ritual pretense they would be treated as if corporeally possessed by the devil, to bring home the malign spiritual influence he had over them by virtue of their descent from Adam. From this theological point of view, therefore, when the devil and his fellow demons were conjured to leave the bodies of the baptizands, they were not actually thought to do so. And yet, the picture of their existence in and around the candidates and the oil and the water was so strongly and lengthily depicted by the prayers that it would have been natural for the ministers and congregation to imagine the evil spirits as actually present, cowering before the exorcists' threats and humiliated by the renunciation that followed.

The failure to follow the lead of Theodore of Mopsuestia in modifying the baptismal rites to accord with a more sophisticated demonology was universal, with one outstanding exception—the area of East Syria and beyond. It was here that Theodore was held in the highest regard, and it was here too that the practice of prebaptismal exorcism had never gained general sway. Theodore coped with the practice as it had developed in Antioch by transforming it into a theological drama. His spiritual heirs, represented today by the "Nestorian" or East Syrian Church and its Uniate counterpart, the Chaldean Rite, went further and eliminated the preliminary ceremony altogether. Theodore's service had been at once the most rational and the most consciously dramatic of all the Christian initiation rites. The Nestorian service, as reformed in the seventh century under the catholicos (patriarch) Ishoyabh III and later adapted for children, became even more rational and eventually completely devoid of drama.

Ishoyabh's service can be reconstructed in large measure from the anonymous commentary edited and translated by R. H. Connolly.[44] The commentator professes to follow Ishoyabh's prescriptions assiduously, and even the elaborate symbolism that he gives to the different ceremonies seems to come, at least partially, from Ishoyabh.[45] As the service is presented here, it is extremely dramatic, though in a much different way from that of Theodore. The history of salvation from the Old Testament to the New is elaborately reenacted several times; but Satan plays almost no role in the drama. Although the time of baptism, on the eve of the feast of the Resurrection, is said to signify our defeat of Satan and death,[46] nothing more is made of it. No antidemonic significance is given to the signings and anointings, nor are there any exorcistic ceremonies, whether in the old-fashioned Western style described by Chrysostom or in the newer courtroom-drama service of Mopsuestia. Instead, the candidates undergo a series of instructions or prayers accompanied by the imposition of hands, which symbolize, for instance, the doctrine imparted to Moses.[47]

We know that there was a ceremony of the renunciation of Satan and a confession of faith in God, for we are told that the candidates are instructed about them, but we are not informed as to how or when they are to be performed.[48] The effect of baptism is to overcome original sin, whereby Satan is crushed,[49] but there is no indica-

[44]R. H. Connolly, *Anonymi auctoris expositio officiorum ecclesiae Georgio Arbelensi vulgo adscripta*, vol. 2, CSCO 76: Scriptores syri 32 = 2.92 (1915 repr. Louvain 1953) 87–106: the Latin translation of the tract on baptism.
[45]Ibid. 92 n. 3.
[46]Ibid. 87–88.
[47]Ibid. 89; cf. 94, 104.
[48]Ibid. 89.
[49]Ibid. 105, cf. 93.

tion whether his downfall is ritually emphasized. We might be tempted to think, of course, that there were no exorcisms for Ishoyabh to discard, since some parts of Syria had proved resistant to the practice. There is clear evidence, however, that a ritual under the name of exorcism had at one time been adopted by the East Syrian-Persian Church. It was stated at the Synod of Seleucia, convened in the year 410 by the catholicos Mar Isaac, that the role of porter was taken by the subdeacons, "who are called exorcists among us." These subdeacons assisted at the baptismal service, for the archdeacon was to inform them, as well as the priests and deacons, of the weeks in which baptism would be administered.[50] But whether they were to serve as porters or exorcists during the service is not clear.

We also possess a description of an early Nestorian baptismal rite, dating from about the middle of the fifth century. It no longer has exorcists, but it preserves the ceremony that Theodore of Mopsuestia called exorcism. The description occurs in one of the *Liturgical Homilies* of Narsai,[51] who founded the school at Nisibis after he and his followers were expelled from Edessa in 457. According to Narsai's account, the candidate approached one of the priests, in order to be set free from the slavery of the Evil One. He brought a charge against his captor and asked the priest to act "as an advocate" (*sunēgoros*).[52] The priest acceded and pleaded the case against Satan, who had led the candidate's father astray.

In his explanation of the renunciation, Narsai followed Theodore in construing the angels of Satan simply as heretics,[53] but he stressed much more than Theodore the prophylactic aspects of the signing and anointing.[54] In Narsai's rite the candidate was told to renounce the Evil One, his power, his angels, his service, and, to judge from

---

[50]Synod of Mar Isaac, canon 15, *Synodicon orientale; ou, Recueil de synodes nestoriens,* ed. and trans. J. B. Chabot (Paris 1902) 267–268.

[51]Hom. 22, ed. A. Mingana, *Narsai doctoris syri homiliae et carmina* (Mosul 1905) 1.356–368; trans. R. H. Connolly, *The Liturgical Homilies of Narsai,* Texts and Studies 8.1 (Cambridge 1909) 33–45; A. Guillaumont, "Poème de Narsai sur le baptême," *L'orient syrien* 1 (1956) 189–207. See William F. Macomber, "The Manuscripts of the Metrical Homilies of Narsai," *Orientalia christiana periodica* 39 (1973) 275–306. Brock, "Commentaries" 56–57, suggests that Narsai was drawing both on Theodore and on the earliest commentary that he edits. But Narsai follows the proper order, as in Theodore, with the "exorcism" before the renunciation.

[52]Narsai, Connolly 39; cf. Guillaumont 198: "Il demande aux prêtres d'être ses avocats dans le procès qui lui est fait."

[53]Narsai, Connolly 36–37; cf. Theodore, *Hom.* 13.7–9 (377–381).

[54]Narsai, Connolly 43–45.

the explanation that follows, also his invention. The formula is not only indirect but impersonal as well: "There is a renunciation of the Evil One, his power," etc. (the construction can be shown more clearly in Latin: "Abrenuntiatur Malo," etc.). It is likely, then, that Catholicos Ishoyabh III had inherited basically the same Mopsuestian ceremonies that Narsai described and that he eliminated them as too fanciful in favor of his own symbolic reenactment of salvation history.

At the time the anonymous commentator wrote, the baptismal service was still performed for adults. But by the time of George of Arbela, who flourished in the tenth century, the practice of baptizing adults had long since become obsolete, and the ritual had been adapted for children.[55] Scholars have often assumed, even after Connolly's time, that the infant ritual in use by modern Nestorians is that of Ishoyabh and that he was primarily motivated in purifying his service of demonological elements by the fact that he was influenced by the Pelagian denial of original sin.[56] As we have seen, however, Ishoyabh did not deny original sin, nor did he eliminate the renunciation of Satan. Moreover, the same seems to be true even of the infant ritual. Though the latter speaks of the infant candidates as undefiled by sin,[57] it is clearly possible that the reference is to personal sins alone and does not entail a rejection of original sin.[58] This interpretation is also possible for similar statements made by George of Arbela[59] and by the patriarch Timotheus II in the fourteenth century.[60] Furthermore, the infant ritual does not omit the renunciation but retains it in modified form. Since children cannot speak for themselves, someone else has to act for them. This is also the case in other rituals, of course, beginning with the *Apostolic Tradition* of Hippolytus. But whereas in the other rituals assistants or sponsors make the declaration, the

[55]See Connolly's preface to the anonymous *Expositio* (n. 44 above) 1–3.

[56]So G. Diettrich, *Die nestorianische Taufliturgie* (Giessen 1903) xxxi; Dölger, *Exorzismus* 66; Puniet, "Baptême" 284; W. de Vries, "Timotheus II (1318–1332) über 'die sieben Gründe der kirchlichen Geheimnisse,'" *Orientalia christiana periodica* 8 (1942) 40–94, esp. 76; Johannes Madey, "Die Riten der *Initiatio christiana* bei den Ostsyrern oder Chaldäern," *Kyrios* 2.10 (1970) 101–109, esp. 205.

[57]Diettrich, *Nest. Tauf.* 7.

[58]Heinrich Denzinger, *Ritus Orientalium, Coptorum, Syrorum, et Armenorum in administrandis sacramentis*, 2 vols. (Würzburg 1863–1864 repr. Graz 1961) 1.365 n., acknowledges this possibility.

[59]Quoted in Connolly, *Expositio* 2.

[60]See de Vries, "Timotheus II" 76.

Nestorian ritual prescribes that the celebrant is to do it. That is, the priest simply declares that the children "are ready to receive the sign of life, while renouncing Satan and all his works and being perfected through the true faith in the Father, Son, and Holy Spirit, so that they might be worthy to receive the wondrous gift of grace and put off the old man, which was corrupted by the lusts of error, in reconciling baptism."[61]

Therefore, in admitting that children had to renounce Satan, and in alluding to "our fall" and man's capture by Satan, who is called "the lord of our world,"[62] the ritual concedes as much to the power of Satan after the fall of the first man as do any of the rituals before it. It clearly follows the tradition of Theodore of Mopsuestia and Narsai, who centered the ceremonies of baptism on the theme of deliverance of the human race from the captivity that resulted from the sin of Adam. This is not so of the other rituals we have examined, except in the interpretations of later commentators, like Augustine, though it is true that, in the course of the liturgy to which the rituals belong, mention is sometimes made of Christ's deliverance of man, fallen through Adam, from the bonds of the devil; or else there is reference in the rituals themselves, or in the baptismal instructions, to the candidates' liberation from the devil at baptism but without specific allusion to Adam's fall.

As for Ishoyabh's alleged elimination of exorcism from the rite, we may suppose that if he had inherited the kind of exorcism introduced elsewhere in the Christian world, even at Antioch in Syria, a man of his reforming temper might have been moved to reject it because of the irrationality of the ceremony, since on the literal level it presupposed the belief that all unbaptized persons were somehow possessed by demons or unclean spirits. If he did reject such a rite, he may have found support for his decision in the fact that Syria as a whole had not taken up the practice. His rejection would have had no bearing upon what he thought of original sin, for, as we have seen, this Western practice of exorcism was at first in no way connected with the notion

[61]Diettrich 19. Another German translation of the rite is given by Johannes Madey and George Vavanikunnel, *Taufe, Firmung, und Busse in den Kirchen des ostsyrischen Ritenkreises* (Zurich 1971) 22–63; the indirect renunciation appears on p. 34. The Chaldean liturgy has added the form of the renunciation for the most part as it appears in the *Roman Ritual,* where the sponsors respond to the questions of the minister. See George Percy Badger, *The Nestorians and Their Rituals* (London 1852) 2.212.

[62]Diettrich 14, 17, 18, 47.

of original sin. It was only later that such a connection was deduced.[63]

It is far more likely, as I have said, that the tradition Ishoyabh inherited was that of Theodore and Narsai, who had in effect replaced the exorcisms with a self-conscious drama of salvation. In "efficacious" and realistic terms, the ceremony had nothing to do with expelling demons, but rather was little more than an elaborate prayer that God would permit the candidate to make an effective renunciation of Satan. Ishoyabh may have found the whole performance, with its courtroom fictions, distracting and superfluous, an element that should be sacrificed in the interests of decorum.

It is important to remember that Ishoyabh also eliminated the apotropaic aspect of baptism. He avoided all mention of it in connection with the signings and anointings both before and after baptism. In the infant ritual, the only reference to this function is the statement that Christ has been baptized and has sanctified the water, so that by the hidden power and armor of the Spirit those who are baptized in faith might be victorious over Satan, "the lord of our world."[64] Thus we have one more indication that Ishoyabh's modification and rearrangement of the demonological elements of the Nestorian baptismal rite were not motivated by a rejection of original sin, since apotropaic prayers and ceremonies had nothing to do with the state of the candidate before baptism but were directed solely towards his protection in the time to come after baptism, when one must resist the temptations and afflictions that were provoked by the devil, according to traditional Christian belief, against all the faithful.

The rite of baptism as reconstituted by Ishoyabh and later simplified and modified for children has remained virtually the same up to the present day. The fact, then, that Timotheus II in the fourteenth century spoke of exorcists and exorcisms in his explanation of baptism has been cause for some puzzlement. But W. de Vries shows that his account, as well as that of Emmanuel bar Shahhare in the tenth century, hearkens back, none too accurately, to the rites of the catechumenate as they were thought to have existed before Ishoyabh's time.[65] Emmanuel does not mention exorcism, and de Vries's suggestion that the imposition of hand that he does speak of might have

[63]Cf. Dölger, *Exorzismus* 39–43; see Chap. 7 at n. 22.
[64]Diettrich 18.
[65]W. de Vries, "Zur Liturgie der Erwachsenentaufe bei den Nestorianern," *Orientalia christiana periodica* 9 (1943) 460–473, esp. 472; cf. "Timotheus II" 69, 76.

had some exorcistic meaning is not at all likely. De Vries himself admits that the prayer that went with the ceremony began with the same words as the prayer of blessing.[66] A similar prayer with laying on of hand opens the Nestorian ritual for infants,[67] which no doubt corresponds to the many similar ceremonies in Ishoyabh's service. These ceremonies can be compared to the imposition of hand and prayer of thanksgiving that occur at the baptismal instruction in the description provided in the *Apostolic Constitutions*.[68] The only specifically exorcistic imposition of hand that occurs in the Syrian documents that we have seen is in the *Testament of Our Lord,* where it is simply taken over from the *Apostolic Tradition* of Hippolytus. Of course, hands are necessarily laid upon the candidates in signings and anointings, but insofar as these ceremonies have demonological significance in the Syrian rituals, they are designed not for the expulsion of demons already present but for the repulsion of evil spirits in the future.

If Ishoyabh eliminated the courtroom defeat of the devil and played down the devil's role in the new series of dramas that he devised for the baptismal services, the infant ritual in turn eliminated all of Ishoyabh's typological dramatics. Perhaps the reason was that the children could not be expected to assume the roles assigned to them nor abide the long period of preparation. Whatever the cause, the result was that from the most dramatic of the early rituals of Christendom, the Nestorians evolved the least dramatic service of all.

We shall study the directions taken by the other main liturgical traditions in Part 3.

[66]De Vries, "Zur Liturgie" 464.
[67]Diettrich 7.
[68]*Ap. Const.* 7.37.4 (Funk 442).

PART III /

THE FORMATION OF
THE MODERN RITUALS

10 /

The Byzantine and
West Syrian Liturgies

It is a commonplace that "drama has developed in every known civilization from the ritual services of religion."[1] We think of the Greek civilization as one of the most important contributors to the dramatic arts. Yet Greek drama did not have nearly the same chronological and geographical scope as Greek poetry, philosophy, and rhetoric. It was, in fact, chiefly restricted to Athens and flourished mainly from the "Old Tragedy" of Aeschylus to the New Comedy of Menander, a matter of two centuries or so. But long after the spark had died out, or had been passed on to Alexandria, Rome, and Constantinople, the dramatic rituals of religion continued to develop with great inventiveness. The same was true not only of the pagan mysteries but of the Christian religion as well. Some of the most interesting rites that we have seen so far were Greek or at least Greek-inspired and were carried on in Greek: those, for example, of the Egyptian gnostic Theodotus, Hippolytus of Rome, Cyril of Jerusalem, Theodore of Mopsuestia, and John Chrysostom of Antioch and Constantinople.

Some of the simpler Greek theatrical traditions, especially miming, continued in popularity in the Byzantine Empire until the victory of the Turks in 1453, despite the opposition of the Church. But no genuine secular theater was created, and the religious drama that did

---

[1] This particular form of the commonplace is quoted from the article on "Drama" in *Everyman's Encyclopedia*, ed. 5 (London 1967) 4.477.

develop for the most part remained tied to the sermon, and was perhaps simply preached, that is, declaimed. It may well be that the nearest approach to effective acted drama was to be found in the liturgical services of the Church, and not the least moving of these quasi-dramatic ceremonies were the initiation rites. But only in the Latin West would the "truism" about drama developing from the rituals of religion come true again in any meaningful sense.

In the last chapter we were able to discover only a few of the characteristics of the baptismal liturgy at Constantinople at the time when Chrysostom became patriarch at the end of the fourth century or during the following century. Our earliest copy of the full-blown Byzantine service, which has remained much the same until the present day, is in the eighth-century Barberini *euchologium* (prayerbook).[2] Our knowledge of how the service evolved is very fragmentary, but it obviously was the result of an extremely vital, though often not terribly intelligent (or theology-minded), creative energy. The rites have much in common with those of West Syria. It has often been supposed that these shared characteristics go back to a time before the Monophysite schism of 451, but it is a mistake to believe that liturgical borrowings cannot take place after a schism has occurred.[3]

The Barberini euchologium contains a Good Friday homily delivered by the Byzantine archbishop that is very close to the thought of Chrysostom in his Antiochene catecheses. It has, however, been attributed instead to Proclus or to some other patriarch of the fifth or sixth century.[4] A date later than the time of Proclus is indicated by the fact that the formula of renunciation in the homily is not addressed directly to Satan, as with Proclus, but rather, as in the rite of Theodore of Mopsuestia, is indirect, in spite of the fact that Satan is visualized as present; and, while the ingredients of the formula are the same as in that of Proclus, they are arranged and worded differently. The formula of the homily coincides with that of the ritual contained in the same Barberini codex and reads: "I renounce Satan and all his

[2]Ed. F. C. Conybeare, "The Greek Baptismal Service from the Barbarini Euchologion," *Rituale Armenorum* (Oxford 1905) 389ff., cf. xxv–xxvii. See Miguel Arranz, "Les sacrements de l'ancien euchologe constantinopolitain," pt. 1: "Etude préliminaire des sources," *Orientalia christiana periodica* 48 (1982) 284–335. Arranz will deal specifically with baptism in a later article.

[3]As Bernard Botte, "Le baptême" 154, justly points out.

[4]Wenger, *Huit catéchèses* 83–85. The homily is edited by Conybeare (438–442) and is translated, after further MS corrections, by Wenger (85–90).

works and all his cult and all his angels and all his pomp."[5] The priest says the formula and the candidate repeats it after him. This is done three times, while the candidate faces west and holds up his hands. The homily presupposes that it is still adults that are being baptized. In the rubrics of the ritual itself, however, the priest turns the candidates to the west rather than commanding them to turn, which would indicate that it had the baptism of infants in view.

In the ritual the priest goes on to ask, "Have you renounced Satan?" and he is answered, "We have renounced him." He then commands them to breathe upon (*emphusan*) Satan.[6] In later practice, the candidates are told to "breathe and spit upon him."[7] The explicit addition of spitting to the rite first appears in a thirteenth-century manuscript,[8] but the notion of spitting may have been contained in the original service too, since the archbishop in his homily says, in referring to this ceremony, "If there is anything of a contrary nature in you, spit it out with your breath." He then says, in words reminiscent of Chrysostom, that the devil stands in the west, "gnashing his teeth, tearing his hair, striking his hands, biting his lips in rage," lamenting his loss and unable to believe that his subjects have been delivered from his power.[9]

The Barberini euchologium also has a service for signing an infant on the eighth day after his birth; the priests prays, "May the cross of your only-begotten Son be a sign in his heart and his thought, so that he may flee the vanity of the world [*kosmos*] and every evil snare of the enemy, and follow your commandments."[10] There is another prayer for the child forty days after birth, which in its older form does not mention the necessity of countering demonic forces,[11] though in its later form it speaks of the routing of all opposing power before baptism.[12]

In the catechumenate service before baptism, three long formulas

[5]Conybeare 440, cf. 395.
[6]Ibid. 395–396 and 440.
[7]Jacques Goar, *Euchologion; sive, Rituale graecorum*, ed. 2 (Venice 1730 repr. Graz 1960) 277; *Service Book of the Holy Orthodox-Catholic Apostolic Church*, trans. Isabel Florence Hapgood from Old Slavonic and collated with the Greek text, ed. 2 (1922 repr. New York 1956) 274.
[8]Puniet, "Baptême" 289 n. 8.
[9]Conybeare 439.
[10]Ibid. 389.
[11]Ibid. 390.
[12]Goar 268 = Conybeare 390 n. f (MS G.b.1).

of exorcism (*aphorkismos*) were recited and continued to be recited to the present century in the various Orthodox and Uniate branches of the Church. The first formula reads:

> May the Lord rebuke you, devil, who came into the world and dwelled among men in order to liberate them by the removal of your tyranny. He triumphed on the wood over the opposing powers, as the sun was obscured and the earth shook and the tombs opened and the bodies of the saints arose. By death he destroyed death and conquered him who has the power of death, that is, you, the devil. I adjure (*horkizō*) you also by God, who manifested the tree of life and appointed the cherubim and the flaming and twisting sword to guard it. Be rebuked and go out, unclean spirit. For I adjure you by him who walked upon the surface of the sea as if upon dry land, and rebuked the storm of winds, whose glance dries up abysses, and whose threat dissolves mountains. For he even now commands you through us. Be afraid, go out, and leave these creatures and do not return or hide in them or encounter any of them or work upon them or attack them either by night or by day or at the hour of noon. But go to your own Tartarus until the determined great day of judgment. Be afraid of God, who sits upon a throne of cherubim and looks upon abysses, before whom angels tremble, and archangels, thrones, dominations, principalities, authorities, powers, and the many-eyed cherubim and six-winged seraphim, before whom the heaven trembles, and the earth and the sea and all that are in them. Go out and depart from the sealed, newly chosen soldiers of Christ our God. For I adjure you by him who walks upon the wings of winds, who makes his angels spirits and his ministers flaming fire; go out and depart from these creatures with all your power and your angels, because the name of the Father and of the Son and of the Holy Spirit has been glorified now and forever and for all ages of ages. Amen.[13]

As is evident, this tirade is addressed directly to Satan. He is envisaged, at least at times, as possessing the candidates corporeally, after the manner of the synoptic-Gospel demons, with whom he is identified. He is presented with reasons, no doubt ideally delivered in a thunderous voice, why he should feel constrained to leave the candidates. The naming of God and his various powers is meant to overawe him, by reminding him that he could be expelled by force if necessary, if he should refuse to depart of his own volition at the command of God's priestly ministers. Undoubtedly the references to hell and the coming judgment and punishment are meant as a threat

---

[13]Conybeare 391–392, cf. Hapgood 271–272.

that the punishment would be more severe if he were not to obey the injunctions to depart from the candidates. The fact that the exorcism is delivered after the catechumen has been sealed, which is to say, signed with the cross, is an indication that this original sealing is not consciously regarded at this point either as an effective exorcistic or apotropaic means. No doubt its principal meaning is to serve as a brand or badge, that is, a mark of ownership or allegiance.

The nature of the devil's presence and mode of operation is variously stated. We can deduce from the injunction not to hide in the candidates that he is regarded as being able to dwell within many persons simultaneously. This trait illustrates a common tendency in Christian discussions of the devil, which can in fact be seen in the New Testament itself, namely, to speak of Satan as if his power were virtually unlimited in carrying out his evil designs in various parts of the world at the same time. Sometimes, no doubt, the devil is simply taken as a collective term for all evil spirits. In the second exorcism perhaps the mention of the devil's assisting or "cooperating" powers is meant to designate individual evil spirits, like the "angels" at the end of the first formula.

The second exorcism is as follows:

> The holy God, fearful and glorious, incomprehensible and inscrutable, in all his works and power, who has predestined the torment of eternal punishment for you, devil, commands you and all of your assisting powers, through us his useless servants, to depart from these who are newly sealed in the name of our Lord Jesus Christ, our true God. I adjure you, therefore, all-wicked and unclean and filthy and abominable and alien spirit, by the power of Jesus Christ, who holds all authority in heaven and on earth, who said to the deaf and dumb demon, "Go out from this man and return no more to him," depart and acknowledge your worthless power that does not have authority even over swine. Remember him who at your request commanded you to go into the herd of swine. Be afraid of God, at whose command the earth was established upon the waters, who created the heaven and placed the mountains with a measure and the valleys with a balance, who set the sand as a boundary for the sea, and a safe path in the turbulent water, who touches mountains and they erupt in smoke, who puts on light like a garment, who stretches out the heaven like a skin, and covers its upper parts with waters, who established it in its firmness—it will never decline—who calls the water of the sea and pours it upon the face of all the earth. Go out and depart from those who are being prepared for the holy illumination. I adjure you by the saving passion of our Lord Jesus Christ, and by his precious body and blood and by his fearful coming;

165

for he will come upon the clouds, he will come and will not delay, judging all the earth, and punishing you and your every assisting power in the gehenna of fire, giving you over to exterior darkness where the worm does not sleep and the fire is not quenched. For the power of Christ our God [is] with the Father . . . and the Holy Spirit now and forever and for ages of ages. Amen.[14]

To the statement of God's power this prayer adds an insulting reference to the devil's lack of real power, as he is identified with the Legion of the Gospel incident.

The third formula is a deprecatory exorcism, since it is addressed to God rather than to the devil. It gives special attention to evil spirits other than the devil. They too are regarded, like Legion, who after all is "many," as dwelling within the candidates: "Lord of Sabaoth, the God of Israel, the healer of every disease and every illness, look upon your servants; seek for, search out, and drive from them all the operations of the devil. Rebuke the evil and unclean spirits, and cast them out, and cleanse the works of your hands, and, using your mighty power, quickly crush Satan under their feet, and give them victory over him and over the unclean spirits, so that finding mercy with you they may be worthy of your immortal and heavenly mysteries, and give glory to you."[15]

In the prayer that follows the exorcisms, there is the more sophisticated concept that man is simply enslaved by the devil. Furthermore we meet here the new notion that each candidate is to receive a guardian angel to protect him from the evil spirits:

O Lord and ruler, who made man according to your image and likeness and gave him the power of eternal life, and did not despise him when he had fallen because of sin, but arranged for the salvation of the world through the incarnation of your Christ, receive this creature of yours into your heavenly kingdom, having redeemed him from the servitude of the enemy; open the eyes of his mind so that the light of the Gospel may shine in him. Join to his life a shining angel to deliver him from every snare of the adversary, from the onslaught of evil, from the noonday demon, from evil phantasms.[16]

It is difficult to know the precise meaning attached to the word *phantasmata,* which appears often in both Eastern and Western prayers

[14]Conybeare 392–393.
[15]Ibid. 394.
[16]Ibid.

of exorcism. It could be translated either as "phantom" in the sense of evil spirit or as "phantasm," that is, phantasy, a thought or image of the mind or an external apparition or hallucination.

Next the minister breathes on (*emphusan*) the candidate three times and seals him on the forehead, mouth, and breast, saying: "Drive out from him every evil and unclean spirit, hiding and lurking in his heart—spirit of error, spirit of evil, spirit of idolatry, and of all greed, spirit of lying, and of all uncleanness that is perpetrated according to the devil's bidding."[17] The obvious assumption of the prayer, whether for purely dramatic purposes or not, is that evil spirits are possibly, or likely, still to be found in the candidates, in spite of the fearful exorcisms that have been spoken over them.

The renunciation of Satan follows, as it was described above. Then comes the blessing of the baptismal water. First it is asked, according to the Barberini codex, that all the power of the belligerent soul slayer be drowned in the water.[18] But the modern ritual substitutes a prayer that also appears in the present-day service for the blessing of the water on the feast of the Epiphany: "that this water may prove effectual unto the averting of every snare of enemies, both visible and invisible."[19] The later prayer, then, looks to the overcoming of diabolical power in the future rather than in the present.

A long prayer then recounts many of God's attributes and describes his acts of creation and redemption. Included is the following statement: "You also sanctified the streams of the Jordan, in sending the Holy Spirit down from heaven, and crushed the heads of the dragons lurking there."[20] These words also appear in the Epiphany service,[21] which seems to have inspired the blessing of the baptismal water.[22] We also read there that "the Lord, the king of ages, reneweth corrupt Adam by the waters of Jordan, and crusheth the heads of the dragons which lurked therein."[23]

We saw in the fourth chapter that some commentators have taken these and similar texts as verifying what they believe to be a tradition of Jesus purifying the water of demons when he was baptized.[24] But it is

[17]Ibid. 394–395.
[18]Ibid. 398.
[19]Hapgood 276, cf. 193.
[20]Conybeare 400.
[21]Conybeare 418, Hapgood 194.
[22]See Botte, "Le baptême" 153–154.
[23]Hapgood 184.
[24]See Chap. 4 at n. 43.

hardly likely that anything more than a metaphor is meant. The allegorical nature of the tradition is clearly emphasized in the Armenian service, where it is said that after the enemy drove men from the garden he pursued them like a wild beast but that the Son called them to the Jordan. "And there he beheld the dread Dragon lurking in the water; opening its mouth it was eager to swallow down mankind. And in the full-flowing eddies of Jordan, it received them in its whirlpools, as Job doth say. But the only-begotten Son by his mighty power having trampled the waters under the soles of his feet sorely punished the mighty brute, according to the prediction of the prophet, that 'thou hast bruised the head of the Dragon upon the waters!' "[25]

Besides the theme of bruising the heads of the dragons on the waters, which comes from Psalm 73.13, another motif from the psalms is employed in the Epiphany service that has also been misinterpreted by commentators. The antiphons taken from Psalm 113.3,5 ("The sea looked and fled, Jordan turned back. . . . What ails you, O sea, that you flee? O Jordan, that you turn back?")[26] have been taken to mean that the demons in the water were frightened at the sight of their divine enemy. But it is far more likely that these verses are taken in the spirit of the psalm as a whole, which simply says that nature was awestruck at the presence of God. This view is supported by another text from the service: "The waters beheld thee and were affrighted. The Baptist became all trembling."[27]

An interesting Ethiopic text adds further confirmation to this interpretation: John the Baptist tells his disciples that the Lord told him that, if he should see the water of the Jordan draw back and turn hot, he should know that the Lamb of God had come. Jesus later tells his own disciples that the day has come when he will bruise the Evil One and demolish his power and destroy him in the waters. The waters draw back in fear when he comes and is baptized. But Satan, far from being crushed in the water, is a spectator at the event and proceeds to tempt Jesus.[28]

If, however, no Eastern liturgical tradition has Jesus cleansing the

[25]Conybeare, *Rituale Armenorum* 168.
[26]Conybeare 415, Hapgood 183.
[27]Hapgood 189.
[28]*Les miracles de Jesus* 30, ed. and trans. Sylvain Grebaut, PO 17 (1923) 841–854. For Syrian traditions of metaphorical reflections, see Sebastian P. Brock, "The Homily of Marutha of Tagrit on the Blessing of the Waters at Epiphany," *Oriens christianus* 66 (1982) 51–74. For variations in the baptismal formulas, see his "The Epiklesis in the Antiochene Baptismal *Ordines*," *Symposium syriacum 1972*, ed. Ignacio Ortiz de Urbina, Orientalia christiana analecta 197 (Rome 1974) 183–215, esp. 186–196; and see p. 206.

water of demons, there is a tradition of the water at the present time being infested with demons and needing to be cleansed. In the Byzantine baptismal service, after the minister breathes on the water and seals (crosses) it three times, he recites a prayer that is exorcistic in the specific sense of being designed to drive away evil spirits that are actually hiding in the water. It is noteworthy also that the fear is expressed that an evil spirit might descend with the baptizand into the water. We recall that this fear prompted the antidemonic exercises before baptism in the ritual of the *Exerpta ex Theodoto.* The prayer reads: "May all the opposing powers be crushed under the signing with the model of the cross of your Christ. Let all the aerial and invisible idols depart from us, and let no dark demon hide in this water, nor let there descend with him who is baptized, we pray you, Lord, an unclean spirit inspiring darkness of thoughts and disturbance of mind."[29]

The consecration of the oil follows, and as with the water, the minister breathes upon it and seals it three times. He prays to have it protect the candidate against the devil in the future, in serving as armor of righteousness for the "turning away of every diabolical operation." The candidate is then signed with the oil on the forehead, on the breast, and between the shoulder blades, and his whole body is anointed. After the baptism, before the "chrismation," the minister asks that the neophyte be delivered from the Evil One and all his machinations, again doubtless referring to the future and not to the present.[30]

Such, then, is the fully articulated ritual of deliverance as it was finally established in the Byzantine liturgy. I have stressed only the satanic aspects, for the sake of economy, in order to give a clear picture of the role projected upon the antagonist of mankind in this tradition. The threefold prototypical plot of exorcism, renunciation, and apotropaism is followed completely and explicitly in abundant detail, without any of the logical or programmatic inconsistencies that we have noticed at times in earlier rituals. (The most obvious example of this kind of failing is the provision of the *Apostolic Tradition* to continue the process of exorcism after the candidates have been pronounced thoroughly cleansed of the alien spirits.)

[29]Conybeare 401.
[30]Ibid. 402, 403–404. As in the West, the usual time for the conferral of baptism in the Byzantine liturgy was at the Easter Vigil on Holy Saturday. See Gabriel Bertonière, *The Historical Development of the Easter Vigil Service and Related Services in the Greek Church,* Orientalia christiana analecta 193 (Rome 1972) 65–66 (tradition of Jerusalem) and 132–134 (tradition of Constantinople).

In examining the baptismal services of West Syria, we shall be chiefly interested in the ways in which they differ from the Byzantine forms. There are three main liturgical traditions: the Maronite, the Syrian Orthodox (or Jacobite or Monophysite), and the Melchite. The latter two traditions have their corresponding Uniate or Catholic forms, while the whole Maronite tradition, centered in Lebanon, has long been in union with Rome. The Maronite rites, by long custom attributed to James of Serug, the doubtfully Monophysite bishop of Batnae near Edessa (d. 521), are the most archaic; they preserve, for instance, the early Syrian modeling of baptism upon Christ's baptism in the Jordan rather than emphasizing the Pauline model of Christ's death. The Orthodox rites, by custom usually assigned to Severus, patriarch of Antioch from 512 to 518, have more Byzantine elements, while the Melchites (that is, "Royalists") avowedly follow the services of Constantinople, translated from Greek into Syriac, but in fact many Syrian elements have been added.

From the demonological point of view, the most interesting set of variations in these rituals is to be found in the formulas and actions connected with the baptismal water.[31] In the oldest Maronite manuscript (Vatican Syriac 313), after the water is consecrated, it is insufflated in the form of a cross and perfumed with incense; each of these actions is accompanied by a nondemonic prayer. There follows a prayer that some scholars have mistakenly translated in an exorcistic sense, thus: "Expel, O Lord, from this water, and from those who descend into it and are baptized in it, and from this place, every rebellious power of the adversary, and give it the power of your Holy

---

[31]Hubert Scheidt, *Die Taufwasserweihegebete,* LQF 29 (Münster 1935) 12–31, has printed some of the different versions of the blessing side by side for purposes of comparison. Puniet gives a table comparing the parts of the entire baptismal ceremony in various versions of the Syrian service ("Baptême" 275–276). For the sake of convenience, I shall refer to the Latin translations of the Syrian orders contained in Denzinger, *Ritus Orientalium* 1.266ff., which are taken from the edition of Bishop Joseph Aloysius Assemani, *Codex liturgicus ecclesiae universae,* vols. 1–3 (Rome 1749–1750). The texts that Assemani edits derive from late medieval manuscripts; see Sebastian Brock, "Studies in the Early History of the Syrian Orthodox Baptismal Liturgy," *Journal of Theological Studies* 2.23 (1972) 16–64, who lists later editions and translations of the Orthodox rituals and describes some of the extant early medieval manuscripts in the British Museum. See also Joseph Marie Sauget, "Le *Codex liturgicus* de J.-L. Assemani et ses sources manuscrites pour les *Ordines* de l'initiation chrétienne selon la tradition syro-occidentale," *Gregorianum* 54 (1973) 339–352. The Maronite services have been studied by Augustin Mouhanna (see n. 32).

Spirit."[32] But the initial verb, *zgur* in Syriac, is more properly translated "restrain" or "curb." Therefore, the import of the prayer is apotropaic or protective.[33]

This sequence of rites and prayers is followed in the modern Maronite office (edition of 1942) except that the perfuming of the water is omitted.[34] But in the Middle Ages there were two divergent traditions: one (represented by Paris Syriac MS 117) eliminated not only the placing of incense in the water but the apotropaic prayer as well. Instead, Christ is asked to consecrate the water as he did when he was baptized at the Jordan.[35] In the other tradition (represented by Paris Syriac MS 118), the apotropaic prayer is kept and apotropaic language added to the following prayer, which originally referred only to the newly baptized as clothed in the armor of salvation. Now it is prayed that the Holy Spirit will "coerce" or "expel" from the water all the power of the adversary and will protect (another version says "enflame") it with His own power; and the armor of faith is to serve against all the darts of the Evil One.[36] The service also multiplies the preceding cross insufflation of the water by three and accompanies the breathings with a version of the Byzantine exorcism of the water (the insufflations are indicated at the places marked with a cross †): "O Lord, † let the head of the dragon, the intellectual manslayer, be

[32]So Augustin Mouhanna, *Les rites de l'initiation dans l'église maronite,* Orientalia christiana analecta 212 (Rome 1980) 53: "Expulse, Seigneur, de cette eau, de ceux qui y descendent et s'y font baptiser, et de ce lieu, toute force rebelle de l'Adversaire; procure-lui la Force de l'Esprit-Saint." Mouhanna gives the Syriac text in facsimile on plate 33: Vat. syr. MS 313 fol. 46v, lines 2ff. Renaudot, translating a later version of the order ascribed to James of Serug, that of Paris Bibl. Nat. Syr. MS 118 (see Mouhanna 95), uses the verb *abige* ("drive away"); see Denzinger 1.345. On pp. 82–83, Mouhanna gives several variants of the text of the prayer.

[33]The verb is literally and correctly translated, "keep back," by Sebastian Brock, "The Anonymous Syriac Baptismal *Ordo* in Add. 14518," *Parole de l'Orient* 8 (1977–1978) 311–346, esp. 329 no. 35: "And keep back from it every power of the enemy, as well as from those who are to be baptized in it, and from this place; and endow them with the might of thy Holy Spirit" (Syriac text on p. 320). But the prayer should not be called an exorcism (p. 343), since the evil spirits are not to be driven out from where they are already present but are to be held at bay and not allowed to be present.

[34]Mouhanna 171.

[35]Mouhanna 133; see also his "La consécration de l'eau dans la liturgie baptismale maronite," *Parole de l'Orient* 8 (1977–1978) 217–233.

[36]Denzinger 1.345, translated from an unidentified manuscript by Assemani (who uses the verb *coerceat*); the variants given by Denzinger from Renaudot's translation are from Paris Bibl. Nat. Syr. MS 118; see Mouhanna 95 nn. 42–43. Mouhanna translates by the verb *expulse* (p. 85).

crushed under the sign and model of your cross. And † may the invisible and aerial shades flee and be removed from these waters, and may there not hide in them a dark demon. Nor † let there descend into these waters with him who is baptized in them, we beseech you, Lord God, an evil and dark spirit with evil thoughts and disturbance of mind."[37] The demonology of the last sentence of this prayer is peculiar, and it has been interpreted in various ways, as is evident from the different versions of the corresponding formula in the Severan Orthodox orders and from modern translations. Sebastian Brock translates the oldest form of the Severan version as follows: "May no unclean spirit of the dark go down with those who are baptized—[no spirit] that introduces thoughts and perturbation of the spirit."[38] This interpretation is like that of recent translations of the Syrian Orthodox and Catholic orders and like Joseph Assemani's rendering of the first Severan order (as classified by Brock). But elsewhere, in the fourth order, Assemani understands the text to say that the *spirit* is introduced with the thoughts.[39]

[37]Denzinger 1.345 (Assemani); cf. Mouhanna 102. Assemani and Renaudot interpret the preceding rubric to mean that the priest recites the prayer "bowed down" (*inclinatus*); Mouhanna takes it to mean that he prays silently (*en secret*), as in later practice. The formula for the third insufflation reads, in Assemani's translation: "Neque descendat in aquas istas cum hoc qui baptizatur in eis, rogamus te, Domine, spiritus malus et tenebrosus cum iniquis cogitationibus et conturbatione mentis." Mouhanna translates: "Nous t'en supplions, Seigneur Dieu, que tout esprit mauvais et ténébreux, et que les pensées mauvaises et le trouble d'esprit ne descendent pas dans cette eau avec celui qui va y être baptisé." In a related manuscript (Vat. syr. 312), the formula is followed by a triple exsufflation of the candidate (Mouhanna 114).

[38]Sebastian P. Brock, "The Consecration of the Water in the Oldest Manuscripts of the Syrian Orthodox Baptismal Liturgy," *Orientalia christiana periodica* 37 (1971) 317–331, esp. 328. He follows the oldest manuscript: London British Library Additional MS 17218 (eighth century). Some versions qualify "thoughts" as "foul" or "deadly," and some specify the descent as "to the water."

[39]See *The Sacrament of Holy Baptism According to the Ancient Rite of the Syrian Orthodox Church of Antioch,* ed. Athanasius Yeshue Samuel, trans. Murad Saliba Barsom (Hackensack 1974) 60: "Let not the evil spirit of darkness be hidden in it, nor the unclean spirits of obscurity, that cause mortal troubles and mental disturbance, be allowed to go down into this water with this child to be baptized." For the Catholic service, see G. Khouri-Sarkis, "Prières et cérémonies du baptême selon le rituel de l'église syrienne," *L'orient syrien* 1 (1956) 156–184, esp. 173–174: "Que ne descende pas avec celui qui est baptisé l'esprit immonde des ténèbres apportant les pensées de mort et la perturbation de l'esprit" (translating the Syriac text edited by I. E. Rahmani, Charfet 1922). For the first Severan order (as numbered by Brock, "Consecration" 319), see Assemani 2.291 (Denzinger 1.306): "Neque cum hoc qui baptizatur descendat immundus tenebrarum spiritus, qui unacum cogitationis et mentis

In the Greek rite, as we have seen, the corresponding formula is a prayer that the candidate not be tempted by the dark thoughts inspired by the evil spirit as he is being baptized. In the Syriac formulas, darkness is not applied to the thoughts. But according to the usual interpretation, the basic concern is still that the candidate may be tempted. If, however, there is any justification for Assemani's alternative interpretation, the prayer may contain the idea, or may have been understood to contain the idea, that the candidate could be at fault by consenting to unworthy thoughts and that this consent or disturbance of mind would give admittance to the unclean spirit. But however the connection between the evil spirit and the evil thoughts is to be interpreted, the notion that the evil spirit might accompany the candidate into the water remains similar to the Theodotan concept. However, in Theodotus's text, we recall, the reason for taking precautions against unwanted demonic companions was the belief and fear that the evil spirits would acquire additional strength from the baptism and would become impervious to future attacks against them.

The original intention of the Severan formula and its Byzantine original was, it seems, simply to protect the candidates from the evil

---

turbationem inducit." For the fourth Severan order, see Assemani 2.229 (Denzinger 1.285): "Neque descendat cum hoc qui baptizatur immundus tenebrarum spiritus, cum mentis cogitationibus introductus." In Assemani's second order, where the Latin translation is that published in 1572 by Guy Lefevre de la Boderie (Assemani 2.290n = Denzinger 1.313), the spirit is said to have spoken the thoughts: "Neque descendat cum iis qui baptizantur immundus tenebrarum spiritus . . . quoniam turpes cogitationes locutus est cum mentis perturbatione." In the third order (Assemani 2.219, Denzinger 1.275), Assemani identifies the spirit whose descent is feared with the dark demon who may be hiding in the water: "Neque delitescat in aquis istis tenebrosus daemon, neque cum iis qui baptizantur descendat." The spirit of darkness and the evil thoughts are then made to figure in the next petition: "Quaeso, Domine, malus tenebrarum spiritus cum mortiferis cogitationibus mentisque perturbatione fac ut procul recedat." But to judge by Brock's listing of variants ("Consecration" 328), the final petition of this version of the order is the same as that for the first order: "Concede ut dissipetur ex eo operatio accusatoris" (Assemani 2.291, Denzinger 1.306) and the fourth order (Assemani 2.229, Denzinger 1.285). This petition, which Brock translates as "And grant that the machination of the accuser may perish," would seem to correspond to the original apotropaic formula of the Maronite services and the anonymous service edited by Brock, "Anonymous Syriac Baptismal *Ordo*" (see n. 33 above and n. 76 below). Cf. the breathing formula in a short Maronite service attributed to St. Basil (Denzinger 1.358–359): "Do you, O Lord, restrain [*compesce*] all the evil spirits and drive [*depelle*] from this water and from everyone who is baptized in it every operation of the wicked, crafty, and terrible adversary."

thoughts and mental perturbations that a demon could inspire; but the prayer could no doubt also be taken to apply to the whole community present at the baptism, especially when only infants were being baptized. Some sort of rationalization or "mental reservation" would be necessary, since the babies could scarcely be troubled by thoughts of any kind at this stage, unless one were to visualize the evil spirit as implanting ideas and attitudes that would emerge as the child matured (an unlikely notion, I think). Realistically, the only disturbance that could be caused in the infants would be a crying tantrum or a similar malaise of an altogether lower order than the evils envisaged in the original formula.

How much concern of this sort there was over the inapplicability of adult rites to infants we do not know. In matters of religious ritual, it is normal for the letter of the formulas and prayers to take on a sacred and unchangeable quality after they have become traditional, unless and until such time as they are subjected to review during a critical and innovative movement of reform. In our study of Christian baptismal services so far, we have seen three such reformations, one under Theodore of Mopsuestia, and the other two in the East Syrian Church, first under Ishoyabh III in the seventh century, and later when the service was adapted for infants. Elsewhere, the adult rituals were simply applied without adjustment to infants. This development was very natural, of course, since even in eras of adult conversions to the Church, infants were always baptized along with adults, with basically the same ceremonies. As time went on and only infants were baptized, that is, in well-established Christian communities, only the rubrics of the rites changed; and rubrics, of course, are, as a rule, purely practical, not theoretical. We are told how to hold the baby or how to answer for him, not how to apply to him the sentiments of the prayers and exorcisms. One later medieval English ritual even provides a distich to instruct the priest on his course of action if the infant should urinate or defecate in the baptismal water. But I have never seen any rubric explain how the devil could "possess" the water before it is blessed.[40]

The conservativeness of liturgical texts is all the more pronounced

---

[40]*Manuale et processionale ad usum insignis ecclesiae Eboracensis,* ed. W. G. Henderson, Surtees Society 63 (Durham 1895) 10: "Infans in fontem si stercoret, eiice lympham; / Si tantum mingat, non moveatur aqua." I should note, however, that theological rubrics do sometimes occur; I cite an example in n. 45 below.

when the language remains the same, especially if that language has become archaic and is no longer spoken by the people at large. But when there is a translation from the original language into a vernacular, as there was in the West Syrian Church, there is more scope for adaptation and emendation. But even in the West Syrian traditions, once the basic formulas were established they usually remained pretty much the same, except for inadvertent variants or "exuberant expansions" or cuts made in the name of economy. But sometimes we can infer that deliberate changes were made in troublesome texts. For instance, in the Mesopotamian version of the Orthodox service, attributed to Barhebraeus, catholicos of Tagrit in the thirteenth century (it is still used today in Iraq and India), the opportunity was taken, while incorporating some local traditions in the rite, to solve the problem of interpreting the odd prayer over the water by eliminating all reference to darkness and disturbing thoughts.[41]

I shall now consider each of the major West Syrian traditions apart from the ceremony of blessing the water, with attention to some of the more striking contributions they make to the ritual struggle against the diabolical antagonist. I will take as the basis of comparison the most demonized of the Maronite rites discussed above[42] and will outline the nondemonic as well as the demonic elements in order to set the latter into their ceremonial context. Noteworthy, first of all, is a ceremony for the reception of the mother and her newborn infant into church, in which, at the outset, the help of the Mother of Christ is enlisted for the overthrow of the devil's power. There follows a signing with oil, which is performed in order to provide those who receive it with weapons of the spirit to resist the devil and his powers and to elude all his deceits.[43]

The ministers of the sacrament are a priest and a deacon. They begin the baptismal service proper by lighting incense and reciting a

[41]Youssef Qōzi, *Le rituel baptismal du Maphrianat de Tagrit et de Mossoul/Ninive: Edition critique de la recension brève,* 2 vols. (Diss. Université Catholique de Louvain 1974) 2.145: "[Je] t'en supplie, Seigneur Dieu, que ne descende point, avec ceux qui [vont] être baptisés dans ces eaux, l'esprit mauvais [fém.] et impur, afin qu'ils méritent de recevoir tes dons divins." The Syriac text is given on p. 146.

[42]I follow Assemani's version, Denzinger 1.329–350, with variants from Paris MS 118 (analyzed and partially translated by Mouhanna 95–109).

[43]Denzinger 1.332–333 (not treated by Mouhanna). For a similar Orthodox rite, see Denzinger 1.267, where the sign of the cross in his mind and heart is to enable the child to flee the vanity of this world and all the wicked deceit of the adversary.

number of prayers, which include a history of the Advent of Christ: the Son of God became man in order to make men the adopted children of God, through water, and to renovate Adam, his image, which had deteriorated with age and the corruption of sin, and to reconstitute it in the healthful and spiritual furnace of baptism. Christ's own baptism is recalled, and God is asked to look with favor upon the candidate and forgive his sins.[44]

The scene is set further by the recitation of verses from the psalms (including the report of the water's fright at the appearance of the Lord), and after more readings and prayers, the candidate is made to face the east, and the priest signs his forehead, making a cross three times with his right thumb, speaking his name and saying: "This lamb who comes to holy baptism is sealed in the flock of Christ, in the name † of the Father, amen. And † of the Son, amen. And † of the Holy Spirit, forever, amen." The catechumens who are not yet scheduled for baptism are then dismissed. After further prayers, the priest takes a container of hot water in his right hand and cold water in his left and pours both into the baptismal font.[45]

The ceremony of exorcism follows. The formula is pronounced by the priest against the demons who supposedly possess the candidate's body. Therefore, the candidate appropriately stands in the west, the devil's direction, and faces the priest, who stands opposite, in the east. The priest first insufflates the candidate's face in the form of a cross. He then pronounces a number of adjurations, for each of which he makes a sign of the cross (presumably with his hand and not with his breath) over the candidate's face. The adjurations are like a series of incantations, each beginning with words such as "I exorcize you and bind you, unclean demons and evils spirits and every power of the enemy, by Him who," and so forth, naming some attribute of God or describing one of his acts of mercy to mankind. The formula

[44]Denzinger 334–335; cf. Vat. 313 (Mouhanna 16–17) and the fifth Severan rite (Denzinger 289–290).

[45]Denzinger 336–337 (Mouhanna 97). Cf. the fourth Severan order, where the rubric rejects the Arian interpretation of the hot and cold water as representing the blood and water that flowed from the side of Christ. The purpose of mixing hot and cold water is simply to make the temperature comfortable for the infants (Denzinger 283). The procedure is not to be found in Vatican 313. In this early version, it is specified that the triple crossing of the baptizand's forehead is to be done without oil, and the verb used is "seal" (*htam*); Mouhanna 26 and plate 10 (fol. 24r line 10). See Brock, *Holy Spirit* 23.

then comes down to particulars about the presence of the demons in the candidate:

> I exorcize you, unclean demons and defiled spirits, by the power of the mighty God, that you go out from this creature that is betrothed to the living God, and that going away from it and departing in banishment, you return no more to stay in this child that has drawn near to be made the dwelling of the Holy Spirit, so that He may remain in him. But you, wicked spirits, flee from him, and as the evil spirit departed from King Saul when David played the lute, † thus let Satan and his power flee from this servant of yours, Lord, when your majesty descends in a cloud and comes upon the waters of baptism. Thus, Lord, let not the evil spirit remain in any part of the soul, body, or spirit—neither in the bones, nerves, veins, arteries, marrow, nor in any of the small or large members of this your servant, who has been called to this sacrament of baptism.

This prayer betrays a very crude concept of demonology, one that hearkens back to the Pseudo-Clementine writings, according to which the spirits can hide in various parts of the body. The priest goes on to declare to the evil spirits that all the heavenly forces are attendant upon the coming ceremony of baptism. He then warns the Wicked One (presumably singling out Satan) to beware lest he perish when the king sits on the throne and judges their audacity and rebellion. He is warned not to come to this servant and is then told (now he is assumed once more to be still within the candidate) not to hurt the candidate in any way when going out from him. The priest continues:

> But if you do not put aside your audacity nor are willing to go away from the holy church, the holy of holies, in which the Lord dwells, † I bind you and anathematize you in the name of the Father and Son and Holy Spirit. Be bound and anathematized by the holy Trinity if you come with him to this holy baptism, which burns with fire and spirit. Rather, begone to the deep hell, where your punishment will last forever. † I bind you and anathematize you, Satan, by that hour in which our Lord was hung on the gibbet of the cross . . . . † I exorcize you and bind you, wicked Satan, by this hour in which we priests stand by, whom the Father placed over his treasures, from the mouth of the Father, who baptizes, and the Son, who receives, and the Holy Spirit, who descends—if you come to this body that is called to the banquet of the Only-Begotten. For behold the pastor descends to his sheep; and if

177

he sees the ravening wolf, he will rout him from before his countenance like smoke before the wind. † But now I seal him, and protect him from all the power of demons in the name of the Father, Son, and Holy Spirit now and always and forever. Amen.[46]

In contrast with the Byzantine exorcism, the threats here are explicit; the devil is warned that he will have a severe time of it if he does not depart before God's sacramental coming. We could perhaps conclude from this adjuration that the formulator considered it impossible for any evil spirit to remain when baptism is actually being conferred. Certainly the devil is meant to reach this conclusion, though he is expected to stay in the vicinity a bit longer, at least long enough to hear himself renounced. In the blessing of the water that follows, as we have seen, there is, if not a firm belief, at least a lively fear that the spirits of evil are still within hearing distance. It would be easy, of course, to make these rituals look ridiculous by subjecting them to such realistic analysis, but we would be wrong to come to such a conclusion. We should acknowledge, rather, that the canons of dramatic convention are as important in assessing the true meaning of such services as are considerations of reality and realism.

After the candidate, facing east, is exorcized, he turns himself around and faces in the devil's direction and speaks for the first time. Like the priest who denounced Satan within him, he now denounces Satan in his own name by pronouncing the words of renunciation. He is given these words by the priest, and he repeats them three times. Or if he is an infant, his sponsor speaks for him while holding up his left hand (an adult candidate, of course, would keep his own hand raised as he spoke). The formula is: "We renounce you, Satan, and all your angels, and all your powers, and all your worldly phantasies, and all your impure and detestable doctrine, and, finally, all that comes from you."[47]

[46]Denzinger 339–340. Cf. the very similar formula of Vatican 313 (see Mouhanna 31–35), which, however, is not preceded by an insufflation. The insufflation is also missing from Paris 118 (Mouhanna 98). The verb for the operation is once again "seal" (*htam*): plate 21, Vatican 313 fol. 34v line 9. For the variants of Vatican 116, see Mouhanna 75–76, and for the additions of Stephen of Edhen, the Maronite patriarch in the last half of the seventeenth century, who was influenced by the Latin rite, see Denzinger 337 n. 1, 338 n. 1.

[47]Denzinger 340; the formula is missing in Assemani's text, and I follow Renaudot's translation. Mouhanna's interpretation is quite different (pp. 36–37): "Nous te renions, Satan, tous tes messagers, toutes tes armées, toute ta pompe mondaine, tout ton enseignement impur et abominable, et tout ce qui vient de toi."

The candidate then turns (or is turned) to the east, and this time his right hand is held up. The confession of allegiance and faith also uses direct address, unlike the early Western forms that we have studied, and is repeated three times: "We confess you, God the Father almighty, and your Son our Lord Jesus Christ, and your living, Holy Spirit, the Advocate [Paraclete], and all your angels, and all your virtues, and all the teaching of the holy, catholic, and apostolic Church, and all that comes from you. We believe, and we believe in Christ."

Thereupon, after the creed and further prayers are said, the priest and the deacon pray over the simple oil. In the deacon's prayer, which has been added to the older service, he asks that the oil serve as a shield against the fiery darts of the enemy. He is looking not primarily to the future, it seems, but more to the present, for he goes on to pray that it remove far away from the candidates all evil and unclean spirits and make them pure temples of the Holy Spirit. Therefore, like the older Maronite formula for the water, this prayer is apotropaic rather than exorcistic.[48]

After the signing (*rushma*) of the candidates' foreheads with the oil, the deacon, in a prayer added to the original service, sets the stage for the blessing of the water. He begins: "How terrible and tremendous is this hour in which the heavenly powers stand in silence upon the waters of baptism. A thousand thousand angels, and myriads of myriads of Seraphim hover with tremulous wing over the holy baptism, the new mother, the spiritual mother giving birth to spiritual children." As he goes on to describe the action of the angels and the Holy Spirit, he moves into the historical present and characterizes the baptism of Christ as taking place here and now.[49]

The blessing of the water follows. We have already studied the demonic aspects of the various versions of the service, but the whole ceremony is much more elaborate than could be gathered from what was said above (though the Maronite rite is simpler than most others). After a series of prayers and a ritual dialogue with the people, the priest seals the water three times with the sign of the cross and then burns more incense while reciting appropriate formulas. Further prayers on the positive aspects of the ceremony follow, and only then does the antidemonic insufflation occur, together with the exorcistic

[48]Denzinger 340–341; see Mouhanna 78–79 and plates 60–61. Mouhanna, however, makes the prayer exorcistic by using the verb *expulse*.
[49]Denzinger 342; Mouhanna 100.

and apotropaic formulas analyzed above. The priest then takes a horn full of myron and pours some of it into the water three times, in the form of a cross, and pronounces a blessing each time. The deacon puts periods to the first and second blessings with alleluias and after the final one bids a blessing of his own for the font, the priest, and the blessed people who receive baptism.

The priest and deacon then prepare to anoint the candidate with holy oil. They pray for all the faithful to be strengthened in their battle against Satan. The priest stands in the eastern part of the baptistery and faces the candidate for a second *rushma*. He anoints his head with the oil in the form of a cross and designates him as a lamb signed with the sign of the Trinity. Before the signing the priest prays with bowed head that the candidate be preserved from all evils in the flock of the Lord, and then, in a louder voice, says, "Thus, O Lord, bless him in your name, and by your cross protect him from the Evil One and all his powers." After the signing, the deacon anoints the candidate's whole body with oil and sings a hymn describing the Old Testament uses of holy oil.[50]

Then the priest lowers the candidate into the font (obviously it is usually an infant that is being spoken of in the rubrics). He stands in the east with the child facing him. Holding his right hand on the candidate's head, he draws water with his left hand first from the east side of the font and pours it over his head. He does the same with water taken from the west, north, and south of the font, and says: "I baptize you, N., a lamb in the flock of Christ, in the name of the Father, amen. And the Son, amen. And the Holy Spirit, forever, amen." He is then sealed with myron on the forehead as a verification of his reception of the grace of the Holy Spirit. The sweet odor of the myron, which is then applied to the neophyte's whole body, is symbolic of true faith. The new Christian is then dressed in white robes and his loins girt, and he becomes a partaker in the holy mysteries. The priest then dismisses the people, commending them to the Holy Trinity.[51] The drama of redemption and regeneration has come to an end once more.

[50]Denzinger 347–348. See Mouhanna 88 and plate 72 lines 1–2 for the *rushma* of Paris 116 fol. 30r. Assemani uses the verbs *ungat* and *obsignatur*.

[51]Denzinger 348–350. Assemani uses *sigillo obsignatur* for the final anointing, Mouhanna 105 *sceau* and *marqué*. In Paris 116 the verb in the rubric is *rsham* (fol. 32v line 10, plate 75), which Mouhanna simply translates *oint* (p. 90), but in the formula it is called a *tab'a* (fol. 33r line 2), rendered *sceau* (p. 90).

It is noteworthy that the chrismation after baptism has no apotropaic significance attached to it. It was rather the prebaptismal anointings that were given this meaning. In fact there was no postbaptismal anointing at all in Chrysostom's time, and the same is true of the original form of the earliest Maronite service (Vatican MS 313).[52] In this respect the ceremony corresponds to early Syrian practice. It should be mentioned, however, that in the Maronite ceremony for the removal of the baptismal cincture and robes seven days after baptism, there is a prayer to make the neophyte unassailable by the opposing spirits.[53]

Of the variations in the other versions of the Maronite tradition, I will mention only a prayer accompanying the ceremony of breathing upon the candidate that recalls St. Augustine's remarks on the exsufflation of infants: "With great fear inspired by the Lord and by prudence, I breathe against you, evil demons and impure spirits. I do not breathe against the image of God, nor against the creature formed by his hands, but I breathe against you, spirits of impure and unclean demons, so that you will flee before the great, fearful, wonderful, holy, strong, and mighty name of the Lord God, whose name is most powerful."[54]

Let us now review, much more briefly, the antidemonic aspects of the services used by the Antiochene Jacobites (Orthodox). I shall use as the basic text Assemani's first order (in Brock's numbering).[55] But first let me cite an opening prayer from the third order: it recounts the history of salvation, including the breaking of the enemy's yoke from the shoulders of mankind. Then God is asked to effect the complete deliverance of the catechumens there present from the slavery of the accuser and to make them formidable to demons and to all the power of the adversary.[56] The petition looks both to the past and to the

[52]Mouhanna 63–64 and plate 42. The myron ceremony has been added in a later hand.

[53]Denzinger 360.

[54]Paris MS 116, Mouhanna 75, Denzinger 353 (Renaudot). For "breathe," Mouhanna uses *insouffle*, while Renaudot uses *inspirat* and *exsufflo*. A longer version of the same prayer appears in Paris 119 (Mouhanna 145). In the exorcism of the candidates the identification of the evil spirit that troubled Saul as Lucifer in Renaudot's translation (Denzinger 354) is not borne out in Mouhanna's translation (p. 75 n. 17 no. 14).

[55]Denzinger 1.302–309, with references to the complete prayers that he gives in the third order, pp. 267–279, as numbered by Brock, "Studies" 18.

[56]Denzinger 1.269.

future. Perhaps the same can be said of the prayer, common to all the orders, which is said when incense is offered: God is first asked that there may depart from the lives of the candidates all the injurious devices of the enemy.[57]

After the prayer over the incense, there follows a prayer similar to that said in the Maronite service when the infant is signed at his first reception into the church. In the Jacobite rite, however, it precedes the first signing. Once again it is quite clearly the future that is being provided for: "Impress upon them the light of your countenance and carve in their hearts and thoughts the cross of your Christ, so that they may flee the vanity of the world and all the evil of the adversary and walk in your commandments."[58] At this point the first order of Severus calls for the priest to breathe upon the candidate's face.[59] (Lefevre's translation of the second order instead has the priest breathing three times into the water.)[60] The prayer continues: "Grant them, O Lord, your holy breath, which your only-begotten Son breathed into his disciples. Expel far from their minds all remnants of the cult of idols."[61] The reference to idolatry is an indication of the archaic or archaizing flavor of the prayer.

The candidates are next signed three times on the forehead, without oil. Their clothes are then removed, and as they face east the priest bows down and says the following prayer: "I call upon you, O Lord, . . . for the driving out of every evil spirit and the casting out of adverse and hidden operation, so that these souls may be pure to receive the indwelling of the Holy Spirit." He then turns to the west, while they are still facing east, and pronounces an adjuration while making a cross over their countenances at every invocation:

> We invoke you, Lord, our God, creator of all things visible and invisible; and laying our hand on this creature of yours, we sign him in your name, Father, Son, and Holy Spirit, and we rebuke in your most holy name every demon and evil and impure spirit, so that they may be far away and depart from your creature and image and from the work of your holy hands. † Hear us, O Lord, and upbraid them, and cleanse your servants from the working of the adversary. † But you listen, O perverse and rebellious one, who injure this creature of God. † I adjure

[57]Ibid. 270, 303.
[58]Ibid. 271; cf. n. 43 above.
[59]Ibid. 304; Khouri-Sarkis 165 is similar.
[60]Denzinger 1.312; see n. 39 above.
[61]Ibid. 271.

you, enemy of justice, and transgressor of divine and holy laws, by the glory of the supreme king, depart in fear and be subject to the terrible Lord, who by his command set up and established the land upon the waters and placed the sand as a boundary to the sea. † I adjure you by him who has all power in heaven and on earth, by him through whom all things were created and are conserved, by him through whom the heavens stay in place and the things upon the earth are made firm. † I adjure you by him who sent the legion of demons into the abyss by means of swine and drowned the heavy-hearted Pharaoh with his chariots and horsemen. † I adjure you by him who with divine power said to the deaf and dumb spirit, "Go out of this man and enter him no more." † Fear the terrible name of God, before whom the whole creation of angels and archangels trembles, in whose sight the whole ministering army stands in fear, at whom neither the seraphim nor the cherubim dare to look, whom the heavens fear and before whom the abysses tremble. † Fear the terrible name of God, who thrust the rebellious demon into the abyss in dark chains. † Fear the judgment to come; be terrified, and do not come to the creature of God, do not cleave to the creature of God; for it is not the dwelling of demons but the temple of God. For he has said, "I will dwell in them and walk in them and I will be their God and they will be my people" You however he put down deformed and empty, and an unclean spirit. † I adjure you by the holy and pure God, the Father, Son, and Holy Spirit; be far from the servants of God, and go away into trackless and waterless regions, because your place is there. Be uprooted and routed and depart, accursed one, from the creature of God, impure spirit, spirit of error, the food for fire. Make haste, do not resist, for God the Father, Son, and Holy Sprit will pluck you out by the roots, casting you out from every creature of his and throwing you into inextinguishable fire, while freeing this work of his hands until the day of redemption.[62]

We may note that though this prayer is obviously connected with the second Byzantine exorcism, the evil spirit addressed here is apparently not the devil himself, since it is presumably the devil who is thought to be chained in the abyss. The exorcism ends with a clear threat: if the spirit does not hasten to get out, God will pluck him out and cast him here and now into hell. In an order adapted for the baptism of girls (counted by Brock as Assemani's fifth order), there is an exorcism that differs to some extent from the one just cited, in that a series of adjurations is inserted in which the evil spirit is consistently

---

[62]Ibid. 271–272, 304. This exorcism is extremely abbreviated in the Tagrit service; see Qōzi 2.115–119.

addressed as "unclean demon" and is reminded of various acts of salvation performed by God, mostly from the Old Testament.[63]

The renunciation of Satan follows the exorcism in most of the Jacobite services, and it is indirect except in the Tagrit version. The candidate faces west while his sponsor holds his left hand and speaks three times the formula of renunciation: "I N. who am baptized renounce Satan and all his angels and all his works and all his army and all his cult and all his worldly error and everyone who agrees with and follows him."[64] After he aligns himself with Christ, all the participants enter the baptistery (the previous ceremonies have taken place in the church proper). The candidate is signed "with the oil of gladness against every operation of the adversary" so that he may be grafted onto the olive tree of the Church. Then follows the blessing of the water, which we discussed above. After the baptism, the candidates are sealed with myron "so that, being filled with every odor of spiritual sweetness, they may not be seized by adverse powers and may fear nothing from the principalities and powers of darkness."[65] In this tradition, therefore, the postbaptismal as well as the prebaptismal anointing has an apotropaic purpose.[66]

In addition to the Syrian Jacobite orders just described, there is a

[63]Denzinger 291.

[64]Ibid. 304. Another formula in Arabic is given, which has: "and all his soldiers and all his works and all his fear and all his worldly error and all who follow him and his filthy opinion." Assemani's translation of the fourth order yields: "and all his soldiers and all his work and all his deeds and all his power and all his worldly error and all who follow him and his filthy opinion" (Denzinger 283); and according to his version of the third order, a person renounces Satan "and all his works and all his army and all his service and all his pomp and all his worldly error and everyone that agrees with and follows him" (ibid. 273). To judge from the analysis of Khouri-Sarkis 168 n. 14, Assemani's *militiae* and *milites* seem to be renderings or expansions of the word for "service." The modern English translation, ed. Samuel 42, reads, "all his deeds, his services, his worship, his vain pomp, his worldly deceitfulness, and all his followers and adherents." The direct renunciation of the Tagrit ritual is as follows: "Je te renie, Satan, . . . [toi] et tous tes anges, et toutes tes armées, et tout ton culte, et toute ton erreur." The Arabic version is also given: "Je te renie, O Satan, . . . [toi] et tous tes anges, et toutes tes forces, et toute ta crainte, et toute ton erreur." See Qōzi 2.121. See n. 76 below for a rite with a different placement of the renunciation and confession.

[65]Denzinger 1.273–277; cf. 2.526–551 for the Jacobite service of consecration of the chrism, from a MS in the hand of the patriarch Michael (Michael I, d. 1199; or Michael II, d. 1319), in which most of the allusions to the devil concern the function of the chrism as a prophylactic; but it is also to serve as a means for the expulsion of evil spirits (541).

[66]The Jacobites also have an order for the removal of the crown and the cincture that were placed on the neophyte at baptism. He is warned as they are taken off to take care lest the adversary despoil him as he did Adam (ibid. 1.328).

shorter service that is also ascribed to Severus, in which the following brief prayer is said: "O God, the lover of men, expel from this soul, which has come to approach your holy baptism, all spirits of evil through the sign of the cross of your only-begotten Son. Do you, O Lord, rebuke all the evil spirits." A cross is breathed on the water: "May it expel from these waters and from these who are baptized in them every evil operation of the opposing power." The candidate is then anointed with oil of gladness "against every power of the accuser."[67]

Another short service, to be used in danger of death, is attributed to Philoxenus, who became metropolitan of Mabbug or Hierapolis in 485. It begins with the rubric: "In place of the renunciation of demons and confession of Christ and the adjuration and other ceremonies of this kind, the priest shall take holy oil and sign the forehead of him who is baptized and say, 'N. is signed as a spiritual lamb in the flock of Christ, in the name of the Father and the Son and the Holy Spirit forever. Amen.'"[68] By the time this order was written, therefore, the antidemonic ceremonies were not considered to be an essential preliminary but were simply gone through for form's sake or for the sake of the "spectacle." It is a confirmation, therefore, of the nonrealistic nature of the ceremonies. The kind of demonic control over the unbaptized that the prayers of the longer services seem to presuppose can hardly have been taken to be an actuality after infant baptism had become the normal rule, if indeed it was literally meant when the prayers were first composed or elaborated.

Finally, let us look at the Melchite tradition. Their service begins with a prayer that those who are prepared for baptism may have harmful influences and all adverse power removed far from their lives.[69] This petition resembles the opening prayer of the Jacobite service, of course, and the prayer that follows is also clearly a variant of the Jacobite prayer: "Lord God, Father almighty, I call upon your holy name through your only-begotten Son, our Lord Jesus Christ, for the expelling of all evil and unclean spirits and for the searching out of all adverse powers, so that these souls, having received the grace of the Spirit, may be pure and come to you."[70]

There follows a version of the Jacobite prayer of exorcism, with an

[67]Ibid. 1.316–317 (Brock's order no. 7, as listed on p. 369 of his 1970 article cited in n. 76 below).
[68]Ibid. 318.
[69]Ibid. 319. The Melchite order is attributed to Saint Basil.
[70]Ibid.

added ceremony in which the minister breathes upon the candidate in the form of a cross.[71] This recalls the Byzantine tradition, as does the prayer that comes next, in which a guardian angel is asked for the candidate:

> Do you even now, in saving this creation of yours from the servitude of the adversary, receive him into your kingdom; open the eyes of his mind, so that he may be illumined with the light of the gospel of your kingdom; grant an angel of light to be a companion to his life, so that he may free him from all harms to the soul, from evil incursions, from demons, from the noonday spirit of the devil, from phantasms and illusions. Drive away from him all spirits and the operation of error that hides and remains in his heart, the spirit of deception, the spirit of idolatry, avarice, and lying, and of all impurity that is accomplished at the bidding of the calumniator, and make them sheep in the flock of your Christ.[72]

There is an interesting form of the renunciation, which includes both direct and indirect formulas. The candidates first say three times: "We renounce you, Satan, and all your angels and all your works and all your cult and all your pomp and all your error in this world." Then the minister asks, "Have you renounced Satan?" They reply, "We have renounced Satan." This too is said three times. As in the Greek rite, the oil is breathed upon three times, and God is prayed to send the Holy Spirit upon it to make it a terrible defense against the working of all the opposing powers of the calumniator, and so on, as well as a means of cleansing away all the remnants of idolatry and every diabolic superstition.[73]

The water is also blessed by breathing three times into it in the form of a cross, and the prayer that follows is a version of that found in both the Greek and West Syrian orders.[74] The postbaptismal chrismation is accompanied by a short prayer in which protection from the adversary is sought.[75]

---

[71]Ibid. 320. The Assemani translation uses *exsufflare*, the word employed in the Western tradition, rather than *insufflare*, which would correspond to the Byzantine *emphusan*. For a similar rite added to a Maronite service, see n. 37 above.

[72]Ibid. 320–321.

[73]Ibid. 321–322.

[74]Ibid. 323–324. The last part of the prayer reads, in part: "Nor let there descend with those who are baptized the evil spirit of rebellion who blinds thoughts and disturbs minds."

[75]Ibid. 326.

These, then, are some of the ceremonies of initiation developed along the Constantinople-Antioch axis of the Byzantine Empire. Some of them, perhaps many of them, were already formulated and in use by the time of St. John Chrysostom at the turn of the fifth century. After a certain amount of regional differentiation and adaptation, they remained basically the same during the succeeding centuries.[76] The most notable linguistic and geographic extension of the rites in later times was their translation into Old Church Slavonic for the use of the new Christians to the north, when adult baptism necessarily came into use once more. But the basic libretto of the ceremonies continued unchanged. Any new life or freshness in their production would have to come from the spontaneous inventiveness of the celebrants. That there was such, on occasion, can hardly be doubted, for Eastern ecclesiastics have long had the reputation for being far more ready to improvise liturgical "business" than their more rubric-bound Latin brethren.

[76]For some more of the intervening variations, see the discussion of Sebastian Brock, "Studies." In "A New Syriac Baptismal *Ordo* Attributed to Timothy of Alexandria," *Le muséon* 83 (1970) 367–431, Brock edits and translates a ritual that goes back, he believes, to the end of the sixth century, the time in which the basic forms of the Maronite, Jacobite, and Melchite orders are thought to have evolved. But unlike them, it did not receive a wide or permanent following. The order shares many features of the rituals we have described above, but it has several peculiarities, the most interesting of which is that it places the renunciation of Satan and confession of Christ *before* the exorcism of the candidates. The similar sequence in the commentary mentioned above, Chap. 9 n. 39, may be coincidental. The formula of renunciation is direct and specifies all Satan's angels, powers, works, service, worship, *phantasia* (which Brock takes as equivalent to pomp), and festivals (372–373). William F. Macomber, "A Theory on the Origins of the Syrian, Maronite, and Chaldean Rites," *Orientalia christiana periodica* 39 (1973) 235–242, esp. 240–241, takes the order and the manuscript in which it is found as evidence that "the Monophysites do not seem to have attained full liturgical uniformity for many centuries." Brock describes yet another ritual in "A Remarkable Syriac Baptismal *Ordo* (B.M. Add. 14518)," *Parole de l'orient* 2 (1971) 365–378, edited ibid. 8 (1977–1978) 311–346 (see n. 33 above). It has no renunciation at all, and it markedly reduces the number of exorcisms. However, we see that while the candidates are being exorcized they are looking to the east, but in the following rubric the priest is instructed to turn them to the east to confess Christ (translation, pp. 323–324). This anomaly may well indicate that an intervening ritual of renunciation, in which the baptizands faced west, was mistakenly omitted.

II /

Armenia and Egypt

As a coda to our examination of the initiation services of the Byzantine Rite and its near variants, let us look at some rituals from
areas that constitute a kind of ecclesiastical outback, where because of
various internal and external pressures the local churches developed
forms or syntheses peculiar to themselves. We have already dealt
with one such region when describing the reforms made in the
Nestorian Church of East Syria and Persia. Armenia provides another example.

According to a twelfth-century source, the Armenian baptismal
service was basically the work of John Mandakuni, who died sometime after the year 480, and this attribution has been accepted as
accurate by some authorities.[1] Mandakuni belonged to the group of
"holy translators" of the fifth century who were trained principally at
Constantinople and Edessa and who translated Greek and Syriac
writings into Armenian. If Mandakuni was responsible for the service, he would doubtless have been familiar with two prebaptismal
traditions: (1) the native Syrian practice of having no exorcistic ceremonies but only an apotropaic anointing before baptism; (2) the typically Western form of exorcism practiced at Constantinople and
Antioch (the forensic drama of Mopsuestia and Edessa, which Ishoyabh seems to have inherited, would not yet have been developed).
Mandakuni was apparently working from the second tradition, for

---

[1]Diettrich, *Nestorianische Taufliturgie* xxv n. 1; cf. Denzinger, *Ritus Orientalium*
1.383.

his ritual presupposes on the literal level that the candidates are corporeally possessed by evil spirits before baptism.

The most important manuscript witnesses to the early Armenian service date from the tenth or possibly even the ninth century. F. C. Conybeare observes that this tradition omits various central portions of the baptismal rite, the result, he believes, of adapting the service to infant baptism.[2] Later, however, the use of adult stand-ins, that is, sponsors, was introduced, and the ceremonies that had been omitted were restored, as appears from more recent manuscripts. But this sequence of events does not adequately explain many of the changes, and it is likely that at least some of the additions were not original to the rite but were inserted under the influence of other rites. A clear example of this process can be seen in another part of the liturgy: the Armenians adopted the Latin minor order of exorcist under pressure from the crusaders.[3]

Like the Greek and West Syrian Churches, the Armenians had an order for the blessing of an eight-day-old child, in which it was prayed that the light of Christ might be a sign in the infant's heart and thoughts "unto the renunciation of the vanities of the world and of all thoughts of the adversary." There was also a ceremony for bringing the child to church on the fortieth day "for the laying on of hands of Christianity," so that "he may become strong and secure against the enemy's inward working" or "the enemy's craftiness."[4]

The baptismal service itself begins with a prayer said at the door of the church, which contains a similar petition: "Cleanse his mind and conscience from all wiles of the adversary." Then follows a short exorcism, which, like the third Byzantine exorcism, is addressed not to the evil spirits but to God:

> Let him be made a partaker in that awful name of thine, which has routed and dispelled the deceit of demons and the folly of idolatry, and

[2]Conybeare, *Rituale Armenorum* ix–xiii. See Winkler, *Armenische Initiationsrituale* 396–397: by the beginning of the eighth century, the renunciation, confession of faith, and prebaptismal anointing were no longer practiced (they were ordered to be reinstated in A.D. 718).

[3]See Denzinger 2.1, 280–281. The Armenians had dealings with the crusaders in the Kingdom of Lesser Armenia, which was founded in Cilicia (north of Antioch) in the year 1080.

[4]Conybeare 86–87. Conybeare xii says that both of these rites are in the purest idiom of the fifth century and were intentionally omitted from the manuscript because they proved that infants were not baptized when they were in use.

has brought to nought all the snares of Satan. Look, O Lord, in thy mercy on this man; remove and set afar from him, by the all-conquering invocation over him by thy name, the thoughts, words, and deeds of lurking unclean spirits, and all the wicked devices whereby evil demons are wont to deceive and undo mankind, to the end that, being affrighted at thy conquering name, they may be troubled and tortured with unseen torments, driven afar from him by adjurations, and may not again return into him.[5]

The last part of this petition shows, as mentioned above, that the evil spirits are envisaged as actually dwelling within the unbaptized person. The reference to "adjurations" is an indication that the rite originally contained formulas addressed to the spirits, which were supposed to operate in the way described by Cyprian in treating of the violently possessed; the demons were tormented by the words of exorcism themselves. We may also recall the "fiery sayings" that made up the exorcisms in Nicetas's account.[6]

The candidate is then turned to the west, and the following formula is repeated three times: "We renounce thee, Satan, and all thy deceitfulness and thy wiles and thy service and thy paths and thine angels." This direct repudiation is followed by an indirect one, as in the Melchite order of St. Basil, which we studied in the previous chapter. The priest asks three times, "Dost thou renounce?" and each time the candidate replies, "I renounce."[7]

A later text[8] has a more elaborate ceremony, one that resembles the modern Byzantine service: "The priest orders the catechumen to turn to the west and to stretch his hand straight out in the same direction, as if thrusting backwards the gloomy darkness. And he bids him spit three times on Satan, that is to deny him; and he adjures him thrice, saying: 'Dost thou renounce Satan and all his deceitfulness and his wiles and his paths and his angels?' Each time the catechumen shall say: 'I renounce,' and withal spits upon Satan."[9]

[5]Ibid. 90–91. For the Armenian text and a German translation, see Winkler, *Arm. Init.* 190–195. For Conybeare's term "devils" I have substituted "demons."

[6]See Chap. 7 at nn. 13 and 41.

[7]Conybeare 92; Winkler, *Arm. Init.* 196–197.

[8]Conybeare's MS B, A.D. 1300 or earlier.

[9]Conybeare 91 n. a. Other MSS as well as the modern Uniate euchologium have other questions that Conybeare believes to be primitive. One response reads: "With faith I ask to be baptized, and on this day to be purified from sin, to be delivered from demons, and to serve God" (105).

In these formulas there is no reference to the world as there was in most of the other rites that I examined in Chapter 10, but, as we have just seen, the prayer over the eight-day-old child makes such a reference when speaking of renunciation. Similarly, in an Armenian rite of penance, the penitents are asked, "Do ye renounce Satan and all his deceit and his service and his paths and his angels?" and they respond three times, "We renounce Satan and the vain and false world and its distractions."[10]

In the prayer over the oil it is asked that the anointing of the candidate may be "unto holiness of spiritual wisdom, that he may manfully fight and triumph over the adversary."[11] When the minister comes to pray over the water, he asks simply that the Holy Spirit cleanse it as Jesus cleansed the Jordan by descending into it. But in the thirteenth-century manuscript just cited as well as in several other manuscripts a long blessing of the water has been inserted that recalls that of the Greek and West Syrian liturgies, with its allusion to the dragon's bruised head. The prayer asks that all the principalities of Satan may tremble and flee from the water along with all their evil influence, or, in an alternative reading, that "the all-filthy Satan may tremble and flee therefrom and be driven with his evil guile out of this creature." Furthermore it is sought from Christ that "by the fear and might of thy holy cross the enemy may be routed and tormented, and being driven away and overthrown may be brought to nought and undone and weakened by thy victorious name, that there may lurk ambushed in the water no demon of darkness."[12]

In the postbaptismal anointing, there are prayers for the various parts of the body; the apotropaic motif of a shield against the devil

---

[10]Conybeare 193–194.

[11]Ibid. 93; Winkler, *Arm. Init.* 200–201. Winkler 405 distinguishes between the initiation-motif (royal or priestly anointing) in this formula and the antidemonic element that I have cited, which she thinks was added later. But she analyzes it as cathartic (purifying) rather than as apotropaic (protective). Regarded as cathartic it would be out of place; regarded as apotropaic, it fits the idea of a mark of initiation: henceforth the signed candidate will be guarded against malign forces. I should note that the ritual does not in fact call for a prebaptismal anointing, though the prayer of blessing refers to such an anointing (see Winkler 394–395).

[12]Conybeare 95 (Winkler, *Arm. Init.* 210–211); Conybeare 101–102. The Assemani text (Denzinger 1.394) goes on to ask that the dark demon might not descend into the water with the baptizand. Bartsch 39–40 seems unfamiliar with Conybeare's work and attempts to reconstruct a direct adjuration of the demon from the Assemani text in order to show how exorcistic elements were made use of in the prayer.

appears, surprisingly, only when the backbone is anointed: "May this seal which is in the name of Christ be for thee a shield and buckler, whereby thou mayst be able to quench all the fiery darts of the Evil One." A similar motif occurs later, however, when the newly baptized person is reclothed. The minister speaks of the helmet of salvation and crown of grace that he has received and characterizes them as "armor without flaw against the adversary." After eight days, the priest lifts off the crown and prays: "Set them afar from the error of the enemy and from his snares, and from the works of iniquity. . . . Send thy angel of peace that he may come and watch over him."[13]

It is clear that this service for all its eclecticism has preserved and later amplified the three movements of the basic antidemonic *agon,* especially as they are set forth in the East's most influential prototype, the Byzantine liturgy.

Let us turn now once more to Egypt, that ancient breeding ground of demons and antidotes against demons. We recall that in the orthodox services of the fourth and fifth centuries, there was great stress upon the use of oil as an aid to prebaptismal exorcism, not only in the versions of the *Apostolic Tradition* of Hippolytus, but also in the rites that showed recognizable dependence upon Hippolytus. A rite that comes from a later time, seemingly the sixth century, continues this tradition. The service in question is contained in the Arabic translation of the *Testament of Our Lord.* After a supplication on behalf of the catechumens in which it is recounted that Christ rescued men from the servitude of Satan, there is a prayer over the oil asking God to "send on this oil your sacred power, and let it be oil that may put to flight all the operations of the adversary and destroy all evil and all injustice." The minister then anoints the candidates' foreheads, eyes, ears, hearts, and hands, saying, "Oil putting to flight all the operations of the adversary, and planting those who are anointed with it in the sacred universal Church."[14]

After the anointing the minister asks God to drive from the baptizands "all the works of error, all unbelief, all worship of idols, all magic, all blasphemy, all satanic weapons," and to protect them from every evil. Then each candidate, or his sponsor, if he is young, faces

---

[13]Conybeare 98, 99, 101; Winkler, *Arm. Init.* 224–225, 226–227, 232–233.

[14]Anton Baumstark, "Eine ägyptische Mess- und Taufliturgie vermutlich des 6. Jahrhunderts," *Oriens christianus* 1 (1909) 1–45, esp. 35.

west and raises his right hand and says, "I renounce you, Satan, and all your angels."[15] This ceremony follows the pattern of the *Canons of Hippolytus* in the fourth century, with its direct address made to the devil while facing west. Cyril of Alexandria in the fifth century knew of a similar practice. "We admonish," he says, "those who have entered to the saving baptism and then turned to the west to cry out: 'I renounce you, Satan, and all your works and all your angels and all your pomp and all your service.'"[16] Cyril has extended the formula of renunciation to include all the elements of the renunciation that were used in fifth-century Constantinople, as witnessed by Proclus.

To continue with the Arabic *Testament:* the priest next prays that God will not destroy them but will guard them from all satanic instigations, and he seeks the grace of the Spirit to give the water and ointment power to cleanse away sin and to put to flight "all works of the adversary." In the postbaptismal sealing with chrism, there is no reference to the devil. In the final prayer of thanksgiving it is simply said that God has nullified in them all the powers of error, injustice, and unbelief.[17]

Another Egyptian baptismal liturgy can be found in the *Canons of St. Basil,* a compilation of ecclesiastical regulations that goes back at least to the period before the Arabic conquest of Egypt in the seventh century.[18] A week of fasting is required before baptism, and then, on Saturday morning at cockcrow, the water is blessed. In the course of the prayer that is said over the water, it is stated that God has crushed the devil under the candidates' feet and has enabled them to be reborn.[19]

The formula recited over the oil is called an exorcism, but it is really a prayer for exorcistic and apotropaic power. God is addressed as the one who has nullified idolatry and all the power of the devil, and he is asked to bring it about that the oil will frighten away all evil spirits from those who are anointed with it and dispel the influences they have upon body and spirit. It is to counteract all the opposition of the devil, thereby allowing God to be served without hindrance. The prayer over the chrism or oil of thanksgiving follows, and it has

---

[15]Ibid. 37.
[16]Cyril of Alexandria, *Explanatio in Ps.* 44.11 (PG 69.1044).
[17]Baumstark 39, 41, 45.
[18]Ed. Wilhelm Riedel, in *Die Kirchenrechtsquellen des Patriarchats Alexandrien* (Leipzig 1900) 232–283.
[19]*Can. Bas.* 101–102 (Riedel 278–279).

a similar purpose: to make the oil a whip with which to drive off Satan.[20]

Then an exorcism properly so called is recited over the candidate himself:

> In the name of the Lord we exorcize every unclean spirit in every deed and every *phantasia,* every evanescent being and vain power and every power that belongs to the slanderer. We exorcize you by the greatest name, which is above all names, more exalted than all captains, powers, and lords, to which the armies of the angels and the leaders of the angels, the cherubim and seraphim, are subject, before whom the whole creation bows down in adoration, and whose commands no one can withstand or oppose. We exorcize you that you flee away from the one who is anointed with this oil and washed in this water so that he may serve the Lord alone all his days, for to him belong glory and power forever and ever. Amen.

Thereupon the candidate faces west and renounces the devil in the following words: "I reject you, devil, I reject your *phantasia,* I reject all your organs, I reject all your satanic service,[21] I reject all your deeds, I reject all magic, I reject all your satanic power that prevails amidst error." He is then anointed with oil of exorcism, after which he makes his confession of faith. Both kinds of oil are poured into the water before he is baptized. After the final anointing after baptism, the bishop prays God to deliver the newly baptized from the evils and snares of their enemy.[22]

The demonology of these two services is complete but still rather restrained, in much the same mode as the earlier rituals. The ceremonies, however, developed later in Egypt by the Coptic Jacobites rival those of the Syrian Jacobites in luxuriance and imaginative detail. But if the expansive impulse of the Egyptian liturgists can be attributed to their brethren to the north, the inspiration for the content of the new formulas came just as often from earlier native tradition as from imperial precedents.

Denzinger published three versions of the Coptic rite, namely (1) that of the manuscript of Raphael Tuki, (2) the text edited by Renaudot, and (3) the Ethiopic version edited and translated by Petrus

[20]Ibid. 103–104 (279–280).
[21]Riedel interprets this word (in German, *Dienerschaft*) as corresponding to "pomp" in the Greek.
[22]Ibid. 105–106 (280–282).

Aethiops (Tesfa Sion).[23] The oldest text is that of Renaudot,[24] and we shall follow it while noting the more important variants from the other versions. The Arabic rubrics in the Tuki service were added in the edition of the rite made by the patriarch Gabriel in 1411.[25]

We find a significant difference early in the service, in the prayer over the oil of the catechumens; the priest prays, according to the Renaudot text, that it might be efficacious for driving away demons. The Ethiopic recension is similar, but Tuki's version of the Coptic reads, "that it might be free from demons" and their magic and incantations and from all idolatry.[26] We recall that among the versions of the *Apostolic Tradition* the Ethiopic rather than the Coptic text suggested that evil spirits were actually present in the oil and had to be removed. Another prayer asks that the oil serve "to destroy every work of the adversary—every witchcraft, incantation, and idolatry— and turn back every evil work."

The infants to be baptized are then given to the priest, who carefully examines each of them to see if they are wearing rings, earrings, or other jewelry and sees to it that all such ornaments are removed. He then makes a sign of the cross over the oil of catechumens and

---

[23]Denzinger, *Ritus Orientalium* 1.191–233. He gives the Tuki version complete (191–214) and cites formulaic variants from the other two versions in footnotes. The Ethiopian rite is also in PL 138.927–950, and the Ethiopic text itself has been given a modern edition by S. Grebaut, "Ordre du baptême et de la confirmation dans l'église éthiopienne," *Revue de l'orient chrétien* 26 (1927–1928) 105–189, but it is accompanied by the old Latin translation of Tesfa Sion. An older and more authentic (but seemingly incomplete) version of the Ethiopian rites was published by Ernst Trumpp, *Das Taufbuch der äthiopische Kirche*, Abhandlungen der philosophisch-philologischen Klasse der Königlich Bayerischen Akademie der Wissenschaften 14 (Munich 1878) 147–183; cf. Puniet, "Baptême" 257. This text lacks most of the ceremonies and prayers of the anointing before baptism and the blessing of the water. The Tesfa Sion version begins with the blessing of a mother, in which both the mother and her newborn child are signed on the forehead with holy ointment; and then the priest imposes his hands and prays that it may be a crown of justice that will not be won away by the devil (Denzinger 222).

[24]Denzinger 214–221; an English translation from MSS of similar antiquity has been made by B. T. A. Evetts, *The Rites of the Coptic Church: The Order of Baptism and the Order of Matrimony* (London 1888) 17–43; see Puniet, "Baptême" 257.

[25]Puniet, "Baptême" 257. A synopsis and partial translation of the present-day ritual, based on the Cairo 1896 edition, is given by O. H. E. Khs-Burmester, *The Egyptian or Coptic Church* (Cairo 1967) 111–126; see also Burmester's "The Baptismal Rite of the Coptic Church (A Critical Study)," *Bulletin de la Société d'Archéologie Copte* 11 (1945) 27–86.

[26]Denzinger 194, cf. Trumpp 170. The modern ritual agrees with Renaudot here, as in most other cases. See Burmester, *Egyptian Church* 115; "Baptismal Rite" 62.

signs them with the oil on the forehead and breast, over the heart, saying to each, "I anoint you, N., with the oil of catechesis, of the holy, one and only, catholic, and apostolic Church of God. Amen." Then he signs the palms and backs of their hands, saying: "May this oil overcome all the assaults of the adversary."[27] It is not clear to me whether some sort of agonistic contest is behind the latter part of this ceremony. In the West, we saw, the oiling of the neophyte's body was sometimes taken as a preparation for wrestling with the devil. But oily hands would appear to be more of a hindrance than a help, both in wrestling and in boxing.[28]

In the course of the succeeding petitions, which qualify as exorcisms, God is asked to "drive away all powers, all opposing and wicked spirits," and to keep them restrained. "O God of truth, scrutinize the hidden places of their hearts . . . and do not permit an evil spirit to hide in them, but grant them cleanness and salvation, give them health, regenerate them by the laver of regeneration and by the remission of sins, make them a temple for your Holy Spirit. . . . And do not permit an unclean or wicked spirit to hide in them, lest from then on they be carnal members in the thoughts and affections of their mind."[29] (Literally, of course, this prayer suggests that the candidates could remain possessed by evil spirits during and after baptism. But we must be cautious about literal interpretations.)

The priest then places his hand on the candidate and says: "In the name of the only-begotten Son Jesus Christ, I cleanse and prepare this body. In the name of the only-begotten Son Jesus Christ, may it be liberated from all demons. May all darkness flee from this body and every thought of infidelity and unbelief flee from this soul. In the name of the only-begotten Son Jesus Christ, may he be cleansed and freed from all demons forever. Amen." He then orders them turned to the west and gives them the words of renunciation, which are addressed directly to the devil: "I renounce you, Satan, and all your works and your evil angels and all your exceedingly evil demons[30]

---

[27]Denzinger 195, 215; Cf. Burmester, *Egyptian Church* 115–116. The Tuki and Ethiopian anointings are similar but more elaborate.

[28]Fisticuffs is the basic metaphor behind *oppugnationes,* the word that Renaudot used to speak of the attacks of the devil (Burmester translates "opposition"). Cf. Tuki's formula: "May this oil destroy all the power [*vis*] of the adversary"; and Tesfa Sion's: "May this oil destroy every work [*opus*] of the opposing enemy."

[29]Denzinger 196–197.

[30]The Tuki MS has, instead of angels and demons: "all your wicked demons and your evil ministers"; and as in Burmester, "Baptismal Rite" 65, the works are called "unclean."

and all your power and filthy service and all your malignant deceits and honor[31] and all your army and all your might and all the rest of your impieties."[32] Then he says three times, "I renounce you." In the Tuki version there follows an Arabic rubric, according to which the priest breathes three times in the candidate's face and says, "Go out, unclean spirit."[33] This interpolated exorcistic action is performed after the renunciation, as if the devil who was being renounced was still within the candidate. We recall that similar kinds of belated exorcisms were found in the best redactions that we possess of the *Apostolic Tradition* of Hippolytus, most of which are Egyptian.

After the confession of faith the priest asks, among other things, that God drive from the candidates all magic and every incantation and every work of Satan.[34] Each candidate is then anointed in seven places on his body with the oil of catechumens. The accompanying prayer reads: "I anoint you with the oil of gladness, to purify you from all the work of the enemy, by grafting you onto the fruitful olive tree of the holy, catholic, and apostolic Church of God. Amen." The Tuki version, however, followed by the modern ritual, seems to interpret the anointing as a prophylactic for the immediate present or future, for it reads: "as a defense against all the works of the evil adversary, so that you may be grafted," and so forth.

The priest goes on to pray for the expulsion of all opposing and rebellious powers, and asks God to examine the candidate's heart to detect any wickedness of Satan that might be hiding in it, and if there be any, to pluck it out and remove it from the soul and body of his faithful servant, and to put on him the garment of salvation, the impregnable armor of faith that cannot be overcome (Tuki adds, "by our adversary"). As in the Byzantine and Melchite liturgies, angelic help is sought for the candidate:

[31]Tuki: "enticements"; Burmester: "error."

[32]Denzinger 198. The Ethiopic formula reads, according to Trumpp's version: "I renounce you, Satan, and all your work and your demons and all your army and all your angels and your whole flock and all your princes and all your perversity" (175), and according to the Tesfa Sion text: "I renounce you, Satan, and all your unclean works, all your evil ministers and incantations and all your power, all your princes, all your evil and dark frauds and adulations and enticements and all your jurisdiction and infidelity" (Denzinger 223). Denzinger cites a formula from the rite mentioned by Ebnassal that reads: "I renounce you, Satan, and all your works, all your armies, your ministers, all that belongs to you, and all your impiety" (198 n.). He also prints a short rite in private use among the Copts, in which the formula of renunciation is: "I renounce you, Satan, and all your error and snares" (234).

[33]Ibid. 198, as in Burmester; see Puniet, "Baptême" 257, 266.

[34]Denzinger 199; Burmester, "Baptismal Rite" 68.

Do you, O Lord, save and deliver this creature of yours from the servitude of the enemy. Receive him into your kingdom, open the eyes of his heart with the light of the knowledge of the Gospel of your kingdom. Let the angels of light guard his life, so that he may be freed from all evils of the adversary and from every manifest encounter of the wicked Satan[35] and from the arrow flying by day and from the business walking in darkness, from the phantasms of the night; take away and keep far from him every unclean spirit, every evil spirit that disturbs his heart, spirit of error and of all wickedness, spirit of love of silver and of idolatry, spirit of lying, and every filthiness that is perpetrated under Satan's direction. Make him a sheep of the holy flock of your Christ.[36]

The consecration of the baptismal water is basically the one common to all of the modern Eastern rites, except the Nestorian. Some Egyptian peculiarities, however, are worth noting. After an infusion of oil, God is asked to strengthen the candidates, "so that all adverse power may be eliminated by this water and by this oil. And keep away all wicked spirits from them. Drive away all magic, sorcery, and all idolatry and every incantation."[37]

The priest then breathes three times in the form of a cross into the water and says a version of the familiar Epiphany prayer over the water. At one point there is the following petition: "Grant that there not remain in the [water] or descend into it, with him who is baptized in it,[38] a wicked spirit, unclean spirit, spirit of the day, spirit of noon, spirit of evening, spirit of night, or spirit of the air, of hell, or of those that are under the earth,[39] but rebuke them with your great power and let them be crushed before the sign of your cross and by your holy name, which we call upon, most glorious and terrible to our adversaries."[40] In the Ethiopic version of the blessing of the water,[41] the priest first asks that everything working evil against his creatures may flee from the water. After the deacon tells everyone to look to

[35]Tuki: "From the noonday demon," a reading that seems more authentic, since the prayer at this point is drawing on Psalm 90.5–6. It is also the reading of a Byzantine formula in Goar, reproduced by Burmester, "Baptismal Rite" 30–31.

[36]Denzinger 200, 216.

[37]Ibid. 201–204, cf. 217–218; Burmester, *Egyptian Church* 119–120.

[38]Tuki: "or descend into it with the baptizand." So Burmester, "Baptismal Rite" 41, 74.

[39]After "spirit of the air" the Tuki text has instead "nor spirit of disturbance nor a specter or spirit of a demon of hell, that dwells under the earth." Burmester: "or any spirit of the deep, or any diabolical spirit of those which are beneath the earth."

[40]Denzinger 204–206.

[41]Denzinger 226–230; Grebaut 177–183; Scheidt 35–51; lacking in Trumpp (cf. 176–177).

the east, the priest continues: "And let there be scattered before the sign of the cross all the powers of those that oppose us, and flee from it all the demons that are in water and on land, who are not seen. Nor let there hide in this water dark pride, nor let a wicked spirit descend with those who are baptized, who would darken their mind and disturb their heart." He goes on to pray that they may expel the old man and put on the new, and then he recounts that God established the sea and broke the heads of the dragon on the water and that the waters in seeing God were afraid. Finally he prays:

> Grant to the [water] that if any wicked spirit is hiding outside of it he may not return any more to those who are baptized. Amen. Neither the spirit of the day. Amen. Nor the spirit of noon. Amen. Nor the spirit of evening. Amen. Nor the spirit of night. Amen. Nor the spirit of the air. Amen. Nor the spirit of pride, pride that is under the earth. Amen. But keep away all wicked spirits with your power and goodness, and may they be broken before the cross of your Son. Amen. In your holy name, which we beseech, which is full of glory and terrible against what opposes us, that everyone who is baptized in it may drive out of himself the old man, which is defiled by the pleasure of error, and put on the new man, which is made new in the likeness of his creator.

The demons assigned to the different parts of the day in this prayer were inspired by the example of the noonday demon in Psalm 90. The spirit of the air could have been a reflection of Saint Paul's references to the principalities and powers, and the spirits of the earth and water an extension along the same line of thought. It is difficult to know whether this liturgical tradition reflects established notions of demonology, such as those that would be expounded by Michael Psellus at Constantinople in the eleventh century. Most probably the various spirits are largely rhetorical creations designed to fill out the lavish prayers that were required in these liturgies but based upon the real belief that evil spirits can be present in any place at any time. We recall that in the first exorcism in the Byzantine liturgy the devil was told not to return to the candidates at night or during the day or at noon. The conferral of baptism itself in the present-day Egyptian rite is accompanied by a breathing upon the face of the candidate at each of the three immersions.[42] But the devil is out of sight and mind at this point, and the ceremony no doubt symbolizes the bestowal of the Holy Spirit.

[42]Denzinger 208; Burmester, *Egyptian Church* 122; "Baptismal Rite" 75; cf. Puniet, "Baptême" 268.

At the postbaptismal chrismation there is nothing specifically anti-demonic in evidence, but in the rite for consecrating the oil of catechumens and the chrism there are a number of petitions to make these unguents effective protection against the evil spirits.[43] A final prayer for the neophytes on the octave of the baptism goes back over ground that has already been covered. God is asked to cleanse them and bless and renew them through his grace and through baptism. Further on, it is said that he has already cleansed them from all spot of body and soul. The prayer continues: "Order them to be defended up to the end by the good angels. . . . Take from their hearts the spirit of disturbance and the spirit of error, so that their hearts may be illumined by the light of your greatness."[44] There seems then still to be a worry about the dwelling of evil spirits within the soul even after all the ceremonies of initiation have been completed. At the moment of baptism, however, as we saw above, there is no hint or suspicion that any demonic influence is still present in the candidate. The exorcisms and renunciations, in other words, were considered completely effective, insofar as the notion of demonic domination was taken realistically rather than symbolically in the first place.

All of the Eastern rites, with the exception of the Nestorian, were caught in a movement aimed at expanding liturgical services to the greatest possible extent in order to add to their solemnity and impressiveness. The Nestorian reform moved in the opposite direction, towards rationality and economy at the expense of obsolete forms and histrionic splendor. The demonological elements were inevitably reduced by this reform; and they were just as inevitably extended in the other rites—to such a degree, as we have seen, the language often outran belief, at least official belief. But after the burst of creative energy in the liturgy came to an end, the forms that resulted remained unchanged through centuries of prescribed repetition until the present day.[45]

---

[43]Denzinger 252, 254, 256, 258, 260, 264.

[44]Ibid. 214.

[45]The short Tagrit service attributed to Barhebraeus is an exception; see Chap. 10 nn. 41, 62.

12 /

The Roman-Frankish Liturgy

In the West, the Roman liturgy must of course occupy the center of our attention, for the forms of worship adopted at Rome eventually came to dominate Europe. Despite this later prominence, however, it is not always easy to determine the precise nature of the Roman ceremonies during the first Christian millennium. For just as the *Apostolic Tradition* of Hippolytus survives only in later adaptations, so too our knowledge of the subsequent Roman liturgy, especially the Gelasian and Gregorian traditions, largely depends upon Frankish manuscripts of the eighth century and later, in which there is certainly some admixture of elements alien to native Roman practices. The liturgy that was reestablished in Rome in the tenth century was a mixed form of this kind.

In the seventh chapter, we studied the baptismal services at Rome as they were described by John the Deacon about the year 500. We recall that in his day there were three preparatory meetings, called scrutinies, held during Lent before the actual ceremony of baptism took place. A hundred years later, the number of scrutinies had increased to seven, as witnessed by *Ordo romanus XI*,[1] which dates from the end of the sixth or beginning of the seventh century. This order made use of the primitive Gelasian liturgy, but the earliest form that we possess of the Gelasian sacramentary, in an eighth-century Frankish manuscript,[2] has only an interpolated scrutinal liturgy; it con-

---

[1]See Andrieu 2.384, 388.
[2]Here designated as Gel; bibliographic details appear in the Abbreviations.

forms to that of *Ordo XI,* except that it is presented as one scrutiny instead of seven.[3]

It is basically the service of *Ordo XI* that has come down to us in the liturgy of the Latin rite in the modern *Rituale romanum.* It was hardly affected by the Gregorian liturgy,[4] and we need not enter into the complicated questions of the original relationships between the Gregorian and Gelasian liturgies (and that of *Ordo XI*) and of their further interaction in Frankish territories. We will study the most important of the resulting amalgamations (that, namely, of *Ordo romanus L*), which was brought to Rome in the tenth century and was subsequently promulgated throughout the whole of Western Christendom.[5]

Ordo XI presents a series of cumulative initiation ceremonies that rival those of the Eastern rites in elaborateness and dramatic invention. Furthermore, these ceremonies were integrated into the larger "drama" of the Easter liturgy, and of the weeks leading up to it, more fully in the West than in the East. O. B. Hardison has analyzed some of the outstanding features of this dramatic ritual, and I refer the reader to his work for the context into which the catechumenal and baptismal rituals fit.[6] Hardison sees the Lenten agon,

[3]Andrieu 2.396–399.

[4]The citations of this liturgy (Greg) will refer to the paragraph numbers of the *Hadrianum* (i.e., the liturgical book sent by Pope Adrian to Charlemagne). See Abbreviations. For recent conclusions on the development of the Gregorian sacramentary, see Jean Deshusses, ed., *Le sacramentaire grégorien,* 3 vols., Spicilegium friburgense 16, 24, 28 (Fribourg 1971–1982) 3.60–63, 78–92, and Antoine Chavasse, "L'organisation générale des sacramentaires dits grégoriens," *Revue des sciences religieuses* 56 (1982) 179–200, 253–273; 57 (1983) 50–56. For sacramentaries in general, see Jean Deshusses, "Les sacramentaires: Etat actuel de la recherche," *ALW* 24 (1982) 19–46.

[5]Cf. Andrieu 5.72.

[6]Hardison, *Christian Rite and Christian Drama,* essay 1: "The Mass as Sacred Drama" (35ff.); essay 2: "The Lenten Agon: From Septuagesima to Good Friday" (80ff.); essay 3: "*Christus Victor:* From Holy Saturday to Low Sunday" (139ff.). See also Lukken 211–214. As I mentioned in the Preface (n. 1), in referring to the article by Jerome Taylor, Hardison uses the term "drama" rather loosely in applying it to the liturgy, though we may acknowledge that it has some dramatic aspects. Hardison is not completely successful in his attempt to recreate a standard liturgy of the ninth-century Frankish Empire. To take one example, the *Liber sacramentorum* in PL 78 upon which he relies (see p. 85 n. 3) is not a ninth-century but a tenth-century work, the *Corbie Sacramentary,* a much-supplemented *Hadrianum* that differs greatly from Benedict of Aniane's prototype (ca. 800); see n. 11 below, and see Andrieu 2.xxxviiiff. The *Liber responsalis* on which Hardison draws is indeed from the ninth century, being part of the *Antiphonary of Compiègne.* But he sometimes prefers to follow later orders: for

that is, the "dramatic conflict between Christ and Satan," as beginning on Septuagesima Sunday (in the earlier liturgy, it would be on Sexagesima Sunday). In the office of Matins for that day, there is related the story of the fall of the first parents of mankind and their subsequent expulsion from Paradise, and the liturgy of the following weeks (or week) takes on a tone of sorrow for sin and expectation of redemption. The second phase begins on Ash Wednesday, the first day of Lent, a time of general fasting and penitence. A dominant theme of the period is the Exodus, chosen because of its application to the catechumens, who were likened to the Israelites passing through the Red Sea. Satan comes noticeably to the fore in the Gospel reading of the first Sunday of Lent, the temptation account of Matthew 4.1–11.

In the days when there were only three scrutinies, these meetings took place on the third, fourth, and fifth Sundays of Lent. When they were expanded to seven, they were held on weekdays, beginning with the Wednesday after the third Sunday. When the first session was announced on Monday, the community prayed that with God's help it could perform with faultless ministry "the celestial mystery in which the devil and his pomp will be destroyed and the gate of the heavenly kingdom opened."[7]

The scrutinies of *Ordo XI* are designed for the initiation of infants into the life of Christianity. But there is abundant evidence from the formulas employed that they were originally intended for adults; and as has been observed before, adults would continue to be baptized in all missionary regions, as, for example, in the kingdom of the Franks during the seventh and eighth centuries, and in England during the sixth and seventh centuries, and again during the ninth century and later, at the time of the Danish invasions and conversions. The *Gela-*

---

instance, in accepting the Creation readings as occurring on Septuagesima rather than on Sexagesima Sunday. The moving of the readings to Septuagesima Sunday is a development that took place only in the twelfth century. See the *Corpus antiphonalium officii*, ed. René Jean Hesbert, 5 vols., REDsmf 7–11 (Rome 1963–1976) 1.126ff., 2.220ff., and *Sources of the Modern Roman Liturgy: The Ordinals of Haymo of Faversham and Related Documents,* ed. Stephen J. P. van Dijk, 2 vols., Studia et documenta franciscana 1–2 (Leiden 1963) 2.62–65. S. J. P. van Dijk and Joan Hazelden Walker, *The Ordinal of the Papal Court from Innocent III to Boniface VIII and Related Documents,* Spicilegium friburgense 22 (Fribourg 1975) 170 n. 2, cite Bernold of Constance, *Micrologus* 47 (PL 151.1012), as attributing the change to Pope Alexander II (1061–1073).

[7]Gel 283.

sianum and the mixed Gelasian and Gregorian sacramentaries ("Gelasian of the Eighth Century") preserve an earlier ceremony for the reception of a pagan adult into the catechumenate, which was no doubt kept in regular use during the Christianization of central Europe.[8] In such circumstances, then, the rubrics of infant services would be tacitly adjusted until the flow of adult converts ceased.

We should note that Alcuin in two letters describes a baptismal process in which he seems to have adult converts in mind. His description has a number of unusual elements to it, particularly in having the renunciation of Satan come at the beginning. He says that "the pagan first becomes a catechumen, approaching towards baptism in order to renounce the malign spirit and all of his damnable pomps." The candidate is then exsufflated, so that, with the devil put to flight, Christ's entry may be prepared for. The malign spirit is exorcized, that is, adjured to go out and depart and to give way to the true God. Next, the candidate receives salt so that his sins may be cleansed by the salt of wisdom. He receives the Apostles' Creed so that the empty house may be adorned and prepared by faith as God's dwelling, "now that it has been abandoned by the original inhabitant." Then scrutinies are performed, "to examine frequently how firmly and rootedly, after the renunciation of Satan, he has fixed in his heart the sacred words of the faith he has received." The candidate's nostrils are touched (and presumably anointed, since the "same oil" is used next on his breast), so that he will persevere in faith as long as he breathes. (The two last-named explanations have been taken as coming directly from John the Deacon's letter to Senarius, but in fact the characterization of the scrutinies is found almost verbatim in the still earlier treatise of Nicetas of Remesiana.) Other anointings follow, and Alcuin gives them a definitely apotropaic significance: "His breast is anointed with the same oil, so that by the sign of the holy cross the devil will be denied entry. His shoulders are also signed, so that he will be fortified on all sides." Then Alcuin proceeds to give a further symbolic meaning to the rites (or perhaps he means that there is a second anointing, as in the *Stowe Missal*): the

---

[8]Gel 598–601: *Ad catechumenum ex pagano faciendum.* In the first formula we read: "Accipe signum crucis tam in fronte quam in corde. . . . Horresce idola, respue simulacra, cole Deum patrem omnipotentem," etc. (599). For an important "Gelasian of the Eighth Century," see *Liber sacramentorum gellonensis,* ed. A. Dumas and J. Deshusses, 2 vols., CCL 159, 159A (1981). The ceremony in question is at nos. 2387–2390. I refer to this *Sacramentary of Gellone* in n. 63 below.

anointing of breast and shoulders signifies strength of faith and per-
severence in good works. Baptism follows, and no diabolical import
is given to it or to the remaining ceremonies.

Alcuin's letters, based in part on earlier authorities, were in turn
used by several of the metropolitans who responded to Charlemagne's questionnaire on baptism. In fact, the questionnaire itself,
which was sent out around the year 800, seems to have been based on
Alcuin's letters, except that it specifies infants as the catechumens.
The order of topics is as follows: the creed and the confession of faith;
the renunciation ("Satan and all his works and pomps"), exsufflation,
and exorcism of the devil; the reception of salt and touching of
nostrils; and the anointing and signing of breast and shoulders.[9] But
whether or not the unusual elements or interpretations given by Alcuin corresponded to actual rituals and formulas in use in his time,
they gave way before the force of the Roman liturgy.

At the first scrutiny in *Ordo XI,* the candidates, children or otherwise, who are to be baptized at the Easter Vigil services, are first
registered. The priest then makes a cross upon the forehead of each
with his thumb, and then, placing his hand on their heads, he says a
prayer in which he asks God to "expel all blindness from their heart
[and] break up the snares of Satan, by which they had been bound."
There follows a blessing of salt:

[9]For Alcuin's letters, see *Epistolae karolini aevi* 2, ed. Ernst Dümmler, MGH Epistolae 4 (Berlin 1895), epis. 134 (pp. 202–203) to Oduin (this letter has been dated ca.
798) and epis. 137 (pp. 210–216) to some monks in Septimania (southern France). The
text at one point in no. 137 ("ut exploretur saepius *quam firmiter* post renuntiationem,"
p. 214) follows the wording in the treatise of Nicetas (see Chap. 7 at n. 40), whereas
that of no. 134 does not ("ut exploretur saepius *an* post renuntiationem"), except in a
variant reading in Dümmler's text. Charlemagne's questionnaire is edited by J. M.
Hanssens, "Deux documents carolingiens sur le baptême," *Ephemerides liturgicae* 41
(1927) 69–82, esp. 74–75; it and some responses are analyzed (especially for the
postbaptismal ceremonies) by Fisher, *Christian Initiation: Baptism in the Medieval West*
58–66. The questionnaire, like Alcuin's letters, suggests that the breast and shoulders
are anointed twice; for this feature in the *Stowe Missal,* see Chap. 13 at nn. 9 and 40. It
is noteworthy that Rabanus Maurus, one of Alcuin's disciples, in a passage in the *De
clericorum institutione* (1.27), which was passed on as a canon by Gratian in the *Decretum*
(3.4.61), speaks of the ceremonies in the following order: confession of faith, renunciation, and exsufflation. In another canon that Gratian took from the same chapter
(*Decretum* 3.4.63), Rabanus gives a mildly apotropaic meaning to the next ceremony,
that of signing the candidate on the forehead and on the heart: the devil is to know
that henceforth he is *alienus* to the vessel that once was his. For other accounts, see
Susan A. Keefe, "Carolingian Baptismal Expositions," in *Carolingian Essays,* ed. Uta-
Renate Blumenthal (Washington, D.C., 1983) 169–237. See also Donald A. Bullough, "Alcuin and the Kingdom of Heaven," ibid. 1–69, esp. 42–48.

I exorcize you, creature of salt, in the name of God the Father almighty and in the charity of our Lord Jesus Christ and in the power of the Holy Spirit. I exorcize you by the living God and by the true God, who procreated you for the safekeeping of the human race, and ordered you to [be] consecrate[d] by his servants for the people coming to belief. Therefore we beseech you, Lord our God, that this creature of salt in the name of the Trinity be made a salutary sacrament for putting the enemy to flight. Do you, Lord, sanctify it with sanctification and bless it with blessing, that it may become a perfect medicine for all who receive it and remain in their bowels, in the name of our Lord Jesus Christ, who is to come to judge the living and the dead and the world by fire.[10]

Another version of the formula, which is that followed by the service of the *Rituale romanum* of 1614, is found in Benedict of Aniane's supplement to the *Hadrianum* (that is, the Gregorian sacramentary sent to the Franks by Pope Adrian). Here the address to God begins only after the antidemonic function of the salt has been specified: "I exorcize you, creature of salt, in the name of God, . . . who . . . ordered you to be consecrated . . . so that . . . you might become a salutary sacrament for putting the enemy to flight. Therefore we beseech you, Lord our God," and so forth.[11] The *Hadrianum* itself has only a prayer to God: "Bless, almighty God, this creature of salt with your heavenly blessing, in the name of our Lord Jesus Christ and in the power of your Holy Spirit, for putting the enemy to flight; sanctify it with sanctification and bless it with blessing, and let it become a perfect medicine for all who receive it and remain in the bowels of those who eat it, in the name of our Lord Jesus Christ."[12]

The fact that the Gregorian liturgy has only a blessing and not an exorcism of the salt is one of the circumstances that leads Hanssens to believe that it antedates *Ordo XI;* that is to say, he regards the exorcism as a later addition to the simple blessing.[13] However, as Bartsch points out, the word "exorcize" is used here in the primitive cultic

[10]*OR* 11.4–5, Andrieu 2.418–419 (it should be noted, by the way, that Hardison uses the old designation *Ordo romanus VII* for *Ordo romanus XI*). The same two prayers are in Gel (285, 288), while only the first is in Greg (357); it is preceded in Greg by a different blessing of the salt (below at n. 12).

[11]Greg sup 1068. The supplement, long ascribed to Alcuin, has recently been attributed by Jean Deshusses to Saint Benedict, abbot of Aniane. See his *Sacramentaire grégorien* 1.63–67 and 3.66–75.

[12]Greg 356.

[13]J. M. Hanssens, "Scrutins et sacramentaires," *Gregorianum* 41 (1960) 692–700, esp. 696. He is commenting upon Alois Stenzel, *Die Taufe* (Innsbruck 1958).

sense of "adjure," that is, "command the attention of" or "address solemnly by way of apostrophe." Only in the interpretation of the Fathers did it always have the meaning of ordering demons to depart.[14] Since therefore the "exorcizing" of the salt cited above has no obvious reference to the expulsion of the devil or demons from the salt, the compiler of the Gregorian ritual may have intentionally omitted it for the reason that it did not correspond to his notion of what an exorcism should be. Bartsch too believes that the Gregorian prayer is an abbreviation of the Gelasian formula, since it is very likely that the phrase "in the name of our Lord Jesus Christ and in the power of your Holy Spirit" in the former was taken over from the latter.[15] But as the prayer stands, even in its shortened Gregorian form, it could perhaps be termed an exorcism in a demonic sense, since God is asked to make the salt an effective instrument for the driving out (hence "exorcizing") of the devil. We have seen the word used in this sense before.[16] The aim of the prayer, however, seems to be in the nature more of preventive than of curative medicine: that is, directed toward staving off diabolic assaults rather than toward the remedying of diabolic possession. In fact, the *Exorcizo* version of the prayer is simply termed a blessing, in Benedict of Aniane's supplement as well as in the *Gelasianum* and in *Ordo XI*. At all events, the immediate function served by the salt is neither exorcistic nor apotropaic. The priest simply places it in the mouth of the infant and says: "Receive the salt of wisdom, having become well disposed for eternal life."[17]

The new catechumens are then taken outside the church, only to be summoned back almost immediately. After they are commanded to pray and bend their knees, they are signed first by their godparents and second by an acolyte, who places his hands first over the boys and then over the girls and recites a prayer for each sex.[18] Neither of these prayers deals directly with the devil, but the one for the males resembles a petition that we saw in the Eastern liturgies: God is asked

---

[14]Bartsch 7–11. On pp. 387–391 Bartsch collects the various versions of the formula for exorcizing the salt cited above.

[15]Ibid. 293–294. Bartsch, however, does not advert at this point to the presence of the formula in the *Hadrianum* but is rather speaking of other occurrences of the prayer.

[16]E.g., in the Egyptian *Canons of Basil* 103 (Chap. 11 at n. 20). Cf. the Ethiopic *Apostolic Tradition* (Chap. 9 at n. 6).

[17]OR 11.6, Gel 289.

[18]OR 11.7–16.

to send his holy angel to protect these servants of his, as he did of old in appointing an angel to guard the Israelites during their exodus from Egypt.[19] Each of the prayers is followed, however, by the *Ergo maledicte,* a direct address to the devil: "Therefore, accursed devil, recollect your sentence and give honor to the living and true God. Give honor too to Jesus Christ his Son, and to the Holy Spirit, and go away from these servants of God, because God our Lord Jesus Christ has deigned to call them to himself, to his holy grace and blessing, and to the font, the gift of baptism, through this sign of the holy cross, which we give to their foreheads. Never dare, you accursed devil, to violate [it]."[20] The mere recalling of his future fate, it seems, is taken as a cogent reason for Satan to leave the candidates and also, presumably, to prevent him from returning. The cross appears to serve as a reminder to the devil of the candidate's status and not of his own defeat by Christ or as a self-sufficient prophylactic—though these meanings may have been implicit, either when the formula was composed or when it was used in later times.

A second acolyte then says the following exorcism, *Audi maledicte,* over the male children, after another double signing and imposition of hands:

> Hear, accursed Satan! Adjured by the name of the eternal God and our Savior, the Son of God, depart in defeat, trembling and groaning, and take your envy with you. Let there be nothing in common between you and the servants of God, who are now thinking heavenly thoughts and are about to renounce you and your world, and to win a blessed immortality. Therefore give honor to the coming Holy Spirit, who, descending from the highest realm of heaven, with your deceits thrown into disorder, is to make the breasts that have been cleansed, that is, sanctified by the divine font, a temple and dwelling for God, so that, completely freed from all the injuries of past crimes, they may as servants of God render thanks at all times to the eternal God and bless his holy name forever.[21]

This exorcism preserves a reference to the act of renunciation that specifies the devil and the world as its objects, a tradition that I treated in Chapter 6. The devil is to leave before he is renounced and before the Holy Spirit prepares the souls as temples of God. The nature of

[19]*OR* 11.14, Gel 291.
[20]Gel 292, given also in Greg sup 1072.
[21]*OR* 11.18, Gel 294.

the devil's presence before his departure is not made clear in this particular formula, that is, whether or not he is thought to dwell within the person. Unlike the following exorcisms, the *Audi maledicte* is not closed with the *Ergo maledicte,* perhaps because it was felt to be its equivalent. The prayer that the second acolyte proceeds to say over the infant girls is simply a petition that God may free them as he did Susanna from the crime falsely charged against her. Then the *Ergo maledicte* is recited.[22]

The imprecatory formulas recited by the third acolyte (again, after a double signing and the laying on of hands), beginning *Exorcizo te immunde,* are exorcisms in the strictest sense of the word, that is, commands to an alien spirit to go out from its victims' bodies (the devil is visualized as dwelling in all of the candidates simultaneously). The formula over the males reads: "I exorcize you, unclean spirit, in the name of the Father, Son, and Holy Spirit, that you go out and depart from these servants of God. For he commands you, accursed [and] damned one, who walked on the sea and extended his right hand to Peter when he was sinking." The formula over the girls is similar, except that different incidents in Jesus's life are recalled, namely, his opening the eyes of the man born blind and the raising of Lazarus after he had been dead four days.[23] These formulas resemble the first exorcism of the Byzantine service, in which examples of Christ's powers are cited as reasons for the departure of the devil. But the few incidents chosen for the Roman formulas are rather inappropriate, and, unless they were simply cross-references to the readings of the day or week, they seem to have been meant originally as prototypes of the saving grace of baptism rather than as reminders of Christ's ability to control evil spirits. It is obvious that the "exemplary" portion of these formulas was quite fluid, in contrast to the basic command to the devil to "go out and depart," which we know to have been used in John the Deacon's time.[24]

The scrutiny comes to a close with yet another double signing, this time performed by the godparents and the priest. In the concluding prayer, there is no reference to the diabolical possession presupposed by the words of the exorcisms. The "show" is over for the time being, and a straightforward, realistic request is addressed to God to

---

[22]*OR* 11.19, Gel 295.

[23]*OR* 11.21–22, Gel 296–297.

[24]Cf. the exorcism's "ut exeas et recedas" with John's "ut exeat et recedat."

cleanse the candidates and sanctify them, giving them true knowledge to become worthy of the grace of baptism.[25]

The original three scrutinies were expanded to seven simply by duplicating the exorcisms and signings of the first in four additional sessions. The original second scrutiny was moved to third place, and the original third session became the seventh. The multiplication of exorcisms should not be taken as demonologically motivated. The reason given for the necessity of having seven scrutinies is not a fear that demons or demonic influence might otherwise continue to lurk in the infants but that the number should correspond to the gifts of the Holy Spirit.[26]

The second scrutiny took place on Saturday, three days after the first, and the third scrutiny during the next week, after the fourth Sunday of Lent. This third session (the old second scrutiny) contained no exorcisms at all but was given over to explaining the Gospels, the creed, and the Lord's Prayer to the catechumens, a practice that was continued even after the only candidates for baptism were infants. Presumably, of course, the review of these fundamentals of the faith would not be wasted on the adult congregation in attendance. The creed (in its Niceno-Constantinopolitan form) was recited in Greek as well as in Latin for the benefit of the large Byzantine community at Rome.

The third scrutiny is concerned with the devil only incidentally, in brief references in the homilies. But these references do bring home to the congregation the "real presence" of Satan in their lives. Thus, the confession of faith (that is, the creed) is characterized as an invincible weapon against the wiles of the enemy. The priest prays that the devil may always find the neophytes armed with this "symbol," so that once the adversary whom they renounce is defeated they may keep the grace of the Lord untainted to the end.[27] Similarly, in the explanation of the Lord's prayer the deacon warns of the snares and temptations of the devil. This time they are mentioned as something that all the faithful must guard against, without specific reference to the candidates for baptism.[28]

The fourth and fifth scrutinies were held during the following week, between Passion Sunday and Palm Sunday, and the sixth was

[25]OR 11.24, Gel 298.
[26]OR 11.81.
[27]OR 11.67, Gel 317.
[28]OR 11.69, Gel 319, 326. See Lukken 39.

held after Palm Sunday, in the early part of Holy Week. On Holy Thursday, the day on which the Last Supper and the institution of the Holy Eucharist were commemorated, the pope (or bishop, outside Rome) celebrated the Mass of the Chrism, during which the postbaptismal oil was prepared.

One of the prayers recited at this service asks God to cleanse the bodies and minds of the candidates when they are anointed with the oil, "so that if any remnants of the opposing spirits still adhere to them they may depart at the touch of this sanctified oil. Let there be no place for the spiritual weaknesses, no faculty for the apostate powers, no permission for the lurking evils to remain hidden."[29]

The content of this prayer seems more appropriate for the oil of catechumens, which is applied before baptism, than for the chrism of the postbaptismal anointing. But Bartsch holds that its position in the *Gelasianum* indicates that it was in fact used here for the consecration of the chrism.[30] He finds the oldest known formula for the consecration of the oil of catechumens elsewhere in the *Gelasianum,* under the rubric of the "Blessing of Exorcized Oil" for use in emergencies. This latter formula, however, though just as unsuitable for chrism as the former, was nevertheless employed by the compiler of *Ordo L* for the consecration of the chrism, and it filled that function in the Roman rite thereafter.[31] It reads:

> I exorcize you, creature of oil, by almighty God, who made heaven and earth, the sea, and all that is in them. Every power of the adversary, every army of the devil, every attack, every phantasm of Satan, be uprooted and be put to flight from this creature of oil, so that it might become for all who are to be anointed with it [a means] for their adoption as sons, through the Holy Spirit, in the name of God the Father almighty, and in the charity of Jesus Christ our Lord, who is to come in the Holy Spirit to judge the living and the dead and the world by fire.[32]

Bartsch believes that this formula was originally a direct address to Satan ("I exorcize you, unclean spirit"), which came to be used both for catechumens and for material things. When it was incorporated into the Roman liturgy, he conjectures, its beginning was changed to conform to the peculiarly Roman habit of exorcizing (that is, address-

[29]Gel 384 (cf. Greg 336).
[30]Bartsch 306. For more on this point, see Lukken 257–258.
[31]OR 50.25.91 (Andrieu 5.220–221); Bartsch 306, 310–311, 399–402.
[32]Gel 617: "Ad succurrendum. Benedictio olei exorcizato [*read* exorcizati]".

ing) the material object. But there remained untouched the concept that the influences of the devil, or perhaps even evil spirits themselves (depending on the meaning of *virtus, exercitus, incursus,* and *fantasma*), were actually present in the objects and had to be removed before they could be used for holy purposes. Bartsch finds indications of Eastern influences not only in the syntax of the formula, especially in the use of the passive imperative, which we saw in the Byzantine liturgy ("be rebuked"),[33] but also in its cosmological view of everything as under the control of the "ruler of this world," a concept that corresponded to the dualistic tendencies of the Celtic and Germanic peoples among whom the Gallican liturgy originated.[34] However, we have observed before that the idea of the indwelling of spirits in objects, especially in water, was widespread throughout the ancient world, and we must not eliminate the possibility that the Christians at Rome shared it and could have originated such formulas.

A later version of this same formula is to be found in the *Gelasianum* Mass of the Chrism. In spite of a misplaced rubric that calls for the mingling of balsam (which would apply only to the chrism), the "prayer" was used for the consecration of the oil of catechumens and continued to be so used to modern times (except that its grammatical inconsistencies were remedied along the way). The original redactor of the formula was apparently disturbed by the sudden shift of address from the oil to the evil powers and attempted to change the last part of the text to the third person without knowing enough grammar to replace the imperative commands with the proper subjunctive forms. The result translates as follows: "I exorcize you, creature of oil, in the name of God the Father almighty and in the name of Jesus Christ his Son and of the Holy Spirit, that in this invocation of the threefold might and in the power of the Godhead every most wicked power of the adversary, every inveterate malice of the devil, every attack of violence, every confused and blind phantasm—be uprooted and be put to flight and depart from the creature of this oil," and so on.[35] The specification of the demonic forces that are to be removed

[33]See Chap. 10 at n. 13. We may also note the use of the word "phantasm" to denote a demonic force.

[34]Bartsch 139–147; cf. Andrieu 2.xiii–xiv.

[35]Gel 339: "*Olei exorcizati confectio.* . . . Exorcizo te, creatura olei, in nomine Dei patris omnipotentis et in nomine Iesu Christi filii eius et Spiritus sancti, ut in hanc invocationem trinae potestatis atque virtutem deitatis omnis nequissima virtus adversarii, omnis inveterata malitia diaboli, omnis violentiae occursio, omne confusum et caecum fantasma—eradicare et effugare et discede a creatura huius olei," etc.

from the oil, especially in the substitution of *malitia* for *exercitus*, perhaps by way of *militia*, seems to indicate that the redactor was thinking not of the evil spirits themselves but only of their harmful influences, which are not personal agents that can go and come by a will of their own and which cannot be addressed except by way of personification. He continues so to address the oil but only half-succeeds in depersonifying the forces of evil.

The liturgy of Good Friday, which commemorates the crucifixion and death of Christ, should, we might expect, lay great stress on the Savior's struggle with his chief adversary, the devil. Instead, however, as in the Gospels, the events are portrayed largely on the level of human guilt and antagonism.[36] This continued to be the case in the *Improperia*, or Reproaches, which came to be chanted during the Adoration of the Cross (sometimes by two deacons concealed behind the altar). In them Christ is portrayed as sorrowfully accusing mankind from the cross: "My people, what have I done to you, or in what have I grieved you? Because I brought you out of the land of Egypt, you have prepared a cross for your Savior." It is true that one of the verses of the *Pange lingua* sung during the Adoration attributes man's first fall to the fraud of the betrayer and characterizes Christ's death on the cross as the result of a scheme designed to remedy the injury inflicted by "the craft of the enemy"; and the prayer recited at the third genuflection addresses Christ "who has through suffering on the cross delivered us this day from the devil's servitude" and asks that the cross may serve to turn back the fiery darts of the most wicked enemy and to heal wounds already inflicted.[37] But though Christ's agon "is described as an heroic victory," by which the prisons of hell were broken open,[38] there is no real articulation of the combat in terms of a personal opponent. In the simple communion

---

[36]In the Gospels Judas is associated with the devil for bringing about Christ's death and Peter for trying to prevent it; but after the Last Supper, or at least after the Agony in the Garden, there is no further reference to Satan. See Kelly, "Devil in the Desert" 214–220.

[37]*OR* 50.27,43, 48. See also the Solemn Prayers before the Adoration, where heretics are said to be "deceived by diabolical fraud" (*OR* 50.27.27). Similar expressions are common in the order for the reconciliation of penitents on Holy Thursday: Gel 354, 358, 363, 367, 374 (*OR* 50.25.28ff.). On the *Improperia*, see Hardison 131–132, and Daniel Frederick Melia, "The Byzantine *Improperia* in the Good Friday Liturgy in Eighth-Century Ireland," *Chronica* (Newsletter of the Medieval Association of the Pacific) no. 34 (Spring 1984) 20–21.

[38]Hardison 133, citing the antiphon sung before the *Pange lingua*.

service of the Mass of the Presanctified, which ends the day's service, there are no further references to the devil, nor is there any further hint of the harrowing of hell.

About the tenth century there began to be added to the Good Friday liturgy in many places a little drama representing the burial of Christ. A consecrated host or a crucifix was taken to a repository designated as the sepulcher, on the altar or elsewhere, and was reverently "buried." Ordinarily a corresponding ceremony of Resurrection or "Elevation" would be enacted early on Easter morning.[39] At times, beginning in the thirteenth century, it seems, there was a reference to or an enactment of the harrowing of hell during the Elevation ceremony. But even here the emphasis on the adversary was minimal. At first it was simply a question of singing the Easter antiphon *Cum rex gloriae,* first found in *Ordo romanus L,* as the priest and his ministers went in procession. The antiphon describes Christ as entering hell prepared for war, with the chorus of angels before him ordering the gates of the princes to be removed (a reference to Vulgate Psalm 23). But no war ensues. Instead the antiphon gives the welcoming cry of the captive people. Only in the fourteenth century do we first find the actual dialogue of the psalm used in this context: "Lift up your gates, O princes, and be lifted up, eternal gates, and the King of Glory shall enter in." "Who is this King of Glory?" "The Lord mighty and powerful, the Lord powerful in battle, he is the King of Glory." A nonliturgical precedent for such use is to be found in the Latin A text of the *Descensus ad inferos* section of the *Gospel of Nicodemus:* here, Inferus (Hell personified), after worried talk with Prince Satan, asks about the identity of the king, and the captive patriarch David answers him. But in the Elevation orders, normally no more than the first verse was sung, and that, of course, by the priest representing Christ. Only in one sixteenth-century Bavarian text (Bamberg, 1587) is the response, "Who is the King of Glory?" sung by the opposition—that is, by someone on the other side of the door "who simulates the person of the devil."[40]

---

[39]See Hardison 136–138; cf. a similar Holy Thursday–Good Friday sequence of ceremonies (123–125, 134–136). For the texts of the surviving services, see Karl Young, *The Drama of the Medieval Church,* 2 vols. (Oxford 1933 repr. 1962) 1.149–177, 552–565, and see n. 64 below.

[40]Young 1.149–176. The relevant passage of the Latin A text of the *Descensus* is given on pp. 149–150. For a parallel presentation of the three main versions of the *Descensus,* see James, *Apocryphal New Testament* 118–137, and see the table of corre-

In a fourteenth-century order from Dublin, the choir, foursquare on the side of Christ, first sings the *Cum rex gloriae* and then joins the priest in singing the psalm verses, not at the gates of hell, but at the sepulcher, which in a sense was Christ's entryway to hell:

Priest: "Be lifted up, eternal gates, and the King of Glory shall enter in."

Choir: "Who is this King of Glory? The Lord of hosts, he is the King of Glory."

The priest repeats his command at a higher pitch, and the choir responds with the same question and gives the answer cited earlier ("The Lord strong and powerful," etc.). At the third command, the choir returns to its first response. While the priest and an assistant

---

spondences on p. 118. In the Latin B text (pp. 132 and 134), Christ himself answers the question, "Who is this King of Glory?" The dating of the various versions of the *Gospel of Nicodemus* is problematic. G. C. O'Ceallaigh, "Dating the *Commentaries of Nicodemus,*" *Harvard Theological Review* 56 (1963) 21–58, dates the original Greek *Commentaries* or *Hypomnemata of Nicodemas* (which did not include the *Descensus*) to sometime after the year 555. H. C. Kim, ed., *The Gospel of Nicodemus* (Toronto 1973) 1–2, citing private communications from O'Ceallaigh, says ca. 600. In his article, O'Ceallaigh postulates, though without offering proof, that during the course of the seventh century a Latin version of the *Commentaries* was produced, along with the Latin B version of the *Descensus* (to use the terminology of Tischendorf and James); according to O'Ceallaigh, the Latin B *Descensus* was the basis of the Greek paraphrase (which he dates to about the end of the seventh century), and the Latin B version was also the basis of the Latin A text (the Latin A version appears in the tenth-century Einsiedeln manuscript, edited by Kim). But this sequence is clearly wrong, for it is Latin A rather than Latin B that is parallel to the Greek version. If Latin A were posterior to Latin B, it would have to be based both on Latin B and on the Greek version. In other words, Tischendorf would seem to be right about Latin A being earlier than Latin B. A late ninth-century (and garbled) copy of the Latin A version is cited by Jackson J. Campbell, "To Hell and Back: Latin Tradition and Literary Use of the *Descensus ad inferos,*" *Viator* 13 (1982) 107–158, esp. 112 n. 9. He follows O'Ceallaigh in calling this version "Late Latin" but makes the mistake of saying that this was also what Tischendorf terms it (Tischendorf, of course, would have called it "Early Latin"). The text of the *Cum rex gloriae* of OR 50.31.3 is given in Andrieu's posthumous vol. 5 as follows: "Cum rex gloriae Christus Infernum debellaturus intraret et chorus angelicus ante faciem eius portas principum tolli praeciperet sanctorum, populus qui tenebatur in morte captivus voce lacrimabili clam[a]verat," etc. (p. 300); this punctuation makes the antiphon refer to the "gates of the holy princes." But Cyrille Vogel and Reinhard Elze, *Le pontifical romano-germanique du dixième siècle,* Studi e testi 226–227, 269 (Vatican City 1963–1972) 2.113, punctuate thus: "portas principum tolli praeciperet, sanctorum populus qui tenebatur in morte captivus," etc. The resulting meaning, "the captive population of saints," seems unusual and awkward.

dramatize the Resurrection, by placing the crucifix corpus on the altar, the choir sings Psalm 29, using verse 4 as the antiphon (that is, it is sung before the psalm and after each verse). This antiphon, "O Lord, thou hast plucked my soul from hell," identifies the choir, for the moment, at least, as the "grateful dead," and it is possible that they were also meant to be playing this role when inquiring about and describing the King of Glory. Then the two priests lead the choir in singing a stanza from the hymn *Ad coenam agni,* in which Christ is described as emerging from the tomb as the conqueror come from hell, where he has put the tyrant in chains and has opened Paradise.[41]

According to the Latin A *Descensus,* Jesus broke into the infernal prison and tore apart the bonds of the saints; then he crushed Death under his feet, seized Satan and handed him over to the power of Inferus, and drew Adam to his divine light. But in the earliest references to or accounts of the descent into hell, Satan does not appear; rather, Death is the principal opponent, accompanied only (at times) by the personification of Hell. These figures were most likely suggested by Hosea 13.14: "De manu Mortis liberabo eos, de Morte redimam eos; ero mors tua, O Mors; ero morsus tuus, O Inferne." The additional role of the devil was no doubt suggested by Habakkuk 3.5: "Ante faciem eius ibit Mors, et egredietur diabolus ante pedes eius."[42] But the suggestion was not taken in the ancient liturgy. The Roman canon makes only the most skeletal reference to the harrowing of hell ("ab inferis resurrectio"), while the Constantinopolitan Creed used in the scrutinies makes none at all.[43] The collect of the Easter mass singles out the personification of death rather than the devil as the defeated adversary ("devicta Morte");[44] in the Easter preface, death is no longer personified ("mortem nostram moriendo destruxit");[45] and in the Easter sequence, *Victimae paschali laudes* (composed in the eleventh century), Death and Life are the adversaries: "Mors et Vita duello conflixere mirando. / Dux Vitae, mortuus, regnat vivus."[46]

In the earliest extant antiphonary, that of Compiègne (ninth cen-

---

[42]See Campbell 115.
[43]Greg 11, Gel 1250; Gel 312, 314.
[44]Greg 383; Gel 463 is different but has the same phrase.
[45]Greg 385; Gel 466 has the same phrase but is longer and says, "the death of us all was redeemed by the cross of Christ."
[46]Young 1.273.

tury), one of the antiphons for Matins of Holy Saturday was inspired by the passage from Hosea: "O Mors, ero mors tua! / Morsus tuus ero, Inferne!"[47] The second nocturn of the same office opens with Psalm 23, and the antiphon is verse 7b: "Elevamini, portae aeternales, et introibit Rex gloriae." The first responsory describes the harrowing of hell, and once again the emphasis is on Death: "she" is said to flee from the sight of Christ. Even the Gates of Death are personified: when they see Christ, they crumble. The phrase, *ille captus est qui captivum tenebat primum hominem,* presumably does not refer to Mors because of the masculine gender; it could therefore refer, or could have been taken to refer, either to Inferus or Satan.[48]

The preface of the Easter Vigil mass, which was said after the baptismal services were completed, either used the same phrase as the Easter preface ("mortem nostram moriendo destruxit"),[49] or, in the first formula given in the *Gelasianum,* spoke of Jesus as breaking up the prisons of hell ("inferorum claustra disrumpens") and bringing out man who had been cast down by the envy of the enemy ("invidia inimici deiectus").[50] Benedict of Aniane in his Supplement to the *Hadrianum* altered the latter preface to identify the devil as Christ's opponent in the harrowing. His preface says that Christ "broke open the prisons of hell and raised the bright banners of his victory, and triumphing over the devil he rose victorious from the dead." The night, personified, is lauded in past, present, and historical-present tenses: "O night, that puts an end to darkness and opens up the way of eternal light! O night, that deserved to see the devil conquered and Christ arise! O night, in which Tartarus is despoiled and the saints liberated from hell, and the entrance to the celestial homeland opened;

---

[47]*Corpus antiphonalium* (n. 6 above) 1.176 and 3.371 (= PL 78.769). See Balthasar Fischer, "'O Mors, ero mors tua': Eine Kurzformel der römischen Liturgie für das Paschamysterium," *Eulogia: Miscellanea liturgica in onore di P. Burkhard Neunheuser O.S.B.,* Studia anselmiana 68 (Rome 1979) 97–113.

[48]*Corpus antiphonalium* 1.174 and 4.375–376 (= PL 78.768): "Recessit Pastor noster, fons aquae vivae, ad cuius transitum sol obscuratus est; nam et ille captus est qui captivum tenebat primum hominem; hodie portas Mortis et seras pariter Salvator noster disrupit. *Vers.* Ante cuius conspectum Mors fugit, ad cuius vocem mortui resurgunt; videntes autem eum Portae Mortis confractae sunt." For more on the theme of the harrowing of hell, see Lukken 37, 131–143, 213, 255–256. An early instance of the devil's being associated with Hell and Death occurs in *The Teachings of Silvanus* (early third century). See M. L. Peel, "The *Descensus ad Inferos* in *The Teachings of Silvanus,*" *Numen* 26 (1979) 23–49.

[49]Greg 379, Gel 458.

[50]Gel 457 (beginning *Adest enim*).

217

in which the swarm of crimes is destroyed in baptism and sons of light arise therefrom."[51]

Benedict was inspired by the *Exultet,* or blessing of the candle, which was chanted at the Easter Vigil before the baptismal rites. But this blessing, which Benedict also included in his Supplement, describes the harrowing much more simply: "Having destroyed the bonds of Death, Christ rose as victor *ab inferis.*" This vulgate version of the *Exultet,*[52] which made its way into the Roman liturgy in Frankish territory in the eighth century, may well go back to the fourth century. Another version, the Beneventan or *vetus itala,* which was common in southern Italy, has a similar treatment of the harrowing of hell: this is the night "in which there occurred the resurrection of the dead *ab inferis* to eternal day; for the bonds were loosened and the sting of Death was trampled, for He arose from the dead who had been unbound (*liber*) among the dead." This version of the blessing was first illustrated in the extraordinary *Exultet* rolls, which developed in Italy around the tenth century, but it was replaced later in most places by the vulgate text. The pictures on the rolls were placed upside down, so that, as the deacon sang about the events commemorated in the text while gradually paying out the roll, the pictures would be revealed to the congregation in front of the ambo, or podium. The number and nature of the scenes varied—in one instance there are thirty-seven separate pictures. A fairly typical shorter version was produced at Montecassino at the end of the eleventh century: the scene is set with a picture of Christ in glory, beneath which is an illustration of the deacon in the ambo, with the paschal candle nearby. Then there appears a picture of the exulting angels, then a female personification of the Earth (suckling a bull and a serpent), followed by a similar personification of Holy Mother the Church. Next comes the harrowing of hell, and then a flashback to the sin of Adam and Eve, then the scene of Magdalen in the garden with the resurrected Christ. Another scene of the candle and deacon follows, then comes a picture of bees with their hives and keepers (the

---

[51]Greg sup 1588. See Edmond Eugène Moeller, *Corpus praefationum,* 4 vols., CCL 161A–D (1980) no. 1525. The language of Benedict's preface about the devil was introduced into the *Adest enim* preface (see previous note) of the St. Gall *Sacramentarium triplex* (n. 75 below); see Moeller no. 17.

[52]Greg sup 1021–1022; for variants of the preface section (1022), see Moeller no. 522, and see below, n. 65.

origin of the wax for the candle), and finally scenes of the pope and the emperor with their respective courts.[53]

The harrowing of hell does not always occur in the rolls, though sometimes it occurs twice—one picture showing Christ's victory and the other the release of the imprisoned saints. At times no adversary appears: Christ simply stands at hell's entrance or leads Adam and Eve and the other redeemed souls out to freedom. At other times, however, the Savior is shown trampling a figure, who is sometimes bound, beneath his feet.[54] In the Latin B version of the *Descensus ad inferos,* it is Satan who is both bound and trampled, but in the roll from Montecassino just described, the figure is labeled *Infernus.*[55] Often Christ is armed with a lance with which he pierces the throat of the chief adversary, whether the latter is portrayed as a monster or as a human-shaped demon, who is sometimes with a companion.[56] However, whether or not the community witnessing Christ's victory on the scrolls would be capable of distinguishing between Satan and Death and Hell, the only "real" adversary to be reckoned with was Satan, prince of death and captain of hell.

The use of illustrated *Exultet* rolls did not extend outside the region of Italy and flourished only from the tenth to the twelfth century, though at some places it did live on; in the Cathedral of Salerno, in fact, it was continued almost until our own time.[57] As demonstrated by the harrowing-of-hell representations, the rolls show the conflict with the powers of evil only in its historical aspect. It is true that the *Exultet,* like the Holy Saturday preface, asserts that the holiness of

[53]Vatican Library Barbarini MS lat. 592, in Myrtilla Avery, *The Exultet Rolls of South Italy,* 2 vols. (Princeton 1936) vol. 2, plates 147–153. The earliest of the rolls, that of Vat. lat. 9820 (Benevento, ca. 985), has been reproduced and commented on by Herbert Douteil and Felix Vongrey, *Exultet Rolle,* Codices selecti 35 (Graz 1974–1975). For the Beneventan *Exultet,* see H. M. Bannister, "The *Vetus itala* Text of the *Exultet,*" *Journal of Theological Studies* 11 (1909) 43–54, esp. 48–50. A good survey of the various forms of the *benedictio cerei* and of the vulgate *Exultet* is given by Guglielmo Cavallo, *Rotoli di Exultet dell'Italia meridionale* (Bari 1973) 3–21; see also Cavallo's article, "La genesi dei rotoli beneventani alla luce del fenomeno storico-librario in Occidente ed Oriente," *Miscellanea in memoria di Giorgio Cencetti* (Turin 1973) 213–229.

[54]Avery, plates 48, 54; in plate 75, Adam and Eve use the crouching black figure as a step in their progress out of hell.

[55]Ibid. 149; James, *Apocryphal New Testament* 134–135.

[56]Avery, plates 36, 120, 137, 188.

[57]Henri Leclercq, "Pâques," *DACL* 13.1522–1574, esp. 1560–1563.

"this night" of Christ's triumph "puts crimes to flight and washes away guilt" in baptism. But the devil's defeat in this act of sanctification is neither alluded to nor represented, though the act of baptism itself sometimes is. It is striking to notice in this connection how infrequently the harrowing of hell is depicted on the baptismal fonts of the High Middle Ages. Even when it does occur, it is normally only as one of many incidents in the life of Christ.[58] More striking still is the rarity of pictorial allusions to the exorcisms and their histories of evil spirits that were recited over the candidates and the water.[59]

In the early liturgy, however, which was developed before Latin became unintelligible to the peoples of the western Roman Empire, Satan as present adversary is very much in evidence on Holy Saturday. The morning was the time set for the seventh scrutiny, which began, curiously, with an exorcism that was called a catechesis. The direction of the *Gelasianum* reads: "In the morning the infants recite the symbol. First you catechize them in these words, with your hand placed upon their head." *Ordo XI* has, "This is the order according to which they are catechized. . . . Making a sign of the cross on the forehead of each," the priest says the following formula (the *Nec te latet,* which seems to be an expansion of the *Ergo maledicte*):

Nor does it escape you, Satan, that punishments threaten you, torments threaten you, the day of judgment threatens you, the day of penalty, the day that is to come like a burning furnace, in which eternal perdition will come for you and all your angels. Therefore, damned one, give honor to the living and true God, give honor to Jesus Christ his Son, and to the Holy Spirit, in whose name and power I command you to go out and depart from this servant of God, whom today the Lord our God

[58]The Princeton Index of Early Christian Art has on file only eight instances of the harrowing on fonts, ranging from the twelfth to the fourteenth century. One of the scenes is destroyed, but of the others, only two, from twelfth-century fonts in Germany and Sweden, show Satan overcome by Christ. See Karl Hölker, *Kreis Warendorf,* Bau- und Kunstdenkmäler von Westfalen 42 (Münster 1936) 81, fig. 113, and William Anderson, "Romanesque Sculpture in South Sweden," *Art Studies* 6 (1928) 49–70, fig. 52.

[59]I am not convinced that the so-called demoniacal figures sometimes seen on fonts are intended to represent the evil spirits cast out at baptism (see, e.g., F. C. Hingeston and William Osmond, *Specimens of Ancient Cornish Crosses, Fonts,* etc., London 1850, no. 29). But a picture in Avery (n. 53 above) plate 113, from a tenth-century illustrated Italian *Benedictio Fontis,* shows at the exorcism *Procul ergo* three angels pushing three reluctant demons on their way. See below at n. 68.

Jesus Christ has deigned to call by his gift to his holy grace and to the blessing and font of baptism, that he may become his temple by the water of regeneration for the remission of all sins.[60]

The puzzling reference to catechizing was eventually dropped, but the exorcism itself, in a somewhat extended form (with some additions taken from the Gregorian version) remained in the modern (post–1614) *Rituale romanum,* in the service for the baptism of adults. In the shortened infant ritual, however, as we shall see, only the final command survived. It is quite evident from the tenor of this address to Satan that there is no thought of the imminent commemoration (later on Holy Saturday) of the attack that was made on him in his fortress of hell by the soul of the dead Jesus (or Jesus in his glorified body just before his resurrection). The devil is simply envisaged as possessing each of the candidates and as not yet suffering the pains of hell. But this logical (or chronological) contradiction did not disturb the overall movement of the ritual plot, as it had developed by the ninth or tenth century: in the historical present of the sacred triduum, the Savior who died yesterday and will rise tomorrow will defeat the forces of evil in hell this very night. In this morning's ceremony, Satan, who has virtual omnipresence, is warned of this defeat. However, the *Nec te latet* was eventually brought more into harmony with the historical harrowing of hell by an important change: after the initial address to Satan, which really looks forward to the Last Judgment, the unclean spirit actually possessing the candidate is distinguished, at least as a possibility, from Satan: he is not only already damned but "to be damned" and is addressed as "whoever you are, unclean spirit."[61]

---

[60]OR 11.83–84; Gel 419. Greg 359 is similar.

[61]OR 50.29.5. Perhaps this is the place to notice a number of prayers in the *Gelasianum* for those baptismal candidates who are thought to be especially dominated by evil spirits, that is, the possessed and the ill. In one, designated as "Imposition of hand [upon] an energumen catechumen," God is besought "that by the invocation of your name the enemy may depart in confusion from the vexation of this servant of yours and that his soul, freed from his possession, may hasten back to the author of his salvation and follow his liberator, diabolical filth having been cast aside and the most sweet odor of the Holy Spirit having been perceived" (Gel 593). The next prayer is for an infant energumen: "Holy Lord, almighty Father, eternal God, I beseech your power with every lamentation for the infancy of this one oppressed by the devil. You who give aid even to the unworthy in oppression, arise on behalf of assaulted infancy, and do not continue vengeance for long, nor let the sins of the parents come before

After the exorcism comes the Effeta, which we discussed at the end of the seventh chapter. The priest touches the nose and ears of each candidate with saliva and says: "Effeta, that is, be opened, to the odor of sweetness. But you, devil, be put to flight from him, for the judgment of God has drawn near."[62] This formula too can obviously be read as referring to the harrowing of hell in the historical or dramatic present as well as to the actual present and to the Last Judgment.

Next, the candidate is anointed, on the breast and between the shoulder blades, with exorcized oil. In later times, the formula "I cover you with the oil of salvation" would be added, but in the *Gelasianum* the priest immediately calls the candidate by name and asks him, "Do you renounce Satan?" He answers, "I renounce him." "And all his works?" "I renounce them." "And all his pomps?" "I renounce them."[63] But even though the priest says nothing about the anointing, its purpose is self-evident: to strengthen and protect the

---

your face, who promised to judge neither the father for the son nor the son for the father; help, we beseech, this one who is vexed by the furor of the enemy, lest you make his soul be possessed by the devil without baptism; rather, let his tender age, free from malignant oppression, give to you eternal thanks" (594). Another prayer, for a sick catechumen, asks that baptism may remove "whatever in him the devil was holding subject to punishment by the transgression of original sin" and bids God to "drive off from him the poisons of every most evil spirit." If he is to be baptized, the priest recites the (Lord's) prayer and creed and "catechizes" him with the *Nec te latet* and then asks the aid of God "lest the enemy begin to triumph over this soul without the redemption of baptism" (595–597).

[62]Gel 420; Greg 360 and OR 11.85 give only part of the formula. In Gel 602, the rite for baptizing a sick catechumen, the future tense is used instead of the perfect: *appropinquabit* instead of *appropinquavit*. See Lukken 31–32.

[63]Gel 421, Greg 361. This ceremony for some reason was omitted from the existing copies of OR 11 (see Andrieu 2.376–377, 401). OR 15.114 (Andrieu 3.119), influenced by the *Sacramentary of Gellone,* divides the renunciation into two questions. The first, coming after the priest has anointed the candidate with two crosses on his breast, is, "Do you renounce Satan and all his works?" The second question is asked after the priest anoints him with a third cross, this time between his shoulders: "And all his pomps?" In both cases, the bystanders reply for the candidate: "He does renounce." OR 28.53 (Andrieu 3.402) and OR 50.29.7 (5.263) have the original sequence outlined in the text above: anointing of breast and shoulders, followed by the three questions. But then comes the formula, "Ego te linio," etc. Logically, the placement of this formula should indicate another anointing or series of anointings after the renunciation. Cf. the question of a double anointing in my discussion of Alcuin, n. 9 above. On the various meanings given to the anointing, see Emil Joseph Lengeling, "Vom Sinn der präbaptismalen Salbung," in *Mélanges liturgiques offerts au R. P.Dom Bernard Botte O.S.B.* (Louvain 1972) 327–357.

neophyte as he takes the step of formally abjuring his association with Satan. The priest then places his hand on the candidate's head and, in the case of infants, chants the creed (an adult, of course, would be expected to make this confession of faith himself). With this, the seventh scrutiny comes to an end.

The next order of the day was the Easter Vigil service. Originally it began after dark and lasted till past midnight. In the eighth century, however, the service began to be anticipated in the afternoon, and eventually it was moved to the morning. Even a midafternoon start would put the Vigil mass much earlier than midnight.[64] In some

[64]See Henri Leclercq, "Semaine sainte," *DACL* 15.1151–1185, esp. 1179–1180. He cites the order of Einsiedeln (*OR* 23, dated by Andrieu 3.266 to the eighth century, perhaps the first half), which begins the vigil around 1:00 P.M. (the seventh hour of the day), and the order of S. Amand (*OR* 30B, end of the eighth century: Andrieu 3.461), which put the start an hour later (the eighth hour), like the *Gelasianum* (Gel 425). The *Gelasianum* was influenced by *OR* 16 (written in the third quarter of the eighth century), which, however, specifies that the vigil is to begin a little after the ninth hour (see Andrieu 3.140). The purpose of the anticipation, Leclercq insists, was to give the faithful more time for sleep. Hardison 144 has surely miscalculated when he supposes that the vigil ceremonies could extend from midafternoon until midnight. A similar supposition is made by Timothy J. McGee, "The Liturgical Placements of the *Quem quaeritis* Dialogue," *Journal of the American Musicological Society* 29 (1976) 1–29, esp. 15: "During that period [the eighth century], the Easter Vigil ceremony began in the late afternoon and lasted well into Sunday morning." McGee cites as his source Michel Huglo, "L'office du dimanche de Pâques dans les monastères bénédictins," *Revue grégorienne* 30 (1951) 191–203, but Huglo makes it quite clear (p. 192) that the mass would start shortly after nightfall. He cites *OR* 17 (ca. 790–800), which is influenced by *OR* 16 and like it starts the vigil a little after the ninth hour; but it specifies that the third litany, which is followed by the mass, is to begin "cum . . . stella in coelo apparuerit" (*OR* 17.109). A similar rubric occurs in *OR* 30A (before 800), where the vigil starts in the eighth hour. It is true that Amalarius of Metz, *De ecclesiasticis officiis* 1.16 (PL 105.1032–1033), says that there is no mass "today," but it is clear that he is contrasting the day with the night. He goes to the Fathers to show that the service took place at night; first he cites Augustine and then Jerome. Of the latter, he remarks that he specified a certain hour for the service (the people should not be dismissed before midnight). But Amalarius himself does not insist upon extending the service to midnight. This question becomes important for Hardison's hypothesis concerning the origin of the *Quem quaeritis* as a Vigil ceremony (see 170, 198–199). It is essential to his theory that the original form of the play developed before the Vigil service was anticipated. But the earliest surviving versions are from the tenth century, well over a hundred years after anticipation has become a common practice. Admittedly, "common" does not mean "universal." According to William de Durantis, writing in the thirteenth century, the Easter Vigil was still being held at night in many places. He says, in the *Rationale divinorum officiorum* 6.78.2 (Venice 1589) fol. 231: "Antiquitus totum officium de nocte dicebatur, et adhuc in plerisque locis fit." I should also note that in his essay, "Gregorian Easter Vespers and

places the ceremonies of the seventh scrutiny were combined with the Vigil, but in general they seem to have remained distinct.

The service opens with the lighting of the new fire and the blessing of the paschal candle, during which the *Exultet* is sung, with its encapsulation of salvation history: "O truly needful sin of Adam, which is blotted out by the death of Christ! O *felix culpa,* which deserved such a great Redeemer! O truly blessed night that alone deserved to know the time and hour in which Christ arose from hell!" Near the end of this hymn of praise occur the words: "May the Lucifer of morning find it burning, that Lucifer, I say, who knows no setting, he who on his return from hell shed a serene light on the human race."[65] The old Lucifer now lies shackled in the midst of torment, but the contrast, if it was intended, was not made explicit.[66]

There follows a long series of readings from the Old Testament, punctuated by prayers. Their specific purpose is to give the catechumens their ultimate preparation for baptism. After this, the Litany of the Saints is chanted, during which the celebrant proceeds to the baptismal font to bless the water. It should be noted that the baptismal ceremonies could be performed even in monastic churches, certainly in minsters and in cathedrals staffed by monks, but also in more secluded abbeys, if only for the children of the lay servants. Thus, in the *Regularis concordia,* the handbook of customs stipulated

---

Early Liturgical Drama," in *The Medieval Drama in Its Claudelian Revival,* ed. E. Catherine Dunn et al. (Washington, D.C., 1970) 27–40, Hardison envisages a much earlier date for a *Quem quaeritis* rite, in suggesting that it influenced the Easter Vespers ceremony, which dates from at least the ninth century and may, he says, go back to the sixth. For a summary of more recent research and speculation on the *Quem quaeritis,* see Sandro Sticca, "Italian Theater of the Middle Ages: From the *Quem quaeritis* to the *Lauda,*" *Forum italicum* 14 (1980) 275–310, esp. 279–292. See also Johann Drumbl, *Quem quaeritis: Teatro sacro dell'alto medioevo* (Rome 1981), and David A. Bjork, "On the Dissemination of *Quem quaeritis* and the *Visitatio sepulchri* and the Chronology of Their Early Sources," *Comparative Drama* 14 (1980–1981) 46–69 (Bjork believes that the *Quem quaeritis* was composed by a northern Frankish monk sometime in the ninth century). For the texts, see Walther Lipphardt, *Lateinische Osterfeiern und Osterspiele,* 6 vols. (Berlin 1975–1981), and Gunilla Bjorkvall, Gunilla Iversen, and Ritva Jonsson, *Corpus troporum,* vol. 3: *Tropes du propre de la messe,* pt. 2: *Cycle de Pâques* (Stockholm 1982) 15–16, 217–223, 316–333.

[65] Greg sup 1021–1022. The somewhat similar blessing of the candle in the *Gelasianum* (Gel 426–428) is followed by a blessing of incense, which asks of God that the incense may expel diabolical wickedness wherever it is used (Gel 429).

[66] On the term "Lucifer" or Morning Star as applied to Jesus and Satan, see Kelly, *Devil* 6–7, 13, 34–35, 37, 127–128, 133–134.

for the reformed monasteries of England in the second half of the tenth century, the abbot is instructed at this point in the Vigil service to go down for the blessing of the font.[67]

The celebrant first addresses a long prayer to God, in which he recounts his acts of salvation in connection with water. Then he recites the *Procul ergo*:

> Therefore at your command, Lord, let there depart far from here every unclean spirit, let all the wickedness of diabolical deceit stand far away, may the mingling of opposing power have no place here, let it not fly around waiting in ambush, nor creep up while remaining concealed, nor corrupt by its infection. May this holy and innocent creature be free from every attack of the assailer and cleansed by the departure of all iniquity. May it be a living fountain, regenerating water, a purifying wave, so that all who are to be washed in this salvation-bearing laver may by the operation of the Holy Spirit in them obtain the gift of perfect purgation.[68]

The priest then signs the water and says a blessing that begins, "Therefore I bless you, creature of water, by the living God, by the holy God, by the God who in the beginning separated you with a word from the dry land," and so forth.[69] Other versions of the

---

[67]*Regularis concordia anglicae nationis monachorum sanctimonialiumque,* ed. and trans. Thomas Symons (London 1953) 48. Hardison 95 was misled into thinking that the baptismal services were omitted altogether. The *Concordia,* however, was not meant as a substitute for the liturgical books but simply gave an outline of the services. When a relatively new ceremony was introduced, full details were given. The burial or deposition play on Good Friday is an example. It was to be performed, if thought fit, "for the strengthening of the faith of unlearned common persons and neophytes" (44). The elaborate *Visitatio sepulchri (Quem quaeritis)* play given at the end of Matins on Easter morning (therefore, about 3:30 A.M.) is described with even greater detail and is not said to be optional (49–50; cf. xxxi, xliv). Sometimes, of course, no baptisms would be performed, but even then the blessing of the font took place and the blessed water was to be distributed to the congregation to be sprinkled in their homes. See *OR* 34.26; 50.32.97.

[68]Gel 445, OR 11.92. C. Coebergh, "Problèmes de l'évolution historique et de la structure littéraire de la *benedictio fontis* du rit romain," *Sacris erudiri* 16 (1965) 260–319, esp. 276–282, argues in effect that this prayer is apotropaic rather than exorcistic in intent; there is, he says, no concern to rid the water of demons or demonic influence, but rather to guard the candidates or ministers from the final attacks of the devil before the triple confession of faith and immersion. But the phrase "totius nequitiae purgata discessu," even granted Coeburgh's claim that *purgata* was used for *pura* for stylistic reasons, indicates that the purity of the water is to be effected by the departure of iniquity: *sit pura discessu nequitiae.*

[69]Gel 446.

prayer begin with *exercizo* or *adiuro* rather than *benedico,* as, for example, the formula for the blessing of baptismal water in emergencies
that is contained in the *Gelasianum* itself.[70] The formula of exorcizing
or adjuring is older than that of blessing (or signing).[71] But, as before, the formula is simply a solemn apostrophe to the water and does
not signify an attempt to remove demonic forces. There is, however,
another exorcism of the water given in the same section of the
Gelasianum based on the Gallican model (according to Bartsch's hypothesis) of a direct address to the devil, except that, as in the case of
the oil of catechumens, the water is first addressed nondemonically,
in the Roman fashion.[72]

In the Irish *Stowe Missal* there is preserved a formula reflecting the
original Gallican form of the address to the unclean spirit, who is
clearly regarded as being present within the water, as in the case of
the *Procul ergo* (which was no doubt inspired by the Gallican prototype). But the water itself is eventually addressed: "Therefore I
command you, every unclean spirit, every phantasm, every lie, be
uprooted and be put to flight from this creature of water, so that it
may be for those who are to descend into it a fountain of water
springing to eternal life. Become, therefore, holy water, water
blessed for regenerating sons for God the Father almighty in the name
of our Lord Jesus Christ who is to come in the Holy Spirit to judge
the world through fire."[73] This formula in the *Stowe Missal* is preceded by the "nonexorcistic exorcism" of water that we discussed
just above. The two formulas were clumsily merged in a single one
that was carried over into the *Roman Ritual,* in which the water is first
addressed: "I exorcize you, creature of water, by the living God . . .
so that you may become holy water, blessed water," and then the evil

[70]Gel 604: "*Benedictio aquae ad succurrendum.* Exorcizo te, creatura aquae, per Deum
vivum. . . . Adiuro te per Iesum Christum," etc. Bartsch collects all the texts,
Sachbeschwörungen 354–358 (cf. 19–20, 260–264).
[71]See Scheidt, *Taufwasserweihegebete* 64, 85; for other studies on the blessing of the
baptismal water, see Bartsch 20, 202–203.
[72]Gel 607: "Exorcizo te, creatura aquae. . . . Omnis virtus adversarii, omnis incursio diaboli, omnes [sic] fantasma, eradicare et effugare ab hac creatura aquae," etc. Cf.
Greg 206: "Exorcizo te, creatura aquae, . . . si qua fantasma, si qua virtus inimici, si
quae [sic] incursio diaboli—eradicare et effugare ab hac creatura aquae," etc. For
parallel texts see Bartsch 358–360. The blessing of oil specifies the *exercitus* (army) of
Satan as well.
[73]*The Stowe Missal,* vol. 2, ed. G. F. Warner, HBS 32 (London 1915) 28–29.

spirits are commanded to depart: "I command you, therefore, every unclean spirit," and so forth.[74]

In the Ambrosian liturgy the merger was made more intelligently. The Gallican formula was transformed so as to eliminate the notion that evil spirits were present in the water, though at the expense of asserting the devil's presence in the candidates themselves; it is asked that the water may be effective for the expulsion of the devil and his influences from those who are to be baptized. The result reads: "I adjure you, creature of water, by the true God. . . . Become therefore water exorcized for putting to flight every infestation of the devil and every phantasm of the enemy, and to uproot the enemy himself and to put him to flight and to supplant him from the servants of God who are to be baptized in you today," and so forth.[75]

After the blessing of the water we hear no more of evil spirits in the Roman baptismal service. The candidates are baptized and then anointed with chrism, first by the priest and then by the bishop. There are no apotropaic overtones to these anointings or to the signings and impositions of hands that accompany them.[76]

The ritual of *Ordo romanus XI,* but as amplified by *Ordo L,* was to provide the main outlines for the later Roman practices. About the middle of the tenth century, a monk of the Abbey of St. Alban's at Mainz set out to unite in one book everything connected with episcopal ceremonies. He was abundantly supplied with materials, including most of the surviving *ordines romani,* and he worked with an "exuberant gaucherie." The result was an awkward mixture that included many superfluous and obsolete or archaic rites. It was adopted as the Roman Pontifical and soon spread throughout Europe. The part that contained the baptismal service was designated as *Ordo romanus antiquus* and is the *Ordo romanus L* of Andrieu's edition.[77]

---

[74]*Rituale romanum: Benedictio fontis seu aquae baptismalis* (Bartsch (357–358).

[75]*Sacramentarium bergomense: Manoscritto del secolo IX,* ed. Angelo Paredi, Monumenta bergomensia 6 (Bergamo 1962) 165, § 534; see also the *Manuale ambrosianum ex codice saec. XI olim in usum canonicae vallis Travaliae,* ed. Marco Magistretti, Monumenta veteris liturgiae ambrosianae 2–3 (Milan 1904–1905) 2.205–206; *Sacramentarium triplex* (early eleventh century) no. 1307, and the *Biasca Sacramentary* (early tenth century) no. 498, both edited by Odilo Heiming, *Corpus ambrosiano-liturgicum* 1.1, LQF 49 (Münster 1968) 120; 2.1 LQF 51 (1969) 72. The passive imperatives of the original formula (*eradicare* and *effugare*) are treated as active infinitives.

[76]*OR* 11.96–101; Gel 449–452.

[77]Andrieu 5.72–79.

At the first scrutiny *Ordo L* prescribes a renunciation of Satan and a threefold confession of faith while preserving the same ceremonies in their traditional place, the renunciation at the seventh scrutiny on Holy Saturday and the confession at the baptism itself. Next there is a ceremony of exsufflation: "Then he exsufflates into his face three times, saying, 'Go out, unclean spirit, and give place to the Holy Spirit the Paraclete.'"[78] We recall that there was no exsufflation in *Ordo XI,* though such a ritual was attested to in the previous sources, up to the time of John the Deacon. It is probable, therefore, that there was an exsufflation in the original *Ordo XI* and that the manuscript of the order that served as an archetype for the existing manuscripts was defective in not preserving it.[79]

It is clear that the compiler of *Ordo L* received at least a partial inspiration for his changes from the Ambrosian liturgy, where there was a renunciation at the first scrutiny, held on the second Saturday of Lent. The Ambrosian form of the ceremony, however, is that of *The Sacraments* and consists of a double question ("Do they renounce the devil and his works? The world and its pomps?").[80] This renunciation is accompanied by an exorcism of ashes, which is also included in *Ordo L*:

> I exorcize you, ashes, in the name of God the Father almighty and Jesus Christ the Son of God and the Holy Spirit, who ordered you to be changed by fire into cinders, that, just as by God's command through his holy servant Moses the ashes of a heifer sprinkled on the people sanctified the whole congregation of Israel, so too you, exorcized in the name of the Trinity, sprinkled on the earth and on sackcloth—[that] the devil may not hide in those who are to be standing upon or passing across [you] in the scrutiny but may be manifested and expelled so that they may be found pure and sincere.[81]

The *Ambrosian Manual* also calls for an exsufflation of the ashes, with the formula: "I exsufflate you, ashes, sprinkled upon sackcloth."[82] I

---

[78]*OR* 50.20.3–5.

[79]So Andrieu 2.376.

[80]*Man. amb.* 2.169.

[81]*Man. amb.* 2.142–143; cf. *Sac. berg.* 349. *OR* 50.19.3 patches up the anacoluthon and faulty cases of the text but in so doing omits the notion of sprinkling the ashes on the earth and on sackcloth.

[82]*Man. amb.* 2.169: "Exsufflo te, cinis, et cilicio asperse" [*sic*]. Beroldus gives a more correct formula but without using the vocative: "Exsufflo te, cinis cilicio aspersus." See M. Magistretti, *Beroldus, sive Ecclesiae ambrosianae mediolanensis kalendarium et ordines saec. XII* (Milan 1894) 92.

shall discuss the meaning of these and other breathing ceremonies in the next chapter.

The first scrutiny of *Ordo L* then carries on as in *Ordo XI,* as do the other six scrutinies, through the remaining weeks of Lent. An exorcism of the palms on Palm Sunday is prescribed; it follows the pattern of a formula that we have seen used before on oil and water: every power of the adversary, the whole army of the devil, every incursion of the demons is to flee from this creature of flowers and fronds.[83] In the blessing of the olive and palm branches that follows, it is recounted that the people strewed branches before Christ, thereby "showing him already the victor over the prince of death." Other blessings ask that the celebration of this triumph today may help God's people to be victorious over the enemy. Once they have overcome his temptations in this world, they may achieve the palm of victory in the next.[84] At the end the priest sums up by describing Christ as he appeared on Palm Sunday, when by the marvelous plan of God he was about to fight with the prince of death for the life of the whole world and was to triumph over him by undergoing death.[85]

On Holy Thursday, the exorcisms and blessings of the oils go on at great length. There is included a sermon on the making of the chrism that gives a definitely apotropaic significance to the final anointings: "In baptism, we are reborn to life; after baptism we are armed and strengthened against enemies, to do battle with them. In baptism we are washed; after baptism we are renewed. In baptism we receive the remission of all sins, both original and actual; after baptism we take up the shield of faith, the helmet of salvation, and the sword of the Spirit against our enemies, so that we may stand armed on all sides."[86] Related ideas, as we saw, are found in the prayer recited at one of the three genuflexions made during the Adoration of the Cross on Good Friday, though here the link is not made with baptism.[87]

On Holy Saturday morning, the seventh scrutiny is held as in *Ordo XI.* But in the Vigil service there is provision made for the "catechizing" (that is, exorcizing) and preparing for baptism of such infants as have not yet partaken in these ceremonies.[88] Before the blessing of

---

[83]*OR* 50.23.11. See above at nn. 35, 74.
[84]*OR* 50.23.12, 18, 19.
[85]*OR* 50.23.41.
[86]*OR* 50.25.144.
[87]*OR* 50.27.41–43.
[88]*OR* 50.29.43.

the font, the exorcism *Procul ergo* is said, while the priest divides the water with his hand in the form of a cross. More crosses are made in the blessing that follows, and the paschal candle is also dipped into the water. At the words "Holy Spirit," the priest breathes into the water in the form of the Greek letter psi (for *psychē*, spirit). He then pours chrism into the font and mixes it with the water and sprinkles the whole font and the bystanders with the mixture.[89]

The act of baptism itself follows. Many of the manuscripts of *Ordo L* call for a repetition of the renunciation of Satan here, before the three credal questions of the baptismal formula are asked. In so doing, they restore the ancient dramatic sequence of the ceremonies and bring to a climax and conclusion the agon with the great antagonist. Thereafter, as in the *Apostolic Tradition,* the earliest of the Roman orders of baptism, no more is heard of Satan. He is drowned in oblivion, in the midst of rejoicing.

The Roman liturgy, then, continued to follow the demonological pattern set for the initiation rites in the West from early times. Extensive exorcisms of the passive candidate are followed by the simple ceremony of the candidate's active renunciation of Satan. There are also subsidiary exorcisms of the elements of water, oil, and salt. Sometimes these exorcisms are truly exorcistic, in the sense that they are aimed at driving the devil and his influence out of the elements. But they can also be considered, at least at times, to be apotropaic with respect to the candidate—not perhaps in the common Eastern sense of protecting the candidate during his life after baptism, but at least in the ad hoc sense of protecting him here and now while he is undergoing the ceremonies of baptism. I inferred, for instance, that the purpose of anointing the baptizand on his breast and on his shoulders with exorcized oil was to strengthen him for the renunciation of

---

[89]*OR* 50.29.49–53. Originally, the priest breathed three times into the water, to signify the sanctifying power of the Holy Spirit, at the words: "Descendat in hac plenitudine fontis virtus spiritus tui, totamque huius substantiam regenerandi fecundet effectu" (Greg 374e, cf. Gel 448). Deshusses reconstructs the original rubric of the *Hadrianum* as: "Hic suffla tribus vicibus in aqua." To this formula was added a direction for dipping the paschal candle or candles into the water (see the variants given by Deshusses at Greg 374e). I must protest against recent Freudian or anthropological interpretations of the candle as a phallic symbol—which of course would entail seeing a corresponding colpic (vaginal) symbol in the water or its container. To my mind, such a meaning would not have occurred to the inventors and promulgators of the gesture, and the suggestion would have struck them as irreverent, to say the very least.

Satan that follows immediately. In Alcuin's interpretation, however, a long-range prophylaxis may have been intended, for in his ritual (whether it was real or only "ideal") the renunciation had already been made. Ministers of the Roman rite may also have intended, at least some of the time, a similar antidemonic effect for the future; but, if so, this meaning was not made explicit by the prayers of the liturgy.

We have seen that the dramatic rituals and prayers of the struggle against Satan that were developed as a part of the preparation for baptism were suggestively incorporated into the general liturgy of Lent and Holy Week, which reviews Christ's redemptive acts. But in the tenth century and later, when the creative period in the production of antidemonic baptismal services was long past (except for the recent combinatory activities of the compiler of *Ordo romanus L*), these services seem to have provided little if any inspiration for the new liturgical dramas that were coming into being. But the baptismal liturgy nevertheless supplied a fitting context for the new developments.

13 /

Milanese, Gallican,
and Spanish Rites

We have just seen in some detail the rites of initiation that came to have the greatest currency in Europe because of the influence of Rome. It will now be worthwhile to study some local variations. As before, we shall be dealing mainly with the ways in which the conflict with the devil is dramatized. We shall see that the Roman rite is quite restrained in comparison to the flamboyance of some of the provincial rites.

Let us begin with the Ambrosian traditions of Milan and northern Italy. We have already seen the way in which the catechumens begin their initiation process, according to the *Ambrosian Manual:* on the second Saturday of Lent, after mass is celebrated, the children to be baptized wait at the doors of the church while the ashes are exorcized and exsufflated. Then two deacons and two subdeacons go to the candidates, and the deacons ask, "What do they seek?"

The subdeacons answer, "Faith."

"Are their parents worthy?"

"They are worthy."

"Do they renounce the devil and his works?"

"They renounce them."

"The world and its pomps?"

"They renounce them."

The deacons then address the children as if they had spoken for themselves: "Be mindful of your words, that they may never depart from you." The children are then taken in and signed and brought before the altar to be exorcized (I shall give the standard form of exorcism below). The same ceremonies are to be repeated on the following two Saturdays.[1]

In other Ambrosian orders, the candidates themselves are exsufflated. According to one, which goes back to the eighth century, the preliminary gatherings of catechumens are called scrutinies. At the first two such meetings, the candidates, who are all infants, are first signed, and the unclean spirits are "interdicted" (adjured) to remove themselves from the children and flee at the sight of the sign of Christ shining in them. The priest then goes into their midst, stands facing east, and exsufflates (or "sufflates") in the form of a cross, saying: "All right" (*Omnia recta*).[2] At the third and final session, there are four exsufflations. After the first, a version of the *Nec te latet* is said. After the second: "In the name of our Lord Jesus Christ we conjure you, whoever you are, most unclean spirit hiding in these bodies, that you go out and depart from the servants of God whom our Lord Jesus Christ has deigned to call to the knowledge of baptism." After the third: "Depart therefore, accursed Satan, from the servants of God and give place to the Holy Spirit, because we interdict you in the name of him who is to come to judge the world and you, enemy, by fire." Before the fourth exsufflation there is an Effeta ceremony (with no mention of the devil), and after it, once again, the strange formula "All right."[3]

In the ninth-century *Bergamo Sacramentary* as well as in the eleventh-century *Ambrosian Manual,* there is an order for the making of a catechumen apart from the traditional system of scrutinies. Here there is an antidemonic breathing ceremony in connection with the Effeta, which comes immediately after the renunciation. As in the Roman Effeta, the minister touches the ears and nose of the candidate with saliva and says: "Effeta, that is, be opened, to the odor of sweetness." Then, however, the rubric directs, according to the Bergamo service, "Insufflate into his face in the form of a cross and say, 'I insufflate you, unclean spirit, in the name of our Lord Jesus Christ. But you, devil, be put to flight, for the judgment of God has drawn near.'" The *Manual* directs: "Exsufflate from foot to head, in

[1]*Manuale ambrosianum* 2.169.
[2]C. Lambot, *North Italian Services of the Eleventh Century,* HBS 67 (London 1931) xxxiii–xxxiv, 11; cf. 4.
[3]Ibid. 16.

ridicule of the devil," while saying, "I exsufflate you, most unclean spirit," and so forth.[4] Then follows an anointing of back and breast with oil that has just been exorcized according to the Romanized Gallican formula.[5] The anointing is accompanied by an exorcistic insufflation, and another version of the Gallican formula is recited but now with the Gallican beginning: "I exorcize you, every most unclean spirit, in the name of our Lord Jesus Christ; every attack, every wrath, every phantasm, be uprooted and be put to flight from this creature of God."[6]

The same ceremony occurs, though not in connection with an anointing, in the early Spanish liturgy, which is basically Gallican in form.[7] The version of the *Liber ordinum,* an eleventh-century manuscript, uses the term *insufflare,* whereas the tenth-century *Antiphonary* now at León has *exsufflare.*[8] In the Irish-Gallican *Stowe Missal,* on the other hand, there is an exsufflation before the anointing but no exorcism. The priest is to exsufflate the candidate and is then to touch his breast and back with oil and chrism, saying, "I anoint you with oil sanctified in the name of the Father, Son, and Holy Spirit."[9] The exsufflation is not specifically said to be against the devil, but the ceremony is both preceded and followed by the Roman form of the renunciation of Satan.

There is an insufflation into the water called for in the Ambrosian liturgy, before the "adjuration" of the water that I discussed earlier,[10] but it is not obvious that this breathing is exorcistic in the sense of antidemonic, as are the ones just cited. It *is* obvious in the order for baptizing a sick infant, however, where the formula of insufflation as well as the exorcism that follows are both directed against the devil:

[4]*Sac. berg.* 1480; *Man. amb.* 2.467. A thirteenth-century MS has a different rubric: "Here exsufflate into his face in the form of a cross" (*Man. amb.* 1.144).

[5]Gel 617. According to Beroldus, who wrote in the twelfth century (see Chap. 12 n. 82), this formula was used at the cathedral at Milan for the consecration of the chrism (*Beroldus* 103).

[6]*Sac. berg.* 1483 (cf. *Man. amb.* 2.467). For the distinction between Roman and Gallican formulas, see Chap. 12 after n. 32.

[7]But see T. C. Akeley, *Christian Initiation in Spain, c. 300–1100* (London 1967) 19.

[8]*Le Liber ordinum en usage dans l'église wisigothique et mozarabe d'Espagne du cinquième au onziéme siécle* chap. 4, ed. M. Férotin, Monumenta ecclesiae liturgica 5 (Paris 1904 repr. 1967–1968) 24–25; *Antifonario visigótico mozárabe de la catedral de León fol. 133,* ed. Louis Brou and José Vives, Monumenta Hispaniae sacra, series liturgica 5.1 (Barcelona 1959) 203.

[9]*Stowe Missal* (above, Chap. 12 n. 73) 25.

[10]*Sac. berg.* 534; *Man. amb.* 2.205; see Chap. 12 at n. 75.

Exorcism of the water. I insufflate you, most unclean spirit, in the name of our Lord Jesus Christ. I exorcize you, creature of water, in the name of God the Father almighty and in the name of Jesus Christ his Son and of the Holy Spirit. If [there be present] any phantasm, if any power of the enemy, if any attack of the devil—be uprooted and be put to flight from this creature of water, so that it may become a fountain of water springing to eternal life. And when this servant of God is baptized, let no infirmity of body have control over him, and let the enemy of the human race not oppose him, but when he is reborn of water and the Holy Spirit let him become a temple of the living God for the remission of sins, in the name of God the Father almighty and in the name of Jesus Christ his Son, who is to come in the Holy Spirit to judge the world through fire. Amen.[11]

Traditionally the term *insufflare* more often referred to the reception of the Holy Spirit, in accord with the Gospel precedent (John 20.22). There is this kind of breathing rite in the eighth-century *Bobbio Missal,* a Gallican sacramentary with signs of Irish influence. The priest insufflates three times into the candidate's face and says, "Receive the Holy Spirit; retain him in your heart."[12] And in the *Roman Ritual* of 1614, in the service for the baptism of adults, an insufflation of the Holy Spirit is placed immediately after the exsufflation of the devil.[13]

Quodvultdeus employed *insufflare* to designate an antidemonic ritual,[14] however, and when the *Liber ordinum* does the same it confirms a seventh-century Spanish usage witnessed to by Isidore and repeated by Ildephonsus.[15] But, like the *León Antiphonary* and the later Ambrosian liturgy, it also uses *exsufflare* for the same purpose, since it has an exsufflation of the font that is followed by an exorcism specifically directed against the evil spirit—although, partway through, the water itself is addressed instead of the evil spirit. The priest comes to

[11] *Sac. berg.* 1490. Cf. Greg 206 (Chap. 12 n. 72 above).

[12] *The Bobbio Missal* 233, ed. E. A. Lowe et al., HBS 53, 58, 61 (London 1917–1924) 2.72.

[13] *Rituale romanum* (rev. ed. Turin 1952): *Ordo baptismi adultorum:* "Tunc sacerdos exsufflat ter in faciem eius et dicit semel: 'Exi ab eo, spiritus immunde, et da locum Spiritui sancto Paraclito.' Hic in modum crucis halat in faciem ipsius et dicit: 'N., accipe Spiritum bonum per istam insufflationem et Dei benedictionem.'" The exorcisms follow, in which it is of course assumed that the devil and not the Holy Spirit is present within the candidate.

[14] See above, Chap. 5 at n. 21.

[15] Isidore, *De ecclesiasticis officiis* 2.21.3 (PL 83.815); Ildephonsus, *De cognitione baptismi* 26 (PL 96.122).

the font and exsufflates three times and speaks while facing west. The text, which is very corrupt, can be translated as follows:

> Depart, unclean spirit, from everything that our faith is to employ in the office of the sacrament of religion. And do not pretend [= "dare to incur"?] the guilt of a crime, for you know the power of the Savior. Our confidence is not in merit but in the command, although the very power of the ministry entails the dignity of the minister. Therefore, creature of water, I admonish [*convenire*] you, by our common God, that you be intelligent in the conserving movement of sensibility and do not refuse to be subject to the service by which we strive to please God. Purge from yourself all communion of demons, all association of iniquity. Being capable of the Lord's protection, eliminate all the stain of phantasm. So that, having acquired the grace of sanctification, those that you receive guilty you may restore innocent to your, as well as our, creator.[16]

The word *convenire* in these Spanish formulas is used as the equivalent of *exorcizare*.[17] The above formula is remarkable for the degree to which it personifies the water or assumes a mind and a will in it.

The central ceremony of the scrutinies of the *Ambrosian Manual* is the recitation of the "Exorcism of St. Ambrose," a long formula that is ascribed to Ambrose but is certainly not by him. There is a preliminary prayer in which each minister seeks the necessary power for confronting the evil spirits:

> Almighty Lord, the Word of God the Father, Christ Jesus, God and Lord of every creature, who gave to your holy apostles the power of treading upon serpents and scorpions; who among the other commands of your wonders deigned to say, "Put demons to flight"; by whose

[16]*Liber ordinum* 4 (29): "Discede, immunde spiritus, ab omnibus quibus fides nostra usura est religionis officio sacramenti. Nec praetendas culpam criminis, qui agnoscis potentiam Salvatoris. Non est meriti confidentia, sed praecepti, licet ipsa potestas ministerii dignitas sit ministri. Te igitur per communem Deum, aquae creatura, convenio, ut conservante motu sensibilitatis intelligens subici servitio, quo placere Deo nitimur, non recuses. Omnem a te communionem daemonum, omne collegium iniquitatis expurges, totam fantasmatis labem capax dominicae praeceptionis [*lege* protectionis] extermines; ut gratia sanctificationis indepta, tuo nostroque pariter Creatori quos acceperis culpabiles restituas innocentes. Amen."

[17]See Bartsch 17–18; cf. his translation of a similar formula, 134–135. There are many patristic precedents for using the word transitively in the sense of "admonish," "accuse," "call to account," etc. See *Thesaurus linguae latinae* 4 (Leipzig 1906–1909) 828–830, senses II B 1, 4.

power Satan was conquered and fell like lightning from heaven; I humbly call on your name with fear and trembling, that having granted forgiveness of all my sins you may deign to bestow confidence and ability, so that I may faithfully and securely go against this cruel dragon, fortified by the might of your arm.

The ministers then recite the exorcism proper, while the children are signed on the forehead with the formula, "I sign you with the sign of the cross in the name of the Father, Son, and Holy Spirit." The exorcism reads:

I adjure you, therefore, every most unclean spirit, every phantasm, every attack of Satan, in the power of the name of Christ, who after the laver of Jordan was led into the desert and conquered you on your home grounds, that you cease to assault him whom he formed from the clay of the earth for the honor of his glory and that you tremble in the miserable man, not at his human frailty but at the image of almighty God. Give way, therefore, to God, who reduced you to servitude in his humbled servant Job. Give way to God, who engulfed you and your forces in the abyss in Pharaoh and his army by his servant Moses. Give way to God, who revealed you in Bel and prostrated you in the dragon by his servant Daniel. Give way to God, who put you to flight, expelled from King Saul with spiritual songs by his most faithful David. Give way to God, who condemned you in the traitor Judas. For he now drives you with divine blows, in whose sight you with your legions trembled and cried out, "What is there between us and you, Jesus son of David? Have you come before the time to torment us?" He impels you with everlasting flames who at the end of time will say to the impious, "Go, accursed ones, into the eternal fire that my Father has prepared for the devil and his angels." For the worm that never dies is for you, impious one, and your angels; for you and your angels inextinguishable fire is prepared; for, accursed one, you are the prince of manslaughter, you are the author of unchastity, the head of sacrileges, the master of the worst arts, the teacher of heretics, the inventor of all that is obscene. Go out, therefore, impious one, go out, wicked one, go out with all your deceit; for it is God's desire that man be his temple. But why do you delay any longer? Give honor to God the Father almighty, to whom every knee is bent. Give place to Christ Jesus, who shed his blood for man; give place to the Holy Spirit, who manifested you in Simon by blessed Peter his apostle, who condemned your deceit in Ananias and Sapphira, who struck you down in King Herod when he would not give honor to God, who covered you with the gloom of blindness in the magician Elymas by his apostle Paul and by the same apostle ordered you with a word of command to go out from the

237

pythoness. Therefore depart now; depart, seducer; for your home is the desert, your habitation the serpent. Be humiliated, be prostrated; there is no time for delay. For behold the Lord and Ruler is near, the fire will quickly burn before him and will swallow in flames his enemies around him. For even if you deceive man, you cannot mock God. For he, to whose eyes nothing is hidden, casts you out. He expels you, to whose power all things are subject; he shuts you out, who has prepared the eternal Gehenna for you and your angels, from whose mouth will issue a two-edged sword, who is to come in the Holy Spirit to judge the world through fire. Amen.[18]

This remarkable dramatic monologue begins by addressing whatever evil spirits are present in the candidates but later singles out the devil himself. (We saw the opposite occur in later versions of the *Nec te latet,* which is directed at first against Satan but then against the unclean spirit, "whoever he is.") The whole history of the divine-demonic conflict is put before us, and at one point the words of the demons' response to Jesus are repeated: Legion objected that they were to be given their freedom until the Day of Judgment. Jesus refuted this claim: they were to be restrained and tormented in the present as well as in the future. The present coming of Jesus is merged with his final advent on Doomsday, and thus the complete cycle of the story of salvation is announced to the devil, much as it would be presented to the people in later times from the stages of the Corpus Christi pageants.

An exorcism somewhat similar to the Ambrosian formula is contained in the *Old Gallican Missal,* an early eighth-century sacramentary:

I come against you, most unclean damned spirit; you are grown old in evil, the substance of crimes, the origin of sin; you delight in deceits, sacrileges, defilements, slaughters. Invoking the name of our Lord Jesus Christ we rebuke you and adjure you through his majesty and power, passion and resurrection, advent and judgment, that in whatever part of the members you are hiding, you manifest yourself by your own confession, and that, shaken by spiritual flames and invisible torments, you flee from the vessel that you believe yourself in possession of, leaving it purged for the Lord after having been your dwelling place. Let it suffice that in former ages you ruled over almost the whole of the world in the hearts of men. Now day by day your kingdom will be destroyed, and

[18]*Man. amb.* 2.123–124 n. (= *Beroldus* 93); ibid. 469–471; *Sac. berg.* 1488.

may your weapons daily grow ineffectual until the end. What you suffer now was long ago prefigured. Already you were devastated by the plagues of the Egyptians, you were drowned in the Pharaoh, destroyed in Jericho, prostrated in the seven Chanaanite nations, defeated by Samson in the Philistines, cut off by David in Goliath, hanged by Mordecai in Haman, cast down by Daniel in Bel, punished in the dragon, pierced through by Judith in Holofernes, subjugated by the Lord to human commands, blinded by Paul in the magician, burned in the serpent, burst open by Peter in Simon; by all the saints you are put to rout, tortured, lacerated, consigned to eternal fires and infernal darkness, from where our Lord Jesus Christ in a second Adam rescues man while he triumphs over you. Depart, depart, wherever you are, and seek no more to enter bodies dedicated to God. May they be forbidden to you forever, in the name of the Father and Son and Holy Spirit, and in the glory of the Lord's passion, by whose blood they are saved, whose advent they await, whose judgment they confess.[19]

The exorcism seems to assume that the very words that are addressed to the devil inflict torture on him and that he will be forced to confess his presence, ideas that can be found in the writings of the early African Fathers, namely, Tertullian, Minucius Felix, and Cyprian.[20] These writers, however, were speaking of the corporeally possessed; and though the *Old Gallican* exorcism is included in the missal as a prebaptismal service, the reference to the *corpora Deo dicata* indicates that it was in fact composed for those who were already baptized but were thought to be possessed by the devil.[21] The "Exorcism of St. Ambrose" underwent the reverse of this process, in that it was taken from its function as a baptismal exorcism in the Ambrosian rite and was included in a modified form in the *Rituale romanum* as an exorcism for use in cases of possession. Dölger suspects that the exorcisms for the possessed attributed to St. John Chrysostom in the Greek *Euchologium* were also originally designed for the exorcizing of catechumens.[22] Such a change of purpose can definitely be said to have happened in the case of exorcisms in the Spanish liturgy. In the *Liber*

---

[19]*Missale gallicanum vetus* 13.61, ed. L. C. Mohlberg et al., REDsmf 3 (Rome 1958) 17.

[20]Tertullian, *Apologeticum* 23.16 (CCL 1.133); Minucius Felix, *Octavius* 27.5–7 (CSEL 2.40); Cyprian, *Ad Demetrianum* 15 (CSEL 3.1. 361–362). See Kelly, *Devil* 74–76.

[21]So Adolphe Franz, *Die kirchlichen Benediktionen im Mittelalter* (Freiburg 1909) 2.579.

[22]Dölger, *Exorzismus* 54; see Goar, *Euchologion* 581–585.

ordinum we find an "order to be celebrated over one who is vexed by an unclean spirit."[23] As I shall show when I take up Spanish services as a whole, the endlessly elaborated exorcisms of the order were originally designed for the baptismal candidates.

There may be a hint in one of the Spanish exorcisms of the idea that the evil spirit can be dwelling or hiding in certain parts of the body, when it is said that Christ pursues the devil "to the marrows of the body." We saw a clear example in the exorcism of the *Gallicanum vetus* (and, in the Eastern tradition, in the Pseudo-Clementines and in one of the prayers of the Maronite baptismal service).[24] But other exorcisms in the Gallican tradition bring out this notion even more strikingly. In the *Bobbio Missal,* the prayer for the prebaptismal anointing, which takes place after the Effeta, reads: "Work, creature of oil, work, so that there may not hide here the unclean spirit, neither in the members nor in the marrows nor in a joint of the members, but let the power of Christ, the Son of the most high God, and of the Holy Spirit, work in you for ever." This formula, which appears in later sacramentaries among the rites for the anointing of the sick, is placed in the *Stowe Missal* at the chrismation after baptism, where it may have been given an apotropaic significance (against future demonic inhabitation). The presence of this prayer in both *Bobbio* and *Stowe* has been taken as an indication of its Celtic origin.[25] *Stowe* has an even more detailed expression of this Gaelic localization of the demonic presence in the following prebaptismal exorcism: "Holy Lord, almighty Father, eternal God, expel the devil and gentleness from this man, from his head, hair, crown, brain, forehead, eyes, ears, nose, mouth, tongue, under-tongue, throat, jaws, neck, breast, heart, from his whole body on the inside, from outside, from his hands, feet, all members, the joints of his members, from his words, works, and all activity now and to come, through you, Jesus Christ, who reign."[26] It is noteworthy that the final phrase, "now and to come," makes the prayer explicitly apotropaic as well as exorcistic. We could argue, of course, that every exorcism is at least implicitly apotropaic: the exorcist always wants the possessing demon to go out and never to return.

[23]*Liber ordinum* 26 (73).
[24]Below, at n. 54 (exorcism no. 12); above, at n. 19; Chap. 8 at n. 3; Chap. 10 at n. 46.
[25]*Bobbio* 243 (2.74; cf. 3.129); *Stowe* 31. See Puniet, "Baptême" 327.
[26]*Stowe* 24.

Our discussion of the Gallican baptismal practices has been somewhat sporadic, and it may be good to summarize the demonological
aspects of each of the major surviving documents. The *Old Gallican
Missal*'s rite "for making a Christian" contains, as we saw, the exorcism *Aggredior te,* a formula originally used for possessed persons
already baptized.[27] There follows a service for the explanation of the
creed and the Gospels and then an order called "Preliminaries for the
Scrutiny." In the latter, there is a collect in which Christ is asked to
"repel from these creatures of yours the invading snares of the devil,
so that, being cast down from every place, every deceit, he can never
harm either soul or body, so that, acknowledging the mark of divine
inscription, the enemy may confess that what has now begun to be
yours is alien to him—through the sign of the cross, which he will
never efface, imprinted for ever."[28]

In the order for baptism on Holy Saturday, the preface before the
exorcism of the water has a petition that "the head of the dragon may
be broken and crushed on these waters," thus paralleling the Eastern
blessing of the water.[29] The exorcism of the water is not antidemonic
but is simply a blessing addressed to the water and is basically the
same prayer that occurs in two forms in the *Gelasianum*.[30]

In the preface for the blessing of the font, there is this petition:
"Whoever here shall have renounced the devil, grant that they may
triumph over the world [*mundus*]." The ceremony of renunciation
itself consists of a single question: "Do you renounce Satan, the
pomps of the world [*saeculum*], and its pleasures?" with the response
"I renounce them."[31] In Chapter 6 I cited many examples of the
inclusion of the world in the renunciation of Satan. In France in the
fourth and fifth centuries instances come from Hilary of Poitiers and
"Hilary of Arles." The *Bobbio Missal* has a comparable formula: "Do
you renounce Satan, his pomps, his luxuries, this world?"[32]

The *Bobbio* order for the making of a Christian comes after the
Exultet on Holy Saturday. It begins with a prayer to God to guard his
servant and, "with the devil crushed," to strengthen him. The Lord
is then asked to assign to him the angel of peace, the angel of mercy,

[27]Above, at n. 19.
[28]*Mis. gal. vet.* 13.77 (23).
[29]Ibid. 27.163 (40).
[30]Ibid. 27.165 (40); Gel 446, 604. See Bartsch 354.
[31]*Mis gal. vet.* 27.168, 171 (41).
[32]*Bobbio* 244 (2.74); see above, Chap. 6 at n. 27.

who may lead him to eternal life with the help of the Holy Spirit and deliver him from the jaws of the enemy through the sign of Jesus Christ.[33] Next, the sign of the cross is made on him and the creed recited. Then comes the triple insufflation discussed above, symbolizing the reception of the Holy Spirit.[34] The order of baptism follows, beginning with a composite exorcism of the water: "I exorcize you, creature of water, . . . so that every power of the adversary, every army of the devil, every attack, every phantasm—be uprooted and be put to flight" and so forth.[35] Then comes a garbled version of the Gelasian *Procul ergo,* followed by the nondemonic blessing of the creature of water.

The *Bobbio* then inserts an exorcism of the candidate before he is baptized. The order of ceremonies is illogical, since presumably he has already received the Holy Spirit. God is besought to admit this servant to the font of eternal salvation, "so that [of] those whom you ordered to come from darkness to light none should be deceived by the frauds of the enemy." Then comes another version of the by now familiar Gallican exorcism formula: "I exorcize you, unclean spirit, by God the Father almighty, who made heaven and earth, the sea and all that is in them, so that every power of the adversary, every army of the devil, every attack, every phantasm be uprooted and put to flight from this creature so that it may become the holy temple of God" and so forth.[36] There follows the Effeta, the anointing with oil and the formula "Work, creature of oil," and the renunciation, which we have just seen.

The baptismal service of the *Missale gothicum,* which is dated between 690 and 710 and is usually ascribed to the church of Autun, has very sparse demonological elements. In the *contestatio* or preface to the blessing of the water, mention is made of God's Holy Spirit over the waters at the beginning of the world, and of the angel of Bethesda, and it is asked that the angel of God's piety be here in these sacred fonts; and then God is besought to pour out his Holy Spirit, the Paraclete, the Angel of Truth. Next the minister makes a cross with the chrism and says the following exorcism:

---

[33]*Bobbio* 228, 230 (2.71).

[34]Ibid. 232–233 (71–72); see above at n. 12.

[35]Ibid. 234. As in Greg 206, the original commands to the demonic forces remain, since the adapter failed to change the imperatives to subjunctives.

[36]Ibid. 240 (73). In this version there was an attempt to change the imperatives (*eradicare* and *effugare*) to subjunctives (*eradicitur* [*sic*] and *fugetur*).

I exorcize you, creature of water. I exorcize you, every army of the devil, every power of the adversary, every shade of demons. I exorcize you in the name of our Lord Jesus Christ of Nazareth, who was incarnated in the Virgin Mary, to whom the Father subjected all things in heaven and on earth. Fear and tremble, you and all your malice. Give place to the Holy Spirit so that it may be for all who descend into this font a laver of the baptism of regeneration for the remission of all sins, through our Lord Jesus Christ, who is to come in the seat of the majesty of his Father with his angels to judge you, enemy, and the world through fire for ever.

There follows a triple insufflation into the water, after which the priest pours in chrism in the form of a cross.[37]

The baptismal section of the *Stowe Missal* is a hodgepodge resulting from an awkward attempt to modify the Celtic ritual in terms of Roman practices. It begins with the Gelasian *Ergo maledicte*[38] and is followed by the strange prayer reproduced above detailing the various parts of the body from which the devil is to be expelled. There follows a misplaced formula for the consecration of holy water (it is to drive away demons and other harmful forces from the houses in which it is sprinkled). Then a consecration of salt: "God, who for the safety of man [constituted] a medicine in this salubrious salt, grant that his soul might be converted and snatched from the error of gentileness and confess the trinitarian God and repel the devil by renunciation and the sign of the cross of our Lord Jesus Christ, who reigns with the Father and the Holy Spirit for ever."[39]

After the Gelasian exorcism of the salt come the two Gelasian renunciations, separated by the exsufflation and anointing, as I described it above.[40] More Roman prayers follow[41] and then an Effeta and another anointing of breast and back with oil and chrism but this time without the exsufflation. After baptism comes the anointing with oil and chrism that is accompanied by the formula "Work, creature of oil."[42] This is virtually the only instance of an antidemonic rite after baptism in the later Western rituals, but although it is capable of an apotropaic (and therefore logical) interpretation, its

---

[37]*Missale gothicum* 33.257–258, ed. L. C. Mohlberg, REDsmf 5 (Rome 1961) 66–67.
[38]Gel 292; see Chap. 12 at n. 20.
[39]*Stowe* 24–25.
[40]Above at n. 9.
[41]E.g., Gel 285, 597, 419.
[42]See above at n. 25.

position here may simply be a mistake, and it may have corresponded to no real practice (or, at least, to no widespread practice).

I turn now to the last major tradition of Christian initiation, the rites of the Visigoths in Spain. Early reports of baptismal practices in the Iberian peninsula, though sparse, show that considerable variations were to be found from place to place. Isidore of Seville in the seventh century has a fair amount to say about baptism, but his testimony has often been dismissed as reflecting only his literary sources and not contemporary local customs. T. C. Akeley is no doubt right, however, in insisting that some native references can be sorted out, though probably not as many as he supposes. Isidore's description of exorcists sounds largely theoretical, and it may well be that the exorcistate did not exist in Spain as an independent order. He quotes the *Statuta ecclesiae antiqua* in its original Gallican form (exorcists are to "lay hands on the energumens, whether baptized or catechumens") and not in the later variation that originated in the Spain of his own day, which directs exorcists to work not only upon demoniacs but upon ordinary (that is, not violently possessed) catechumens as well: they are to lay hands "on energumens or on those who are to be baptized." Ildephonsus of Toledo simply repeats Isidore's version of the formula.[43]

When Isidore speaks of the exorcisms undergone by the catechumens, he does not explicitly say that they are performed by exorcists, as Ildephonsus does, but perhaps his use of the terms energumens and catechumens indicates that he has the *Statuta* formula in mind. He describes the preliminary ceremonies thus: "They are exorcized first, then they receive salt and are anointed. Now, exorcism is a speech of rebuke made against the unclean spirit in energumens or in catechumens, by which the most wicked power and inveterate malice or violent incursion of the devil is expelled from them and put to flight." It is obvious that basically the same exorcism was in use in Isidore's day as that used in later times. Ildephonsus repeats Isidore's description of exorcism as well as his statement that the power of the devil is insufflated in the candidates.[44] But before he mentions the insufflation, he goes on to describe exorcism further and to name the

<hr/>

[43]Isidore, *De eccl. off.* 2.13.4 (PL 83.793); Ildephonsus, *De cog. bapt.* 22 (PL 96.121); *Statuta ecclesiae antiqua* 95, ed. C. Munier, *Concilia Galliae, A. 314–A. 506,* CCL 148 (Turnhout 1963) 182–183. On the *Statuta* see Kelly, *Devil* 79–80. See Akeley, *Christian Initiation in Spain* 59ff., for his discussion of Isidore.

[44]Isidore 2.21.2 (814–815); Ildephonsus 23 (121). See above at n. 8.

formulas of the long order for the possessed mentioned earlier.[45] As we shall see shortly, this order was used on Palm Sunday.

According to the tenth-century *Antiphonary of León* (Akeley is inclined to classify this and the *Liber ordinum* as northern Spanish or late Visigothic), the candidates are exsufflated, exorcized (with the simple formula reflected in Isidore's description), and signed every day from the fourth Sunday of Lent until Palm Sunday. On the fourth Sunday itself, the sermon *Homo ille* is read. This exhortation, which has recently been attributed to Nicetas of Remesiana, speaks not of diabolical possession but of diabolical influence; it does, however, use what might be called the exorcistic subjunctive: "Let there depart all vain superstition, let there depart the respect given to the devil and his angels, let there depart the worship of idols, let there depart the error of the Gentiles." After the sermon (in which there is no specific reference to exorcism), the exorcisms are performed by subdeacons in the presence of the bishop; they sign the infants and touch them with their hands, praying God to let the candidates pass from darkness and wrath to his kingdom: "Let them depart from the domination of him who, since he was unwilling to be your subject, was not able to depart from the law of your power [and] is bound as befits his condition [?], so that from now on they may cease to be subject to the domination of the adversary; from this time now they begin to belong to the hope of salvation and to the grace of the Redeemer." A deacon then prays God to defend them so that, "with the ancient enemy and his machinations repulsed," the Church may rejoice in him. The bishop then signs them from a distance.[46]

The two weeks of preliminary exorcism lead up to what can only be described as a "Solemn High Exorcism" on Palm Sunday. There is first a triple exsufflation and exorcism of the oil. Then the lower clergy and the deacons or priests divide themselves into two choirs and chant a series of exorcisms. The formulas were fixed, to a certain extent, by the time of Ildephonsus (who died in the year 667), for he gives an incipit (*Deprehensae sunt insidiae*) that is repeated by the *León*

---

[45]Above at n. 23.

[46]*Ant. León* 133r–v (203–204). The sermon *Homo ille* is referred to in the *Liber comicus,* the seventh-century lectionary of Toledo, and is given by Johannes Krinke, "Der spanischen Taufritus im frühen Mittelalter," *Gesammelte Aufsätze zur Kulturgeschichte Spaniens* 9, Spanische Forschungen der Görresgesellschaft ser. 1 (Münster 1954) 33–116, esp. 40–42, as it appears in the tenth-century *Sacramentarium fuldense.* For Nicetas, see Chap. 7 at n. 40.

Antiphonary. However, it was apparently still the practice in his day to use a certain amount of improvisation, since he specifies that

> the language of the exorcism shall not be overly polished, or difficult to understand, or contain unusual expressions, but shall be simple, orderly, ardent, so shining with the intent of virtue that it may truly demonstrate the expelling of the prince of this world by the strength of its rebuke, and thereby too the hurling of bolts of terror in the spiritual combat that is waged against the aerial powers, so that the very expulsion of the invisible enemy may be observed in action in a kind of visible conquest, with the result that the catechumen is terrified by the thought of what he hears and the faithful are encouraged by the assault of the conflict.[47]

Ildephonsus's instructions are reminiscent of earlier accounts, especially John Chrysostom's,[48] and can be taken as stage directions to the participants. When the catechumens are infants, of course, only the effect on the "audience" remains pertinent. Even when there are adult candidates, however, the combat is not real or literal but moral and symbolic. Only when the same rite is applied to persons actually possessed physically by the devil, as in the *Liber ordinum,* is the combat thought actually to take place in the terms of the exorcisms.

In the baptismal order of the *Liber ordinum,* there is given only the first exorcism (*Recordare Satan*) of the series of thirteen found in the order for the possessed. We know, however, from the incipits of the *León Antiphonary* and from the presence of the exorcisms in the Romanized Catalan-Narbonne rite (which goes back to the beginning of the ninth century) that the whole series was used for the baptizands in the Palm Sunday service.[49] I will translate all of them in order to

[47]Ildephonsus 24 (121). The phrase that I translate "not overly polished" is "non turno verborum," literally "not with a lathe of words."

[48]See Chap. 9 at n. 17.

[49]Ildephonsus 25 (121–122); *Ant. León* 152v–153 (244–245); cf. Pierre de Puniet, "Catéchumenat," *DACL* 2.2579–2621, esp. 2601–2602; Akeley, *Christian Initiation* 153–154. *León* gives the incipits of formulas 1, 2, and 8, but formulas 3–7 and 8–13 were regarded as single units, to judge from M. S. Gros, "El antiguo ordo bautismal catalano-narbonense," *Hispania sacra* 28 (1975) 37–101, esp. 47–48, 51. Gros calendars the rite from two manuscripts, Paris B. N. lat. 933 (mid-eleventh century) from the abbey of Lagrasse near Carcassonne and Vic Cathedral 104 (twelfth century). Formula 8 (according to my numbering) covers five pages in the manuscripts (Lagrasse, fols. fv–hv; Vic, fols. 139–141); Gros refers only to the first column number of the corresponding material in the *Liber ordinum* (viz., col. 76), but I think that we can assume it to include everything from no. 8 to no. 13 (viz., cols. 76–78). The Vic *ordo* places the exorcisms on the day before Palm Sunday, whereas in the Lagrasse *ordo* they have been put with the Roman exorcisms at the beginning of the catechumenate.

illustrate the range and variety of images and concepts that could be brought into play in the combat against the forces of evil.

The ceremony begins with the deacon reciting the *Recordare Satan:*

> 1. Remember, Satan, what punishment is in store for you. When you see the man that my Lord and God is to call to his grace, flee and depart in confusion. But if you act deceitfully, Christ himself will be present in the judgment prepared for you. You will give an account to the living God and will not unsign the signed vessel, adjured as you are in the name of the Father, Son, and Holy Spirit, to whom this sign and unvanquished name belong.[50]

The clerics in choirs respond with this antiphon: "Resist the devil and he will flee from you. Approach God and he will approach you." The exorcism and antiphon are then twice repeated.[51]

The bishop thereupon recites the following three "chapters," "making a cross against the west." The three texts listed are those that Ildephonsus said were the basis of the prebaptismal exorcisms, namely, "May the Lord who has chosen Jerusalem rebuke you" (Zechariah 3.2); "It is said to you, Satan, go back" (cf. Matthew 4.10); "The lion from the tribe of Judah has conquered, the root of David" (Revelation 5.5).

The deacon and the other clerics then recite further exorcisms, beginning with the *Deprehensae sunt insidiae:*

> 2. Your snares have been apprehended, accursed damnable devil, and you no longer have power to deceive further those whom you thought to have conquered with the everlasting unhappiness of your evils. We advance against your raving madness, devil, and we exert our efforts against your evils, unclean spirit. Your snares, ancient enemy, have been exposed so that the breasts dedicated to Christ may be cleansed of all your works. Let the madness of your error desist from them and let the error of your malice entangle them no further. Depart in confusion from these servants of Christ and be shut out by the Spirit of adoption. Depart, adjured by the true God, and flee from these obsessed bodies. Do not dare now to do anything further in them, nor henceforward deceive them by the instigation of your work. But given over to the darkness of your wickedness and awaiting the punishment of raging

---

[50]*Liber ordinum* 26 (74); cf. 4 (26); thus far the *Liber* order for the possessed is identical to the León baptismal service. In the directions that follow, the *Liber* specifies that the presiding clergyman can be either the bishop or senior priest and says that he makes the sign of the cross against the west "towards the aforesaid sick man," that is, the demoniac.

[51]Ibid. 26 (74).

Gehenna, depart from these who are being redeemed by the Lord. And therefore depart, irremediable one, from these who have renounced you and have conceived the Lord Christ in heart, body, and mind. Dwell therefore outside of human activity and give honor to him who lives forever.[52]

This formula as it stands refers to a previous renunciation of Satan, which may be the result of an adjustment of the text to fit the case of a baptized demoniac, since the baptismal order of the *Liber* places the renunciation after the exorcism of the candidates as well as after the Effeta and the exsufflation and exorcism of the water.[53] However, in one of the formulas below (no. 7) there may be the suggestion that the persons in question have renounced the devil but have not yet been baptized.

3. We come against you, devil, with spiritual words and fiery speech. We ignite the hiding places in which you are concealed. We torment you with speech from our own mouth but with the power of our God. Flee, rebellious enemy. How long does your pride puff you up? How long will envy inflame you? Do you not recall, wretched one, that on this account you were shut out from the society of angels and that, cast down by the sentence of almighty God, you fell from heaven? Why do you not moderate your crimes? Why do you persecute the creature of God that God does not wish to perish? Fear, miserable one, fear the day of judgment that will be revealed to you in fire. Fear Christ, the punisher of your offenses. Let there be nothing between you and the human race, for which Christ died and arose.

4. We interdict you through him who delivered his people from the servitude of Egypt. We interdict you by him in whose name the wave of the Red Sea was divided and water became firm like a wall contrary to the nature of a flowing element. We interdict you by him in whose name the kingdoms of powerful kings are laid low. We interdict you by him who deigned to preserve the three boys in the furnace of burning fire before the eyes of the hostile king; by him in whose name Daniel trod upon the hunger-maddened lions, their ferocity subdued; by him who opened the eyes of the blind, made the deaf to hear, restored paralytics to their members; by him who loosed the tongues of the dumb, by him who healed those disturbed by a demon, by him who made the lame to run, who raised the dead to life. We interdict you by him who walked with his feet upon the waters, who established the sea and set a boundary for it, saying: "Up to here shall you come and here

[52]Ibid. (74–75).
[53]Ibid. 4(32). This is the order of Silos MS 4; Silos 3 and Madrid 56 agree.

shall you break your swelling waves." We admonish [*convenire*] you by his power to whom you yourself revealed your name, that you were Legion. We address you by his power who restored Lazarus to life and salvation and changed lamenting to joy when he had been undone by death, when his flesh had already dissolved in decay.

5. You have heard, therefore, accursed one, the great works and powers of the Lord. Fear, miserable one, the exterior darkness and the eternal fire that is prepared to burn you. Flee, Satan, from God's artifact, and leave the prepared work of the divine likeness.

6. We adjure you, unclean spirit, by God the Father almighty and the spotless Lamb, the Son of the most high God, who came to wash away our sins by baptism and the Holy Spirit and to bring us to the eternal kingdom, who chose the patriarchs, set up the prophets, predestined the apostles, who holds the key of David and closes what no one opens and opens what no one closes, who cast you, condemned for your pride, from the kingdom of heaven and assigned you to the darkness of hell. We exorcize † you by his power, unclean spirit, by God the Father, in whose name these are signed † with the most sacred sign. Henceforth do not dare to unsign them, devil, who are marked with the banner of Christ for the safeguarding of their salvation.

7. We interdict you before Christ and his angels that you do not hold or possess these persons further or pervert them from the way of truth, because in renouncing you they have been made servants of God and have made their refuge in the living God in order that they can be exalted and cleansed by the laver of water and by the Holy Spirit so that they can most fully know the living God, our Lord and Savior, who is blessed forever.

8. We act against you, devil, author of crimes, fugitive from heaven, slayer of unhappy souls, tempter of the world, envious of the just, enemy of chastity and of the continent, unclean demon, multiform spirit, crafty foe, horrendous damnable serpent. The unconquered name of Christ and the glorious banner of his power impel you to depart from these. We are the ministers of God; by invoking God's name we pursue you. You will be [or: are being] cast out to be burned, the head of evils, the deceiver of minds, the constructor of all crimes, the accursed audacious tempter, living amidst stench, dwelling in filth. We impel you, contemner of divine power; we threaten you to go out, we compel you to depart; we are waging a holy war against you, with the aid not of a humble foe but of the sword-bearer of old.

9. You are he who contemned God through the swelling of your heart and wished to be not only his equal but even his superior. You deluded man immediately after the world began and deceived simple souls, flattering them with lying words. You endeavored to tempt the Lord himself; you secretly approached, crept up in the hope of deceiving once again; but you were found out and repulsed and so laid low,

249

because you were recognized and detected. You set up for worship stone and wooden gods, which are to be burned along with you. You form the minds of the wretched with flattering error, fill them with pride, corrupt them with lust. You blind the hearts of men with cupidity, incite them with discord, impel them with wrath. You blockade roads with bandits, besiege the seas with pirates, and stir up wars and mutual bloodshed the whole world over.

10. Depart, ulcer of the world, savage, unclean, horrendous, enemy of the whole human race. Go out, flee far away, flee between heaven and earth, you who lost the high seat of heaven, where you were once an angel. For the salvation of nations has now come, and the salutary light has shone upon the men who are to be saved. Behold your idols abandoned and your dwellings and temples deserted because of the faith of the believing people. The Son of God excluded [excludes?] you from the soil of the earth, you are [will be?] seized by winds, whirled about by storms. Christ excluded [excludes?] you from all these. Depart to Tartarus, depart to beyond the seas. Acknowledge the Lord, give him honor, fear the creator of you and of all things, who for our sake put on a body in order to deliver us from bodily vices and to shut you out from our bodies. Behold, he now torments you who you said was to be tormented. Behold, he now saves men whom you thought to be only a man. Behold you now confess him to be unconquered whom you once handed over to persecution.

11. Depart, flee at the power of his name, by whose command the elements minister, the winds serve, the seas obey, the deeps give way, in terror of whom and by the power of whose name you and all demons are cast out of possessed bodies. Fear him, the maker of the world, the leader of the kingdom, the prince of light, the author of salvation, who illuminated the world by his birth and redeemed it by his passion, who alone among the dead was free and could not be held by Death, who crushed the strongholds of Tartarus and wrested away by the power of his majesty those whom you were holding captive in hell, who, with Death overcome, carried the flesh he had taken from the earth up to heaven, after his victory over the world, who sits at the right hand of the Father, receiving from him the eternal power of the kingdom, who is to come from heaven for your punishment, having the force of a magistrate and the power of a judge, to render rewards to the just and the penalty of eternal punishment to you and to all the impious.

12. By the invocation of this name you are cast out from these, by this saving sign you are shut out from their members. He now pursues you, to torment you while you are hidden and concealed within the marrows of the body. Henceforth do not dare to summon these souls and subvert them from the truth of faith to your superstition. Henceforth do not shut them off from the commandments of God and defile them with the filth of sin. Remove, wretched one, the sway of your

wickedness from the servants of Christ. For Christ has trodden upon your head, the world has shuddered at you, faith has crushed you. Go away from the bodies of the innocent; the name of Christ has its dwelling here. You entered as a transient, not as a resident; go out of your own accord, for you will be cast out against your will. Do not delay, enemy, go out, flee. Flee between heaven and earth where you were cast of old when you lost your dignity. From the soil of the earth the Son of God excludes you, casts you out, and sinks you in the depths of Tartarus. Seek the lower regions; you hold there the destined souls of the impious, to whom you may adhere in fellowship or be the torturer in their punishments.

13. Depart from the bodies of men; may perpetual night possess you, eternal gloom enfold you, so that after you have been cast out by the sign of Christ, the faithful souls may have peace and their bodies eternal salvation; so that adjured in the name of the Father, Son, and Holy Spirit, by the sign of holy anointing, you may never follow their footsteps.[54]

After these exorcisms have been said, the bishop or presiding priest goes on to recite a number of prayers, asking God to come to the aid of his oppressed servants. But all of these prayers seem to have reference to baptized demoniacs and therefore would not have been taken from the Palm Sunday order for catechumens. The final prayer speaks of Satan as persecutor of the faithful and of the sheep of God's house, who have been created and redeemed by him. However, like some prebaptismal prayers we have seen, it asks that the devil's victim may merit an angel of piety as a guardian.[55]

After this cosmic survey of the events of Satan's tragedy, past and future, the infants who have thus been exorcized are signed and anointed: the bishop makes the sign of the cross on their ears and mouths, singing, "Effeta, effeta with the Holy Spirit into the odor of sweetness, effeta."[56] Unlike the Roman rite, the Spanish service has no final enjoinder to the devil to begone. Isidore, as we saw, spoke of a reception of salt and an anointing but not of an Effeta. Ildephonsus says he hears that the salt ceremony takes place in some areas but affirms that he is opposed to the custom. According to him, the exorcisms are followed by the Effeta, as in the *Antiphonary*, but no formula is given.[57] After the Effeta, there is a laying on of hands and

[54]*Lib. ord.* 26 (75–78).
[55]Ibid. (79–80).
[56]Ibid. 4(27); *Ant. León* 153 (245).
[57]Ildephonsus 26–29 (123–124).

then a credal interrogation ("Will N. believe in God?" etc.). Finally, the palms are blessed and the mass for Palm Sunday is said. After the gospel, a sermon explaining the creed is to be given.

On Holy Saturday, after the blessing of the paschal candle and the reading of the third of the twelve lessons, the baptismal font is blessed and baptism administered. Few details of the rites are given at this point, but their general nature can be gathered from elsewhere in the *Liber ordinum,* in an "order for baptism to be celebrated at any time," which begins with the insufflation and exorcizing of the infant that I cited earlier.[58] He is then signed on the forehead and given his name, and the exorcism *Recordare Satan* is said facing west. After the Effeta, imposition of hands, and credal interrogation, the water is exsufflated and exorcized by means of the odd formula cited earlier.[59] One of the manuscripts has an additional exorcism of the water, which is a version of the Romanized Gallican formula,[60] and yet another formula is to be found in the section on holy water earlier in the *Liber;* it is said facing west:

> We invoke the help of the divine majesty against you, enemy serpent, so that your art may prevail by no poison of your vices in the element of this water, which we prepare by the mystery of Father, Son, and Holy Spirit for the saving of souls, the washing away of the crimes of sins. And therefore, accursed devil, after the invocation of the threefold sanctification, depart trembling, and let all devices [*machinamenta*] disappear from this water, that this water may remain pure and immaculate, sanctified by the divine richness for sanctifying souls, by this sign of the cross of our Lord Jesus Christ, who ordered you to be expelled from here.[61]

The renunciation of Satan and confession of faith follow. The priest first asks, "Do you, servant of God, renounce the devil and his angels?"

One of the ministers replies: "I renounce them."

"His works?"

---

[58]Above, at n. 8.

[59]Above, at n. 16.

[60]*Lib. ord.* 4 (30 n. 2: codex 3 of Silos, A.D. 1039): "Exorcidio te, creatura aquae, . . . ut omnis a te invidia et fantasmas diabolica procul abscedat, omnisque incursus daemonum et infestatio Satanae velociter separentur abs te," etc.

[61]Ibid. 2 (18). See also the insufflation and exorcism (both nondemonic?) of the water in the Ximenes *Missale mixtum* cited in Chap. 14 at n. 5.

"I renounce them."

"His empires?"

"I renounce them."[62]

"What is your name?"

The minister pronounces the child's name, and the priest repeats it at the beginning of his next question:

"N., do you believe in God the Father almighty?"

"I believe."

"And in Jesus Christ his only Son our Lord?"

"I believe."

"And in the Holy Spirit?"

"I believe."

"Then I baptize you in the name of the Father and of the Son and of the Holy Spirit, that you may have life eternal."

After the infant is baptized and clothed, the priest seals him with chrism, saying: "The sign of eternal life which God the Father almighty has given through Jesus Christ his Son to those who believe, to be saved." He lays his hands upon him and sums up the saving action that has taken place and prays for the seven gifts of the Holy Spirit to be poured into him.[63] As elsewhere in the Western tradition, the devil is now forgotten. The struggle is over, and the Vigil celebration of the Savior's Resurrection continues.

---

[62]Ibid. 4 (32). For the term *imperia* in the renunciation, see Chap. 6 at nn. 20, 31, 33. For the variants of the Vic *ordo,* see Gros (n. 49 above) 92, 98.

[63]*Lib. ord.* 4 (32).

14 /

Western Reforms

The baptismal service of *Ordo romanus XI*, as expanded in *Ordo romanus L*, came into use all over Europe after the tenth century; and it survived into modern times in its basic outlines, after a thousand years, in the rite for the baptism of adults in the *Roman Ritual*. The Protestant reformers of the sixteenth century, however, made radical changes in this service, as in other areas of the public worship of the Church.

Luther at first took over most of the demonological elements of the Latin, since he was firmly convinced of the need to combat the devil. According to the instruction that accompanies his revision of the baptismal ritual, Satan possesses the child before baptism and remains his enemy his whole life long.[1] He made an exception however, regarding the exorcisms of the material elements, all of which he omitted, no doubt considering them superstitious abuses. One of his disciples, Olavus Petri, explained that it was not necessary to exorcize salt, since it was a pure creature of God.[2] He obviously assumed that it was the purpose of the exorcism to free the salt of demonic ele-

---

[1]Martin Luther, *Das Taufbuchlin verdeutscht* (1523), ed. Emil Sehling, *Die evangelischen Kirchenordnungen des XVI Jahrhunderts* 1 (Leipzig 1902) 20. An English translation of this and many other orders of baptism can be found in J. D. C. Fisher, *Christian Initiation: The Reformation Period: Some Early Reformed Rites of Baptism and Confirmation and Other Contemporary Documents,* Alcuin Club Collections 51 (London 1970). See also Bruno Jordahn, "Der Taufgottesdienst im Mittelalter bis zur Gegenwart," *Leiturgia,* ed. K. F. Müller and W. Blankenburg, 5 (Kassel 1970) 349–640.

[2]*The Manual of Olavus Petri, 1529,* trans. Eric F. Yelverton (London 1953) 66.

ments. It is true that such a purpose was clearly expressed in the exorcisms and blessings of the water and oil used at baptism. But in the exorcism of salt, the salt is explicitly said to have been created by God for the safeguarding of the human race, and its only connection with the devil is to occur after its consecration, when it is to serve as a means for repelling him. Other formulas for the consecration of salt are similar.[3] However, the fact that these formulas begin with the words "I exorcize you, creature of salt," inevitably gave rise to the assumption that the purpose envisaged in the formulas was the purification of the salt. This interpretation of the word in an originally nondemonic formula of blessing can be seen in a modern English Catholic ritual, where the words "exorcizo te" in the consecration of the baptismal font are translated as "I command all evil to be gone from you."[4]

Sometimes a truly antidemonic formula would be retained but de-demonized. An example can be found in the Anglican Book of Common Prayer. In the original Prayer Book of 1549, the blessing of the baptismal water was inspired by the *Missale mixtum,* which was issued at the beginning of the sixteenth century under Cardinal Ximenes. This missal called for a triple insufflation and an exorcism, the purpose of which was to remove from the water "every evil of the spirit of wickedness."[5] It was followed by a blessing of the water (the latter also appears as a preface in the *Missale gallicanum vetus,* part of which I quoted above).[6] The English adaptation eliminates both the apostrophe to the water and reference to evil in the water and transforms the whole into a prayer of blessing:

O most merciful God, our Savior Jesu Christ, who hast ordained the element of water for the regeneration of thy faithful people, upon whom being baptized in the river of Jordan the Holy Ghost came down in the likeness of a dove, send down we beseech thee the same thy Holy Spirit to assist us, and to be present at this our invocation of thy holy name. Sanctify † this fountain of baptism, thou that art the sanctifier of all things, that by the power of thy word all those that shall be baptized

[3]See Chap. 12 at n. 10, and see the collection in Bartsch 387–389.
[4]*The Small Ritual: Being Extracts from the Rituale romanum in Latin and in English* (London 1964) 54–55. The same phrase is translated elsewhere in the ritual simply as "I adjure thee."
[5]*Missale mixtum* (PL 85.464–465).
[6]See Chap. 13 at n. 29.

therein may be spiritually regenerated and made the children of ever-lasting adoption. Amen.

O merciful God, grant that the old Adam, in them that shall be baptized in this fountain, may so be buried that the new man may be raised up again. Amen.

Grant that all carnal affections may die in them, and that all things belonging to the spirit may live and grow in them. Amen.

Grant to all them which at this fountain forsake the devil and all his works that they may have power and strength to have victory and to triumph against him, the world, and the flesh. Amen.[7]

The *Gallicanum vetus* and *Missale mixtum* speak only of triumphing over the world, but the English version adds the devil and the flesh, thus making it a prayer for victory over the devil in the future.

Further alterations were made in the 1552 edition. The initial paragraph was omitted, and the remaining petitions were so altered as to remove all suggestion of their having been part of a blessing of water:

O merciful God, grant that the old Adam in these children may be so buried that the new man may be raised up in them. Amen.

Grant that all carnal affections may die in them, and that all things belonging to the spirit may live and grow in them. Amen.

Grant that they may have power and strength to have victory and to triumph against the devil, the world, and the flesh. Amen.[8]

In the first edition of his *Taufbuchlin,* Luther kept all the ancillary ceremonies like exsufflation, the giving of salt, and so on, but he said in his instruction that they were not essential for the rite, since baptism could be administered without them; and he added that they were not the proper means to make the devil frightened or to put him to flight, for the evil spirit was contemptuous of greater things than they. Such a literalist interpretation of the liturgy is typical of a reform mentality, which is usually puritan or at least purist in outlook; there is always a drive to pare away the accidentals, the trimmings, and to preserve only the essential and "appropriate" aspects, narrowly conceived. Thus Luther did not consider the possibility that these ceremonies were symbolic of greater things than themselves or

[7]F. E. Brightman, *The English Rite: Being a Synopsis of the Sources and Revisions of the Book of Common Prayer* (London 1915) 2.738. Brightman's work was reissued in 1921 as "second edition revised" with the same pagination (and presumably with minimal corrections), and this edition was reprinted in 1970 at Farnborough.
[8]Ibid. 739.

that they could be regarded as efficacious because of the underlying premise of appeal to God and trust in his aid.

The inevitable result of such an attitude is the elimination of the purely dramatic aspects of ritual and a new emphasis on straightforward declaration. Thus, in the second edition of his baptismal service, issued in 1526, Luther reprinted his instruction but omitted all the ceremonies that he had labeled as nonessential. For instance, he dropped the exsufflation but kept the formula that accompanied it ("Go out, you unclean spirit, and give place to the Holy Spirit"). He also made drastic cuts in the other prayers and formulas, both demonic and nondemonic. The first edition contained the three major Roman exorcisms said over the male infants, namely the *Ergo maledicte,* the *Audi maledicte,* and the *Exorcizo te immunde.*[9] But the second edition kept only the first part of the third, thus: "I exorcize you, you unclean spirit, in the name of the Father † and the Son † and the Holy Spirit, that you go out and retreat from this servant of Jesus Christ."[10]

The fact that Luther included any exorcism at all suggests that he took the prebaptismal indwelling of the devil literally. He eliminated the other formulas because, presumably, one word of command was thought to be sufficient. Sometimes, however, his followers in later times reverted to the full complement of exorcisms as given in the first edition.[11] Only at the end of the sixteenth century was the efficacy of exorcism seriously called into question. It was in due course rejected as a superstitious practice, and even the brief exorcism retained in the 1526 *Taufbuchlin,* along with the formula of exsufflation, was eliminated.[12] The renunciation of Satan (and all his works and all his ways) was retained, however, and survives in most Lutheran denominations to the present time. The Church of Sweden is a notable exception; there it was eliminated, and the very existence of the devil was abjured.[13]

---

[9]Gel 292, 294, 296; see Chap. 12 at nn. 20–23.

[10]Luther, *Das Taufbuchlin verdeudscht aufs neu zu gericht* (1526), Sehling 1.22: "Ich beschwere dich, du unreiner Geist, bei dem Namen des Vaters † und des Sons † und des heiligen Geistes, das du aus farest und weichest von diesem Diener Jhesu Christi."

[11]E.g., in the *Kirchenagenda* of Mansfeld, published in 1580 (Sehling 2.219), which omits only the last part of the first and first part of the second exorcism.

[12]See Wallace Notestein, *A History of Witchcraft in England from 1558 to 1718* (Washington, D.C., 1911) 87 n. 36; Jordahn (n. 1 above) 511–520.

[13]The renunciation was also lacking in the Swedish Lutheran Church in America until its merger with the American Lutheran Church.

The Calvinists for their part, being puritans par excellence, rejected exorcism from the beginning and also eliminated the renunciation and the other ceremonies that had collected around the central act of baptism. The Church of England at first followed Lutheran precedents[14] and included an exorcism, modeled on various parts of the Roman formulas:

> I command thee, unclean spirit, in the name of the Father, of the Son, and of the Holy Ghost, that thou come out and depart from these infants, whom our Lord Jesus Christ hath vouchsafed to call to his holy baptism, to be made members of his body and of his holy congregation. Therefore, thou cursed spirit, remember thy sentence, remember thy judgment, remember the day to be at hand wherein thou shalt burn in fire everlasting, prepared for thee and thy angels. And presume not hereafter to exercise any tyranny towards these infants whom Christ hath bought with his precious blood, and by this his holy baptism calleth to be of his flock.[15]

But in 1552, under Swiss Calvinist influence (that especially of Bucer), the exorcism was dropped. There was no exsufflation rite or formula even in the 1549 version, but the same was true of the service of the Sarum rite, which had previously been in force in England.[16]

In another detail the Book of Common Prayer, again inspired by Lutheran sources, adds to rather than subtracts from the demonological elements of the baptismal service. When the candidate is signed before baptism, the priest says, "Receive the sign of the holy cross, both in thy forehead and in thy breast, in token that thou shalt not be ashamed to confess thy faith in Christ crucified, and manfully to fight under his banner against sin, the world, and the devil, and to continue his faithful soldier and servant unto thy life's end. Amen."[17] It is noteworthy that in the 1552 and later editions this ceremony is placed after the actual baptism, as being more appropriate to one who has already been fully admitted into the Church. It thereby fits the

---

[14]For a comparison of Catholic, Lutheran, and Anglican rites, see Brightman, *English Rite* 1.cxii–cxxii; 2.724–777.

[15]Ibid. 2.730.

[16]See *Manuale ad usum percelebris ecclesiae sarisburiensis,* ed. A. Jeffries Collins, HBS 91 (London 1960) 25ff.

[17]Brightman, *English Rite* 2.728. Brightman traces the formula to the *Encheiridion* of Cologne, published under Archbishop Hermann von Wied in 1538.

traditional pattern, for the most part neglected in the West, of taking prophylactic measures against the devil after baptism.

The same Lutheran sources were drawn upon for the alteration of the renunciation ceremony to include specific mention of the world. The third question concerning the flesh seems to have been an independent addition; we may compare the addition of the devil and the flesh to the Anglican blessing of the water. The questions are as follows: "Dost thou forsake the devil and all his works? Dost thou forsake the vain pomp and glory of the world, with all the covetous desires of the same? Dost thou forsake the carnal desires of the flesh, so that thou wilt not follow nor be led by them?"[18]

The Anglican service, therefore, became a model of "rational demonology." Gone is the fiction of diabolical possession in the unbaptized, the histrionic fulminations against the devil and the unclean spirits, the embarrassing addresses to water, oil, and salt, and the anointings. There remains nothing but an address to the faithful, a subdued prayer or two, a Gospel reading, a simple dialogue involving a calm renunciation of the devil and the world, a confession of faith, and a desire to be baptized. Then, after the baptism, a discreet sign of the cross on the child's forehead (the oil of the 1549 service has been dropped), and indirect address: "We receive this child into the congregation of Christ's flock, and do sign him with the sign of the cross, in token that hereafter he shall not be ashamed to confess the faith of Christ crucified, and manfully to fight under his banner against sin, the world, and the devil, and to continue Christ's faithful soldier and servant unto his life's end. Amen." The service ends with a recitation of the Lord's Prayer and an admonition to the godparents, beginning with these words: "Forasmuch as these children have promised by you to forsake the devil and all his works, to believe in God, and to serve him, you must remember that it is your parts and duties to see that these infants be taught, so soon as they shall be able to learn, what a solemn vow and promise they have made by you."

They are to be brought back for confirmation when they shall have reached the age for learning their prayers and catechism. This cere-

[18]Brightman 734–736. The second question combines the *omnes pompae eius* of Sarum, the *vanitas et gloria saeculi* of the *Encheiridion,* and the *mundus et omnes concupiscentiae eius* of Hermann von Wied's Protestant *Einfaltigs Bedencken* (Cologne 1543). From 1552 on the three questions were combined into a single one.

mony, performed by the bishop, had long since been separated from the baptismal service.[19] Originally, of course, it was an anointing with chrism, but Cranmer was content with a sign of the cross and the laying on of hands.[20] As in the Roman service, this "confirmation," or strengthening, is left abstract, with the foe remaining unnamed.

The Anglican services continued virtually unchanged until 1968, when an experimental ritual was put into use. In this order, the great adversary's name has been banished even from the renunciation. And in the case of infants, the sponsors (and parents) speak not for their charges but for themselves. The priest addresses them: "Those who bring children to be baptized must affirm their allegiance to Christ and their rejection of all that is evil. It is your duty to bring up these children to fight against evil and to follow Christ. Therefore I ask, 'Do you turn to Christ?' They answer, 'I turn to Christ.' 'Do you repent of your sins?' 'I repent of my sins.' 'Do you renounce evil?' 'I renounce evil.'" But Satan does not lurk under the global designation of "evil" throughout the entire service, since the old formula accompanying the signation is preserved with the admonition to fight against sin, the world, and the devil.[21]

In addition to diminishing the demonological aspects of baptism, the reformers of the sixteenth century also translated the services into the vernacular languages. This change made the whole more intelligible to the "audience," but at the same time it had the effect of reducing the mystery and impressiveness of the rites. In contrast, the Roman service continued to be said in Latin; but it too had lost something of its dramatic aspects. Well before the sixteenth century, the practice of celebrating the seven scrutinies during Lent had died out, and baptism itself was usually no longer conferred during the Easter Vigil service—though the font was still blessed at this time. What remained was a one-act presentation of the soul's redemption from the powers of evil, abstracted now from the ritual drama of the

[19]See Fisher, *Christian Initiation: Baptism in the Medieval West,* which has the sub-subtitle *A Study in the Disintegration of the Primitive Rite of Initiation.*

[20]For further details, see Leonel L. Mitchell, *Baptismal Anointing,* Alcuin Club Collections 48 (London 1966) 177–187: Appendix I, "Anglican Use of Baptismal Oil."

[21]Peter Jagger, *Christian Initiation, 1552–1969: Rites of Baptism and Confirmation since the Reformation Period,* Alcuin Club Collections 52 (London 1970) 140–141. In the separate confirmation service, the rejection of evil is repeated.

life, death, and resurrection of Christ in the temporal cycle of the liturgy.

During the sixteenth century, the Roman rite remained that of *Ordo romanus L.*[22] The Protestant prejudice against exorcism and material sacramentals had the effect of strengthening Catholic determination to continue using them, in spite of sometimes quite justifiable charges of inappropriateness or obsoleteness. In 1614, in the *Roman Ritual* issued by Pope Paul V, some changes were introduced, but none of them qualitative. A distinction was made at last between adult and infant baptism. *Ordo L* remained the basis for the adult service, though some of the ceremonies, like the exorcism of ashes and the explanation of Gospels, creed, and Lord's Prayer, were omitted and others were added, like the elaborate (but nondemonic) signation of the five senses and the insufflation of the Holy Spirit.[23] One important change was made regarding the anointing with the oil of catechumens. Instead of preceding the renunciation, it now followed it, and this exorcism was added: "Go out, unclean spirit, and give honor to the living and true God. Flee, unclean spirit, and give place to Jesus Christ his Son. Depart, unclean spirit, and give place to the Holy Spirit the Paraclete." The whole service, of course, was to be performed on one occasion.

In the 1614 order for the baptism of infants, the first renunciation was omitted (as it was in Luther's ritual), but a triple exsufflation and the accompanying formula ("Go out from him, unclean spirit, and give place to the Holy Spirit the Paraclete") remained, as did the exorcism of salt and the prayer asking that the bonds of Satan be broken. The double signings before the exorcisms were omitted, and only the third of the three sets of exorcisms was kept, which comprised the *Exorcizo te immunde* (male version) and the *Ergo maledicte*. Before entering the baptistery, the priest was to stand with his back to it and say an exorcism over the infant based on the last part of the *Nec te latet:* "I exorcize you, every unclean spirit, in the name of God the Father almighty, and in the name of Jesus Christ his Son, our Lord and judge, and in the power of the Holy Spirit, that you depart

---

[22]This can be seen from the service in the edition of Cardinal Giulio Antonio Santorio, *Rituale sacramentorum romanum Gregorii papae XIII pont. max. iussu editum* (Rome 1584) 29–74. For some peculiarities in the printed *Ritual romanum* of 1487, see Fisher (n. 19 above) 113–114.

[23]See Chap. 13 at n. 13.

from this creature of God that our Lord has deigned to call to his holy temple that he himself may become a temple of the living God and that the Holy Spirit may dwell in him, through the same Christ our Lord, who is to come to judge the living and the dead and the world by fire." The Effeta (with the admonition to the devil to flee) and renunciation followed. The exorcisms of the water and the oil of catechumens and the chrism remained the same.

In 1962, there appeared the first of a series of new rites for the Roman Catholic Church. The Sacred Congregation of Rites published an optional version of the adult service divided into seven sessions, in imitation of the seven scrutinies of the old order.[24] A renunciation of Satan and profession of faith was included in the first session and repeated in the final one, on Holy Saturday, but the earlier set was omitted in the first draft (October 1965) produced by the commission established during the Second Vatican Council for the reform of the liturgy.[25] Meanwhile, in 1964, in conformity with the decree on the liturgy by the Second Vatican Council, the rite of infant baptism was translated into the vernacular languages. The exorcisms, with their presupposition that the child was possessed by the devil, immediately became an embarrassment. In Ireland, the problem was met by leaving the formulas in Latin.

In the October 1965 draft the exsufflation ceremony at the beginning was made optional. The explanation was that recent converts from agnosticism would not yet have a sufficiently developed faith to permit them to perceive the influence of spiritual powers and accept the sign of exsufflation, while others—for example, converts from animism—were truly in need of such an exorcism and would understand its form.[26] The formula for the rite was somewhat modified,

---

[24]*Acta apostolicae sedis* 54 (1962) 310–338, decree of 16 April 1962. This new "catechumenate" service as well as the usual adult service and that for the baptism of infants (discussed below) can be found in both Latin and English in *Collectio rituum pro dioecesibus Civitatum foederatarum Americae septentrionalis: Ritual Approved by the National Conference of Bishops of the United States of America* (New York 1964). The new service allowed the laying on of hands to be substituted for the exsufflation, insufflation, or anointing, if it were thought to be more appropriate.

[25]Robert D. Duggan, "Conversion in the *Ordo initiationis christianae adultorum,*" *Ephemerides liturgicae* 96 (1982) 57–83, 209–252; 97 (1983) 141–223, esp. 96.229.

[26]Ibid. 96.229 n. 133, quoting the report of August 1965. Balthasar Fischer, "De initiatione christiana adultorum," *Notitiae* 3 (1967) 55–70, esp. 60–61, uses the same language but goes on to say that the 1962 rite had proposed instead of the exsufflation the gesture of extending the right hand towards the candidates. But even this gesture,

but the devil was still addressed: "The Lord repels you, devil, by the breath [*spiritus*] of his mouth and orders you to depart, because his kingdom has drawn near." According to the accompanying explanation, this formula makes it clear that the Lord, whose kingdom has come, repels the devil, not the priest and certainly not his breath. Moreover, the words "from him" (*ab eo*) were deliberately omitted, lest the impression be revived that the Church considered the candidate to be possessed.[27]

However, by the time that the candidates were to be brought to the phase of the "major exorcisms" or scrutinies, they were all to be considered sufficiently prepared not only to be told about the devil and his angels but also to hear the devil addressed and denounced in formulas modeled upon the traditional exorcisms of the scrutinies. The chief exemplar was the *Exorcizo te immunde* in its various forms,[28] but the command to "go out and depart" (*ut exeas et recedas*) was reduced simply to "depart," no doubt for the same reason that the phrase *ab eo* was removed from the exsufflation formula, to avoid the implication of actual diabolical possession.[29]

But upon further consideration, the commissioners came to the conclusion that any sort of address to the devil would imply physical possession. As Balthasar Fischer, the chief spokesman for the commissioners, later explained (referring specifically to the new infant ritual): "Such an utterance cannot but suggest the presence *here*—and prac-

---

Fischer says, which is as "apotropaic" as the exsufflation, would not be understood by new converts from agnosticism. He adds that all converts would be clearly instructed about the devil and his angels in later stages of the initiation process.

[27]Duggan 96.230 n. 137. See Fischer, "De initiatione" 61.

[28]See Chap. 12 at n. 23.

[29]The texts are given by Duggan. For the first scrutiny, see 97.176 n. 334, draft of March 1966. I translate: "I exorcize you, malign spirit; give honor to the living and true God, give honor to Jesus Christ his son and to the Holy Spirit, and depart, and no longer lead these servants of God to the filth of sin. For he commands you who mercifully revealed to the sinful Samaritan woman the fountain of water springing to eternal life." For the formula of the second scrutiny, see 97.184 n. 352, which translates: "I exorcize you, malign spirit, through the Father and Son and Holy Spirit, that you depart and no longer dare to blind these servants of God by your fallaciousness. For he commands you who told the light to shine from the darkness and who opened the eyes of the man born blind, so that we too would believe in the Son of God." For the exorcism of the third scrutiny, see 97.189 n. 358; it runs: "I exorcize you, malign spirit, in the name of the Father and Son and Holy Spirit, that you depart and no longer lead these servants of God into the path of death. For he commands you who restored Lazarus from the tomb and, destroying the rule of death, freed us by his own resurrection."

tically speaking, that means in this candidate for baptism, in this truly 'innocent' infant—of the Devil, who has to give way so that the Holy Spirit can enter."[30] But in addition to this practical consideration, Fischer puts forth a theoretical justification for the change that in my opinion is based on a serious misreading of history. He says:

> What has taken place is purely and simply an adaptation necessitated by the theological understanding of the situations and relationships referred to in these texts, for that understanding has grown organically since the texts themselves first saw the light. A developed theology of original sin has made possible a sharper distinction than was possible in the early centuries between demonic possession and the status of belonging to the realm of Satan's dominion—a status which is to be predicated of infants without any suggestion of personal guilt. From this vantage-point, it would seem mandatory to surrender the formula of a direct scolding of the Devil, for all its unique and undeniable majesty.[31]

This analysis seems to be based on the fallacy, which Dölger exposed, that the prebaptismal exorcisms were originally formulated as a ritual response to the doctrine of original sin, whereas, if anything, the doctrine of original sin was formulated as an explanation for the exorcisms.[32] We have seen that Saint Augustine developed his theology of original sin long after belief in the literal, corporeal demonic possession of the unbaptized had evaporated and that nevertheless long after Augustine's time formulas of baptismal exorcism continued to be elaborated. Fischer and his colleagues have apparently failed to appreciate that these formulas were to be taken not literally but symbolically. They have missed the dramatic and allegorical dimensions of

---

[30]Balthasar Fischer, "Baptismal Exorcism in the Catholic Baptismal Rites after Vatican II," *Studia liturgica* 10 (1974) 48–55, esp. 53. Further light on the thinking of the commission can be glimpsed in two articles by a student of Fischer's, Rudy Kriegisch, "Do You Give up the Glamor of Evil?" and "Go Out from Him, Unclean Spirit," *African Ecclesial Review* 22 (1980) 22–28, 91–97.

[31]Fischer, "Baptismal Exorcism" 53.

[32]See Dölger, *Exorzismus* 39–43; Kelly, *Devil* 41. Cf. Aidan Kavanagh, *The Shape of Baptism: The Rite of Christian Initiation* (New York 1978) 91: "A doctrine of original sin involving personal culpability for everyone did not produce change in liturgical practice; rather, change in liturgical practice concerning infant baptism produced the Augustinian concept of original sin as necessarily implying personal guilt." On the question of whether infants were exorcized at the beginning, see my conclusion to Chap. 5 above.

the rites in spite of Fischer's acknowledgment of the impressive nature of the baptismal confrontations with the devil.

Fischer sums up the change from "imprecatory" to "deprecatory" exorcisms as follows: "We no longer speak to the Devil (considered as being present); we speak with God about the Devil (still seriously considered as personal)."[33] Robert Duggan, who has given a detailed analysis of the proceedings of the baptismal commission, in my opinion goes beyond what the commissioners intended in this instance when he says that the "more theologically correct" mode of the final form of the exorcistic rituals "refuses to envision the Devil as being present. The 'myth' of an actually present Devil has been substituted for by a more reflectively aware form of expression."[34] As I understand him, Fischer does not mean to deny the spiritual presence of the devil; the devil is still considered a personal being of great angelic powers who is "within hearing"—who can realistically be confronted by direct address. Rather, Fischer and his colleagues feared that treating the devil as spiritually present could give rise to the mistaken impression that the devil is regarded as inhabiting the baptismal candidates by physical possession. But it is true, as we shall see, that the formulas finally enshrined in the new rituals give little or no sense of the possibility that the devil or other evil spirits might be witnesses to, or even obstructors of, the ceremony. Fischer justifies the deprecatory form of exorcism as traditional, and so it is. But since he and his fellow commissioners have attempted to avoid the language of corporeal possession, most of the resulting formulas designated as exorcisms can hardly be considered to be exorcisms in any traditional sense.

Let me summarize the changes that have occurred, by looking at the final versions of the new baptismal services. I begin with the infant ritual, which was officially issued in 1969.[35] The exorcisms of the water and salt have been eliminated; salt, in fact, is no longer to be given at all, and the Effeta, which is optional, is not taken as an occasion to order the flight of the devil (or to request, in deprecatory fashion, that God put him to flight). The rubrics announce a "prayer of exorcism" before the prebaptismal anointing, but it is not exorcistic in

[33]Fischer, "Baptismal Exorcism" 53.

[34]Duggan 96.231.

[35]*Rituale romanum: Ordo baptismi parvulorum* (Vatican City 1969; ed. 2 1973). The translation issued in December 1969 by the International Committee on English in the Liturgy is in Jagger 275–288.

any accepted meaning of the word. It simply acknowledges that God sent his son into the world to expel from man the power of Satan, the spirit of iniquity, and to bring man out of the kingdom of darkness to the splendor of his kingdom of light. It ends with a petition to set the children free from original sin and make them temples of the Holy Spirit. An alternative formula speaks of man's rescue from the slavery of sin and prays for these children, "who will have to face the world with its temptations, and fight the devil in all his cunning." Since it looks forward to the future, this part of the prayer is apotropaic in character. But as it proceeds, there is a trace of the exorcistic, rationalized after the manner of the Fathers to imply, not demonic possession, but pervasive diabolic influence: "Your Son died and rose again to save us. By his victory over sin and death, bring these children out of the power of darkness." It ends by reverting to an apotropaic note: "Strengthen them with the grace of Christ, and watch over them at every step in life's journey."

As in Archbishop Cranmer's reformed service, the priest does not address the infants as if they were adults but rather speaks to the parents and godparents: they are to take care to keep the child from the contagion of sin, and as in the new Anglican service, it is they who make the acts of renunciation and profession. The renunciation may take the traditional pattern of the rejection of Satan, and all his works, and all his pomps (or as the English translation puts it, "all his empty promises"); or it may take the following form:

> "Do you reject sin, so as to live in the freedom of God's children?"
> "I do."
> "Do you reject the glamor of evil, and refuse to be mastered by sin?"
> "I do."
> "Do you reject Satan, father of sin and prince of darkness?"
> "I do."

The new ritual therefore recognizes that the infants have no personal sins to renounce. It is true that the doctrine of original sin is still stressed, but this sin is removed by God rather than renounced by the infant (or in the infant's name). Satan is still singled out as the great adversary in the alternative form of renunciation, but no personal allegiance to him is hinted at. There is simply the presumption that in committing sin a person follows Satan.

266

The new ritual for adults was issued at the beginning of 1972.[36] It resembles the infant ritual in suppressing the demonic aspects of the various "material" ceremonies. As already indicated, the devil is no longer addressed and therefore plays no part in the ritual except as someone who is talked about. There is no sense of re-presenting salvation history, and none of the participants assume roles other than their own. Except in the rite of exsufflation, which is retained as an option for use in primitive cultures (as we shall see), there is almost no dramatic aspect remaining, apart from that arising from the fundamental symbolism of the various rituals of anointing, washing, clothing, and so on. The full-scale adult ritual is divided into three periods or degrees: (1) the making of the catechumens; (2) the rite of election and the time of purification and illumination; and (3) the celebration of the sacraments of initiation.

The first degree begins by having the candidates express their first adherence, and the ceremony includes an elaborate signing of the forehead and senses. There are no demonic references in the standard ritual, but an alternative form is given for use, at the discretion of the local episcopal conferences, in regions where there are active cults for the worship of "spiritual powers," or for calling up the shades of the dead, or for obtaining benefits by the use of magic arts. The candidates are first exsufflated, and the following exorcism is pronounced: "Repel the malign spirits by the spirit of your mouth, O Lord; command them to go back, for your kingdom has drawn near."[37]

In spite of the efforts of the authors of the ritual to avoid the implication of actual corporeal possession, the combination of blowing into the candidates' faces and a prayer to repel evil spirits would seem to make the conclusion of actual demonic inhabitation a natural one unless the candidates were to be carefully instructed in the symbolism of the ceremony. The nature of the evil spirits referred to, both here and in the suggested formulas of cult renunciation that follow, remains rather vague. It is, however, assumed that they have real existence, and they are to be renounced by their native names. The candidates are instructed publicly to reject the powers that are not God

---

[36]*Rituale romanum: Ordo initiationis christianae adultorum* (Vatican City 1972 corr. repr. 1974); provisional translation, *Rite of Christian Initiation of Adults* (Washington, D.C., 1974); commentary (by Barbara O'Dea et al.), *Christian Initiation of Adults* (Washington, D. C., 1985).

[37]Ibid. 34 no. 79.

and to renounce those cults in which veneration is not paid to God. But in the actual formula used, they promise not to abandon God and Christ in the future and return to the service of alien powers.[38] In an alternative formula, the traditional demonic nature of the alien spirits is made clear when Christ is described as the Lord of the living and the dead, who commands all spirits and demons. But in the renunciations of magic and magicians that follow, there is no suggestion that the magic is demonically operative or connected to demon worship.[39]

All catechumens (not just those in pagan countries, therefore) may partake in celebrations of the word of God, which can include a series of "minor exorcisms."[40] The stated purpose of the prayers of exorcism, all of which are addressed to God or Christ, is to show the catechumens the true nature of the spiritual life, the struggle between the flesh and the spirit, the place (*momentum*) of renunciation in achieving the beatitudes of the kingdom of God, and the continual necessity of divine aid.[41]

The first formula asks God to turn away (*avertere*) from the catechumens every malign spirit and every working of error and sin, so that they may deserve to become the temple of the Holy Spirit (no. 113). This phraseology could be interpeted not only as exorcistic (in the sense of seeking the removal of all evil spirits that are now present with them) but also as apotropaic (keeping all such spirits away from them until they can be baptized). The prayer ends with a reference to Christ's deliverance of the world *a malo,* the ambiguous Gospel phrase that can be taken as referring either to abstract evil or to the Evil One.

But the word *spiritus* as used in this prayer is also capable of abstract as well as personal meaning, as is evident from some of the other formulas. In one, God is asked to deliver his servants "from all evils and the servitude of the enemy" and to take from them "the spirit of falsehood, cupidity, and wickedness" (no. 115). This is the language of sin demons; but it could also be understood as referring to attitudes or habits, as it does in the previous formula, where there is no demonic reference: God is asked to remove incredulity and doubt and other

---

[38]Ibid. 34–35 no. 80: "Absit ergo a vobis, ut Deum eiusque Christum deseratis et alienis potestatibus serviatis. (R. Absit a nobis.) Absit a vobis ut N. et N. colatis. (R. Absit a nobis)."

[39]Ibid. 151–152 no. 371.

[40]Ibid. 46–49 nos. 113–118; five alternative formulas are given as well, 152–155 no. 373.

[41]Ibid. 44 no. 101.

vices from his servants and to renew in them "the spirit of faith and
piety" and so on (no. 114).[42] The fourth formula is apotropaic,
whether in an abstract or personal sense ("A spiritu cupiditatis et
avaritiae, voluptatis et superbiae serventur immunes"), but the last
two "exorcisms" are completely positive and have no reference to evil
at all.[43] The anointing with the oil of catechumens can take place at this
time. But though the celebrant is instructed to precede the ceremony
with one of the foregoing exorcisms, there is nothing demonic either
in the formula for blessing the oil or in applying it to the catechumens.[44]

The second stage of initiation begins with the rite of election on the
First Sunday of Lent. Three scrutinies are held on the Third, Fourth,
and Fifth Sundays, and they follow the ancient forms in giving a
prominent place to exorcism. The formula of the first scrutiny is not so
much exorcistic as apotropaic, though with reference to the limited
future of the time remaining before baptism; and part of it seems
almost a paraphrase of the final petitions of the Lord's Prayer: "Do not
permit them, relying on empty self-confidence, to be deceived by the
devil's power, but deliver them from the spirit of fallaciousness."
Christ is asked to command the malign spirit whom he conquered by
his resurrection.[45] The provisional English version mistranslates,
"Command the spirit of evil *to leave them*," thus adding the sort of
phrase that the authors of the rite were careful to excise.[46] In the second
scrutiny, the celebrant asks Christ to deliver all those who suffer under
the yoke of the father of falsehood;[47] and in the final scrutiny, the elect

[42]One of the formulas of confirmation combines the personal and impersonal use of
spiritus: "Immitte in eos Spiritum Sanctum Paraclitum; da eis spiritum sapientiae et
intellectus," etc. (95 no. 230).

[43]The same is true of the last alternative formula (no. 373.5); the fourth alternative
formula speaks only of deliverance from vice; the second is similar except for an
ambiguous reference to the spirit of unbelief ("spiritui diffidentiae oboedientes"). The
first formula, however, asks for the removal of every temptation and all the envy of
the enemy. The third addresses Christ and recalls his quieting of the storm and his
deliverance of demoniacs and asks him to repress the adverse power of the enemy.

[44]Ibid. 52–53 nos. 127–132.

[45]Ibid. 65–66 no. 164. The earlier drafts spoke of "malign spirits," in the plural
(Duggan 97.177 n. 337). The alternative formula asks for deliverance from the servitude of sin and Satan's heavy yoke and from Satan's pernicious deceits (162 no. 379).

[46]Duggan 97.175–176 gives both the Latin and the English and comments on the
inexactness of the translation (n. 333). See n. 36 above.

[47]*Ordo init.* 70 no. 171. The alternative formula asks for deliverance from all the
power of the prince of darkness (165 no. 383).

seek deliverance from the death-dealing power of the malign spirit, from death itself, and from the spirit of depravity.[48]

In the new services designed for children who have reached the age of reason, there are no minor exorcisms given during the preliminary catechumenate; and the formulas of exorcism suggested for the scrutinies make no overt mention of the devil but speak only of darkness and the servitude of sin and of the adverse impulse and the spirit of cowardice and evil.[49]

In the shorter ritual for adults, there is only a single "prayer of exorcism" asking for deliverance from the power of darkness by Christ's passion and resurrection; it also notes that Christ was tempted by the snares of the devil.[50] The service designed for adults in danger of death has no prayer of exorcism at all. In the full adult ritual, the *traditiones* of the creed and the Lord's Prayer are celebrated during the course of Lent; and Holy Saturday is the prescribed time for the recitation (*redditio*) of the creed, the Effeta (which is nondemonic), and the choosing of a Christian name. If the anointing with the oil of catechumens is put off until this point, or until after the renunciation at the Easter Vigil, it is not preceded by an exorcism.[51]

The baptism itself is to be celebrated, in accord with ancient practice, during the Easter Vigil service. As I indicated earlier, there is no exorcism of the water but only a blessing.[52] A choice of three formulas of renunciation is given; in addition to the traditional Roman threefold question and the new form introduced in the infant ritual, the traditional form is presented in a single question, with *seductiones* substituting for *pompae*: "Abrenuntiatis Satanae et omnibus operibus et seductionibus eius?"[53] Other formulas of renunciation more closely adapted to the needs of each region, like those suggested after the optional exsufflation, can be established by the local episcopal conferences.

Then follows the anointing with oil of catechumens (if it has not already been performed), the confession of faith, and the baptism itself. Next comes the postbaptismal chrismation, the bestowal of the

[48]Ibid. 73–74 no. 178. The alternative formula speaks only of the devil's servitude (168 no. 387).
[49]Ibid. 137 no. 339 and 179 no. 392.
[50]Ibid. 103 no. 255.
[51]Ibid. 83–84 nos. 206–207 and 90–91 no. 218.
[52]Ibid. 88–89 no. 215; 173–175 no. 389.
[53]Ibid. 89 no. 217.

white garment and the lighted candle, and, as of old, the administration of the sacrament of confirmation, followed by the celebration of the Eucharist. In keeping with the oldest Roman tradition, there is no mention of the adverse powers at any point after baptism.

15 /

Conclusion

From the very beginning the Christian message of salvation was given a demonological dimension. The Gospels show Jesus delivering men from the oppression of unclean spirits and overthrowing the ruler of this world, and the epistles of Paul affirm the Christian's deliverance from servitude to the principalities and powers. It was almost inevitable that this aspect of redemption should be incorporated into the liturgical expressions of the initiation of the followers of Christ into their new life.

It seems that the impulse to liturgize the antidemonic was first given systematic expression by the Egyptian gnostics of the second century, who took practical measures to separate themselves from the evil intelligences of the universe before being baptized. For in spite of occasional passages in orthodox sources of the first two centuries referring to baptism as a release from the power of the devil, there is no decisive evidence that the process of release was ever acted out in a cultic fashion in these circles until well after the gnostics had articulated their precautionary rites against evil spirits.

At the beginning of the third century in Rome we encounter, in the *Apostolic Tradition* of Hippolytus, the ceremony of exorcizing candidates for baptism in order to remove the alien spirits from them. It is entirely possible that this practice was partially inspired by the doctrine and example of Valentinus, who resided in Rome in the middle of the second century. According to Valentinus, the unredeemed state entailed the indwelling of numerous demons. We may suppose that he had some sort of ritual means of eliminating these evil spirits comparable to those of his disciples in Egypt. The Christians in

272

Rome had at their disposal a similar demonological theory independent of the gnostic tradition. This was the Jewish-Christian notion of sin demons, the evil spirits who dwelled in a man when he committed sin. Although this theory, as it was expounded in the *Shepherd* of Hermas, referred to people who were already Christians, the inference could easily have been made that those who had not yet received the forgiveness of their sins in baptism were infested with demons to an eminent degree. And though the demons of the *Shepherd* were eliminated by simple will power and a resolution to commit sin no longer, it was only natural that the candidates should be assisted in ridding themselves of evil spirits. A ready means was at hand—the exorcism that had been traditionally used, beginning with Jesus and the apostles, to cast out the more obvious kind of possessing demons. So that even if these new preliminary exercises of the orthodox community were to some extent prompted by the heretical gnostics, it could be claimed that they involved nothing that could not be justified by the holiest and most respectable of traditions.

The initiation service as Hippolytus explained it also allowed for the voluntary repudiation of the spirits of evil, as can be seen from his remark that the lack of success in expelling the alien spirits was due to the candidate's failure to receive his instructions in good faith. There was, in addition, a formal renunciation of Satan. We know from the witness of the Church of Africa at the same time that the purpose of the renunciation was primarily the rejection of the practices of idolatry, and it reflected the notion that the pagan deities were none other than the fallen angels and demons of Christian teaching.

Another aspect of demonology that has been prominent in Christianity from the beginning is the continual warfare of the evil spirits against those who have been baptized as Christians. A number of liturgical usages reflecting this doctrine were developed at an early date, particularly in connection with the anointing ceremonies performed before and after baptism. By such means the new Christians were strengthened in their future combats with the devil.

Taken together, the rituals of expulsion, repudiation, and prophylaxis or apotropaism formed a series of ceremonies that dramatized in a striking way the very real struggle that every Christian waged with the devil. At first, the ceremonies corresponded very closely to reality, but soon symbolic or fictive elements were introduced or perceived, which had the effect of making the service more figurative and less realistic. This was particularly true of the exorcisms. The notion that all sinners were literally possessed by demons

did not find much favor with the Fathers, and when they were confronted with baptismal ceremonies that presupposed it, they were
forced to interpret them allegorically: the candidates were treated as if
corporeally possessed to illustrate the spiritual subjection that Satan
had brought upon mankind, which could not be removed by the
subjects' own volition alone but required primarily the free benev-
olence of God.

The notion of god demons also waned with the subsidence of
paganism, but the ceremony of renunciation was quite naturally reinterpreted in the sense of a longer-lived demonology and was simply
considered to be a rejection of everything that the devil could offer by
way of temptation to entice men away from the path to salvation. It
was often given aspects of a real confrontation between the candidate
and the devil, a stylized representation of the actual decision taken to
avoid from thenceforth all that was evil.

The third aspect of the antidemonic scenario, the apotropaic, was
the only one that remained absolutely literal and realistic in terms of
the systematic demonology developed by the Fathers. Even here,
sometimes, a dramatic metaphor was used, as when the neophytes
were rubbed down with sacred oil in preparation for the wrestling
match they were to undergo with Satan during their lifetime. Still,
this feature of the services was almost completely neglected in the
services of the West. Perhaps the reason was that the original Roman
service, that of the *Apostolic Tradition,* failed to exploit it. But it may
also be that there was a greater inclination to expand the more specifically dramatic aspects.

The Western liturgies incorporated the initiation services into the
cosmic drama of salvation celebrated in the Church's temporal cycle
and placed the climactic act of regeneration in the Easter Vigil, at the
moment when Christ's victory over hell, death, and Satan was being
celebrated. At the same time that the Roman baptismal rite received
its final form and began to supersede all other rites in the West, the
dramatic impulse was felt anew and expressed itself in adjacent parts
of the liturgy, in representations of the burial and resurrection of
Christ, the harrowing of hell, and the events that followed the
resurrection.

As time went on, the unity and impact of the services of the Good
Friday-to-Easter triduum began to disintegrate. The scrutinies and
baptism were removed from the Lenten liturgy, and the representa-
tional tropes and orders fell into disuse. The demonological substance

of the baptismal order, however, remained intact in the Roman Catholic ritual. But in the new order for infant baptism issued in 1969, all of the explicitly exorcistic elements were removed, and only a trace of other antidemonic elements was included. In my summary of the service in the last chapter, I concentrated only on these elements and not upon the order as a whole. It is, in fact, a very effective ritual reflecting a still quite conservative theology. But its effect is quite obviously something very different from that of the older service. The existence of Satan is still presupposed, as is his responsibility for the original sin of mankind. But there is no longer the repeated confrontation with him that constituted the chief dramatic interest of the earlier rites.

In the new ritual for children who have reached the age for catechizing, which appeared in 1972, even the references to original sin and Satan's domination of the world have been eliminated, and the same is true of the simpler forms of the adult ritual issued at the same time. In the full adult ritual, an elaborate catechumenal liturgy was reinstituted; but the accompanying prayers of exorcisms are not exorcisms in the traditional sense of adjurations addressed to possessing demons or prayers addressed to God seeking to expel possessing demons.

Such literal exorcisms were removed for the same reason that was doubtless acted upon by the Protestant reformers (and presumably by the Nestorians centuries earlier), namely, their failure to correspond to a "real" concept of demonology. Yet the Church as a whole had long been able to live with this discrepancy, by resorting to the sort of dramaturgical rationalization that Saint Augustine and others had hit upon.

A similar sort of rationalization is necessary even for the reformed Roman rite of infant baptism, for those individuals who accept some of the recent theological revaluations of the doctrines of the origin of man, of original sin, and of the existence of Satan and other evil spirits, according to which the story of the fall of man is taken simply as a moving allegory for the human condition and the general sinfulness of the world, and Satan is regarded merely as a powerful symbol of the allurements of the sinful world.[1] Such a reinterpreta-

[1]I argue against the need to accept the existence of evil spirits as "real" or personal beings in my book *The Devil, Demonology, and Witchcraft*, ed. 1 (New York 1968), as is brought out in the title of the British edition, *Towards the Death of Satan* (London 1968); for other editions, see Chap. 8 n. 1. This was also the thrust of my articles

tion on the part of some, of course, would not preclude others from adhering to the literal traditional interpretation, just as it was entirely possible for the faithful in times past to believe in the literal diabolic possession of infants before baptism.

Once the basic symbolic and dramatic nature of the antidemonic ceremonies of the ancient baptismal services is made clear, therefore, there should be no theological objection to their revival in the present-day Western liturgy (they are still in use in the Eastern rites). Late in 1972, in departing from the text of an address in which he reaffirmed traditional notions of demonology, Pope Paul VI questioned the wisdom of eliminating the old forms of exorcism from the baptismal liturgy.[2] But it would seem possible even within the terms of the new ritual to employ any of the traditional formulas that are considered appropriate; one of the rubrics states that when the Roman ritual offers several formulas ad libitum, particular rituals can employ other formulas of the same nature.[3] It might also be feasible at times to perform the other dramatic ceremonies that evolved in the West during the course of time, for example, the Deposition and Elevation rites, the harrowing-of-hell processions, the use of *Exultet* rolls, and the plays that developed from the *Quem quaeritis* trope. And if a personal appearance of the great antagonist is not to be permitted, at least we might be allowed to hear his voice calling out from behind closed doors, "Quis est iste Rex Gloriae?"

But if these traditional dramatic or quasi-dramatic ceremonies could be accommodated to a wide range of theological opinion by means of a similar range of symbolic interpretations, there may well be valid reasons for objecting to them on pastoral and psychological

---

"Devil in the Desert" (1964) and "Demonology and Diabolical Temptation," *Thought* 40 (1965) 165–194, condensed in *Theology Digest* 14 (1966) 131–136. For a listing of later writers who question the tenets of traditional demonology, see Hans Urs von Balthasar, *Theodramatik,* 4 vols. (Einsiedeln 1973–1983) 2.2.431.

[2]Associated Press, 15 November 1972, as reported in the Rome *Daily American,* 16 November 1972, p. 1: "The pope deplored that in the revised rite of baptism less emphasis is put on exorcism, the part in which the priest orders the devil to leave the person to be christened. 'I don't know whether this is realistic,' the pope said of the revised baptismal exorcism he himself approved three years ago as part of the reform of church services." Nothing corresponding to these remarks appears in the official text of the discourse, given in *L'osservatore romano* 112.265 [34.145] (16 November 1972) 1–2; English translation by Austin Vaughan in *The Pope Speaks* 17 (1973) 315–319. Lukken 265 also calls for a reconsideration in this matter.

[3]*Ordo initiationis christianae adultorum* 13 no. 33.

grounds. The members of the liturgical commission who prepared the new services were properly concerned about giving the false impression that the unbaptized were considered to be demonically possessed. We could further note that emphasis on the devil can have a deleterious effect on impressionable or unbalanced minds (especially those with paranoid tendencies) and can even induce symptoms of diabolical possession.[4] From this point of view we can be grateful that "the texts have been purged of too morbid a concern with demons,"[5] while we may share the commissioners' regret at the loss of the "unique and undeniable majesty" of the old ceremonies.[6]

I have tried to characterize the impressive forcefulness of these ceremonies in the different forms they took in the various rites of Christendom. I shall conclude by referring to a much-quoted passage in which R. W. Southern sums up the predominant theological view of the Redemption from the fifth or sixth century to the end of the eleventh. Because of man's original sin, it was believed, the devil had acquired rights over the race, which were lost when he overstepped his authority by putting the God-Man to death. "We have here a view of a struggle in which Man is assigned a very static role. Man was a helpless spectator in a cosmic struggle which determined his chances of salvation. The war was one between God and Devil, and God won because he proved himself the master-strategist. That God should become Man was a great mystery, a majestic, awe-inspiring act, justly acclaimed in such a triumphant expression of victory as the *Te Deum*. But there was little or no place for tender compassion for the sufferings of Jesus. The earthly incidents of his life were swallowed up in a drama enacted between Heaven and Hell."[7]

The last phrase, "a drama enacted between Heaven and Hell," could well serve as a description of the rituals of Christian initiation that were developed at this time, and for the liturgy of Holy Week. But it should be very evident that the liturgical drama is of a quite different quality from the theological. Though there are frequent references to man's servitude to the devil in the various services, it was only in the highly theatrical courtroom drama conjured up in Theodore of Mopsuestia's homilies that the theory of the rights of the devil was given full play. Other rituals, especially those with elabo-

---

[4]See Kelly, *Devil* 92–94.
[5]Kavanagh, *Shape of Baptism* 168.
[6]See Chap. 14 at n. 32.
[7]R. W. Southern, *The Making of the Middle Ages* (New Haven 1953 repr. 1968) 235.

rate formulas of exorcism, show that Satan was constantly suffering defeat before the coming of Christ and also during the life of Christ, before his death. Furthermore, the roles played by the exorcists and the candidates themselves show that a great deal of importance was given to man's cooperation with the grace of redemption. God, the God-Man, and man acted in concert. The devil, overpowered and humiliated, gave up his victims. On Good Friday, as he hangs from the cross, Jesus reproaches mankind for crucifying him: "My people, what have I done to you, or in what have I grieved you? I gave you the water of salvation from the rock to drink, and you have given me gall and vinegar." But once they repent for their guilt in this tragedy, they witness Jesus in a very different guise on the next day—as the victorious hero who breaks down the prison of the evil lord of the underworld and delivers from his grasp all of his fellow men who have been unjustly kept in captivity.

Bibliographical Index

to the Notes

Numbers in the following index refer to chapter and note or note number. For example, "3.8, 10, @16" means "Chapter 3, note 8, note 10, and at note 16 (that is, in the text near note superscript 16)." Full bibliographical details are normally to be found in the first place cited or in the Abbreviations. Multiple editions or translations of a work are usually not listed in this index, whether under the work itself or under the names of the editors or translators, when such information is readily attainable by looking up a single entry such as "*Gospel of Truth,* 4.36." In note 36 of Chapter 4 one finds that the *Gospel of Truth* under the title of *Evangelium veritatis* was edited by Michel Malinine and others and translated by R. M. Wilson in 1961; that it was translated by George McRae (in 1977); and that it was edited and translated into French by J. E. Ménard in 1972 under title of *L'évangile de verité* in 1972.

Ackerman, J. S. "The Rabbinic Interpretation of Psalm 82 and the Gospel of John" (1966), 1.5
Acta sancti Sebastiani, 6.38
Acts of John, 8.25–26
Acts of Paul, 4.17
Acts of Peter, 2.33–34; 4.16
Acts of Thomas, 8.19–22
Akeley, T. C. *Christian Initiation in Spain* (1967), 13.7, 43, 49
Alcuin. *Epistles,* 12.9, 63
Altaner, B., and A. Stuiber. *Patrologie,* ed. 8 (1978), 8.2, 11
Amalarius of Metz. *De ecclesiasticis officiis,* 12.64
Ambrose. *De fuga saeculi,* 6.19
———. *De mysteriis,* 6.19
———. *Hexameron,* 6.20
Ambrose, Pseudo- (?). See *De sacramentis*
Andersen, F. I., trans. *2 Enoch* (*OTP*), 1.1

Bieder, W. *Die Verheissung der Taufe im Neuen Testament* (1966), 2.22

Bjork, D. A. "On the Dissemination of *Quem quaeritis* and the *Visitatio sepulchri* and the Chronology of Their Early Sources" (1980–1981), 12.64

Bjorkvall, G., et al. *Corpus troporum* 3.2 (1982), 12.64

Black, M. *The Scrolls and Christian Origins* (1961), 2.20; 5.17

Bloomfield, M. W. *The Seven Deadly Sins* (1952), 3.1

Bobbio Missal, ed. E. A. Lowe (1917–1924), 6.36; 13.12, 25, 32–36.

Böcher, O. *Christus exorcista* (1972), 2.1

_____. *Dämonenfurcht und Dämonenabwehr* (1970), 2.1

Boismard, M. E. "I Renounce Satan, His Pomps, and His Works" (*BNT*), 1.26; 6.4

_____. *Quatre hymnes baptismales dans la première épître de Pierre* (1961), 1.27

Boniface of Mainz. *Sermons,* 6.37

Botte, B. "Le baptême dans l'église syrienne" (1956), 9.43; 10.3, 22

_____. "L'Eucologe de Sérapion est-il authentique?" (1964), 9.8

_____. "L'onction postbaptismale dans l'ancien patriarcat d'Antioche" (1967), 9.38

_____. *La Tradition apostolique de saint Hippolyte* (1963), 5.2, 4; 6.14; 9.2, 11, 34

Bowman, J. *The Gospel of Mark* (1965), 2.3, 13, 30; 4.56

Braun, F. M. "L'énigme des *Odes de Salomon*" (1957), 4.50

Brightman, F. E. *The English Rite* (1915), 14.7–8, 17–18

Brock, S. P. The Anonymous Syriac Baptismal *Ordo* in Add. 14518" (1977–1978), 10.33, 39, 76

_____. "A Baptismal Address Attributed to Athanasius" (1977), 9.33

_____. "Baptismal Themes in the Writings of Jacob of Serugh" (1978), 9.38

_____. "The Consecration of the Water in the Oldest Manuscripts of the Syrian Orthodox Baptismal Liturgy" (1971), 10.38–39

_____. "The Epiklesis in the Antiochene Baptismal *Ordines*" (1974), 10.28

_____. *The Holy Spirit in the Syrian Baptismal Tradition* (1979), 4.43; 8.28; 10.45

_____. "The Homily of Marutha of Tagrit on the Blessing of the Waters at Epiphany" (1982), 10.28

_____. "Jacob of Edessa's Discourse on the Myron" (1979), 8.15

_____. "A New Syriac Baptismal *Ordo* Attributed to Timothy of Alexandria" (1970), 10.67, 76

_____. "A Remarkable Syriac Baptismal *Ordo* (B. M. Add. 14518)" (1971), 10.76

_____. "Some Early Syriac Baptismal Commentaries" (1980), 9.39, 51; 10.76

_____. "Studies in the Early History of the Syrian Orthodox Baptismal Liturgy" (1972), 10.31, 55, 76

_____. "The Syrian Baptismal *Ordines*" (1977), 8.15

_____. "The Transition to a Post-Baptismal Anointing in the Antiochene Rite" (1981), 8.15; 9.38; cf. 8.1

Bullough, D. A. "Alcuin and the Kingdom of Heaven" (1983), 12.9.

Burmester, O. H. E. "The Baptismal Rite of the Coptic Church" (1945), 11.25–26, 30–31, 33–35, 38–39, 42

_____. *The Egyptian or Coptic Church* (1967), 11.25–28, 37, 42

Busch, B. "De modo quo S. Augustinus descripserit initiationem christianam" (1938), 7.16

Caesarius of Arles. *Sermons,* 6.28

Caird, G. B. *Principalities and Powers* (1956), 1.6–7

Campbell, J. J. "To Hell and Back: Latin Tradition and Literary Use of the *Descensus ad inferos*" (1982), 12.40, 42

Canones ad Gallos, 7.36

Firth, R. "Society and Its Symbols" (1974), Intro. 1
Fischer, B. "Baptismal Exorcism in the Catholic Baptismal Rites after Vatican II" (1974), 14.30–31, 33
———. "De initiatione christiana adultorum" (1967), 14.26–27
———. "'O Mors, ero mors tua': Eine Kurzformel der römischen Liturgie für das Paschamysterium" (1979), 12.47
Fisher, J. D. C. *Christian Initiation: Baptism in the Medieval West* (1965), 7.37; 12.9; 14.19, 22
———. *Christian Initiation: The Reformation Period* (1970), 14.1
Fitzmyer, J. A. "Qumran and the Interpolated Paragraph in 2 Cor. 6.14–7.1" (1961), 1.19
Franz, A. *Die kirchlichen Benediktionen im Mittelalter* (1909), 13.21
Friedrich, G. "Das Lied vom Hohenpriester in Zusammenhang von Hebr. 4.14–15.10" (1962), 1.30
———. "Ein Tauflied hellenisticher Judenchristen: 1 Thess. 1.9f." (1965), 1.30

Gamber, K. *Die Autorschaft von De sacramentis* (1966), 6.26
———. Response to Schmitz (1969), 6.26
———, ed. Nicetas of Remesiana, *Instructio ad competentes* (1964), 6.23, 26; 7.42
Gaster, T. H. *The Scriptures of the Dead Sea Sect* (1957), 2.14
Gelasian Sacramentary (Gel) = *Liber sacramentorum romanae aeclesiae ordinis anni circuli,* ed. L. C. Mohlberg et al. (1960), 6.35; 7.19, 43, 45; 12.2, 7–8, 10, 17, 19–23, 25, 27–29, 32, 35, 37, 43–45, 49–50, 60–63, 65, 68–70, 72, 76, 89; 13.5, 30, 38, 41; 14.9
Genesis Apocryphon, 4.27
Giet, S. *Hermas et les Pasteurs* (1963), 3.13
Goar, J. *Euchologion* (1730), 10.7, 12; 11.35; 13.22
Gospel of Nicodemus, 12.40
Gospel of Philip, 4.17, 25, 33, 42
Gospel of Truth, 4.36
Grant, R. M. *Gnosticism and Early Christianity,* ed. 2 (1966), 4.50
Gratian. *Decretum,* 12.9
Grebaut, S. *Les miracles de Jésus* (1923), 10.28
———. "Ordre du baptême et de la confirmation dans l'église éthiopienne" (1927–1928), 11.23, 41
Green, H. B. "The Significance of the Prebaptismal Seal in St. John Chrysostom" (1962), 9.23
Gregorian Sacramentary (Greg) = *Hadrianum,* ed. J. Deshusses, *Le sacramentaire grégorien,* vol. 1 (1971), 12.4, 11–12, 29 43–45, 49, 60, 62–63, 72, 89; 13.11, 35
———. *Supplement of Benedict of Aniane* (Greg sup), ed. Deshusses, 12.11, 20, 51–52, 65
Gregory Nazianzen. *Oratio,* 8.27
Gros, M. S. "El antiguo ordo bautismal catalano-narbonense" (1975), 13.49, 62

Hadrianum. See *Gregorian Sacramentary*
Hall, S. G. "Paschal Baptism" (1973), 3.28
Hanssens, J. M. "Deux documents carolingiens sur le baptême" (1927), 12.9
———. *La liturgie d'Hippolyte* (1959), 5.3; 6.20, 22
———. "Scrutins et sacramentaires" (1960), 12.13
———. "La synopse des ordonnances apparentées à la *Tradition apostolique*" (1970), 5.2
Hapgood, I. F. *Service Book of the Holy Orthodox-Catholic Apostolic Church,* ed. 2 (1922), 10.7, 13, 19, 21, 23, 26–27

Hardison, O. B. *Christian Rite and Christian Drama in the Middle Ages* (1965), Intro. 1–2; 12.6, 38–39, 64, 67

———. "Gregorian Easter Vespers and Early Liturgical Drama" (1970), 12.64

Heitmüller, W. *Im Namen Jesu* (1903), 1.25

Henrichs, A., and L. Koenen, "Ein griechischen Mani-Codex" (1970), 2.6

Hermas. *The Shepherd*, 2.23; 3.14–17

Hesbert, R. J. *Corpus antiphonalium officii*, 5 vols. (1963–1976), 12.6, 47–48

Hilary of Arles (?). *Expositio de fide catholica*, 6.27

Hilary of Poitiers. *Tractatus super psalmos*, 6.27

Hingeston, F. C., and W. Osmond. *Specimens of Ancient Cornish Crosses, Fonts*, etc. (1850), 12.59

Hippocrates, Pseudo-. *The Sacred Disease*, 2.35

Hippolytus. *Apostolic Tradition*, 5.2, 6–16, 19–20, 23–29, 31, 33, 36–37; 7.16; 9.1; 12.16

———. *Canons of Hippolytus* (q.v.)

———. *Refutatio omnium haeresium*, 2.6

Hölker, K. *Kreis Warendorf* (1936), 12.58

Horner, G. *The Statutes of the Apostles* (1904), 5.10, 13, 29; 9.3

Hort, F. J. A. "Adam, Books of" (1877), 4.54

Huglo, M. "L'office du dimanche de Pâques dans les monastères bénédictins" (1951), 12.64

Ignatius of Antioch. *Epistle to the Ephesians*, 4.43

Ildephonsus of Toledo. *De cognitione baptismi*, 6.31; 13.15, 43–44, 47, 49, 57

Irenaeus. *Adversus haereses*, 3.23; 4.1, 11–12, 24, 26, 30; 6.5–6

Isidore of Seville. *De ecclesiasticis officiis*, 6.31; 13.15, 43–44

Jagger, P. *Christian Initiation, 1552–1969* (1970), 14.21

James, M. R. *The Apocryphal New Testament* (1924), 4.17; 8.20–21; 12.40, 55

———. "A Fragment of the Apocalypse of Adam in Greek" (1893), 4.55

Jansen, H. L. "The Consecration in the Eighth Chapter of Testamentum Levi" (1959), 3.10

Jerome. *Commentary on Amos*, 6.21

———. *Commentary on Matthew*, 6.21

———. *Epistles*, 6.20–21

Jeu, Books of, 4.63–67

John Chrysostom. *Catecheses*, 9.15–21, 24

———. *Homilies on Colossians*, 9.21

John of Jerusalem (?). *Mystagogical Catecheses*, 9.30–32

John the Deacon. *Epistle to Senarius*, 6.34; 7.18, 37, 39; 12.24; cf. 5.4

Jonge, M. de. "The Interpretation of the *Testaments of the Twelve Patriarchs* in Recent Years" (1975), 3.3

Jordahn, B. "Der Taufgottesdienst im Mittelalter bis zur Gegenwart" (1970), 14.1, 12

Jubilees, 1.3; 2.12

Jürgens, H. *Pompa diaboli* (1972), 6.16

Justin Martyr. *1 Apology*, 2.24, 26, 42

———. *2 Apology*, 2.42

———. *Dialogue with Trypho*, 2.42; 6.8

Käsemann, E. "A Primitive Christian Baptismal Liturgy" (*BNT*), 1.24

Kavanagh, A. *The Shape of Baptism* (1978), 14.32; 15.5

Keefe, S. A. "Carolingian Baptismal Expositions" (1983), 12.9.
Kelly, H. A. "Demonology and Diabolical Temptation" (1965), 15.1
———. *The Devil, Demonology, and Witchcraft,* ed. 1 (1968), 8.1; 15.1
———. *The Devil, Demonology, and Witchcraft,* ed. 2 (1974), 1.1; 3.30; 6.7; 12.66; 13.20, 43; 14.32; 15.4
———. "The Devil in the Desert" (1964), 1.1, 5, 10; 6.7; 12.36; 15.1
———. *Le diable et ses démons* (1977), 1.1; 8.1
———. "The Metamorphoses of the Eden Serpent During the Middle Ages and Renaissance" (1971), 4.46
———. *La morte de Satana* (1969), 8.1
———. Review of B. Gerhardsson, *Testing of God's Son* (1968), 2.12
———. Review of J. B. Russell, *Satan* (1983), 1.1
———. *Towards the Death of Satan* (1968), 8.1; 15.1
Khouri-Sarkis, G. "Prières et cérémonies du baptême selon le rituel de l'église syrienne" (1956), 10.39, 59, 64
Kim, H. C. *The Gospel of Nicodemus* (1973), 12.40
Kirchenagenda of Mansfeld, 14.11
Kirsten, H. *Die Taufabsage* (1960), 6.1, 25
Klijn, A. F. J. *The Acts of Thomas* (1962), 8.17–18
Köbert, R. Review of Lattke, *Oden* (1980), 4.50
Koester, H. *"Gnomai diaphoroi"* (1965), 1.20
Kohler, K. "Demonology" (1905), 4.56
Kretschmar, G. "Die Bedeutung der Liturgiegeschichte für die Frage nach der Kontinuität des Judenchristentums im nachapostolischer Zeit" (1965), 3.11
———. "Beiträge zur Geschichte der Liturgie" (1963), 9.4
———. "Die Geschichte des Taufgottesdienstes in der alten Kirche" (1970), 8.18
———. "La liturgie ancienne dans les recherches historiques actuelles" (1982), 5.2, 4; 9.1
———. "Recent Research on Christian Initiation" (1977), 2.6, 16; 4.57
Kriegisch, R. "Do You Give up the Glamor of Evil?" and "Go out from Him, Unclean Spirit" (1980), 14.30
Krinke, J. "Der spanischen Taufritus im frühen Mittelalter" (1954), 13.46
Kuhn, K. G. "Der Epheserbrief im Licht der Qumrantexte" (1960–1961), 1.20

Lambot, C. *North Italian Services of the Eleventh Century* (1931), 13.2–3
Lampe, G. W. H. *The Seal of the Spirit* (1951), 4.12, 18, 57
Latte, R. de. "Saint Augustine et le baptême" (1975–1976), 7.15
Lattke, M. *Die Oden Salomos in ihrer Bedeutung für Neues Testament* (1979–), 4.50
Leaney, A. R. C. *The Rule of Qumran and Its Meaning* (1966), 2.10, 14
Leclercq, H. "Pâques" (*DACL*), 12.57
———. "Semaine sainte" (*DACL*), 12.64
Le Déaut, R. *Introduction à la littérature targumique* (1966), 2.2
Lengeling, E. J. "Vom Sinn der präbaptismalen Salbung" (1972), 12.63
Leo the Great. *Sermons,* 7.35
Liber ordinum en usage dans l'église wisigothique et mozarabe d'Espagne du cinquième au onzième siècle, ed. M. Férotin (1904), 6.33; 13.8, 16, 23–24, 49–56, 60–63
Lipphardt, W. *Lateinische Osterfeiern und Osterspiele,* 6 vols. (1975–1981), 12.64
Lukken, G. M. *Original Sin in the Roman Liturgy* (1973), 5.32; 6.39; 9.28; 12.6, 28, 30, 48; 15.2
Lundberg, P. *La typologie baptismale dans l'ancienne église* (1942), 4.45
Luther, M. *Das Taufbuchlin verdeutscht* (1523), 14.1
———. *Das Taufbuchlin verdeudscht* (1526), 14.10

Bibliographical Index to the Notes

Optatus of Mileve. *Libri VII*, 7.23, 33
———. *Sermo in natali sanctorum innocentium*, 6.11
Ordines romani (OR): OR XI, 6.35; 12.1, 10, 17–19, 21–28, 60, 62–63, 68, 76; *OR* XV, 12.63; *OR* XVI, 12.64; *OR* XVII, 12.64; *OR* XXIII, 12.64; *OR* XXVIII, 12.63; *OR* XXXA, 12.64; *OR* XXXB, 12.64; *OR* XXXIV, 12.67; *OR* L, 12.31, 37, 40, 61, 63, 67, 78, 81, 83–89; 14.@22, @23
Ordo baptismi parvulorum (1969), 14.35
Ordo initiationis christianae adultorum (1962), 14.24
Ordo initiationis christianae adultorum (1972), 14.36–53; 15.3; cf. 9.39
Origen. *Catena on John*, 4.59
———. *Homilies on Exodus*, 4.58, 60
· ———. *Homilies on Joshua*, 4.28; 6.9
———. *Homilies on Luke*, 4.61
———. *Homilies on Numbers*, 3.21; 6.12, 18
———. *Selecta in Psalmos*, 4.15
Ovid. *Amores*, 6.17

Pacian of Barcelona. *Sermo de baptismo*, 6.31
Paris Magical Papyrus, 2.31; 4.32
Passio sanctae Caeciliae, 6.25
Paul VI. Homily of 15 November 1972, 15.2
Peel, M. L. "The *Descensus ad inferos* in *The Teachings of Silvanus*" (1979), 12.48
Peter Chrysologus. *Sermons*, 7.46
Petri, O. *Manual* (1529), 14.2
Pirmin. *De singulis libris canonicis scarapsus*, 6.37
Pliny. *Naturalis historia*, 2.36
Potterie, I. de la. "L'onction du chrétien par foi" (1959), 8.18
Proclus of Constantinople. *Mystagogic Catechesis*, 9.22
Procopius of Gaza. *Commentary on Genesis*, 9.20
Pryke, J. "The Sacraments of Holy Baptism and Holy Communion in the Light of the Ritual Worship and Sacred Meals at Qumran" (1966), 2.8
Pseudo-Clementine writings. See Clement of Rome, Pseudo-
Puniet, P. de. "Baptême" (*DACL*), 6.37; 8.15; 9.56; 10.8, 31; 11.23–25, 33, 42; 13.25
———. "Catéchumenat" (*DACL*), 13.49

Qõzi, Y. *Le rituel baptismal du Maphrianat de Tagrit et de Mossoul/Nineve* (1974), 10.41, 62, 64; 11.45
Quasten, J. *Patrology*, 3 vols. (1950–1960), 2.32, 40; 3.29; 5.5; 8.11
Quodvultdeus. *Contra Iudaeos, paganos, et Arianos*, 6.10; 7.33
———. *De symbolo ad catechumenos*, 5.21; 6.10; 7.33
Qumran Scriptures, 2.10, 14–15, 21–22; 4.27

Rabanus Maurus. *De clericorum institutione*, 12.9
Raffa, V. Review of Botte, *Tradition* (1964), 5.2
Regularis concordia, 12.67
Reitzenstein, R. "Eine frühchristliche Schrift von den dreierlei Früchten des christlichen Lebens" (1914), 6.10
Renaux, C. "Hierosolymitana," pt. 2 (1981), 9.29
Riley, H. M. *Christian Initiation* (1974), Intro. 1
Rite of Christian Initiation of Adults (1974), 14.36,46
Robinson, J. A. T. "The Baptism of John and the Qumran Community" (1957), 2.8

Robinson, J. M., ed. *The Nag Hammadi Library in English* (1977), 4.12, etc.
Roman Ritual (1487), 14.22
—— (1584), 14.22
—— (1614), 9.61; 12.74; 13.13; 14.23
——, English trans. (1964), 14.4
—— (1969), see *Ordo baptismi parvulorum*
—— (1972), see *Ordo initiationis christianae adultorum*
Rordorf, W. "Le baptême selon la *Didaché*" (1972), 2.16
Russell, D. S. *The Method and Message of Jewish Apocalyptic* (1964), 1.7; 3.3
Russell, J. B. *Lucifer* (1984), 6.35
——. *Satan* (1981), 1.1; 7.3

Sacramentaire grégorien, see *Gregorian Sacramentary*
Sacramentarium bergomense, ed. A. Paredi (1962), 12.75, 81; 13.4, 6, 10–11, 18
Sacramentarium fuldense, 13.46
Sacramentarium triplex, ed. O. Heiming (1968), 12.51, 75
Sacramentary of Gellone, ed. A. Dumas and J. Deshusses (1981), 12.8, 63
Sagnard, F. *La gnose valentienne et le témoignage de saint Irénée* (1947), 4.2
——, ed. *Extraits de Théodote* (1948), 4.2, 6–7, 10, 21, 23, 41
Salles, A. *Trois antiques rituels du baptême* (1958), 9.4–7
Salvian of Marseilles. *De gubernatione Dei*, 6.27
Samuel, Y. S., ed. *The Sacrament of Holy Baptism According to the Ancient Rite of the Syrian Orthodox Church of Antioch* (1974), 10.39, 64
Sarum Manual, 14.16
Sauget, J. M. "Le *Codex liturgicus* de J. L. Assemani" (1973), 10.31
Scheidt, H. *Die Taufwasserweihegebete* (1935), 10.31; 11.41; 12.71
Schmitz, J. *Gottesdienst im altchristlichen Mailand* (1975), 6.26
——. Rejoinder to Gamber (1969), 6.26
——. "Zum Autor des Schrift *De sacramentis*" (1969), 6.26
Schoeps, H. J. "Die Dämonologie der Pseudoklementinen" (1950), 8.2
Segelberg, E. "The Baptismal Rite According to Some of the Coptic-Gnostic Texts of Nag-Hammadi" (1962), 4.37
——. "The Coptic-Gnostic Gospel According to Philip and Its Sacramental System" (1960), 4.17, 26
Sehling, E. *Die evangelischen Kirchenordnungen des XVI Jahrhunderts,* 2 vols. (1902), 14.1, 10–11
Selwyn, E. G. *The First Epistle of St. Peter* (1947), 1.34, 36
Serapion. *Sacramentarium*, 9.8–10
Siricius, Pope. *Epistle to Himerius of Tarracona*, 7.36
Smith, M. A. "Did Justin Know the *Didaché*?" (1966), 2.25
Southern, R. W. *The Making of the Middle Ages* (1953), 15.7
Standaert, B. *L'Evangile selon Marc* (1978), 1.32
Statuta ecclesiae antiqua, 13.43
Stenzel, A. *Die Taufe* (1958), 12.13
Sticca, S. "Italian Theater of the Middle Ages: From the *Quem quaeritis* to the *Lauda*" (1980), 12.64
Stowe Missal. Vol. 2. Ed. G. F. Warner (1915), 12.9, 73; 13.9, 25–26, 39, 42
Strack, H. L., P. Billerbeck, et al. *Kommentar zum Neuen Testament,* 6 vols. (1922–1961), 1.5; 2.1–2, 11, 18, 29; 4.56
Swanston, H. "The Lukan Temptation Narrative" (1966), 1.5
Sybilline Oracles, 2.22

Werblowsky, R. J. Z. "On the Baptismal Rite According to St. Hippolytus" (1957), 5.18, 31
Whitaker, E. C. "Unction in the Syrian Baptismal Rite" (1961), 8.24
Winkler, G. *Das armenische Initiationsrituale* (1982), 8.1, 15, 18, 22–23, 25, 27; 11.2, 5, 7, 11–13
———. "The Original Meaning of the Prebaptismal Anointing and Its Implications" (1978), 8.1

Ximenes de Cisneros, Cardinal. *Missale mixtum*, 13.61; 14.5

York Manual, 10.40
Young, K. *The Drama of the Medieval Church*, 2 vols. (1933), 12.39–41, 46
Ysebaert, J. *Greek Baptismal Terminology* (1962), 3.11; 7.7; 8.8, 15, 18; 9.34, 38

General Index

I do not list secondary authors in this index. As for primary authors and works, I limit myself to those that figure prominently in the text. For all others, and for references to specific works, see the Bibliographical Index to the Notes.

295

cross *(cont'd.)*
   metaphor for baptism, 62–63. *See also*
   anointing; sealings and signings
Cyprian, 30, 36, 97, 109–111, 128, 190, 239
Cyril of Jerusalem, 145–146, 161

Dead Sea scrolls. *See* Qumran community
Death, personification of, 73, 145, 216–219, 250
demoniacs. *See* possession
demonology, 10, 12, 17–18, 43, 77, 83, 170, 172, 177, 267–268; realistic, 56, 113, 274–276
demons: baptism of, 64, 86, 136–137 *(see also* Theodotus); of disease, 20, 23, 35, 127–128, 139 *(see also* possession); female, 68, 137, 175n; as gods, 30, 36–37, 41, 98–99, 104, 250, 273–274; "guardian," 107; name for all evil spirits, 20; in parts of body, 124, 177, 238, 240, 250; in synoptic Gospels, 18, 164–166; tempting *(see* sin demons); in water, 70–74, 108–109, 169, 212 *(see also* dragon in the water; water)
Deposition drama, 12, 214, 225, 274, 276
Deprehensae sunt insidiae, 245, 247
Descensus ad inferos, 214–216, 219
devil (Satan): as enforcer and punisher, 19; existence of denied, 257, 275 and n; gnostic, 66–67; in hell, 71–73, 214, 216, 219; as Lucifer (postbiblical), 17, 18n; nature of, 165, 265; in New Testament, 17–19, 165
Didache, 37–38, 40–41
Didascalia apostolorum, 75, 128–130, 147
Donatus, Donatists, 112, 115n
dragon in the water, 71–73, 145–146, 167–169, 171–172, 191, 199, 241
drama: defined and discussed, 9, 11–12, 161–162, 202n; aspects of in baptism, 87–88, 92–93, 99–105, 113, 129n, 141–144, 148–152, 157, 167, 169, 178, 185, 188, 209, 221, 230–231, 238, 246, 260–261, 273–278; eliminated from baptismal ceremonies, 152, 156–157, 256–257, 259, 267, 275, 277; imaginary, 21; liturgical, 12, 214–216, 225n, 231, 274

Easter: baptism at, 115; liturgy of *(see* Easter day; Easter Vigil)
Easter day: mass, 216–217; morning ceremonies, 214, 225n; vespers, 225n
Easter Vigil (Holy Saturday) services, 32n, 52, 152, 169n, 205, 217–219, 229–230, 260, 270, 274; times (of day) held, 223

Eastern liturgies, 127, 187, 200, 202, 207–208, 276
Ebionites, 43, 124
Edessa, 131, 170, 188
Effeta, 88, 121, 222, 233, 240, 242, 248, 251–252, 262, 265, 270
Egypt, 42, 44, 50–77, 136–139, 147n, 192–200, 272. *See also* Alexandria; Exodus from Egypt
Elevation dramas, 12, 214, 276, cf. 274
Elkasaites, 34–35, 43
energoumenoi, 60, 67–68, 135, 244; infant, 221n. *See also* possession
English rites. *See* Alcuin; Anglican services; Sarum; York rite
Enoch, First Book of, 17–18, 20, 36n, 72n
Enoch, Second Book of, medieval recension, 18n
Ephraem, 132, 135
Epiphany, 132, 167–168, 198
Ergo maledicte, 208–209, 220, 243, 257, 261
Essenes. *See* Qumran community
Ethiopian texts and rites, 83n–84n, 89n, 91, 138, 168, 194–198, 207n
Exodus from Egypt, 203, 208, 213, 248. *See also* Pharaoh
exorcism:
   apostrophe (nondemonic), 70, 85, 90–91, 206–207, 211–212, 254–255
   demonic (action or formula for expelling indwelling demons), 20–21, 48, 67–68. *See also* fasting;
   hands, laying on of
      distinguished from apotropaic measures, 123n, 170–171
   exorcistic subjunctive, 245
   in Gospels (synoptic), 21. *See also* Jesus, as exorcist
   imprecatory (addressed to demons) and deprecatory (addressed to God), 127, 142, 149n, 166, 209, 265
   Jewish, 42
   mechanics of, 110, 120, 144, 145n, 146, 164, 190, 208–209, 221, 230, 239
   of baptismal candidates
      absence of in early Africa and Levant, 75, 106, 109
      absence of in East Syria, 123–135, 151–152
      belated, 86–88, 138, 169, 197
      eliminated, 147, 149–151, 155–157, 257–258, 275–276
      in Gnostic rites, 64–65, 67–68

Library of Congress Cataloging in Publication Data

Kelly, Henry Ansgar, 1934–
    The Devil at baptism.

    Includes bibliographical references and indexes.
    1. Devil. 2. Demonology. 3. Baptism (Liturgy) 4. Initiation
rites—Religious aspects—Christianity. 5. Liturgical drama. I. Title.
BT981.K44 1985   235'.4   85–404
ISBN 0–8014–1806–2 (alk. paper)